CONTEMPORARY PERSPECTIVES ON CHILDHOOD AND ADOLESCENCE

This book offers fresh perspectives on childhood, adolescence, human diversity, and learning. With novel theoretical backing of Indian research studies that confirm, bolster, extend, or challenge established theories, it explores connections between prevailing ideas in educational psychology and the issues relevant to young learners of today.

Authored by leading scholars and practitioners of Indian education, the volume covers a wide range of topics, including early childhood care and education, sociocultural, philosophical, and psychological perspectives on childhood and adolescence, contemporary lifestyle changes, and concerns about diversity. These concerns range from multilingualism and gender to intelligence and the development of self and identity. Structured in terms of historical progression, each chapter offers a theoretical context, emphasizing contemporary perspectives within the specific area of focus. Additionally, independent research studies are integrated into the chapters to provide a comprehensive framework of the addressed issues rather than existing as standalone research papers.

A valuable resource relevant to multiple disciplines, this book caters to educators, researchers, and teacher trainers, as well as students of Education, Psychology, Counselling, Development Studies, Social Work, and Sociology. It's also a useful tool for parents, policymakers, and governmental and non-governmental organizations involved in education.

Namita Ranganathan is a Professor in the Department of Education, University of Delhi. She has 38 years of teaching and research experience in the fields of Childhood and Adolescence Studies. She was the Head and Dean, Faculty of Education from 2016–2019.

CONTEMPORARY PERSPECTIVES ON CHILDHOOD AND ADOLESCENCE

Development, Diversity and Inclusion

Edited by Namita Ranganathan

Routledge
Taylor & Francis Group
LONDON AND NEW YORK

Designed cover image: Getty Images

First published 2025
by Routledge
4 Park Square, Milton Park, Abingdon, Oxon OX14 4RN

and by Routledge
605 Third Avenue, New York, NY 10158

Routledge is an imprint of the Taylor & Francis Group, an informa business

British Library Cataloguing-in-Publication Data
A catalogue record for this book is available from the British Library

ISBN: 978-1-032-69913-4 (hbk)
ISBN: 978-1-032-82660-8 (pbk)
ISBN: 978-1-003-50550-1 (ebk)

DOI: 10.4324/ 9781003505501

Typeset in Sabon
by Deanta Global Publishing Services, Chennai, India

For my son, TCA Jayant

CONTENTS

FIGURES

TABLES

LIST OF CONTRIBUTORS

Shivani Arora is a Professor of Education at Shyama Prasad Mukherji College, University of Delhi. Her areas of research and teaching include Childhood and Adolescence Studies and Gender. She teaches in diverse Teacher Education Programmes.

Vikas Baniwal is an Assistant Professor in the Department of Education, University of Delhi. His fields of academic engagement include Philosophical and Psychological Foundations of Education, Philosophy for Children and Education for Mental Health.

Neema Chaurasiya completed her PhD from the Department of Education, University of Delhi. She has taught as Guest Faculty in a few colleges of the University of Delhi. She works extensively in Language Education and Gender Studies.

Nidhi Gulati is a Professor at the Institute of Home Economics, University of Delhi. She has vast teaching and research experience in the fields of Childhood and Adolescence Studies and Elementary Teacher Education.

Ravneet Kaur is a Professor in Mata Sundari College, University of Delhi. She has fifteen years of teaching and research experience. She engages extensively with Teacher Education Programmes in Elementary and Secondary Education.

Sandeep Kumar is a Professor in the Department of Education, University of Delhi. His fields of academic work include Social Theory of Education, Research Methods and Psychological Foundations of Education. He has over fifteen years of teaching experience.

Vishakha Kumar served as an Assistant Professor in Jesus and Mary College, University of Delhi, for five years. She is presently the Director of a group of Institutions for children and adolescents, including an Intermediate College in Rishikesh.

Rashi Mukhopadhayay served as an Assistant Professor for ten years in Jesus and Mary College, University of Delhi. At present she works with an International Institution in Cork, Ireland, which deals with adolescents. She is also an Independent Researcher and Consultant for projects on Childhood and Adolescence.

Charu Sharma is an Assistant Professor at Shyama Prasad Mukherji College, University of Delhi. She teaches courses related to Childhood and Adolescence and Diversity and Inclusion in different Teacher Education Programmes.

Yukti Sharma is a Professor in the Department of Education, University of Delhi. She is currently the Joint Director of the Institute of Lifelong Learning, Delhi University. Her fields of engagement include Diversity and Inclusion, Environmental Education and Science Education.

Chandan Shrivastava is an Assistant Professor in the Department of Education, Banaras Hindu University. He has done seminal work in training teachers in the rural belts of Bihar, Jharkhand and Odisha in a UNICEF-funded project. He works extensively in the fields of Social Science and Teacher Education.

Toolika Wadhwa is a Professor in Shyama Prasad Mukherji College, University of Delhi. She has over fifteen years of teaching experience in diverse Teacher Education Programmes. Her areas of academic engagement and interest include Pedagogy, Commerce, Education for Mental Health and Psychology.

1

UNDERSTANDING DEVELOPMENT AND DIVERSITY

Key Concepts and Ideas

Namita Ranganathan

For any student or scholar of Education and for those who wish to become educational practitioners – be it teachers, counsellors, curriculum developers, textbook writers, researchers or even activists who want to work for children – a detailed understanding of concepts, ideas and theories related to human development and diversity is imperative since they subsume many significant issues concerning children and adolescents. Some of these issues include: When does childhood begin and end? Is it a singular stage or stratified into sub-stages? How do children think, feel and deal with the world? Is childhood a universal experience? Why do children enjoy play so much? What is the right age to admit a child to school? How should the school curriculum be structured for different age groups of children? How do children's emotions develop and get expressed? Do children have a sense of morality or not? At what age do they move away from fantasy to reality? When do they become capable of learning two to three languages? How do language skills and abilities develop in them? Does their capacity to think undergo a change with age? How are language and thought related? Do girls and boys grow and develop in the same way, as also children in rural and urban areas? How do children with disabilities grow and develop? Do children from socially and culturally backward areas have different childhoods? Can children who are different in their ability to learn study in regular schools or do they have to go to a special school? Will their curriculum and how they are evaluated be different? Will it have to be customised to their needs and abilities? Will they be able to complete schooling? Why are some children very active while others are nervous and passive? Why do some children grasp what they read or are taught quickly while others don't? How is it that some children are

DOI: 10.4324/9781003505501-1

very confident? Why is it that some children are good in studies, some good in sports, some in art, dancing, etc.?

The list of questions is endless. Very similar to this is the list of questions related to adolescence. For example, What is the age at which adolescence begins? When does puberty begin? What happens during puberty? Why do children suddenly start growing into adults when they are twelve to fifteen years old? Is adolescence a biological construct? Does it happen to everyone? Is it a bridge stage between childhood and adolescence? When does it end? Why is it considered a stage of storm and stress? Do sexual feelings arise at this stage? Are love, romance, daydreams and fantasy part of adolescence? Why is friendship so important? Why is there so much rebellion during adolescence against parents and teachers, and even questioning of some of the beliefs in society? Does the adolescent's capacity to think and reason change? Why do the school curriculum and the number of subjects to be studied expand so much? Why are adolescents so moody? Why do they run after sports heroes and film stars? Do boys and girls in rural areas have adolescence at all? Do children from low-income families experience adolescence? For girls who are married early, is there adolescence at all? Is there one or are there many adolescences that exist?

From the questions and issues raised above, it is clear that human development and diversity are pervasive areas and cover a spectrum of ideas, issues, theories and debates. In the present chapter, an attempt has been made to acquaint the reader with some important concepts and ideas pertaining to development, diversity and inclusion. The idea is to enable the beginning readers to build an understanding of these areas and find answers to their questions. For the educational practitioners, the idea is to re-visit their existing concepts and notions, add value to them and build further perspective on them, drawing from their educational practices and experiences. An important assumption underlying human development, diversity and inclusion is that they are very dynamic fields of research, so the body of knowledge related to them keeps on expanding and changing from time to time. This chapter will also set the base for understanding the rest of the chapters in this anthology.

1.1 Understanding Human Growth and Development

This section discusses human growth and development, the nature of their relationship, the importance and implications of the growth curve and principles of development for policies and practices in education. It also provides a preliminary understanding of some stage theories that explain how development takes place in specific areas of importance to childhood and adolescence.

Growth and development are terms that are often used synonymously. While they are highly interrelated, it is important to understand what they specifically mean and how they are actually related. Growth refers to change/s which is/are measurable, tangible and visible. It is an augmentation or a reduction in shape, size, specific dimensions and skills such that they can be quantified. For example, changes in the physical contours of the body are one of the best examples of growth. Increases in height, weight, musculature and overall body size are examples of growth. Phrases like 'you have become very tall', or 'you have become very thin', or 'from the chubby little boy that I knew, you have acquired a great athletic figure', all imply growth since there is an earlier reference point from which the comparison is being made. The important point is that the changes can be seen and estimated.

Similarly, from a set of simple skills that an individual may have learnt, like swimming, cycling, dancing, singing, etc., he/she may have, over the years, acquired advanced skills in any one of them and may thus be able to do very complex and intricate tasks. For example, from swimming 18 lengths of a standard-sized swimming pool in one hour, an individual may, with time, be able to do 30 lengths. There is a measurable change in speed and capacity. From singing basic ragas, the individual may move to composing pieces based on them. This is a sign of growth as the child's skills are expanding in terms of what she/he could do earlier and what she/he can do now.

Many children who enjoy assembling jigsaw puzzles move from simple to complex compositions. Their dexterity from a 100-piece puzzle may change to assembling 300 pieces, then 500 pieces and so on. The changes in capacity in all the examples are often attributed to growth. However, it is important to understand that growth is not an automatic process. Very closely allied to growth is the concept of maturation. 'Maturation' is a biological term and suggests that changes in human capacity, often seen as 'growth', take place through naturally evolving changes in the body as it unfolds. There appears to be a developmental blueprint which underlies the process of growth in all human beings. Thus, improvement or change in the skills of swimming, dancing, application of mind, etc., can be seen as growth and maturation. Growth cannot take place without maturation. All infants, for example, first turn over, then learn to sit, then crawl, then stand, then walk and then hop, skip, run and jump. The sequence is somewhat predictable, and the age at which each of these will occur is also predictable. This suggests that maturation is what enables growth to take place.

At times, as in the example given above, it is very difficult to explain the changes that take place in an individual merely as growth, especially when there are many changes to the qualities, characteristics, efficiency and performance of the individual. It appears that a more complex process of change has taken place. When the changes are qualitative in nature and cannot be specifically pinpointed or measured but are visible and reflected in the individual's behaviour, attitudes or performance, we are actually referring to the process of development. 'Development' suggests refinement, improvement and qualitative change in a person reflected through demonstration of these in his/her thoughts, behaviour, attitudes and preferences. For example, when we say that Maya has developed into a 'fine young woman', we are talking of the qualities of Maya, which are many, which have undergone change and which are appreciable. Here, there is no specific factor of change that can be identified or measured. Hence, the changes in Maya are more process-based; several aspects have changed, and these changes are what have made her a fine young woman. Such changes may be attributed to the process of development.

When students who perform poorly in the early years of schooling become high achievers and very good at their studies, it is clear that the changes are not sudden but have taken place over a period of time. This exemplifies development. Development takes place in all aspects and spheres of an individual's life.

In real terms, it is not easy to separate growth from development. Yet, it is important to understand that they cannot be used interchangeably. Development is the larger and more permanent process of change, which subsumes growth. However, since development cannot be quantified, growth is often used to mark the parameters of change. Both growth and development occur simultaneously and are supported by 'maturation'. In the development of language abilities in humans, this can be seen very clearly. It is with biological maturation that there is an expansion in a child's brain's capacity to learn new words and build upon his/her vocabulary. The child develops skills of language and communication based on the growth of his/her vocabulary and language comprehension abilities. Here, the processes of growth and development are interwoven, and it may be concluded that language development subsumes growth in language abilities. The child's vocabulary grows and enables him/her to develop better language comprehension and communication skills.

1.1.1 Growth Curve

The growth curve, which denotes how growth and development proceed across the human development life span, is an important concept in the field of education. Its importance lies in the fact that it helps to identify and describe the pattern of growth and development in human beings and also helps to establish some basic assumptions and principles of development which apply universally. It is called the growth curve because it is only growth that can be quantified and plotted as a curve. However, imbued within the growth curve is also the process of development as it unfolds. Let us try to study the implications of the growth curve for education and understand how the human development lifespan is categorised into different life stages (Figure 1.1).

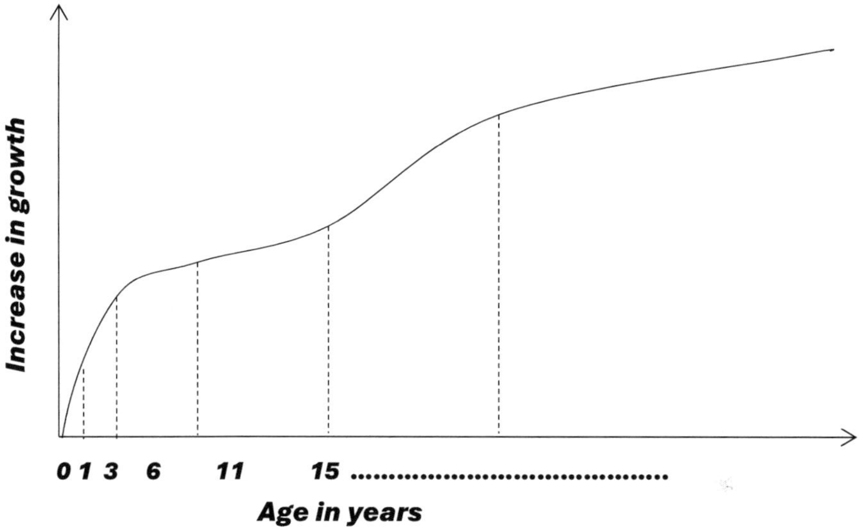

FIGURE 1.1 Growth Curve

Source: Author

TABLE 1.1 Growth Curve Across Life Span

	Age	*Stage*	*Pattern of Growth and Development*
1	Birth–1 year	Infancy	Most Rapid
2	1–3 years	Early childhood	Very rapid
3	3–6 years	Middle childhood	Somewhat rapid
4	6–11 years	Late childhood	Slow, almost like a plateau stage
5	11–18 years	Puberty and adolescence	Sharp spurt in growth and development
6	18–40 years	Young adulthood	Steady growth and development
7	40–60 years	Middle adulthood	Slow growth and development
8	60 years to the end of life	Mature adulthood	Slow growth and development

Source: Author

The growth curve clearly shows the following stages in the human development life span (Table 1.1).

As can be seen in Table 1.1, the human development life span is categorised into eight stages. In the field of Education, our concern is more with the first five stages which cover childhood and adolescence. If we examine the slope of the curve, it clearly shows that growth and development are continuous, ongoing processes with no sudden break or changes. It also highlights two phases of maximal growth: Childhood, particularly early childhood, and puberty and adolescence. In fact, going by the descriptions of the curve (see Table 1.1), infancy or the first year of life is seen to be the most rapid stage of growth. This can clearly be seen in the vast array of abilities and skills that the infant acquires. He/she learns how to sit, crawl, stand and even walk. Recognition of familiar and non-familiar objects and persons takes place. Early beginnings of language are visible. He/she begins to follow instructions, gets into a predictable schedule of daily activities and into a more set pattern of toilet habits. The ability to eat expands with the acquisition of teeth. Socially, the infant begins to respond to persons who try to reach out to him/her.

During early and middle childhood, growth and development continue to be very rapid. The physical and motor abilities of children expand. They can run, hop, skip, jump, ride a cycle and negotiate physical games, get into swings, slides and merry go rounds in a public park.

They can comprehend at least two languages and can express themselves in the home language with ease. As they start formal schooling, they develop a fair amount of competence in reading, writing, comprehending and communicating in the language which is their medium of instruction. Language helps them to give words to their thoughts and form concepts which they can store. By the time a child is six years old, he/she can communicate quite clearly and speak the language he/she knows quite fluently.

Schooling also helps to expand the social and emotional world of children. They learn to relate to others, make friends, engage in simple group activities and express their emotions in socially acceptable ways in public. They begin to follow the rules and schedules set up for them by the home and school. Their energy levels steadily increase, leading to visible engagement in outdoor play.

During late childhood, the rate of growth becomes slower. It is almost like a plateau stage. Children appear to be refining and enriching the skills acquired in the prior stage. There is thus discernible improvement in their language expression, vocabulary, thought processes, formation of ideas and concepts, the intellectual tasks that they can perform, the number of subjects they learn in school and their ability to deal with the school curriculum. Socially, their worlds expand. They make many friends and can engage in several social activities at home, at school and in their neighbourhood. They learn to follow norms and schedules set up by the home and school with more ease and understanding. It is not just blind compliance but compliance with understanding. Energy levels are high and seen to be distributed across a variety of tasks and activities. Hence, what is seen at this stage is a consolidation of all that had been learnt at the earlier stage with a noticeable qualitative improvement in capacity and ability.

It is during puberty and adolescence that the gradient of the slope of the growth curve is very steep, showing a spurt in growth and development. This can be seen very clearly since it is during this stage that puberty takes place, leading to a large number of changes in the body contours of the adolescent. Increases in height, weight, musculature and physical appearance, in general, take place. The child gets transformed into an approximation of what he/she is likely to become as an adult. These changes are mediated by the activation of the gonads, which secrete sex hormones. This, in turn, leads to concomitant emotional changes, pre-occupation with one's body and appearance, attraction to members of the opposite sex, emergence of questions about one's sense of identity and a strong desire to have one's sense of independence. The ability to think, analyse and question also expands exponentially. It is almost like an inner psychological revolution. Thus, the adolescent experiences rapid changes and challenges which he/she has to negotiate.

The subsequent stages represent the cycle of adulthood. The slope of the curve moves upward in a very gradual manner, showing that development continues to take place, but the rate is slow. It appears as if with ongoing experiences, the human being is becoming more mature and moving towards more conviction and personal wisdom.

1.1.2 Significance of the Growth Curve in Education

From the standpoint of Education, the growth curve is extremely important, for it helps to establish that infancy, childhood and adolescence are extremely critical life stages for development and learning. Within childhood, too, it spells out that early and middle childhood are the two stages during which maximum growth and development take place. Late childhood, in contrast, is the age for assimilation and consolidation. The correlation of these life stages with the structuring of the schooling process is also very important to understand. Since the potential for growth and development is so strong, there is a clear implication that the early childhood curriculum must be very stimulating, especially in areas of physical and motor development, and language and cognition. Children have to be encouraged to develop and hone their skills in these areas.

Middle childhood correlates with the pre-primary level of schooling, often called the nursery-kindergarten stage. It marks the first tier of formal schooling, where the child is introduced to a structured curriculum of which language, mathematics and environmental science are a part. The child is taught how to read and write and acquire a foundational understanding of language and mathematics, which is very important since it fuels all future learning and helps to develop an early interest in these subjects. Given that children develop and learn very rapidly at this stage, it is up to schools to plan their pre-primary curriculum accordingly. Children continue to need to develop and hone their physical and motor skills and dabble in imaginative play and art, crafts, music and drama activities. Very often, these generate lifelong interests and pursuits. Early talent identification may also happen. Because energy levels are high, activity-based curricula seem appropriate.

Late childhood corresponds with the primary level of schooling. The child is now positioned from class one to five. Since the rate of growth is slow and the child is basically improving upon previously acquired skills and abilities, the primary school curriculum is usually organised sequentially and in a spiral of levels of difficulty of conceptual understanding. For instance, by the time the child is in class five, he/she is expected to engage in fairly complex mathematical functions in arithmetic and geometry and build an understanding of variables and relationships as the basis for beginning algebra. So from class one onwards, the engagement with knowledge of numbers, number functions, computations, linking numbers with word statements, drawing inferences, recognition of shapes, sizes and volume and simple construction geometry are taught through classes two, three and four. Variables denoted by different alphabets are also introduced.

Similarly, in language, from simple words, there is movement to more complex words, multiple connotations that they might have synonyms, opposites and introduction to simple proverbs where the figurative meaning of words is introduced. The use of grammar to enable appropriate language construction and use also follows movement from simple to more complex forms. So the sequence is nouns, verbs, adjectives, adverbs, conjunctions and prepositions and then learning how to combine all these parts of language into different forms of language expression like direct speech, indirect or reported speech, descriptions, narrations of one's experience, etc. These are targeted sequentially through the primary years. The child's dexterity and competence in language expression correspondingly increase. The focus is on augmenting the child's inherent capacity to learn. Prose and poetry as important genres of language begin to be understood. The pattern is similar in terms of concept organisation and how it is learnt in environmental science as well.

The physical and motor abilities of children also become more specific, with much better levels of body coordination and muscular control. Group games, sports, exercises, yoga, simple gymnastics and dancing rhythmically are all part of the primary school curriculum. They clearly illustrate refinement in physical development over what the child could do during early and middle childhood. Social development during late childhood focuses on building friendship skills, an elementary understanding of society and the worlds of home, school and the environment in which the child lives. By the time children are ten or eleven, they learn how to live in these parallel social worlds in accordance with the standards expected of them.

They learn to follow rules, respect authority and comply with the norms and traditions of their home, school, neighbourhood, community and peer group. They also acquire a sense of right and wrong, good and bad, and learn appropriate forms of social, emotional and moral behaviour and conduct.

It is at the next stage that the physical and psychological revolution occurs. As the child enters the stage of puberty, which launches him/her into the world of adolescence, the hormonal activation of the gonads transforms the child into rapid progression towards his/her adult form. The process is marked by visible bodily changes that alter body contours' shape, size and dimension. These will be discussed in greater detail in the chapter that deals with adolescence. Accompanying body changes are also a multitude of emotions that arise, ranging from excitation, passion and idealism on the one hand to shyness, bewilderment and self-doubt on the other. Attraction to the opposite sex, hero worship and identifying role models connected with glamour or high levels of celebrated achievement, particularly in sports or research contributions, are characteristic features of adolescence. Adolescence has been stratified developmentally into early, middle, and late adolescence because bodily changes and corresponding physiological functioning of the reproductive system take a few years to unfold to full maturity. In terms of schooling years, the stage of puberty and adolescence corresponds with the secondary and senior secondary years from classes six to twelve. Cognitively, the thinking and reasoning capacities of adolescents keep on expanding, and they can engage in fairly complex abstraction.

They can engage in analysis, making judgements, induction, deduction, hypothesising and floating simple theories. Since the need to establish an identity of their own is felt very strongly, striving for autonomy, questioning authority and non-compliance with rules and standards are also often seen. Language and communication skills improve considerably, so it is not unusual to see adolescents in arguments, debates and passionate discussions. Friends and peer communities become very important. In fact, there is a movement in most adolescents from family approval and dependence towards peer group dependence and acceptance. Energy levels are high, and the social needs for recognition, achievement, prestige, esteem and belongingness become very strong. It is because of this augmentation in capacity that the curriculum of the secondary and senior secondary years becomes very expansive and includes many subjects – ascending levels of conceptual organisation, different modes of evaluation, project work, a variety of co-curricular activities, life skills and application of various parameters of performance and achievement. School is like a miniature society, and so it is during adolescence that the skills required to survive in the adult years are honed and built up. The stage of early adulthood deals with higher education and ongoing professional development.

What is seen in the descriptions given above is that the growth curve helps us to link innate capacity with expectations of skills and standards at different levels of education. It also helps to establish the standards and norms based on what most persons at a particular age are able to do. It thus legitimises age and stage linkages, spelling out the stage relations expectations, which may be called 'normative' standards. When these are established, deviations from them also become important to recognise and address. So in many ways, implicit in the growth curve is also an ideational concern for inclusion.

1.2 Principles of Development

A very important concept that helps us to understand the nature and course of human development relates to the principles of growth and development. These apply universally and have been established by developmental psychologists over a period of time. For all those involved in the process of education, they have immense relevance since they put the process of human development into perspective, explaining its various contours and dimensions. They also help to make decisions about teaching–learning, curriculum management and development.

1.2.1 Development Is a Sequential and Orderly Process

This principle suggests that for all human beings, the course of development is the same. Infancy is always followed by childhood, adolescence, adulthood and, finally, old age. This is true for any part of the world. Language development in human beings moves from non-discrete sounds in infancy to more discrete sounds and syllables in early childhood, the beginning of simple words, then phrases, then short sentences to more complex ones and complex language expression by adolescence.

All developmental processes in human beings are based on sequence and order of progression. This helps greatly in setting expectations, goals and targets.

1.2.2 Development Is a Continuous Process

This is very important to understand since it implies that the experiences that an individual has keep on adding value to him/her. There are phases of heightened growth and development, but at no stage is development complete. So, dynamism and change are natural to human beings. Further, one stage paves the way for the next, but there is developmental continuity between stages. For example, even with the advent of puberty and adolescence, many features of late childhood continue to show up in the behaviour of the adolescent. Chronological age sets the normative standards for stage-wise classification, but an individual's behaviour, attitudes and skills maintain a continuum of development.

1.2.3 Development Is Influenced by Heredity and the Environment

This principle of development throws light on what is known as the nature-nurture debate in Education. It suggests that many aspects of our development are influenced by genetic factors, such as how we look, our temperament, our intelligence and our emotional disposition; however, the environment in which these unfold also influences us greatly. In fact, it is difficult to separate one from the other. There are many examples of children who are originally from a particular country who move to another country to pursue education or find their families relocating to a new place. They pick up the language, culture, ways of dressing, food habits, etc., characteristic of the place which is their new habitat with considerable ease, showing that the environment has a significant influence on how we develop. Similarly, individuals who migrate to towns from rural areas learn the ways of the new urban environment very quickly and often find it difficult to return to their earlier lifestyle. It is from this principle that another very important inference is made. Rather than the environment remaining generically defined, what happens is that it is the local cultural context that determines the course and direction of development. So, although some universal dimensions related to maturation and growth unfold in all individuals, the specific ways they manifest will depend on the context in which they have been shaped. The examples already given amply illustrate this aspect. Development is thus both a universal and contextual process.

1.2.4 Development Proceeds from 'Global' to 'Analytical' to 'Synthetical'

There are three keywords which require understanding in this principle of development. 'Global' refers to a 'generic' or what may be called an 'all or none' response. Initially, babies respond with their entire body and later learn to use their hands and legs specifically. For example, babies cry in the same way in the early months to signal hunger, excretory needs and physical discomfort. Later, as they are five to six months old, they have differentiated cries, emerging syllables, sounds, discrete words, simple sentences and full language usage. When the analytical moves to integration or synthesis of the specific parts, it is called synthetical. If we reflect on our ideas as adults, we can trace them back to a set of analytical points which emerged from some generic or global ideas that we initially had. We then typically use our analytical ideas to weave together a perspective representing our view/ideology. This process is seen in all aspects of human development.

1.2.5 Development Proceeds from 'Ego-Centrism to Allocentricism (Self-Centredness to Others' Centredness)

Initially, young children are very self-centred and pleasure-seeking. For them, their needs, wants and sources of joy are important. They are unable to factor in the needs of others. So, it is not uncommon to see them demanding objects at any hour of the day; often, they want eatables, toys, etc., without knowing the difficulties that their caregivers go through, especially when the demand is in the middle of the night! They also often ask for things which their families cannot afford since they are unable to factor this into their cognitive scheme of things when they are very young. As they grow older, however, they begin to relate to others, start understanding their perspective, their contexts, the situation of the family, etc., and so there is a visible shift towards other-centredness. Their behaviour and attitude begin to reflect the spirit of their family, school, etc. The ego-centredness of early childhood should not be confused with the ego-centricism of the adult years. Adults with 'ego' are fully aware of their life situation and become 'self-centred' as a personality stance. In early childhood, it is entirely a developmental issue and not due to a determined behavioural stance.

1.2.6 Development Proceeds from Heteronomy to Autonomy (Dependence to Independence)

This is seen as a universal trend. Initially, infants and children depend on their caregivers for support and facilitation of their development. However, as they grow, they start doing things themselves and want to do them in their own way. Whether it is physical movement, decisions, relationships, studies and career pursuits, this shift towards independence is visible. For example, parental supervision of a child's homework is not required after a certain age. Adolescents learn to travel to school and back on their own. They also go for various activities on their own. Children decide their preferences in clothes, shows and what they like or dislike quite independently from their parents. They begin making independent programmes with their peers and friends as they age. Choices pertaining to the subjects they would like to study, the stream they would like to specialise in and the envisioned career goals all have a strong element of their personal benefits and wishes.

1.2.7 All Dimensions/Spheres of Development Are Interrelated

It is important to understand that while development is process-based and is a holistic concept, there are different dimensions or spheres in which it can be seen. The most significant are physical, intellectual, social, emotional and moral development. There is considerable interdependence among each of these dimensions. For instance, if physical development is delayed, social and emotional development is affected. Likewise, if there is any form of intellectual impairment in a person, his/her social and emotional life, physical activities and sense of morality all get affected. At the same time, as we grow older, any aspect/dimension may develop at a more rapid pace based on our interests. In the case of individuals wanting to be scientists, for instance, intellectual development will be dominant; for a social worker, it would be social development; or for a sports person, it would be physical development.

1.2.8 Individuals Differ in the Rate/Pace of Development

In all the earlier principles of development, it was seen that there is an element of prediction in the pace of development. There are expected norms and standards about when each aspect of a child will develop. There is a stronger propensity for correlating age and stage development. However, often, it is seen that the developmental process cannot be predicted with such accuracy, and so to overcome this phenomenon, the notion of a 'range' is used. 'Range' provides flexibility and variation, which is commonly seen. For example, some babies cut their first tooth at the age of six months, some at eight or nine months and some even at the age of one year. So the question of the normal age when this should happen arises. The answer lies in specifying that infants cut their first tooth any time between six months and one year of age. Such variations are seen at every stage, for instance, when children learn to speak, when they can make decisions on their own, when they can operate a computer, when they attain puberty, when they can travel on public transport on their own, etc. All such similar questions follow the notion of a range. At times, there may be a gross departure from the range. For instance, with respect to puberty, there may be early or late puberty as well. So, norms and standards remain important within a 'range' of operation.

The principles of development help educators to find answers to many questions, some of which were raised at the beginning of the chapter. They also help establish the enormity, magnitude and importance of the development process, especially in the field of education. In the following sections, we will discuss some of the theories of development in the various domains discussed above.

1.3 Piaget's Theory of Cognitive Development

Cognitive development goes beyond the mere addition of facts and new information. It refers to developing new ways of thinking that are qualitatively different from how the world has been perceived. Jean Piaget was a Swiss biologist who worked closely with the famous psychologist Alfred Binet, who has been credited with developing the first intelligence test. In his work in the field of intelligence testing, he noticed that children of the same age group tend to make similar errors while solving problems. In studying patterns of children's problem-solving processes, he concluded that children's thought processes are qualitatively different from those of adults. This led him to understand that children are not illogical but 'pre-logical'. In the following paragraphs, Piaget's theory of cognitive development has been described. This understanding of cognitive development is significant for teachers as it influences their perceptions about how children think and learn.

1.3.1 Key Concepts in Piaget's Theory

Piaget believed that cognitive development takes place as children grow up. To make sense of the world, children interact with the world around them. In describing the different stages of Piaget's theory, it is seen that the nature of this interaction tends to change with the growth and maturation of children. Maturation is one of the four factors that Piaget identified as having a significant influence on how we think. Besides *biological maturation, activity, social experiences* and *equilibration* are other factors that influence how we make sense of the world. Maturation refers to the natural and biological changes accompanying growth processes across various life stages. Activity refers to engagement with the environment and learning from it. Cognitive development also takes place in engagement with others around us. Social transmission, or learning from others, ensures that we are able to build upon the knowledge that others in our culture have already developed. Equilibration refers to the process of reaching a balance in thought in the face of new information. This has been addressed in greater detail in subsequent paragraphs.

Besides these four factors, cognitive development is influenced by two basic tendencies inherited by all species. These are organisation and adaptation. *Organisation* refers to the process of arranging and combining thoughts and behaviours to make coherent sense. People organise their thoughts into 'psychological structures' called *schemas*. According to Piaget, these are the basic building blocks of cognition. As people grow, they develop more sophisticated cognitive structures that help them engage with the world more effectively. For example, an infant uses his hands to grasp objects within his reach. Through touch, she develops a schema of a milk bottle. However, she is not able to coordinate this with other schemas that she may have developed through 'seeing' a bottle, satiation of hunger or the caregiver. As the infant grows, these individual schemas expand, rearrange themselves and develop more meaningfully, independently and together.

Adaptation refers to the process of adjustment to the environment. Adaptation includes two processes: assimilation and accommodation.

Assimilation refers to the process of including new information into existing schemas or what we already know. For example, when a child walks into a mall and observes a mannequin draped in women's clothes, the child is likely to address it by referring to it as an older woman. The child may wonder how or why the woman is standing completely still or how the skin tone is different. This additional information will either be discarded or included in the existing schema of an older woman's appearance. In accommodation, existing schemas are changed in response to new situations and experiences. For example, a child has a schema of a dog. But when he sees a cow, he will need to modify the schema, as the new schema of size variation in the body, such as the tail or the presence of horns, will not fit into the existing schema of a dog.

In everyday settings, the processes of assimilation and accommodation are not disconnected and tend to take place simultaneously. Thus, these processes are not an either/or choice but are used together to make more efficient and elaborate schemas.

At this point, it is important to re-visit the concept of equilibration that was discussed above. Piaget believed that the processes of organisation and adaptation serve the larger purpose of equilibration, or finding a balance. The balance is constantly disturbed by new information from the world. Equilibration exists if an existing schema is adequate to explain an event encountered. Where the new event causes a sense of discomfort or dissonance, it demands a change in how we think or our schemas. This disequilibrium triggers the processes of assimilation and accommodation.

1.3.2 Stages of Cognitive Development

Piaget believed that all children pass through four stages of cognitive development that correspond roughly with their age. These stages are universal, which means that all children, irrespective of cultural background, pass through these stages in the same order. However, these stages are not definitive. This means that people may exhibit thinking associated with one stage in one situation and another stage in another situation. The change process from one stage to another is also a slow transition process. Thus, children's age is insufficient to label them as belonging to a particular stage. The four stages of Piaget's theory have been discussed in the subsequent paragraphs.

1.3.2.1 Sensorimotor Stage

This stage lasts from zero to two years. At this stage, the child's understanding of the world is determined by his/her sensory engagement. This is responded to through motor movements that include reflex actions and exploration of the environment through reaching out for objects and people. In addition, goal-directed behaviour develops at this stage. Thus, realising that the child is not able to carry all the toys in one go, he/she may choose to put them in a bag/trolley to meet the goal. Another key characteristic of the sensorimotor stage is object permanence. For a young child, out of sight is often also out of mind. As the child grows, he/she develops the notion that an object exists even when he/she is not able to see it. This is manifested through children's behaviour in looking for toys/objects that have rolled under the bed, looking for people behind curtains or in the simple game of peek-a-boo. The development of object permanence marks the transition to the next stage.

1.3.2.2 Pre-Operational Stage

This stage lasts from two to seven years of age. Children at this age are incapable of establishing cause-and-effect relationships. They are, thus, often presumed to be illogical. Piaget argued that they are, in fact, pre-logical and not illogical. In other words, they haven't reached a stage of cognitive development to establish cause-and-effect relationships. This stage has been subdivided into the pre-conceptual stage and the intuitive stage.

In the pre-conceptual stage, Piaget believed that children could display some concept formation; however, this was not akin to concept formation in adults. While some classification and categorisation are evident, e.g. being able to identify objects, sub-categorisation and differentiation are often missing, e.g. while playing with blocks, children will be able to classify blocks according to colour or according to shape. But when asked to identify only blocks of a particular colour/shape, they may be unable to do it. For example, a box containing multi-coloured blocks of square, triangle and circle shape may be sorted by a child. The child will place all squares, circles and triangles in three separate groups. At the same time, red triangles and red squares may be placed together, as may be green circles and green squares. Thus, the criteria of classification may keep changing. This is known as syncretic reasoning. Other forms of reasoning that pre-conceptual children display are transductive reasoning and animistic reasoning. An example of transductive reasoning is to mistake all vehicles with wheels for cars, thus not differentiating between buses, trucks, cars, bicycles or animal carts. The characteristic of such reasoning is that it is based on a single criterion and may lead to faulty conclusions. This also gives rise to animistic reasoning, wherein children attribute animate or life-like characteristics to inanimate objects, such as assuming the television to be alive since it can speak!

The pre-conceptual stage lasts from two to four years. The second sub-stage of the pre-operational stage is the intuitive stage. It is referred to as intuitive as during this stage, children's beliefs are based on what they 'think' to be true rather than what they have logically deduced. Questions are thus answered based on what seems to be the right answer. They would not try to logically attempt to arrive at a solution.

Another key characteristic of this stage is egocentrism. This refers to children's thoughts being centred on themselves. Thus, they expect everyone to understand when they have a headache or are hurt. But they would not understand when others have been hurt.

1.3.2.3 Concrete Operational Stage

The third stage begins around seven years of age and lasts up to eleven years. This stage is marked by the transition in children's use of logical thinking. Their thinking continues to be concrete. In other words, they are unable to think in abstract terms. Thus, they focus on 'what is' and not in terms of 'what may be'.

In contrast to syncretic reasoning, children now understand that things and people can belong to multiple categories simultaneously. This is coupled with the ability to seriate. Children would now be able to correctly categorise objects according to shape and colour in the problem discussed in the previous stage. They would also now be able to comprehend that a box containing four red and six blue squares has more squares than red squares. In others, they would develop the ability to understand that one category (red squares) is subsumed under the larger category of squares. Another example is developing the understanding that people can be Assamese and Indian at the same time. This ability leads to numeration. A better understanding of numbers develops with the ability to seriate. Children understand that addition always leads to more of a product.

A key ability developed at this stage is understanding the reversibility of operations. Things taken out of a box can be put back inside. Play dough can be repeatedly reused. Egocentrism is replaced with decentration, which marks the ability to comprehend multiple perspectives simultaneously. This is supplemented by the ability to conserve. Conservation refers to the understanding that the amount of a substance does not change unless something is added to or subtracted from it, even though its shape or form may change. In the play dough example taken above, the child who can conserve will know that rolled-out play dough is the same amount even when made into a ball, a house or a caterpillar!

Finally, logical reasoning at this stage assumes an inductive character. Children can generalise from their own experiences at home and school.

1.3.2.4 Formal Operations Stage

This stage begins around the age of twelve years. Piaget proposed that this was the final stage of cognitive development. The key ability developed at this stage is operating at the abstract/ideational level. Adolescents no longer need concrete objects for deductive reasoning and solving complex problems. They can systematically construct and test hypotheses and perceive abstract relationships. This is known as hypothetico-deductive reasoning, involving thinking steps beyond the realm of concrete reality. Instead, adolescents who can operate formally shift to thinking about possibilities and often construct a utopian world for themselves.

1.3.3 Critique of Piaget's Theory

Piaget's work is considered one of the most insightful descriptions that have contributed to understanding how children think. However, his work is not free from limitations. Although psychologists agree that children go through the changes that Piaget has described, they question the existence of stages. There is also an inconsistency in Piaget's notion of conservation and when children achieve conservation in various domains of number, weight, etc.

Further, Piaget has been accused of having underestimated children's mental abilities. In areas of expertise, children perform much beyond what they are expected to be able to cognise. Finally, Piaget's work seems to ignore the influence of children's cultural and social groups. Thus, people will use cultural knowledge to classify objects in accordance with what makes sense to them.

This brings us to another significant contributor to the understanding of cognitive development – Lev Vygotsky.

1.4 Lev Vygotsky's Sociocultural Learning

Vygotsky was a Russian psychologist who worked towards developing an understanding of learning and development. He began work to improve his teaching but became a key proponent of the sociocultural approach. His early works were banned in Russia as he referred to many Western theories. However, the last quarter of the twentieth century saw a rediscovery of his work and a resurgence in the field of sociocultural psychology.

Vygotsky believed that all children's cultural development appears first at the social level and then at the individual level. In other words, mental processes are co-constructed first at the 'inter-psychological' level during common or shared activities. In the second stage, these processes are internalised by the individual and become a part of his/her cognitive development. This is known as the 'intrapsychological' level. Thus, Vygotsky saw social interaction as not just an influence but as the origin of higher mental processes. He proposed that social interactions with peers, parents and teachers serve as a model for constructing knowledge. This includes learning problem-solving skills and thought patterns that can help to function better. For example, when a young child complains to the teacher about a peer who has taken his pencil, the teacher's questions about where and with whom the pencil was last seen help the child learn how to retrace steps and locate the pencil. The child then uses the same strategy in other settings.

1.4.1 Cultural Tools

Vygotsky believed that 'cultural tools' play an important role in cognitive development. The term 'cultural tools' describes all tools, including 'real tools' such as rulers, books, printing press, computers, etc., and 'symbolic tools' such as language, mathematical operations, formulae, and the like. These real and symbolic tools support thinking, learning and cognitive development. Higher-order mental processes, such as thinking and problem-solving, are accomplished through the use of these tools. This process is referred to as mediation. Children learn to use these tools through their everyday interaction with adults. This may also occur in formal educational settings, such as schools or informal home environments. An example of this is a geography class where children learn to use maps to represent spaces. Thus, children develop knowledge and ideas by learning ways of thinking from their environment and engaging with more capable adults and peers. Vygotsky believed that language was the most important tool for children. It helps them to develop other tools using the symbol system of their language.

1.4.2 Speech and Self-Regulation

Language is, in fact, considered critical for cognitive development. Not only is it a means of expressing oneself but also a tool to ask questions. It is often considered a tool to voice one's thoughts when encountering difficult problems. Different cultures develop a repertoire of words to represent what is important to their culture. Vygotsky also believed that language serves as a guide to cognitive development through 'private speech'. Unlike Piaget's notion of children's speech being egocentric, Vygotsky believed that private speech was important in self-regulation. Children tend to use private speech to direct their own behaviour. Over a period of time, private speech is replaced by inner speech. This transition from audible to inner speech is considered an important aspect of cognitive development. Private speech generally disappears by the age of nine years. However, when faced with a tough problem, older children and even adults are seen engaging in private speech.

1.4.3 Scaffolding and Zone of Proximal Development

A significant implication of Vygotsky's theory is that merely creating an environment for discovery will not be sufficient to support learning. Children cannot be expected to discover on their own. Assisted learning or guided learning in the classroom can be provided through appropriate scaffolds.

This may be in the form of giving appropriate information, prompting, reminding about earlier learning, etc.

In order to understand what kind of assistance children may require, it will be important for the teacher to identify the student's zone of proximal development. This is the level of learning where the child requires assistance in learning. Thus, the child will work independently till the stage that she/he can. This will be followed by scaffolds in the form of questions or directions that can help the child to proceed further.

1.4.4 Critique of Vygotsky's Work

Vygotsky's approach has been criticised for its lack of clarity in understanding the development process. Further, it disregards the role of the individual and does not address differences in learning that arise out of engagement in groups.

1.5 Moral Development

Stage theorists have argued for a synergic development in the moral and cognitive domains. One of the key thinkers in the area of moral development was American psychologist Lawrence Kohlberg. Kohlberg furthered Piaget's theory of moral development. Both Piaget and Kohlberg used a storytelling technique that served as a case in which people were asked to reason out and choose an alternative.

1.5.1 Jean Piaget

Piaget believed that children aged five to ten years make sense of the world through a heteronomous morality that is external to them. Rules are governed by authority figures and not by the children themselves. Thus, the words of parents, teachers and the government are considered to be absolute and unquestionably asked. Rules are considered to be unchangeable, universal and everlasting. No conditions justify breaking the rules. Most children tend to reason by following rules with the expectation of negative consequences. In avoiding punishment, children follow the rules completely.

By the time children reach middle childhood, they have developed perspective-taking abilities that allow them to shift from an absolutist stance towards moral decision-making. They are now able to understand situations from the viewpoint of others. Piaget termed this as the 'morality of cooperation'. Children are now able to think and reason independently. They also understand that rules are formed by society and are changeable to benefit the larger society. Children will continue to follow rules as it will be considered important for society. However, they will understand that these are negotiable guidelines that are meant to improve society at large. This stage is referred to as autonomous morality.

1.5.2 Lawrence Kohlberg

The two stages of heteronomous and autonomous morality were developed further by Kohlberg, who proposed a three-level, six-stage theory of morality. His work is best remembered by his use of the story, often referred to as the Heinz dilemma. Heinz's wife was suffering from cancer and was dying. Doctors had told Heinz that a new medicine could save her. The medicine had been developed by a chemist who had kept a high price for it. Heinz desperately wanted to purchase that medicine but could not afford it. He pleaded with the chemist to sell the medicine to him at a cheaper rate, but the chemist disagreed. In his desperation, Heinz stole the medicine from the store.

The story is followed by questions on whether Heinz was right in stealing the medicine and the moral obligation of Heinz and the chemist to save the woman.

Kohlberg presented this story to seventy-two young boys aged sixteen years living in Chicago. The answers were studied from a life span perspective to present a stage theory that documents the development of moral reasoning across various ages. He eventually presented three levels of moral reasoning that develop in the sequence in which they are presented. Everyone does not reach the third level of reasoning.

1.5.2.1 Level 1 – Pre-Conventional Moral Reasoning

This level of morality is typical of children around nine years of age. Here, morality is developed according to the standards set by adults around us. The consequences of moral behaviour determine whether rules are broken or not. This level is marked by two stages:

Stage 1 – Obedience and Punishment Orientation: This typifies children's behaviour as being directed by the fear of punishment. All children will engage in 'good' behaviour to avoid punishment.

Stage 2 – Personal Reward Orientation: This refers to a focus on self-interest. Children of this age group tend to believe that whatever is beneficial for them personally is the right thing to do.

1.5.2.2 Level 2 – Conventional Moral Reasoning

This stage is generally reached by adolescents. Many adults also tend to stay in this stage and do not move beyond post-conventional moral reasoning. At the conventional stage, the moral standards of adults are internalised by adolescents. Much of moral reasoning is based on the social norms of the group to which the person belongs. This level is divided into stages.

Stage 3 – 'Good Boy'–'Nice Girl' Orientation: In this stage, the person chooses to act morally to win the approval and appreciation of others.
Stage 4 – Law and Order Orientation: In this stage, the person is more aware of the social rules and logic behind them. The focus is on behaving in accordance with the larger social order, upholding the law and avoiding guilt.

1.5.2.3 Level 3 - Post-Conventional Moral Reasoning

At this level, moral reasoning is based on a reflected sense of justice and rights. The person acts in accordance with what one has arrived at through his or her thinking. This is similar to Piaget's idea of autonomous morality. This is the highest level of moral reasoning, according to Kohlberg. This also necessitates the ability to think in abstract terms. Kohlberg believed that only ten to fifteen per cent of the general population reaches this level. This level has been divided into two stages.

Stage 5 – Social Contract Orientation: At this stage, moral behaviour is seen to be guided by what is socially agreed-upon standards. Thus, morality is dependent on the society in which one lives.
Stage 6 – Universal Ethical Principle Orientation: In this stage, the person looks at what is right in terms of what his/her conscience allows. Here, the notions of justice, human dignity and equality become very important.

Kohlberg's theory has been critiqued on several grounds. The sample studied comprised a white male population. It is debated whether his theory applies to other cultural settings. Further, the Heinz dilemma was unfamiliar to young boys who were unmarried and had never been in such life-threatening situations. It is debated whether his sample was able to understand the problem situation at all. Kohlberg's work has also been criticised for being gender-specific. Having studied only males, his theory is considered inapplicable to women. Gilligan, in particular, argued that his sample led him to give greater importance to justice in place of care. She argued that women tend to be guided by compassion and care more than reason and justice, as is argued to be the highest stage of Kohlbergian moral reasoning. This argument also applies to collectivist cultures where the 'ethic of care' is more relevant than the 'ethic of justice'.

This brings us to the end of the discussion on development. In the following section, key issues in understanding diversity have been highlighted.

1.6 Understanding Diversity

Imbued in the process of development is the concept of diversity. Diversity is not a new concept but fundamental to all living species. However, in the field of education, it has acquired significance and focus only very recently. Earlier, it was understood in terms of the variation and heterogeneity across individuals. It was referred to as individual differences. Let us try to understand why this was so. For this, we will have to go back to how Psychology as a discipline developed and understand how it impacted and informed ideas in the field of Education. Basically, there are three important movements in Psychology that have impacted ideas in Education. The first movement was that of Psychoanalysis, through which the importance of the unconscious mind, personality development, sexuality and adjustment and psychotherapy was established. This was followed by Behaviourism, which focused on measurement, establishing norms and standards and externally mediating and controlling behaviour. The overarching assumption in behaviourism is that all behaviour is learnt either through association, conditioning, shaping or reinforcement. The personal wishes, violations and needs of the individual are not given any importance. All forms of mediation are external. Recognising the limitations of such an approach arose the Humanistic movement with a quest to understand the individual from the lens of his/her abilities, personal wishes and agency. Here, the uniqueness of every individual was important and required to be valued.

So, what is clearly seen is that both Psychoanalysis and Behaviourism focus on understanding a person in relation to norms and standards. In effect, the extent to which there was conformity to norms and standards was the critical feature. Any digression from this was seen as a variation. This could be clinically testified as was the case in Psychoanalysis or measured statistically through objectively designed tests as is the practice in behaviourism. The basic difference between Psychoanalysis and Behaviourism was that the former looked at individuals as cases but from the lens of normality and abnormality. Behaviourists were interested in prediction and control; hence, the 'normative' was the standard. Anyone at variance with the norm or standard was seen as deviant.

If we examine any school in terms of its composition, we can very clearly see both variation and heterogeneity. Variation is seen in students' learning abilities, intelligence, behaviour, attitudes, interests, goals, motivation, needs, achievement scores and talents. The variation is in terms of the measured levels of each of these variables being different, as of how they manifest in the person. For instance, intelligence can be average, below average or above average. Learning abilities can be subject-specific or generic in nature. Motivation can range from low to high, and interests and talents can be in different domains and areas. When a discrete variable is selected and measured, then a range of scores is likely to emerge. This measured approach looks at individual differences as variations. However, if in the same school, the same variables are studied in terms of how they are represented in different students without getting into norms, standards or measurement; we look at differences across students as heterogeneity. There will still be differences, but these will be attributed to students from different genetic and environmental backgrounds. 'Heterogeneity' as a concept does not 'standardise' or 'uniformise'. It acknowledges that there will be individual differences because individuals have different genetic makeup, grow up in different environments and have different life experiences.

In the last decade, individual differences have begun to be understood as 'diversity'. Diversity as a concept refers to living things of different shapes, sizes, intrinsic nature and species types co-existing harmoniously. If we look at a large expanse of forest land, different kinds of vegetation are seen to exist in sync with each other. In bio-diversity parks, which have replaced traditional botanical gardens now, the assumption is that flora and fauna co-exist in a relationship of mutual interdependence, and this is what represents diversity.

In society, diversity is seen in many ways – individuals belong to different social and cultural contexts, giving rise to social and cultural diversity. Some individuals are challenged on account of disabilities. This is also another kind of diversity. In a school, diversity stems from differences in caste, region and economic background.

1.7 Concluding Remarks

In this chapter, we have built up an overview of development, including its various stages and the principles of development. The approaches to understanding development were discussed through the works of Piaget and Vygotsky. Moral development, another important dimension of development, has been presented through the key ideas propounded by Piaget and Kohlberg. The theories of cognitive development and moral development by Piaget and Kohlberg present a universal, stage-oriented pattern of development. Vygotsky, on the other hand, shifted the focus to cultural situatedness in learning and development. This also brings to light the need to understand the diverse personal and social contexts in which children grow and learn. This has been briefly discussed in the last section of the chapter. The discussion in this chapter serves as the background in which subsequent chapters in this book can be understood.

Bibliography

Berk, L. E. (2011). *Child development* (8th ed.). New Delhi: Pearson Prentice Hall.

Berk, L. E. (2014). *Development through the lifespan* (6th ed.). Hoboken: Pearson.

Driscoll, M. P. (2005). *Psychology of learning for instruction* (3rd ed.) Boston: Allyn and Bacon.

Santrock, J. W. (2010). *Life span development* (13th ed.). New York: McGraw Hill Higher Education.

Santrock, J. W. (2017). *Child development* (13th ed.) New Delhi: McGraw Hill Education.

Saraswathi, T., Madan, A., & Menon, S. (Eds.). (2018). *Childhoods in India: Traditions, trends and transformations*. London: Routledge.

Vygotsky, L. (1978). *Mind in society: The development of higher psychological processes*. Cambridge: Harvard University Press.

Vygotsky, L. (1986). *Thought and language*. Cambridge: The MIT Press.

2

CHILDHOOD OR CHILDHOODS?

Diverse Perspectives on Understanding Children

Ravneet Kaur

2.1 Introduction

We are often curious to find answers to certain perplexing questions pertaining to children and childhood, such as 'Who' and 'What' is a child? What images do we bring to mind when we think about a child? Are children really as adults perceive them to be? Are children entities in their own right? As individuals, how do children live and experience the world? What is childhood all about? Does the form of childhood remain static and universal, or does it change over time and place? Indeed, the intrigues of children and childhood are many, each raising a set of questions to be probed and understood.

Childhood was once thought of as a life stage that was considered to be universal and invariant. The dominant ways of understanding childhood within the courses and books in Education, Psychology and Child Development rested extensively on the concepts of development and progression. It is only very recently that the cultural constructions of childhood have begun to get acknowledged and researched, leading to acceptance of the idea that several forms of childhood can and do actually coexist. Similarly, assumptions of the traditional developmental theories that viewed childhood as uniform and fixed have been refuted. They find articulation in this chapter. Some alternate approaches to understanding childhood have also been presented. The chapter begins by describing the dominant perspectives on children's development. It then deconstructs the myth of childhood's universality by presenting arguments supporting socially and historically constructed ideas of childhood. It also brings to the fore the multiple views and forms of childhood by tracing their origins in the historical past, their evolution and how

DOI: 10.4324/9781003505501-2

they exist in contemporary times. The chapter foregrounds the existence of multiple childhoods, especially in India, as seen through the lens of social class and gender. The primary findings presented in the chapter have been drawn from my doctoral research, where the focus is on the sociocultural contours of childhood in India.

2.2 Dominant Perspectives on Children's Development

Among the dominant ways of understanding childhood, the major paradigm for studying children was established through Developmental Psychology (Walkerdine, 2009; Woodhead, 2003), where there is extensive reliance on the development metaphor (Hogan, 2005). Within the academic imagery of the disciplines of Developmental Psychology, Child Development and Education, childhood was traditionally understood in terms of development and progression (Burman, 2008; Woodhead, 2006). In recognising development as 'lifespan' to death, most textbooks follow a chronological age and stage approach in delineating development. Some go on to specify age limits on periods of development in childhood, such as Beginnings: 0–1 years; Early Childhood: 1–6 years; Middle Childhood: 6–12 years; and Adolescence; 12–18 years (Dworetzky & Davis, 1989). Likewise, educational discourse tends to categorise children as preschoolers, primary school children, middle school children and high school children. In the Indian context, these correspond to levels of schooling designated as pre-primary, primary, secondary and senior secondary.

The developmental approach largely draws on the works of Piaget (1968), Kohlberg (1969, 1971) and Erikson (1950), among others, in which universal features of change and growth through predictable chronological age and stage-based theories are identified and described. Although they have been described in Chapter 1, it is imperative to briefly dwell upon some of the ideas they carry, particularly those that have attempted to theorise children's development.

In Piaget's account of cognitive development, children's development is linear and has a particular structure, consisting of a series of predetermined stages, leading to the eventual achievement of logical competence. This is the mark of adult rationality. This leads us to believe in a universal childhood and expectations of qualitatively different natures of thought as children pass through different stages. Piaget divided cognitive development into four broad stages. The first is the Sensorimotor Stage, extending from 0 to 2 years. At this stage, schemes are built on the sensory capacities of infants, and what is also seen is the development of object permanence, imitation, goal-directionality and symbolic thought. This is followed by the Pre-operational Stage, which extends from 2 to 7 years and is characterised by illogical, irrational, rigid, and egocentric thought, especially when seen from the adult lens. As was described in Chapter 1, children at this stage have intuitive thought, transductive reasoning and centration on only one idea, which often leads to the development of faulty concepts and poor ability for conservation. They do not fully understand seriation, numeration and reversibility, either. So, they end up forming pre-concepts rather than full concepts. The next stage is the Concrete Operational Stage from 7 to 11 years. This stage is marked by increased logic, flexibility in thinking, ability to perform 'operations', reversible and decentred thinking, and ability to hierarchically classify, seriate and recognise different components of concrete objects and experiences. The final stage is the Formal Operational Stage, extending from 11 years and beyond, characterised by rational, systematic, hypothetico-deductive reasoning and reflexive thought, eventually leading to the formation of complex and abstract notions and ideas, which mirror how adults think and reason.

Piaget (1968) also worked on moral development in children and proposed a two-stage theory that explained the development of morality in children. The first stage was called the heteronomous stage, where rules were seen to be fixed and taken as given by external authority. So, any act is judged as moral or immoral regardless of the intentions of the act. The second stage is the Autonomous Stage, in which judgements are based on cooperation and reciprocity of human relationships and do not go by fixed and given rules. He found heteronomous morality in younger children and autonomous morality emerging in older children. Kohlberg (1969, 1971) extended Piaget's work and described moral development in six stages. At Stage 1 (Punishment and Obedience Orientation), the individual considers something morally correct if he/she can avoid punishment by obeying the rules. At Stage 2 (Instrumental-Relativist Orientation), an act is considered morally right if it serves personal interest and constitutes a social exchange. In Stage 3 (Good Boy-Good Girl Orientation), an act's rightness and wrongness are based on whether that act leads to social approval and good interpersonal relationships or hampers them. Stage 4 (Law and Order Orientation) is based on the criterion that fulfilling duty and upholding laws do the common good to society. Stage 5 (Social Contract Orientation) follows that the laws of the society may be changed to serve people's welfare and be beneficial to society. At Stage 6 (Universal Ethical Principle), moral judgement depends on a person's criteria against the backdrop of a belief in certain universal moral principles.

Piaget believed that all children worldwide pass through pre-determined stages, and no stage can be skipped. These stages are thus theorised as sacrosanct and invariant, applicable across cultures, which is not without contradictions. His view underscores the function that environment and cultural variations can play. According to Piaget, children construct knowledge through activity in a responsive environment, but children's own 'active' role in the construction is given primacy and social dimensions of either the activity or environment are not so important. Likewise, the moral development theories proposed by Piaget and Kohlberg rest on the assumptions that the highest moral sense emerges with age, implying that children move from childhood immorality to adulthood morality due to improvements in cognitive reasoning and justice being the highest moral value. These theories underscore social influences and assign secondary roles to learning and environmental influences.

The importance of environmental influences in children's development can be seen in Bronfenbrenner's theory (1986). He viewed the environment in terms of the nested hierarchy of 'micro', 'meso', 'exo' and 'macro' systemic contexts, each influencing each other and the child interactively. The importance of learning emanating from environmental influences, particularly from the sociocultural context of the child's world, was emphasised by Vygotsky (1978) through his concept of the 'Zone of Proximal Development' (ZPD). He argued that social agents such as parents, peers, adults and others play a significant role in the internalisation of tools and the development of higher psychological functions such as deliberate memory, attention and goal-directionality. Children's thinking, cognition and related skills develop in their attempts to apply the tools of culture. Bruner (1986) added that children gradually appropriated the adult world through the communal processes of culture. Jenks (1982) emphasised an evolutionary model where the child developing into an adult represented a progression from simplicity to complexity of thought and behaviour. However, he acknowledged the diversity of childhoods on the way to adulthood (Jenks, 1996).

Thus, the developmental approach was based on an evolutionary model where development was viewed as orderly, unfolding in a predetermined sequence related to age with universal application to all cultures and societies. It is imperative to note that such categorisations into age and grade levels also tend to push children to achieve developmental and educational milestones within the specified periods. This suggests that children are 'human becomings', in a state of 'not yet being' (Corsaro, 2011; James & Prout, 1997), lacking the skills, capacities and powers of adults (Archard, 2004), and thus, on a stage like a journey to adult competence, which is characterised as rational, mature and responsible (Verhellen, 1997; Walkerdine, 1993).

It is important to highlight here that the assumptions of these traditional developmental theories that viewed childhood as universal, uniform and fixed, rather than being a sociocultural phenomenon influenced by culture and context, have in the last decade been challenged, and alternate approaches to understanding childhood have been floated. The section that follows presents some of them.

2.3 Childhood as Socially and Historically Constructed

This approach to the study of childhood is committed to the view that 'child' is not just a 'biological' category and that childhood is not necessarily a 'natural' phenomenon (Aries, 1962). It emphasises that children are socially constituted (Jenks, 1992; Qvortrup, 1993; Stainton Rogers, Hevey, Roche, & Ash, 1991), and childhood is culture-specific and socially constructed (Misra & Srivastava, 2003). This approach alludes to the work of James and James (2004), who explicated the socially constructed nature of childhood. It finds roots in the new paradigm of childhood studies (James & Prout, 1990). It highlights the view that it is impossible to imagine universal and invariant characteristics of childhood (Aries, 1962; Gergen, Gloger-Tippelt & Berkowitz, 1990). Neither can childhood be seen as static and timeless. Childhood varies as a function of time and space (James, Jenks & Prout, 1998). The notions of childhood thus need to be situated and understood through a cultural lens, recognising the varying social contexts (Jenks, 1996) and processes through which human development takes shape (Sharma & Chaudhary, 2009). There is no finite form of childhood, which has been established historically (Aries, 1962) and cross-culturally (Mead & Wolfenstein, 1954; Whiting & Whiting, 1975). James and Prout (1997) support this by explaining that the immaturity of children may be a biological fact of life, but how this immaturity is understood and provided with a meaning depends on the cultural context in which it is situated. Each culture defines children and childhood differently, and these beliefs mediate what it means to be a child and help to understand when childhood begins and ends (Richards & Light, 1986; Schaffer, 1996; Woodhead, Faulkner, & Littleton, 1998).

The way children are viewed today was not how they were viewed till a century ago. The modern concept of childhood as we know it today is a product of relatively recent technological societies. Such a view of childhood was non-existent at other times. Phillipe Aries (1962), in his book Centuries of Childhood, offers an account of the lives of European children in the Middle Ages. He highlighted that although children were always present, they were not viewed as a separate category worthy of adult attention. Childhood was a stage that came and went rather quickly. Children until the age of 6 or 7 were considered 'infants' and, after that, as little adults. They were expected to behave as adults with adult thinking and interactions. They were looked down upon as a burden, and there was little empathy towards the needs of the children in the West until the thirteenth century. This led to atrocities against them in the form of abandonment, sale of children, infanticide and so forth. By the sixteenth and seventeenth centuries, there was a shift in this form of physical suppression. It moved from overt physical torture to covert and relatively subtle forms of internal suppression, in which 'disciplining the child's desires and child training' was most important to socialise the child, make the child fit in and become acceptable for society. There was a felt need to discipline the 'wants' of the child from the beginning of life. This was done to curb the 'satan' in the child. It was believed that a child was born corrupt and selfish and was unfit to be a part of society. This selfish nature of the child was seen to pose difficulties for the parents. Hence, curbing it in the name of disciplining became mandatory. It was only in the eighteenth century that childhood came to be recognised as a distinct category. After that, there was a noticeable positive shift to a 'nurturing and caring' attitude towards children.

French philosopher Rousseau contributed to the modern idea of childhood and emphasised the 'needs' of the child, which he believed were to be protected and nurtured. He also spoke about the inherent capacities of the child, which would unfold over time. The need for stimulation and education was further accentuated. The work of Saraswathi (1999) on childhood drew attention to socialisation settings, processes, outcomes and ways of studying childhood in the sociocultural matrix. She highlighted that out of the three models of socialisation (Jahoda & Lewis, 1987) that had emerged from European thought – the unfolding model based on the belief of inherent potentials for which nurture only provides a forum; the moulding model with emphasis on shaping, training and dominance of nurture; and the interactive model which acknowledges the role of both nature and nurture – the last two models are what stand as the best representations of Indian ethnotheories about children and their development. She added that the Indian psyche sees the child being born with basic predispositions based on his/her genetic makeup and carried over from his/her previous birth. The role of the family is to nurture the child so that his/her potential is actualised and negative tendencies constrained.

2.4 Childhood in Contemporary Times

The twentieth century was characterised by defining childhood as a special period of the life cycle and recognising the 'needs' and 'natural development' of children. This impacted early education, where the need to give space for play and the child's emotional and physical well-being started getting important (Burman, 2008). This also brought to the fore the concern about the welfare of children of working parents. There were improvements in health care and other facilities for children. With the introduction of compulsory schooling in the 1930s, childhood became a period for learning. More and more schools were established to socialise children.

Some scholars believe that childhood as a life stage is a product of the Industrial Revolution, which required parents to be available to work at factories, made possible by placing children in institutionalised care, such as schools. The working class was deliberately removed for labour, and their children were placed in schools, which gave them a 'childhood'. Thus, childhood as a category was 'created' to suit the market's needs. The childhood we see today is a result of cultural and political conditions constructed by the society of adults in recent times. With the direct impact of new theoretical perspectives and the influence of current research on policy formulation, an overall attitude of empathy and welfare for children has emerged. The United Nations adopted the Convention on the Rights of the Child (CRC) in 1989, where member countries were bound by international laws to partner in protecting children's rights. It spelt out the rights of the children (any human being under the age of 18), restricted the involvement of children in military conflicts and prohibited the sale of children, child prostitution and child pornography. India, too, is a member of the CRC and follows numerous policies and schemes dedicated to the welfare of children.

In the following sections, childhood, as seen through the lens of social class and gender, is discussed.

2.4.1 Social Class as a Dimension of Socially Constructed Childhood

Two major dimensions that colour the social construction of childhood are class and gender. Gittins (2009) pointed out that childhood, historically, was not just differentiated by age but also by class and gender. While collectivising children into childhood, there is an inherent threat of losing the differences between children with regard to their social class, gender, disability (James & Prout, 1997) and ethnicity (Ferreira, 2004). This section discusses how social class is a significant variable that provides different contours to childhood, followed by the notion of multiple childhood(s).

Vasanta (2004) argued that there is a dominance of the middle-class white, male urban childhood as the norm in psychology, education, welfare policies and legislation for children. She thus sounded the urgent need to rethink some of the prevalent notions about childhood, work and schooling and incorporate social class differences into the study of childhood. Cannella and Viruru (2004) emphasised that a universal claim that each child finds opportunities to play, experiment and discover their world is indeed exclusionary. Mehta (1997) believed that despite these being 'universals' that bind children, they still work for exclusion. In his understanding, all children across cultures do not grow up in similar environments. Within cultural anthropology, Das (2003) and Nieuwenhuys (1999) focussed on the meanings children give to issues of violence and labour that affect them.

Further, child labour and schooling (Balagopalan, 2008) have also been studied over time. The micro-lives of 300 children and the processes involved in curriculum transactions by children from working-class families studying in government schools in Andhra Pradesh were taken up by Pappu and Vasanta (2010). The authors flagged a lack of fit between quality and inequality in school education because much of educational theory assumes that every child in the classroom is the same. The study challenged the fixed meanings of childhood across economic classes and communities.

In addition, it is important that childhood gets contextualised in the familial-sociocultural milieu and the overall social dynamics of the culture and context where it is being lived and experienced. For instance, dependency, emotionalism, compliance and group-mindedness are some of the defining characteristics of Indian culture that provide flavour to all aspects of the lives of Indians (Sharma & Chaudhary, 2009), including their notions pertaining to children and childhood. The variables of economic status, parental education and family type were used by Devi and Rani (1997) to capture associations between the quality of social environment and children's intellectual performance. Chaudhary (1995) found that personal space, privacy and exclusion have become highly valued in upper-class urban homes. Further, some researchers point out that child-rearing practices were communicated within extended family ties, but with the erosion of the extended norms, there appear to be class differences between mothers who rely on their mothers' advice and those who reach out for professional help for raising their children (Jones, 1987; Vukelich & Kumar, 1985). Hence, child rearing must also be seen through the lens of social class. Sharma (2003) points out that while understanding the contemporary Indian family and society, the changes in the economic and socio-political life of Indians must also find space.

The seminal work of Saraswathi (1999) on constructions of adolescence in relation to social class and gender, wherein she identified and described specific portraits of adolescence stemming from variations in the socio-demographic landscape in which they were embedded, inspired me to research and paint different portraits of childhood that got created as a function of variations in income levels and gender during my doctoral research. Keeping the Indian social context at the centre of discussion, the following section brings to the fore the existence of multiple childhoods in India, as also endorsed in my research.

2.4.2 Multiple Childhoods in India

As stated in the sections above, research has shown that children's lives are intricately entangled within the mesh of their familial contexts, which in turn draw from the larger framework of the societal context in which they live. To unpack the nature and forms of diversity in childhood, it is thus imperative to consider children's familial contexts and experiences within families. Families belonging to particular income levels share some common features which create particular patterns of childhood. Parental income, education of family members, financial assets, lifestyle and the type of school that the children study in become some of the defining parameters of income of the families. I researched twelve family units consisting of children, parents and grandparents for the study. Data were gathered through semi-structured interviews, home observations, children's drawings and pictures adapted from the Indian adaptation of the Rosenzweig Picture-Frustration (P-F) Study (Children's Form) (1959). Some specific family processes that were studied included ways in which families structure their daily lives, interact, share experiences and deal with conflicts; the nature of parent–child relations with special emphasis on parental support, responsibilities, care and nurturance; and parent–child interaction focussing on the level of engagement between them and children's contribution in household responsibilities. In addition, data were gathered by recounting the lived childhoods of parents' and grandparents' generations. The text that follows presents descriptions of the unique social contexts, which include the social profile, resources with children, aspirations of parents for their children, daily rhythm and routines of children and any other features of significance. These have been located in families typifying different income levels, namely higher, middle and lower-income families, and the childhoods lived by the children in these families.

2.4.2.1 Childhood of Children Belonging to Higher-Income Families

The higher-income families resided in relatively large houses in high-end urban localities. All the families hired domestic helpers and drivers. The parents, as well as the grandparents, were well educated. Fathers either ran their businesses or worked in senior positions in reputed companies. Fathers' work involved long working hours and frequent travelling both within the country and abroad. The mothers either contributed to the family business, worked in reputed companies, or were homemakers. In all the families, paid domestic help was arranged to take care of the children. The grandparents, who were also educated, mostly supervised the children to ensure they were cared for by the nanny.

The children from high-income families studied in high-fee-charging schools catering to the elite population segment. The decision about which school the child would be enrolled in was crucial for the parents of this income group. The school was accorded immense importance for it was seen as a place where children were likely to build on their cultural capital ideas, and values; engage with suitable peer communities; and also dream and aspire. Hence, the parents were very particular about selecting an appropriate school for their children. For the parents from high-income families, their children's education remained a priority, and they wanted to provide their children with a good learning base. Education was, however, valued not only for its instrumental value but also for the knowledge and thought that it provides. Parents wanted their children to settle professionally into respected professions such as doctors, lawyers or business. At the same time, they were favourably disposed towards their children's inclinations and talents in acting and singing and were open to accepting their children's own professional choices. Children were expected to do well in their studies, but hobby classes and learning specific skills were also valued. Children's education was perceived as a long-term investment for securing their future. Securing the future meant making them financially strong, with a legacy of money, property, fixed deposits, bonds, policies, etc., and also emotionally strong and resilient.

The children of these families usually had many amenities at their disposal. Most of the time, they had separate rooms in their respective homes. The children's rooms were installed with television sets, and they also possessed a tablet, which they shared only with their siblings. Each child had his/her own cupboard, study table, toys, books, and clothes to be worn at home and parties. The children decided and chose for themselves what they wished to wear for which occasion, with minimal interference from anyone, including their mother, who sometimes gave suggestions. The parents bought expensive toys and branded clothes for the children, believing that 'their children deserve the best'.

A regular day in the lives of children from high-income families began with getting ready for school. They were assisted by their mother or some other caregiver, such as the grandmother, in getting ready. They got help in taking a bath and getting ready; were provided a clean and ironed school uniform from the child's cupboard; were served breakfast; provided lunch to be eaten at school; and were either driven by the driver of the family to the school or the child was dropped to the pick-up point of the school bus, escorted either by the mother or the grandparents or by the domestic help. The accompanying adult carried the child's school bag as it was felt 'the school bag was too heavy to be carried by the child'. In the afternoon, the children returned from school escorted by one of the adults in the family or with the driver or the domestic help. After returning from school, the children were not expected to do anything except keep their school shoes and books at their appropriate places, which most children did not usually do. They dropped their schoolbag, shoes, water bottles, ties and other stuff here and there in the home, only to be picked up later by the mother or any other caregivers, such as the grandmother or the domestic helper. Most children usually had their lunch in front of the television in their rooms. The mothers, along with the help of the grandmother and/or the domestic help, served freshly cooked, hot food immediately to them. Children's eating patterns from these families were tightly monitored, and they were expected to 'eat right'. However, children from this income group ate relatively more junk food than children from middle- and lower-income families. The children of working mothers phone and report to them what they were doing after returning from school. On television, usually, the children watch the programmes of their own choice and often play alongside their board games or tablets. They mostly played unattended on the tablet. Grandparents often sat around when the children played on their tablets or phones but were clueless about what the children were doing on their gadgets. When the children were asked to put aside their gadgets, they often negotiated with their parents to play on them for a little longer.

In the evening, after having milk with energy supplements, the children usually went for hobby classes such as dancing and drawing or playing in the housing society's park. They were escorted to both places. Upon return from the park, they were usually served snacks, after which they completed their homework under the supervision of either their mother or someone else from the family or a paid tutor. Dinner was a full family meal at the dining table. The food was laid out, and ample choices were available for eating. The children could choose what they wanted and did not want to eat. While the dinner table was laid out, the children were not expected to carry out any task related to the dinner preparation. Thus, the children from these families were generally not expected to contribute to domestic chores and were given everything that qualifies for a comfortable living. Regarding interaction, the parents spent 'quality time' with their children by listening to them and taking them out to a mall, market or park for recreation.

From the above-mentioned social context and experiences of the children in these families, what can be seen is that in the high-income group, childhood was protected and celebrated. The adults thought childhood was a stage of pampering and indulgence by the caregivers. This somewhat romanticised version of childhood compels the parents to celebrate their children's childhood and ensure that their child lives that childhood. As a result, the children from high-income families lived a pampered and protected life. They were provided, nurtured and cared for. Their wishes were usually fulfilled. They were provided with all amenities, sometimes in excess.

2.4.2.2 Childhood of Children Belonging to Middle-Income Families

The children from middle-income families resided in relatively small houses, generally a living room and a single-bedroom flat or house. Most of the parents in this income group were educated. Typically, the fathers were the income generators, with some help from the mothers and the grandparents. The sample families functioned as single-income cohorts. The women of the family shared responsibilities for the household chores.

The families had limited resources as their income funds were either diverted or kept safe for buying a house and providing for their children's educational needs, like tuition and upcoming coaching fees for 'engineering and medical' professions. The children of these families were provided with all the basic amenities, which included food, clothing, shelter, books, etc. Usually, the families had a single television set mounted in the living room, and the entire family watched television together as routine. Although at certain hours of the day the children watched what they chose to watch, for example, cartoons, most of the time, the children watched what the rest of the family watched, which included serials, news and other content that was sometimes appropriate for adult audiences only. The grandparents in most families insisted that children should watch serials like *Ramayana* and other religious programmes and refrain from watching serials with violent content. The parents pressed the need to watch programmes with educational content, such as those on Discovery and National Geographic Channels. The children were provided with course books and toys that were not very expensive, but the parents bought books on general knowledge, autobiographies of eminent people and story books for their children whenever they got a chance to visit any bookshop or book fair. The parents wished to inspire children to do well in life and inculcate the values of hard work and dedication in them. The children were seen to be well dressed, although they sometimes shared the clothes and books with the older sibling and were even passed down to the younger siblings. Often, the mother decided what the child would wear for particular occasions. So, the children were inducted into economising on the available resources from an early stage in life. The parents encouraged sharing among children and often brought only one set of colours, toys and eatables for all the children. Many families did not have any internet facility at home, neither did the families own any computer or tablet. However, the parents arranged for printouts from their office or any nearby cyber cafe whenever the children needed them. Most middle-income families recognised the growing need for computers and the internet and planned to buy them in the future for their children. The parents instated that learning has become technology-oriented and for a better future for their children, they must be provided with the basic learning tools which now extend from books to computers.

As mentioned above, the families had limited space available to them in their homes. Separate rooms were not available for the children. So, the younger children usually slept with their parents in their bedroom. The older child of the family, along with the grandparents and other family members, usually slept on folding beds that the families laid out either in the living room or lobby of the house at night and stacked away in the morning. In some middle-income families, verandahs or balconies were covered and made into a room for the children, recognising that the children, who were 'growing up', needed a separate space. Here, 'growing up' had multiple connotations, such as growing physically in size, needing space to study, becoming sexually aware and mature and so forth. Due to space constraints, the children were mostly in the company of adults. So, while the adults discuss all types of issues, the children of the family sit around and hear their conversations.

The children in this group usually went to privately run schools that catered to children from middle-income families. These schools charge a moderate fee. They do not provide personality-building activities such as swimming and horse-riding like the high-end elite schools, but they adequately provide children with the basic infrastructure. The education of their children was considered very important by the middle-income families. They believed that education could be a means to ensure a better future for their children and their families. They stressed saving money to provide a better educational experience to their children.

A brief description of the contexts in which children from middle-income families grow up provides insights into the kinds of childhood experiences children in such contexts were likely to have. As in the case of children from high-income families, the day of these children too began by getting ready for school. The children were woken up by their mothers, who helped them prepare for school. While the mothers prepared breakfast and packed lunch for the children, the children got ready. The mothers helped the children dress and tie their hair in the case of girls. The clothes were kept on the bed for them. Since the children usually had only two sets of school uniforms, the mothers ensured they washed the school dress daily. The fathers or any other family member accompanied the children to the bus stop from where the school bus or van picked up the children. In the afternoon, the mothers, the grandmothers or anyone else from the family picked up the children from where the school bus dropped them. The children carried their school bags. After returning from school, while the children changed their clothes, the mothers served food for them. The children kept their dirty clothes in the bathroom and other things in their designated places (sometimes, the grandmother helped them change clothes and keep their belongings in their places). For many things, the parents emphasised that their children should learn to do their work themselves, without anybody's assistance. The children brought their food from the kitchen themselves. They watched television while having lunch. After this, they often took a short nap. In the evening, most children from this income group went for tuition. Their mothers dropped them off at the tuition centres, which were nearby. College-going students often took tuition. The parents reasoned that children were in the age of competition and needed extra inputs they could not provide. So, tuition was considered necessary for those inputs and regularity in studying. Although some mothers, fathers and grandmothers helped the children with their homework, they believed additional input would benefit them. Overall, children's schedules were tightly packed around educational activities.

After returning from their tuition, the children usually played either in the street, on the verandah of the house or in the park outside the house. While the children played in the park outside their homes, the mothers kept a watchful eye on them either through the kitchen or accompanying them downstairs. Most of the fathers returned in late evening, and this was the time when the children were called back home. After this, they were expected to maintain 'discipline' at home and complete their homework, which either their fathers or grandmothers helped. The younger children were also generally made to sit and draw or flip pages of any book with pictorials. The families assumed that this would generate interest in them for studying. Some children were seen to study while the television was switched on in the background.

The time spent jointly between the children and parents mainly included playing, watching television and studying together. On holidays, the fathers took the children for outings to markets, temples and/or relatives' places so that they could give them some time and provide them with some enjoyment. In their summer vacations, the children often accompanied their parents to their native villages. They were seen to spend time with the mothers, assisting them in the family chores. As a matter of routine, the children were not expected to do any household chores, but throughout the day, they were asked to run small errands of fetching things, handing things to the mother while she cooked, checking things, clearing up, bringing milk from the market, dusting the home and so on. The girls, in particular, helped their mothers wash the dishes and sweep the floor. In the absence of the parents, the children cared for the younger siblings by serving them food, helping them complete their homework and so on.

Thus, the type of childhood lived by the children from the middle-income families was 'disciplined' and 'regimented'. It was seen as a preparatory stage for subsequent adult life responsibilities and was thereby crafted to prepare children for the same. Although the children were loved, cared for and protected, unlike in the higher-income families where being cared meant 'being provided everything', here love, care and protection translate into 'being prepared to face the challenges of life'. The children were inducted into more middle-class practices of economy of resources and time. Thus, children's activities were goal-oriented and with a distinct instrumental purpose. Education was seen as a means of employment and upward mobility. Hence, the parents invest heavily in the education of their children. Pushing the child for studies was identified as a common phenomenon for the middle class (Saraswathi, 1999), which Elkind (2001) perceives as a feature of 'hurried childhood'. While Viruru (2000) relates this to 'a sense of insecurity which pervades the Indian middle class', Kumar (1993) interprets it as an expression of adult-child continuity. Likewise, in decisions pertaining to children's choices of food, clothing and play materials, the children were provided with what the parents could best provide, and the children were encouraged to optimally use them and learn to share those resources with their siblings. High value was placed on making the children 'cultured' and '*sanskari*' (culturally approved behaviour).

2.4.2.3 Childhood of Children Belonging to Low-Income Families

The lower-income families lived in small houses, either in slum clusters or in other unauthorised constructions. Given the size of the home, exclusive spaces were not available for children. All the members of the family coexisted in the common living space. Since the space inside the house was limited, most family members, including children, moved freely and frequently in and out of the house. The adults and the children often sat outside the home, and the neighbours often came and sat with them. The children played and roamed in the streets and the areas surrounding the home. The family's income was minimal, and the families lived under severe financial constraints. The parent's education level was usually below eighth standard, and the grandparents were either illiterate or had only basic literacy. The mothers either engaged in paid employment or helped their husbands from home in occupations like jewellery making, ironing clothes and street vending.

The children went to government-run or government-aided schools that provide free education, mid-day meals, uniforms, books and other scholarships to all children. In lower-income families, education was valued for its instrumental returns. The educational process was not valued the way it was by families belonging to the middle-income group. In fact, for the parents, especially boys, getting a good job, learning any skill or settling into some income-generating activity was what they aspire for. Children's employment was seen as a means of sustenance and upward mobility for the child, and the family. Interestingly, unlike the case in the higher and middle-income families, the children in these families were valued more for their economic contribution to the family rather than being the source of joy, solace and psychological comfort. The parents, however, wished for them to get 'better and more respectable' jobs and lead a better life than them.

The children in these families grew up in poverty and hardships. The parents were barely able to provide basic amenities to their children. The children were seen to have limited clothes, bought from the weekly markets or obtained from the benevolence of their parent's employers. Employers often distributed the clothes that their children no longer wore. So, many times, the children wore second-hand clothes. The parents tried to buy new clothes for the children at festivals. Most of the children from lower-income families did not have the complete set of schoolbooks that they required. This was partly because of the government's poor distribution and inadequate home purchasing power. They had few toys to play with. However, this did not limit their playing capacity. They either made symbolic toys like paper balls and dolls from old torn clothes to play with or played games with other children that did not require any materials. The children did not have access to the internet at home, but the boys visited nearby internet cafes to play games. The children, however, had access to their parents' phones, which they used to play games on. Since the families had limited space available to them at their homes, children had no space of their own. There was, thus, continuity in the spaces inhabited by the adults and the children of the family. As a fallout of this, there was continuity in the conversations heard by the children, of the adults and vice versa. The children either watched television in their homes, with other family members or in their neighbours' homes. Generally, along with cartoons, because of common watching time, they also ended up watching what the family's adults preferred watching. These programmes were often meant for adult consumption, but the children ended up watching them.

A regular day in the life of the children from low-income families began with getting ready for school. The children either woke up on their own (as some slept in the open, outside the home) or were woken up by someone in the family. They used community toilets, so they queued up in front of them. After getting ready on their own, they sometimes ate something cooked by their mother; they relied on the mid-day meal at school. Since the schools were in their neighbourhood, the children walked across to the school, sometimes accompanied by adults but often on their own or with peers. They carried their bags and, at times, the bags of their younger siblings, too. Since the family's adults were engaged in paid jobs, the children were not picked up from school by any adult family members. After returning from school, the children helped themselves to lunch their mothers prepared. If the mother were available, she would serve the food. If the mother was absent, the older siblings served food to the younger siblings. The children usually changed their school dress and wore home clothes after lunch. In the evening, the boys went for tuition to centres nearby. The parents provided little input since they were not well educated. The mothers sometimes sat with their children to give solidarity and support when they were studying. The girls usually played with their peers near their homes, while the boys ventured out to places farther away from home as well.

After coming home from school, till night, some of the children helped their parents in their occupations, such as beading jewellery that the father sold in the market; collecting clothes for ironing from people's homes and returning ironed clothes to their respective homes, and keeping tab of the money collected from ironing; helping the mother spread the washed clothes on clothes lines; filling chutney in packets while the father or mother makes momos or chaat to be sold in the market; and so forth. The girls, in particular, helped with household chores like washing dishes, sweeping and fetching water in utensils they could carry. The boys cleaned the cooler, stood in queue to fetch water from the community tap and completed market-related tasks. Since the families operated on a daily economy and food items were bought daily, the children were sent to the market often to buy different things required by the family. These tasks became part of the children's daily routine. The adults from these families held that the children should contribute to household chores as early as possible since this was a combined family responsibility. The children seemed to comply with this expectation with ease.

In low-income families, owing to limited income resources, the children were observed to have what may be termed as early adultification, which involves adult-like responsibilities of sibling care, 'parenting' the parents and the grandparents by keeping tab of their medicines, providing them assistance in their ill health, and witnessing circumstances such as financial constraints, violence, street culture and sexual exposure. All these tacitly communicate to them the reality of their social circumstances. Unlike in middle- and high-income families, the children here do not grow up in protected environments. This is a significant finding as it brings out the continuity between childhood and adulthood in this income group. Unlike the childhood in the higher-income group, the childhood of children in this income group cannot be called 'tension-free' and 'devoid of responsibility'.

Also, the nature of engagement with parents was different. It was interwoven into sharing tasks and coping with life. There were no vacant indulgences or what may be called quality time together, as was the case in high- and middle-income families. The parenting practices were based on what was required for survival. The children sometimes accompanied their parents to the places they visited, like family functions, weddings and community gatherings in the locality like '*ram katha, ramlila, bhandara*' and so forth. There were no specially planned activities or outings for the children.

Here, the appropriate metaphors that describe the childhood of children from low-income families were 'struggle' and 'early adultification'. The struggle was for everyday survival, and the early adultification came from the child-adult continuity, which existed in terms of children taking on adult roles in their childhood. Here, the children's education was considered necessary but not significant by the adults in the family. Income generation by boys and discharging domestic responsibilities by girls remain the key family expectations that commence in childhood. The nature of childhood lived and experienced by children from lower-income families nowhere reflects the idealised or normative image of childhood (Mohanty & Misra, 2000; Pappu & Vasanta, 2010) as depicted in early childhood policies (Viruru, 2005) and as mentioned in the United Nations CRC(1989), wherein any human being below the age of 18 years was considered a child, and regardless of the way different communities and societies consider their children, all children were to be provided uniform rights as recognised by the CRC.

Thus, there were three distinct childhoods and not one common childhood that coexisted, influenced by the socio-demographic profile of the families. The nature of childhood was varied, and the income level determined the kind of experiences the children would have. There was a stark difference in the lifestyles, daily lives and expectations from children of the three income groups. This led to differences in their childhoods.

Another significant dimension that colours children's experiences and, subsequently, their childhoods to a large extent is gender. The following section reveals the gendered nature of childhood as observed in Indian society.

2.4.3 Gender as a Dimension of Socially Constructed Childhood

Bartholomaeus and Senekevics (2015) argue that gender is under-theorised and rarely addressed, and any mention of gender tends to be fleeting. Although historically and socially, childhood appears as a gendered space, Aries (1962) highlights that the history of childhood in the West largely represents boyhood. The differences between boys and girls are often reduced to a list of differences wherever they are talked about. How gendered childhoods are constructed and what they mean for children themselves have yet to receive adequate attention (Bartholomaeus & Senekevics, 2015). Gender usually gets discussed when children's bodies and their play become the focus of analysis. Prendergast (2000) draws attention to girls' knowledge about their bodies and experiences of menstruation. Corsaro (2011) refers to gender in his work on children's interactions during play in their peer cultures. However, his focus remains on the differences in the patterns of interactions of boys and girls and does not specifically consider the constructions behind being a boy or a girl.

Childhood as a gendered construction has been taken up by Bartholomaeus and Senekevics (2015), who looked at gendered family practices among children from working-class backgrounds. Connell (2000, 2005) examined gender relations and patterns among children by investigating their daily routines. Anandalakshmy and Bajaj (1981) conducted an ethnographic study of the lives of children from the Momin Ansari community in Varanasi. This silk-weaving community from North India restricted the movement of their girl children, as young as 4 years of age, to their known houses in the neighbourhood. Girls were encouraged to stay indoors and inducted into household chores. Post-puberty, their marriage became a central concern.

In contrast, by 3 or 4, boys were inducted into basket weaving and later valued for their economic potential. Although this study is three decades old, the pattern of gender stereotypy and gendered roles and practices continues to determine the experience of childhood in many parts of rural and semi-urban India. Ilaiah (1996), in his work on the Kuruma community, shared that boys were taught sheep-rearing activities such as what to feed the sheep, how to identify different sheep, how to alleviate their diseased conditions, how to assist sheep in delivering the young ones, how to shear the wool and so on.

On the other hand, girls of the community were socialised to handle young children, husk paddy, powder dry chillies, weave wool into threads and cook in mud-pots. Marak (2010), commenting on the matrilineal Garos of Assam in North-East India, highlighted that the tasks allocated to boys and girls differed for the Garos. While boys fed cows, helped in agriculture and fetching the produce from the fields, and fetched firewood, girls took on sibling care, fetching water from the well, serving tea, feeding pigs, washing clothes, cleaning the house and cooking. Such studies point out the differential socialisation that girl and boy children receive in different communities. This is what largely accounts for different childhood experiences for both genders.

Considering gendered childhood in relation to sexuality, Kehily and Montgomery (2009) point out that drawing on the romantic discourses of childhood, children are positioned as sexually innocent. This Western idea retains its strength, as adults would ideally like children to be sexually innocent. Kumar (2006) argues that sexual innocence has been seen as the hallmark of childhood. Since the mid-nineteenth century, childhood continues to be seen as a category protected psycho-socially. These characteristics of childhood have remained unchallenged and continue to dominate the world's norms and educational ideals.

In the Indian context, studies of sexuality in the context of childhood are scant, as children, especially pre-pubertal girls in the Indian tradition, are considered pure and sexually 'non-polluting'. In traditional Indian society, before puberty, a girl is described as pure and comparable to a goddess. The fact of a girl's pubertal maturity and thereby symbolically communicating about her growing body and sexuality is done through pubertal rites. In Andhra Pradesh, it is customary for pre-pubertal girls to wear a long skirt and a blouse, and after attaining puberty, the dress changes to wearing a half sari, which serves the main function of providing an outer cover for the upper portion of the body. In sync with emergent sexuality and prospective motherhood, certain regulations on the girls' diet and movement seem to express the value of restrained and controlled sexuality and motherhood (Dube, 1988).

The context within which female sexuality takes shape is rooted in the ideology. The social rootedness of female sexuality stems from cultural and religious ideology. How female sexuality is viewed by society impacts the education of girl children. Chanana (2003) argues that reforms in women's education indeed underline 'domesticity and motherhood' as the goals of education. Since the protection of women's sexuality, i.e., their virginity and purity, is linked to the honour of their families, agnatic group and caste (Dube, 1997), the spaces they can occupy, including schools, are constrained. As formal schooling involves travelling beyond the vicinity of the homes, moving into public spaces and interacting with males (male teachers as well as boys) in co-educational schools, in some parts of rural India, when a girl attains puberty, she is pulled out of the school (Nambissan, 2004). Chanana (2003) adds that the reluctance of parents to send girls to school unescorted stems from the social need to protect the sexuality and virginity of girls. This will 'tarnish' the entire family's image and bring social stigma to the family of the abused girl. Hence, to safeguard the sexuality of girls, their education takes a back seat and gets restricted to the primary grades.

Parental neglect and discrimination of the girl child in India is reflected in various statistics (Bennett, 2004). Sharma and Chaudhary (2009) point out the gaps in the developmental journey of the girl child from childhood to adolescence and later life in India.

Analysing the relationship between modernity and female childhood, Kakar (1997) wrote about how, in urban middle-class families, the birth of a son is more welcomed than a daughter, especially when a son is born after a succession of girls. Nevertheless, the birth of a girl in a daughterless family is also an event that is wished for. Roopnarine et al. (1990) reveal that fathers and mothers do not prefer boys over girls in middle-class, educated families in New Delhi after birth. This evinces that parental discrimination between boys and girls is declining in urban India, although the trend is slow. Verma and Ghadially (1985) found that modern mothers from Bombay did not differentiate between sons and daughters and made the same demands on the child irrespective of sex. The mothers, however, prepared their daughters for work, achievement and motherhood.

The findings of my doctoral research, too, resonate with some of the research studies mentioned above. It stands true that the normative childhood of Indian society largely coincides with the childhood of middle-class boys. I explored the dominant constructions of childhood from children, parents and grandparents. In the data gathered from these participants, there was no mention of 'female childhood' as a prototype of a 'child'. The male child was present in the rituals and ceremonies associated with children. The silent exclusion of the female child was noticeable.

The aspirations and expectations from boys and girls differ, as a result of which their training for adult roles differs. Girls were socialised for taking on domestic tasks much earlier than boys. So, the girls babysat, played with younger siblings to keep them engaged, swept and mopped the house floor and washed the dishes. For boys, preparing for adult social roles meant learning to take on chores outside the domain of the home, but for the girls, it was related to chores done within the confines of the homes. In middle- and low-income families, since girls' aspirations revolved around getting married and settling into good families, induction into domestic work and being good wives and mothers was considered appropriate training. What was also being formed was a relational sense of identity, which Kakar (1997) highlights as the dominant construction of identity that prevails among women in Indian society. To be good daughters, wives and mothers was what became the *summum bonum* of their existence.

Considering gendered childhood in relation to sexuality, in my research work, children were considered sexually pure and innocent. Specifically, girls were considered sexually pure before puberty and celebrated for the same. However, both pre-pubertal and post-pubertal girls were considered vulnerable to sexual abuse. Consequently, a watchful attitude towards them on matters of sexuality and prevention of sexual abuse prevailed in all the income groups.

At this juncture, it is important to highlight that childhood cannot be understood exclusively in relation to either gender or income level. Significant intersections between the two factors bring out a more 'real' and 'nuanced' image of childhood. For instance, the childhood of a girl from a lower-income family is very different from that of a girl from a higher-income one. While one lives an adultified childhood, the other remains protected and free. For that matter, if the childhood of a girl from a higher-income family is compared to that of a boy from a lower-income family, one finds that the former has more provisioning and privileges despite being a girl. She is provided for and indulged more than boys from the other income group families. She does not have to partake of any family responsibilities, unlike boys from other income group families, who have to contribute in many ways. In the higher-income group, the same care, protection, discipline and controls are given to both genders. They are seen as children and not as sons and daughters. Both are equally given a protected environment, recognising their needs as children. Thus, the children are spontaneous, wilful and free of tensions and responsibility. Their wishes are honoured by both parents and grandparents. The parenting practices for both sons and daughters are the same, as are the dreams and expectations from them. Further, while continuity in childhood and adulthood was observed in the middle and lower-income families for both boys and girls, this was most apparent in low-income families for girls. Thus, the social construction of gender has to take cognisance of the intersection of all social factors and variables and the multiple ways they play out to create different childhoods.

2.5 Concluding Remarks

In this chapter, I have foregrounded that the experiences of Indian children and, subsequently, the childhoods that they inhabit have considerable variability. Hence, Indian childhood cannot be seen in monolithic ways. The insights generated in this chapter on multiple childhoods make us aware that generalised statements about childhood need to be viewed cautiously. The normative childhood aligns with the middle-class male childhood, which also fits, if not perfectly, with the Westernised normalised childhood. In contrast, Indian childhood and the lives of Indian children are vastly different. Hence, an understanding of the sociocultural matrix of the Indian child is necessary before importing the Western notions of childhood and assuming the middle-class childhood as the normative childhood. For a substantial period of time, most discourses on children remained largely Eurocentric (Raman, 2000). There has been a predominance of the developmental paradigm and the use of Western discourses in understanding childhood in India. Only in the last two decades has there been a significantly more contextual focus. The pluralism which marks Indian society in terms of region, caste, class, community, religion, gender and linguistic group creates several childhoods. Multiple childhoods are thus a visible reality in India, as in other parts of the world.

Bibliography

Anandalakshmy, S., & Bajaj, M. (1981). Childhood in the weaver's community in Varanasi: Socialisation for adult roles. In D. Sinha (Ed.), *Socialization of the Indian child* (pp. 3–39). Delhi: Concept.

Anandalakshmy, S. (1994). *The girl child and the family*. New Delhi: Department of Women and Child Development, Ministry of Human Resource Development.

Archard, D. (2004). *Children: Rights and childhood* (2nd ed.). London: Routledge.

Aries, P. (1962). *Centuries of childhood*. New York: Random House.

Balagopalan, S. (2008). Memories of tomorrow: Children, labour, and the panacea of formal schooling. *Journal of the History of Childhood and Youth*, 1(2), 267–285.

Bartholomaeus, C., & Senekevics, A. S. (2015). Accounting for gender in the sociology of childhood: Reflections from research in Australia and Brazil. *SAGE Open*, 5(2), 1–9.

Bennett, M. (2004). Children and social identity. *Psychologist*, 17(9), 512–514.

Bronfenbrenner, U. (1986). Ecology of the family as a context for Human Development research perspectives. *Developmental Psychology*, 22(6), 723–742. Retrieved from https://pdfs.semanticscholar.org/1737/8413f37060b3b705b71 58af59d61d3cb3385.pdf

Bruner, J. (1986). *Actual minds, possible worlds*. Cambridge, MA: Harvard University Press.

Buckingham, D. (2000). *After the death of childhood: Growing up in the age of electronic media*. Cambridge: Polity Press.

Burman, E. (2008). *Deconstructing developmental psychology* (2nd ed.). London: Routledge.

Cannella, G. S., & Viruru, R. (2004). *Childhood and (post-colonization): Power, education and contemporary practice*. London and New York: Routledge.

Chanana, K. (2003). Female sexuality and education of Hindu girls in India. In Sharmila Rege (Ed.), *Sociology of gender: The challenge of feminist sociological knowledge* (pp. 287–317). New Delhi: Sage.

Chaudhary, N. (1995). Researching communities: Travails of working with Indian communities. *Cross-cultural Psychology Bulletin, International Association for Cross-Cultural Psychology*, 43(4), 5–13.
Connell, R. W. (2000). *The men and the boys*. St. Leonards, Australia: Allen & Unwin.
Connell, R. W. (2005). *Masculinities* (2nd ed.). Crows Nest, Australia: Allen & Unwin.
Corsaro, W. A. (2011). *Sociology of childhood* (3rd ed.). London: Sage.
Das, V. (Ed.). (2003). *The Oxford companion to sociology and social anthropology*. New Delhi: Oxford University Press.
Devi, U. L., & Rani, S. J. (1997). Intellectual abilities of urban school children: Relationship with selected personal-social variables. *Indian Journal of Psychometry and Education*, 28(1), 9–14.
Dube, L. (1988). Socialisation of Hindu girls in patrilineal India. In K. Chanana (Ed.), *Socialisation, education and women: Explorations in gender identity* (pp. 166–192). New Delhi: Orient Longman for Nehru Memorial Museum and Library.
Dube, L. (1997). *Women and Kinship: Comparative perspectives in South and South-East Asia*. Tokyo: United Nations University Press.
Dworetzky, J., & Davis, N. (1989). *Human development: A lifespan approach*. St Paul, MN: West.
Elkind, D. (2001). *The hurried child: Growing up too fast, too soon* (3rd ed.). Cambridge: MA: Perseus.
Erikson, E. H. (1950). *Childhood and society*. New York: W.W. Norton.
Ferreira, M. (2004). *We like to play with the other boys! Social relations among children in kindergarten*. Porto, Portugal: Afrontamento.
Gergen, K. J., Gloger-Tippelt G., & Berkowitz, P. (1990). The cultural construction of the developing child. In G. Semin & K. J. Gergen (Eds.), *Everyday understanding: Social and scientific implications* (pp. 108–129). London: Sage.
Gittins, D. (2009). The historical construction of childhood. In M. J. Kehily (Ed.), *An introduction to childhood studies* (2nd ed., pp. 35–49). Maidenhead: Open University Press.
Hogan, D. (2005). Researching 'the child' in developmental psychology. In S. Greene & D. Hogan (Eds.), *Researching children's experiences: Approaches and methods* (pp. 1–21). New Delhi: Sage.
Ilaiah, K. (1996). *Why I am not a Hindu?* Kolkata: Samya.
International Institute for Population Studies. (2007). *National Family Health Survey (NFHS-3), 2005–06: India*. Mumbai, India: International Institute for Population Studies.
Jahoda, G., & Lewis, I. (1987). *Acquiring culture: Cross-cultural studies in child development*. London: Academic Press.
James, A., & Prout, A. (Eds.). (1990). *Constructing and reconstructing childhood: New directions in the sociological study of childhood*. Oxford: Routledge.
James, A., & Prout, A. (Eds.). (1997). *Constructing and reconstructing childhood: Contemporary issues in the sociological study of childhood*. (2nd ed.). Basingstoke: Falmer Press.
James, A., Jenks, C., & Prout, A. (1998). *Theorising childhood*. Cambridge: Polity Press.
James, A. L. & James, A. (2004). *Constructing childhood: Theory, policy and practice*. Basingstoke: Palgrave Macmillan.
Jenks, C. (1982). *The sociology of childhood: Essential readings*. Batsford: Academic and Educational Ltd.
Jenks, C. (1992). *The sociology of childhood*. Aldershot. Batsford.

Jenks, C. (1996). *Childhood*. London: Routledge.
Jones, D. (1987). The choice to breast feed or bottle feed and influences upon that choice: A survey of 1525 mothers. *Child Care, Health and Development*, 13(1), 75–85.
Kakkar, S. (1979). *Indian childhood: Cultural ideals and social reality*. Delhi: Oxford University Press.
Kakar, S. (1981). *The inner world: A psycho-analytic study of childhood and society in India* (2nd ed.). Delhi: Oxford Univ Press
Kakar, S. (1997). *Culture and psyche: Selected essays*. New Delhi: Oxford Univ. Press.
Kehily, M. J., & Montgomery, H. (2009). Innocence and experience: A historical approach to childhood sexuality. In M. J. Kehily (Ed.). *An introduction to childhood studies*. Maidenhead: Open University Press.
Kohlberg, L. (1969). Stage and sequence: The cognitive-developmental approach to socialization. In D. A. Goslin (Ed.), *Handbook of socialization theory and research* (pp. 347–480). Chicago: Rand-McNally.
Kohlberg, L. (1971). From is to ought: How to commit the naturalistic fallacy and get away with it in the study of moral development. In T. Mischel (Ed.), *Cognitive development and epistemology* (pp. 151–284). New York: Academic Press.
Kumar, K. (1993). Study of childhood and family. In T. S. Saraswathi & B. Kaur (Eds.), *Human development and family studies in India* (pp. 67–76). New Delhi: Sage.
Kumar, K. (2006). Childhood in a globalising world. *Economic and Political Weekly*, 41(38), 4030–4034.
Marak, Q. (2010). Sex typing of children's tasks: A study among the Garos of Assam. *The Oriental Anthropologist*, 10(2), 301–310.
Mead, M., & Wolfenstein, M. (1954). *Childhood in contemporary cultures*. Chicago: Chicago University Press.
Mehta, U. (1997). Liberal strategies of exclusion. In F. Cooper & A. L. Stoler (Eds.), *Tensions of empire: Colonial cultures in a bourgeois world* (pp. 59–87). Berkeley, CA: University of California Press.
Misra, G., & Srivastava, A. K. (2003). Childhood in India: An overview of psychological research. In A. Agarwal & A. K. Saxena (Eds.), *Psychological perspectives in environmental and developmental issues* (pp. 210–249). New Delhi: Concept.
Misra, G., Srivastava, A. K., & Gupta, S. (1999). The cultural construction of childhood in India: Some observations. *Indian Psychological Abstract and Reviews*, 6(2), 191–218.
Mohanty, A. K., & Misra, G. (2000). *Psychology of poverty and disadvantage*. New Delhi: Concept.
Nambissan, G. (2004). Integrating gender concerns. *Seminar*, 536, 1–9.
Nieuwenhuys, O. (1999). *Children's life worlds: Gender, welfare and labour in the developing world*. New Delhi: Social Science Press.
Pappu, R., & Vasanta, D. (2010). Educational quality and social inequality: Reflecting on the link. *Contemporary Education Dialogue*, 7(1), 96–111.
Piaget, J. (1968). *Six psychological studies*. New York: Vintage.
Prendergast, S. (2000). To become dizzy in our turning: Girls, body-maps and gender as childhood ends. In A. Prout (Ed.), *The body, childhood and society* (pp. 101–124). Houndmills, United Kingdom: MacMillan.
Qvortrup, J. (Ed.). (1993). *Childhood as a social phenomenon: Lessons from an International Project (Eurosocial report* 47). Vienna: European Centre.
Raman, V. (2000). Politics of childhood: Perspectives from the South. *Economic and Political Weekly*, 35(46), 40–55.

Richards, M., & Light, P. (Eds.). (1986). *Children for social worlds*. Cambridge: Polity Press.

Roopnarine, J. L., Talukder, E., Jain, D, Joshi, P., & Srivastav, P. (1990). Characteristics of holding, patterns of play, and social behaviours between parents and infants in New Delhi, India. *Developmental Psychology*, 26, 667–673.

Rosenzweig Picture-Frustration (P-F) Study (Children's Form). (1959).

Rousseau, Jean-Jacques. (1979). *Emile* (Allan Bloom, Trans.). New York: Basic Books.

Saraswathi, T. S. (1999). Adult-child continuity in India: Is adolescence a myth or an emerging reality? In T. S. Saraswathi (Ed.), *Culture, socialization and human development: Theory, research and applications in India* (pp. 213–232). New Delhi: Sage.

Schaffer, H. R. (1996). *Social development*. Oxford: Blackwell.

Sharma, D. (Ed.). (2003). *Childhood, family and sociocultural change in India: Reinterpreting the inner world*. New Delhi: Oxford University Press.

Sharma, N., & Chaudhary, N. (2009). Human development: Contexts and processes. In G. Misra. (Ed.), *Psychology in India: Basic psychological processes and human development* (Vol. 1, pp. 69–110). Delhi: Pearson-Longman.

Stainton Rogers, W., Hevey, D., Roche, J., & Ash, E. (1991). *Child abuse and neglect: Facing the challenge*. London: Batsford/The Open University.

U.N. (1989). *United Nations Convention on the rights of children*. United Nations. Retrieved from www.unicef.org/crc/crc.htm

Vasanta, D. (2004). Childhood, work and schooling: Some reflections. *Contemporary Education Dialogue*, 2(1), 5–29.

Verhellen, E. (1997). *Convention on the rights of the child*. Leuven: Garant Publishers.

Verma, R. K., & Ghadially, R. (1985). Effects of mother's sex role attitudes on need for achievement and expectancy for success in children. *Psychological Studies*, 30(1), 1–4.

Viruru, R. (2000). *Early childhood education: Postcolonial perspectives from India*. New Delhi: Sage.

Viruru, R. (2005). The impact of postcolonial theory on early childhood education. *Journal of Education*, 35, 7–29.

Vukelich, C., & Kumar, D. S. (1985). Mature and teenage mothers infant growth expectation and use of child development sources. *Family Relations: Journal of Applied Family and Child Studies*, 34, 189–196.

Vygotsky, L. S. (1978). Mind in society: The development of higher psychological processes. Cambridge, MA: Harvard University Press.

Walkerdine, V. (1993). Beyond developmentalism? *Theory and Psychology*, 3, 451–470.

Walkerdine, V. (2009). Developmental psychology and the study of childhood. In M. J. Kehily (Ed.), *An introduction to childhood studies* (pp. 112–123). Milton Keynes: Open University Press.

Whiting, B., & Whiting, J. W. (1975). *Children of six cultures*. Cambridge, MA: Harvard University Press.

Woodhead, M. (2003). The child in development. In M. Woodhead & H. Montgomery (Eds.), *Understanding childhood: An interdisciplinary approach* (Vol. 1 in Childhood, pp. 35–124). Chichester: Wiley/Open University.

Woodhead, M. (2006). *Changing perspectives on early childhood: Theory, research and policy*. Paper commissioned for the EFA Global monitoring report 2007 titled, Strong foundations: Early childhood care and education.

Woodhead, M., Faulkner, D., & Littleton, K. (Eds.). (1998). *Cultural worlds of early childhood*. London: Routledge/Open University.

3

CHILDHOOD IN INDIA

Socio-Historical Perspective

Nidhi Gulati

The present chapter attempts to outline the varied notions of childhood that have existed over different time periods from ancient to contemporary in India. However, before dwelling on the history of childhood, we need to spell out our understanding of 'childhood' and how we arrive at the history of childhood in our context. There is a dearth of scholarship on childhood in the Indian context, and several scholars have pointed this out. For instance, Kumar (2005) argues that childhood is a latecomer to social science scholarship in India. Even though the past two decades have witnessed a proliferation of work in areas of family history, women in political and family life, socialisation and education, empirical research on the construct of childhood, especially from a historical perspective, is scarce and sparse. Barring a few studies, the child has rarely been the central focus of such investigations. Our insight about the child in history is thus 'incidental'.

In the absence of a documented history of childhood in the ancient and the early medieval period in the Indian context, texts from various disciplines, viz., anthropology, sociology, feminist histories, mythology and histories of education, are used in this chapter to construct a narrative of childhood in India. Anthropological research on family also brings an insight into children's life experiences in cultural contexts. The history of children needs to be demarcated from the history of childhood. While the former includes accounts of real children at particular points in time in particular communities, the latter includes ideologies – the child as an idea or a figure of existence (Pande, 2013) – assumptions and beliefs about childhood. When we look at the child as an 'idea', the child is more than a biological entity. The child becomes a social and political subject, and the notion of childhood is based on ideology.

DOI: 10.4324/9781003505501-3

3.1 Overview of the Chapter

The first section draws from images of childhood in ancient folklore and oral history and includes influences from the twin epic texts, the Ramayana and the Mahabharata. The persistence of these influences can be seen even today in Hindu culture's image of the 'child as Krishna'. A deeply entrenched belief exists that each child embodies aspects of the divine. This section is followed by an empirical understanding of the construct of childhood in medieval times. The second section draws from the social and educational life of the colonial period. It highlights the experience of colonialism, the national freedom struggle and its intersection with childhood. The child had uses for both the colonial and the national projects, which are delineated in the second section. The third section of the chapter looks at social history in post-independent India, focusing on family, urbanisation and industrialisation. One aspect that appears to be continuous over time is the attitude towards young children, who are seen as pure and innocent. The chapter draws on ethnographic research from the 1950s to the 1980s, which revealed primarily indulgent and permissive attitudes towards children, where social control, boundaries and obligations did not restrict childhood. The last section focuses on the more recent impact of market forces on what constitutes childhood in neo-liberal India. This understanding is further deepened by the changes in economy and polity, reflected in the portrayal of family, the shifting nature of productive work and its relationship to schooling, the positioning of the child as a potential citizen and the persistence of folk motifs and beliefs. Following a historical trajectory, the chapter reveals how our understanding of childhood has been carved by various cultural, social and economic forces and continues to do so.

Which notions of the 'ideal child' do not accommodate the realities of children across the developing societies in the Indian subcontinent? A reflection on this question helps open up multiple childhoods which accommodate the lived experiences of children from diverse backgrounds. If childhoods differ, we must ask how various cultural, social and economic forces have carved the trajectory of understanding of childhood. In what ways does it continue to do so? The chapter attempts to answer some of these questions.

3.2 Childhood in History: Dominant Cultural Images

Childhood as a conception has found its place in diverse cultural forms in India. Folklore, mythological texts and literary work inform our notions and ideas of childhood. Without documented historical research, the oral and mythological tradition, which is majoritarian Hindu, informs much of what little we know about the history of childhood in ancient and medieval India. The available sources are linked to not only Hindus but also particular social classes and castes, where the imagery is centred mainly on *Kshatriyas, Brahmins* or the upper social classes.

Among these, the epic texts of the Ramayana and the Mahabharata have influenced our history of childhood, especially in ancient times. A significant image of childhood that appears across the Indian subcontinent is that of Krishna. There are several tales and devotional songs dedicated to young Krishna playing pranks. In these tales, adults are always indulgent in Krishna's pranks, laughing at him as he steals butter, tells lies or steals the clothes of young women. During his childhood in *Vrindavan*, Krishna is celebrated, loved and nurtured by the entire community. Krishna's childhood, as seen in the context of the Bhakti tradition, is filled with the imagery of taking cows to graze at sunrise and playing the flute by the river *Yamuna* amidst trees and creepers. This attitude of indulgence towards children is quite different from other cultures, which are stricter at parenting and reprimand bad behaviour. The pan-Indian belief that all children are made in the image of God and are divine continues to have a considerable influence on the attitudes and behaviour of parents and how society looks at young children. The Krishna myth has been an illustration of one of the dominant images of childhood in Indian society. The following section navigates available evidence from ethnological and select biographical histories to understand childhood in dominant (Hindu) traditions.

3.2.1 'Sanskaras' and Socialisation

Across various regions of India, considerable diversity exists in how children are socialised and what '*sanskaras*' or values guide their socialisation. Some of the variations in cultural practices are discussed in this section. Research in anthropology has found evidence that cuts across barriers of time and appears repeatedly in various cultural practices. Anandalakshmy (2010) explored 'ethnological evidence, across time and found constancy in (predominantly Hindu) cultural modes and practices' (p. 5). Her analysis of some select sources of Tamil and Sanskrit texts highlights *sanskaras*, where each *sanskara* symbolises a critical period in biological and social development. Some such *sanskaras* in the Hindu tradition are *chhati* ceremony (purification rites and clothing ceremony) on the sixth day after birth, *namakarana* (naming ceremony), which happens on the tenth to twelfth day after birth, *mukha dekhna* (viewing of the child's face), *raksha homam* (seeking protection from gods) in the first month, *annaprasana* (first feeding of solid food) in the fifth or the sixth month, *mundan* (shaving of infant's head) towards the end of the first year, *Vidyarambha* (formal beginning of education) between the fifth and seventh year and the *Upanayana* ceremony (opening of the inward eye and wearing of the sacred thread). These *sanskaras* are also celebrated as *rites of passage* – the transition from one phase of childhood to another. In some communities, menarche is also marked by a ceremony.

The child's socialisation in the Indian context differs from how it unfolds in the Western context. In India, there are categorised and organised influences of caste, social class, joint family and community on shaping children into adults. One view asserts that in predominantly Hindu cultures, there is a strong emphasis on following one's dharma, which includes duties and obligations towards one's family and society, which is the 'right' path of life. Life's trajectories are directed towards the right action rooted in cultural sensibilities. The rewards and trials during one's lifetime are linked to actions in past lives, which appear as an inherent 'psycho-biological' reserve that a child is born with. Thus, in Hindu cosmology, a child is born as a 'soul' (*Atman*) that already knows reality. Wisdom and Bhakti (devotion) to one's parents, family and God are ways to free the soul from endless repetitive cycles of rebirth. Attitudes towards young children and their socialisation are ultimately directed at these aims. The preparation for adulthood to fulfil the goals by conformity and compliance to one's family – community networks – and God is made by suitable investments in childhood. This psycho-analytic perspective links the goals and methods of children's socialisation to the wider Hindu cosmology, with variations and indigenous ways between different communities and cultures. Such linkages inform not only the tasks of each developmental stage but also the milestones in the context of rites and ceremonies and the child's social interactions with members of the family and community. The *rites de passage* discussed above can be understood as milestones that mark the transition from one period of childhood to the other. Continuity is visible in how these practices and '*sanskaras*' mark the passage of childhood among most Hindus in contemporary society (Anandalakshmy, 2010; Kakar, 1981).

3.3 Childhood in Medieval India

Examining historical biographies of emperors in medieval India also contributes to understanding childhood in this period. Vanina (2012) found that the virtues of children born to kings or destined to be kings or those who would attain sainthood are extolled from birth onwards. Parenting and parental joy or affection on observing the playful child are discussed extensively in folklore. One important source that informs our knowledge of childhood in India is the scholarship on the princely states. Though not so rigorously studied, several biographies present a graphic picture of the childhoods of kings or the spiritually high classes. There appears to be an underlying belief that some children's physical and mental development was perceived to be 'naturally' gifted. For instance, it has been documented that Prithviraj Chauhan (a Chauhan dynasty king in medieval India) was physically strong, gallant and generous even as a child. Childhoods of such heroes have been described to make the readers enjoy their sweet nature, revel in their naughtiness and reveal that these children had an innate gift.

Vanina's research in medieval India includes records which reveal indulgent and permissive attitudes towards children. Children were believed to be precious, and to love them was considered a service to God. Akbar once said, 'children are young saplings in the garden of life. To love them is to turn our minds to the Bountiful Creator' (Allami, 2006, p. 450). The folk tales about Akbar-Birbal often mention indulgence towards children. In one tale, a child is allowed to pull at 'Akbar's beard'. Various historical records also reveal that permissive and indulgent parenting has continued to mark attitudes towards children across social class and caste boundaries. Pranks, naughtiness and whims were considered natural for a child, for which children were not reprimanded. These practices continue into more recent times. As an illustration from his research with predominantly Hindu families, Kakar (1981) observes that children enjoy the liberal and indulgent affection of parents, extended family and society.

In the pan-Indian context, infancy can be understood as a phase extending to four to five years of age. In comparison, in developmental psychology and medicine, only the first year of life is seen as infancy. In these initial years, the child is indulged by parents and the extended family in daily activities such as feeding, toileting, rudimentary self-care, and walking and talking. Kakar (1981) cites the Indian idiomatic expression that a person spends the first five years of his life as a 'Badshah' (king), the next ten years as a slave and after that as a friend (p. 127). This period of indulgence and freedom comes to a halt between the ages of four and seven when native customs and hierarchical considerations of family, caste and society gain prominence. At this point, boys are separated from the world of women and immersed in the most disciplined world of men.

Several issues emerge from the historical and biographical narratives about childhood of the earlier centuries. Firstly, the history of childhood appears to draw more from images, stories and metaphysical themes rather than from empirical evidence. For instance, the Harappa, Mohenjo-Daro and Hampi excavations have several artefacts such as archaeological figures, toys, masks and articles. These artefacts provided a window into children's everyday life in the Indus Valley more than six thousand years ago. The figurines are made of terracotta and are small in size (about 2–3 inches) and include birds, animals and human figures. All this gives them the appearance of being a toy. It is, however, still being determined whether these were toys or were made for purposes of rituals. In the absence of clear historical evidence, the reconstruction of a history of childhood is selective in its reliance on images, stories and biographies primarily from mythical sources. The folklore and stories of the time reflect the 'image' of the child rather than the *real* child.

The second concern is that the descriptions of childhood centre around the higher social caste(s) and class(es). There is an absence of research on what childhoods of the lower caste(s) were like, what spaces, toys, and clothes were available to them, and the attitudes towards children. Given the diversity of religion in Indian society, notions of childhood have also not been examined around religious communities – for instance, the Jain tradition or the varied sects within Hinduism, Islam or Christianity, or tribal communities. Did some communities see magical realism closely linked to the world of a small child? What are the beliefs that came into play when a child fell sick? What are the beliefs that guided investments in children's socialisation and education? These questions need more systematic historical research.

The above section focused on the sparse nature of research on childhood in India from a historical perspective and the problems associated with the construction of childhood in India in the pre-colonial period. In the next section, we move towards a period which provides a clearer empirical basis for discerning notions of childhood in the colony, viz., the eighteenth and nineteenth centuries.

3.4 Childhood in the Colony

This theme focuses on the experience of colonialism and its impact on childhood in the colony. Do you think that the experience of colonialism continues to influence the socialisation and education of children today? Have you ever felt that certain schooling practices remind you of our colonised history? As you ponder over these questions, we attempt to understand childhood in the colonial period.

Childhood in the colony emerged at the juncture of the consolidation of colonialism, the growth of industrialisation, the persistent prevalence of folk beliefs in Indian society and the spread of rationalist ideas in education. In the colonial period, there were two conflicting views on childhood. The first perspective was the colonisers. The child in the colony was seen as closer to nature and pure, a view closely linked to European notions. The native children reminded the British of their children left in Britain. They saw children as valuable to the civilising agenda. Ideas of children's purity, playfulness, discipline and regimentation were seen as valuable for the children of the colony. These ideas were also impacted by the wider assumptions of the inferiority of race and moral and political status. Like the native adult considered morally inferior and primitive, the child was seen as savage, uncivilised and needed reform (Nandy, 2011).

Opposed to the above perspective, the colonised natives viewed children as valuable to the nationalist project in the colony struggling for freedom. Between 1850 and 1940, adults who participated in the freedom struggle directly or indirectly socialised children to develop nationalism to enable them to become adults who could take on the British (Nandy, 1987/2011; Sen, 2005). The social and political position of the families also marked these influences. Children of the Indian elite were provided with an English education and exposed to ideas of enlightenment. Children of the provincial kings and rulers experienced immense pressure to either succumb to or stand up to the British. Their socialisation was seen as an urgent project to salvage the province. Socialisation and education of the children of the poor and lower castes were also seen to be given attention.

The perception of the British, who believed that the 'colonised culture' was inferior and childlike, fed into the civilising agenda. They aimed to bring the native colonised to maturity by spreading rational ideas. To create the 'colonial citizen', the native child needed to be educated and 'brought up' to the level of Western civilisation (Nandy, 2011). Such a conception of childhood, which is inferior and primitive, continues to lend itself to civilising agendas in various aspects of education. These include practices and structures, which may include curriculum and school practices.

Children were treated as marked entities and socialised in ways that suited the colonial agenda as well as the resistance against it. They were considered helpful for both colonising and nationalist projects. On one side, education in the colony aimed to produce colonised subjects; on the other, education in English and exposure to the ideas of Enlightenment helped provide a unifying thread for the colonised subjects across the country. This furthered the strengthening of the nationalist struggle. Thus, the child in the colony was inadvertently shaped by a unifying education.

During the colonial period, they also witnessed industrialisation, which has been linked to the emergence of adolescence – a specific period in childhood. Ariés (1962) writes that industrialisation in the late 19th century led to the emergence of adolescence as a distinct period of the lifespan in Europe. However, especially before industrialisation, children in the Indian subcontinent did not have formal schooling. A greater continuity existed between adulthood and childhood without the rupture of the storm and stress of adolescence, a period marked by conflict between teenage children and parents, emotional upheaval, pressures and crises.

Saraswathi (1999) asserts that adolescence as a conception was not indigenous to India and is an import. She documents that adolescence is a middle-class phenomenon, more pronounced in boys than girls, who experience greater continuity with adulthood. Exposure to education in English and ideologies can also be seen as a significant contributor to this new developmental period in the lives of Indian children.

These aspects of childhood, such as adolescence or the continuity with education in the colony, continue to influence Indian society and may appear as 'natural' childhoods of an increasing number of middle-class families. How this middle-class childhood shaped the imagination of 'normative' childhood is discussed later in the chapter. It is important to point out here that there exists continued resistance to borrowing ideas from what is commonly called 'the global west'. Contemporary attitudes and notions about childhood continue to link and engage with the colonial past and the European context. There are, however, some departures and points of significant transformation from the linear narrative.

A violent partition marked the Independence of India, and women, especially pregnant women and children, were at the receiving end of violence (Butalia, 1998; Das, 1995; Menon & Bhasin, 1998; Pandey, 2001). Scholars have documented memories of people who witnessed partition and write about the 'violence that erupted so fiercely between Hindus – Sikhs and Muslims in 1946 and 1947 as "a war on each other's women" or a war waged "especially" on women and children' (Pandey, 2001, p. 69)

3.5 Childhood in India: Post-Independence

This section of the chapter deals with childhood in the Indian context, post-Independence. Childhood in Independent India can be identified through several markers – the changing family (increase in nuclear families and a focus on the conjugal bond), the influence of industrialisation (need for schooling, availability of unproductive engagement in household economy, better health care) and exposure to ideas of modernity through education. These factors, coupled with influences of the spread of capitalism, marked an extended childhood, where the period of a child's dependence on the adult increased. The child was kept away from the world of production and reproduction for longer. This meant the possibilities of investing in cultural and social capital in childhood also increased. The returns of this investment could be reaped later in the productivity of the 'adult'. These returns in the form of a prepared adult who could engage in productive, skilled work were accentuated in capitalist economies (Harvey, 1985, 2005). At the same time, the investments in their socialisation and education also changed. Some of these factors are discussed in the section that follows.

3.5.1 Childhood, Socialisation and Family

Ethnographic research in the late 1950s and 1960s focused on studying families and socialisation patterns. These researches reveal social norms and obligations, restrictions and attitudes towards childhood and provide an insight into the patterns of caregiving and relationships in various regions of India. Some of these include Carstairs' (1958) research on caregiving and relationships in a Rajasthan town, Madan's (1962) study of Pundit families in a village in Kashmir and Minturn and Hitchcock's (1963) research with Rajputs of Khalapur. In these families, it was observed that children enjoyed liberal affection from parents, the extended family and society at large. Their pranks, naughtiness and whims were considered natural and not reprimanded.

At the same time, there were variations across regions and communities in how they valued children and privileged or restricted them. In contrast to the Kashmiri Pundit families and the Rajputs of Khalapur, ethnographic research among the Nayars of Angadi village revealed that parents were reluctant to praise children publicly (Minturn & Hitchcock, 1963). Across regions and communities, differences were recorded in the extension of the child's 'circle of love', which was not limited to the family but extended to women in the neighbourhood and the larger extended family.

The notion and exercise of power and control by the patriarch over the women and children of the household are pivotal hinges on which joint family life functions. In her research in the community of Karimpur in rural Uttar Pradesh from 1967 to 1998, Wadley (2010) found that varied forms of control existed, which included physical surveillance, silencing of the women and children, denying them opportunities to speak, seclusion and 'through rituals which mark the superiority of male kin and the importance of the family unit, and through daily practices such as eating routines that mark the male as superior' (p. 17). Many such practices, rules and rituals are the glue that keeps the family together and maintains family honour (p. 22).

In joint families, the maternal-child bond is extended to all women in the household. Many caregivers shaped the early rearing of the Hindu child and consciously moved the child away from the mother towards more participation with the larger familial group and social network. Thus, child-rearing was majorly communitarian and not just relegated to the mother or the immediate family. Wadley (2010) reports that in rural Uttar Pradesh, all residents use fictive kin terms towards all nonrelated village residents of whatever caste group, and traditionally, they see the village community as one family (pp.14–15). Fictive relational terms such as '*masi*' (or mother's sister) are extended to all middle-aged women and '*dadi*' (paternal grandmother) or '*tayi / chachi / bua*' (paternal aunt) to all other women in the village. The young child enjoys the affection of most village women, reminiscent of the affection that Krishna enjoyed in Vrindavana.

Seymour (1999) conducted longitudinal research with twenty-four Hindu families from different social classes and social caste groups in Bhubaneshwar. He highlighted that apart from the mother, grandmothers, older siblings, aunts and neighbour's children provide care and attention to the child. However, later research in the area finds that there are not as many 'multiple mothers' as in the 1960s and 1970s. Sharma (2003), in his fieldwork at Shanti Nagar, a village on the outskirts of Delhi, does not find the same indulgence that earlier ethnographers reported. He asserts that most mothers were 'impersonal and passive when caring'. In contemporary times, the mother appears to be the primary emotional anchor to the child in infancy and early childhood.

Thus, a significant point of departure in how children experience social and familial life emerges from the collective/individual or the nuclear/joint family types. However, these axes of parental love and family size are not uniformly applicable across families and communities in India. There are variations in families and communities on concerns related to the upbringing and socialisation of the child.

In the 1980s and 1990s, several researchers noted the changes in both urban and rural families. Changes in family structure resulted in the changing nature of parent–child relationships. In larger families, the rearing of the child took place within the larger community and not by individual mothers or parents. In contrast, smaller families were marked by closer intimacy between parents and children, and fathers began to participate more in child care and socialisation. One possible explanation for the change in the community-based upbringing of children, characteristic of several parts of Indian society, is perhaps the changes in the family structure in this period. Sini (2011) chronicles the changes that took place in family relationships after the 1980s, which are lessening of control exercised by the community and extended family members, a trend of fixing marriages not purely as social and economic arrangements but out of love, changes in relationships between parents and children to increased care and concern, change in gender equations and increased autonomy of family members.

Several researchers have argued that childhood itself is varied as a consequence of family size and structure; socio-cultural, economic and political milieu; birth order and gender (Chowdhury, Muni, Rath, & Pati, 1996; Saraswathi & Dutta, 1987). They have also pointed out that even when families are nuclear in structure, the spirit of the family is joint, as there are frequent visits, phone calls and extended stays. Despite the underlying universal attitudes, there is considerable heterogeneity in the ideals of childhood. Socialisation patterns are mediated in complex ways (Chaudhary, 2004; Mandelbaum, 1970/2016; Roland, 1989; Uberoi, 2009).

3.5.2 Identity Formation, Socialisation and Divinity

In most Hindu communities across India, the child is believed to be born as an image of the divine. Divinity is heightened in infancy and earlier stages of childhood. Later, the child comes to be seen as human and part of the family and community. Misri's (1985) anthropological research on Kashmiri *Pundits* shows that the conceptualisation of the child lies at the intersection of three overlapping axes: (i) the divine–human axis wherein the child is seen as a gift from God and at the same time, an outcome of human copulation; (ii) the collective individual axis wherein the child is seen as sharing bodily and spiritual substance with *patri* and *matri* kin, yet an individual with unique karma and pre-ordained destiny; and (iii) the unchangeable transformative axis wherein the child is seen as gifted with fixed qualities yet undergoes transformation through the agency of life crisis (*sanskaras*).

Soon after birth, the child is seen as pure and impure and is not subject to the ritual taboos and restrictions that constrain adult conduct. As the child grows, he/she transforms through life crises or *sanskaras*. On the one hand, the focus on maternal and paternal family emphasises relationships with family, indicating a collective identity; on the other hand, karma emphasises the individual born with fixed inclinations, which can be overcome with rituals and *dharma,* i.e. one's duty.

As elaborated in the earlier part of this chapter, there is continuity in how the child is seen as an embodiment of the divine from ancient, medieval and recent times. This cultural belief has continued to inform mothering and social attitudes towards children and childhood. These beliefs coexist with the modern notions of childhood, where the child holds 'emotional value' and is cherished and protected. The family in the modern times becomes a 'prison of love', and the child is not left with a choice but to reciprocate the affection and attention of the parents towards him. The conjugal couple came to occupy a space as an essential unit of everyday life. In modern times, the family is thus closed compared to its previously intense, warm-hearted human community.

The protected child was also to be kept away from the adult world of production and reproduction. Changes in the modes of production and economic activities further impacted childhood, which is elaborated in the next section of the chapter.

3.5.3 Impact of Industrialisation

Several parts of India witnessed rapid industrialisation from the 1950s to the 1980s. Organised industrialisation has also led to several changes in the family structures. As discussed above, family structure is redefined because of the demands of production and work. Dube (2001) cites several reasons that explain the breakup of the joint family-based households in these decades. These are diversity of occupations, migration, and professional considerations such as transfers and distance between the place of work and residence. The conjugal couple comes to be the central focus of the family. An increase in women working outside the home (especially in the informal sector) is also witnessed.

Parry (2005) captures the impact of rapid industrialisation from the 1950s to the 1980s in his research in Chhattisgarh. He documents that the new working class gained a stronghold even though it was polarised between the aristocracy of the organised public sector labour and workers in the informal economy. Though children in rural Chhattisgarh were productively engaged from an early age, they were kept away from hard labour till their 'bones were cooked and hardened' or their 'growth would be stunted' (p. 288). This is so because modern urban employment offers enough opportunities to engage them later. However, schoolwork and a hobby (cultivating a purposeful and disciplined activity) redefine what constitutes work, and childhood is seen as preparation for a blue-collar job in the Bhilai Steel Plant. Childhoods also last longer, as marriage, parenthood and serious engagement with work are consciously delayed. Children from the working classes and the marginal sections of society in the 1960s to 1980s have documented their struggles to get an education to be recognised as someone with 'potential' or 'capability' of getting an education and a job. Parry shows clearly through his research how, with increasing industrialisation, childhood came to be seen as preparation for adult life.

3.5.3.1 Adult-Child Continuity

Communities that had moved to an industrial economy and still engaged in traditional occupations such as farming and weaving did not have similar influences. Anandalakshmy and Bajaj (1981), in their ethnographic study on the weavers' community in Varanasi, indicate an early allocation of responsibilities and tasks to children. The community believed this helped foster competence among children and maintain adult-child continuity.

Parry (2005) also shows how industrialisation led to significant changes in the structuring of childhood. For the children of the aristocracy of the Bhilai Steel Plant, aspiring for secure jobs and the modern notion of life-as-a-plan structured their lives. On the other hand, the children of families from the informal sector came to terms with the fact that when they grow up, '*naukri*' (job) may be beyond their reach, and they could only aspire to reproduce their parents' occupation. Thus, childhoods were differentiated according to social class, and that social class determined preparation for adult life and entitlements. The adult–child binary is thus affected not only by time and locale but also by the occupation of the family and community and the family's social class.

Modernity is characterised by a gradual separation of the world of the adult and the child. The relationship between the school and the home became increasingly distant, with the school becoming the formal agent of socialisation and family, the informal and often 'deficient' agent. Besides industrialisation, modernity brought various ramifications: the centrality of the conjugal couple, changes in the nature of the institutions of schooling and education, and the obsessive focus on the child as the unique instrument of the family's social and material aspirations in bourgeois society. Childhood was considered the natural stage in the individual life cycle based on middle-class norms. This form of urban, middle-class childhood, free of work and labour, is economically dependent on the adult for long periods, is protected from adult vices and is considered the 'norm' to which all childhoods should align. The rights-based approaches and ratification of the United Nations Convention on the Protection of Child Rights reiterate this 'ideal' normative model. The other, non-normative, non-middle-class forms of childhood are either pathologised or are considered pre-modern or 'traditional' (Balagopalan, 2011, 2014).

3.6 Unequal Childhoods: Class, Caste and Socio-Cultural Background

This section of the chapter problematises the notion of an ideal childhood. The critique of the universal 'normative' understanding of childhood locates childhood in socio-cultural locations, emphasising rural/urban differences, social class, caste and religion differences. It includes children's experiences from families and schooling.

3.6.1 Notions of Work and School

Other forms of childhood, which may be non-middle class, are considered pre-modern or 'traditional'. The separation between the adult and the child, where the child does not participate in productive work and is dependent on the adult, is not a homogenous reality across regions and communities in India. Research evidence shows that in communities primarily based on agriculture, craftsmanship or fisheries, children continue to contribute to the productive work in their families.

Within the household, age and gender inequality play a role in allocating responsibilities and duties. The kind of tasks a young girl is expected to perform in the household depends on the family's life cycle. If there are some younger children in the household, girls spend much of their time in childcare activities. Anandalakshmy (2010) documents the life of Kali, a young girl in the village of Ghatiyali, District Ajmer, Rajasthan. She writes that during her research, Kali was married but lived in her parents' home and did not attend school. Her happy disposition and energetic contribution to the farming activities of her family were valued. Kali was aware of the dichotomy of her life – while she took ownership of the economic aspect of her non-education, she was also aware of her loss by not attending school (p. 85).

Nieuwenhuys (2005) explored the compatibility between school and work in Poomkara, a village in Kerala. She highlights how class, kinship, gender, household organisation, state ideology and education influence the lives of children. She shows how local society sees children as a source of free labour and security and as increasing the productive capacity of the family. The local society comprises a household family circle and is situated in complex structures of kinship and caste. Nieuwenhuys observed that 'little children' are perceived as 'little angels' and considered closer to heaven and the gods. The infant mortality rates are high, and children are named only after they have attained the age of five years. She found most children to be unkempt and disordered, often inflicted with ailments and illnesses. Only a significantly small percentage of money is spent on their medical care. Within the household, she finds that age and gender inequality also contribute to allocating responsibilities and duties. The kind of tasks a young girl is expected to perform in the household, in turn, depends on the family's life cycle. If some younger children are in the household, the girls spend much of their time in childcare activities. She also finds that girls devote, on average, six hours a day to domestic chores and only a little more than one hour to 'productive' work.

Nieuwenhuys (2005) maps the social relations, especially in the coir and fishery-based industrial sites in both the Muslim and *Ezhava* communities in Poomkara. She finds that though children participate in these activities, they are considered workers only in limited work arrangements. Their work yields small earnings and is held in low esteem. The meagre earnings contribute to the overall household income and are particularly useful in lean seasons and times of starvation.

Several researchers have attempted to problematise the world of children's work and its association with free and cheap labour (Bissell, 2003; Swaminathan, 2008; Weiner, 1995). The issue of how to position childhood in a third-world country, where economically productive work is valued, is complex and not easily discernable.

There are several contradicting viewpoints about child rights. For instance, despite the existence of the Prevention of Child Labour Act (1986/2016), children can still be seen at worksites (construction, stone quarry, brick kilns, sugarcane industry, salt pans, bangle making, jewellery making, mining, carpet making, *beedi* making, plantations, etc.). The Rights activists, for instance, the National Commission for Protection of Child Rights, argue for universal coverage, which means all children below the age of fourteen should be in school and not participate in work. Another group of scholars argues that to understand childhood in the Indian rural or semi-urban contexts, the defining feature of childhood, according to which children should be kept away from productive labour/work, needs to be opened up. The issue of how to position childhood in a third-world country where economically productive work is valued is complex. According to this view, there exists a deep-seated cultural, gender and class bias and power dynamics, and the notion of 'ideal childhood' is dominant in mainstream developmental psychology as well as international organisations for the welfare of children (Vasantha, 2004; Saraswathi, Madan, & Menon, 2017).

3.7 'Ideal' Childhood

There is a dominance of middle class, white, male urban childhood as the norm in mainstream developmental psychology. This is concomitant with the 'national child' who is imagined only in these ways, negating social class, rural residence, and gender.

An international welfare perspective like that of the United Nations Convention of Child Rights and other international bodies places the 'needs of children' and 'facts for life' at the centre of the rights perspective, where each child has to be free from the world of work and has the right to go to school. Such 'ideal' and 'normative' childhoods do not accommodate perspectives from diverse children's lifeworlds (Vasantha, 2004).

As discussed above, the modern conception of childhood, popularised in the ideology which emerged in Europe in the 18th century, appears to be naturalised and internalised in the childhoods of increasing numbers of middle-class Indian children. It informs the imagination of a 'normative' childhood. In response, a rich body of work presents the narratives of growing up as a Dalit, a non-Hindu, a Muslim or the lower caste. These narratives about growing up, socialisation and schooling as the 'other' also create the normative child (Murali, 2012). The normative child is (and has been) the middle-class, urban, Hindu male child (and non-disabled). It can be argued that all children (for instance, a Dalit girl) are not typical children in how the middle class imagines it to be free from the economic, psychological and socio-political stresses of their family or community. Such children do not have a choice not to be involved in adult issues, carrying the tensions and burden of their stigmatised identities with them (Murali, 2012).

These notions percolate into schooling practices, curriculum, examinations and extra-curricular activities. Concerns arising from economic inequality impact schooling, too. Prevalent discourses locate poverty within the labour, effort and 'will' of the individual poor and not as a systemic concern arising out of economic policies and choices of the country. Batra (2015) argues that such a view sees 'poverty as an individual condition' where discourse builds responsibility for the poor quality of life on the 'poor' people themselves as individuals. Within schooling, categories of 'educational deprivation' and 'capability deprivation' lurk in attitudes impacting the everyday experiences of poor children in school.

Several research studies have reported that classroom teaching-learning is uninteresting and often discriminatory. Teachers have implicit beliefs about deficits in children's backgrounds and cognitive levels. The home is not necessarily print-rich, and what is learnt at school may not be supported at school. All children do not have access to the facilities and the apparatus – like the newspaper, radio and extra reading materials that school education requires. Murali (2012) recalls his school experiences as a poor *Dalit* student, participating and not doing well in a general knowledge test because the test preparation material was not available to all students.

Children from marginalised communities experience childhoods which are not only different but also disadvantaged in how they experience schooling. Several studies have indicated that there is a low participation of Muslim children, especially girls, in schooling. The Sachar Committee report (Sachar, 2005) highlighted that the Mean Years of Schooling (which is also an indicator of retention in the system) is the lowest for rural Muslim boys, closely followed by rural Muslim girls, and this was more so mainly in West Bengal and Uttar Pradesh. As many as 25 per cent of Muslim children in the six- to fourteen--year age group had either never attended school or had or had dropped out.

Another disadvantaged group of children belongs to families which migrate seasonally. Factors such as the availability of work, social networks, proximity and concepts about space influence the choice of a destination made by migrants, who must find a balance between constraints and ambitions. Children from such families do not belong to a particular state. Schools need to recognise the frequent mobility of families and be open to accepting students either with temporary hutments as addresses or with no address at all, which may mean a lack of entitlement to the child.

In addition to these realities, children living in observation homes or juvenile homes are part of institutional care; children of sex workers; HIV affected, leprosy affected; children affected by civil strife/Left Wing Extremism; children recruited in armed conflict/other conflicts – Kashmir. These also constitute a vulnerable group with specific needs of care, empathy and understanding of political rift and strife.

Children from minority, indigenous or migrant backgrounds face discrimination in many ways. These children are involved in issues of identity, caste and poverty, and they carry with them tensions arising from the weight of exploitation and their experiences within the school as well. Children from the margins – Muslims, Dalits, tribal and migrant children – feel a sense of alienation when they first encounter school – every aspect of the school is new for them. The school has certain expectations – of hygiene, of regularity, of reaching school in time, of bringing school-related things to school, of wearing a uniform and so on. A child has to 'make herself over' and accumulate 'cultural capital' to succeed in school.

Researchers have variously discussed how caste and social class impact schooling, which may be access to drinking water, distribution of food, *prarthana bulvana* – recital of the prayer, cleaning the school, children being called out to pick the dead cattle, peer relationships and corporal punishments (Valmiki, 2007; Nambissan, 2010; Murali, 2012). The school is a place they would prefer to avoid going to. They remain largely silent in class, neither answering nor asking questions themselves. Some authors speak of this pain of alienation and the stigma of being considered low among their peers. Their life experiences find no place in the classroom; a 'culture of silence' is their pedagogic encounter with the school. Sharma's (1996) essay on Tharu tribals in West Champaran (Bihar) illustrates how tribal children get pushed out of schools and how their experiences contribute to their alienation. Discriminatory practices, dull and unimaginative pedagogic experiences, and no recognition of the child's own cultural identity in the school system are the factors that lead to their dropping out. This aspect was also emphasised in the PROBE Report Field (1999). Research has also shown that most primary school leavers do not join secondary schools. Learning has to be worthwhile for every student. Therefore, the larger question is how we provide an inclusive mainstream curriculum and teacher education that speaks to all students with sensitivity.

3.8 Childhood in India: Post-Economic Liberalisation

Childhood as a construct has also been studied and redefined post-liberalisation of the economy and the opening up of free markets. In this context, the aspirational values of middle-class children have emerged as having a 'global lifestyle' and 'significantly felt Facebook presence'. However, the impact of privatisation of services and intrusion of technology on childhood needs to be problematised and interrogated further.

3.8.1 Impact of Neo-Liberalism: Shifting Ideologies and Lives

Neo-liberalism is an array of political, social and economic societal alignments based on market relations. It rearranges the state's role and, in turn, gloats over individual responsibility. The most significant impact of neo-liberalism is felt in education and health care, where policies and provisions are increasingly privatised and deregulated.

The opening of the economy to private players is characterised by changing patterns of money flow. There is a significant movement of capital across geographical spaces and investments, service industry growth, gradual de-industrialisation and distress of subsistence economies, primarily agriculture. All these have led to rediscovering the 'nature of work'. There are changes in forms of cultural production, which are now consumed worldwide through electronic media, internet, television, cable, films and videos. This production and circulation address expanding desires to acquire capital, goods and services, and many means to satisfy burgeoning desires. On face value, it appears that people's decisions and lives are based on free choices; however, these choices are structured through the market.

Another essential characteristic is that ideas and ideologies travel easily across local, national and international boundaries. According to Appadurai (1996a, 1996b), post these changes in a capitalist economy, contemporary lives are markedly influenced in many ways, which are by ideascapes (crossing over of ideologies), technoscapes (sharing of technology across the world), mediascapes (influence of availability of global television and internet), ethnoscapes (movement of people across countries and the cosmopolitan nature of urban life across the world) and financescapes (flow of capital and investment). So, ideas and changes permeate and circulate freely across boundaries, which may be local, national or international. These deeply perspective-based constructions or 'scapes' are modulated by nation-states, multinationals and diasporic communities. Such political-economic and social-cultural changes have influenced the lives of children by impacting their living conditions, experiences and futures. One example is the increased circulation of ideas on 'protecting' children and ensuring their survival, health and well-being. Such ideas also include changing notions about 'how children's lives are', 'what is a good family', 'parenting', and 'education'.

3.8.2 The Market and the Child

With the emergence of market forces, children's lives are being increasingly defined by what they consume. The market has produced the child as a consumer, where the market reads children's interest and encourages consumptive patterns of food (fast food chains), internet, television, movies (several cartoon-based series from Disney and anime), and entertainment mini-worlds (Waterworld and Jurassic Parks in India, Disneyland abroad). Markets can observe and capture 'what is of value' to the consumer and package it as a commodified object. For instance, changing patterns of mother–child interactions where mothers want to spend quality time, play more with their children and are increasingly worried about their child's health have been captured by market analysts. Illustratively, these are then packaged as 'Alpenliebe' candies, 'Colgate' toothpaste or nutrition-packed juices and supplements.

Consumer culture uses pleasure as a weapon and commodifies social and cultural life. Social and cultural life and relations become objects to be purchased and owned instead of the child learning to contemplate them, think responsibly and be self-reliant. Happiness, affection towards one's family or freedom to play uninhibitedly are all cultural insignia which can be purchased at the market in the form of a greeting card for a parent, a tea-drinking mug, playtime in artificial environments at a mall or celebrated as international happiness day. It is not just leisure objects and services, but also festivals, rituals and ceremonies; works of art and music; play and sports; school work; and health and well-being – the production of capital and consumerism defines all these spheres of social and cultural life.

Consumption thus comes to define and inform children's lives by shaping identities. Their education and socialisation become central to the goal of furthering the capitalist agenda and are seen as 'investments'. The goal of the parents and teachers is to shape and develop this 'commodity'. This is achieved by equipping children with skills, competencies, knowledge, attitudes and attributes useful to the neo-liberal markets. In this scenario, parenting and education are invested with the responsibility to deliver quality that is not antithetical to the market's demands.

The market is made real for children by shaping their identities and worldviews. Disney offers one case in point in describing how images, representations and values are offered to children. Disney plays on childhood innocence by creating a dream-like world where children can situate themselves emotionally. It has been argued that Disney films are forms of relevant 'public pedagogy', as these films appear to inspire at least as much cultural authority and legitimacy for teaching specific roles, values and ideals as more traditional sites of learning such as public schools, religious institutions and the family. Disney creates meta-narratives about society – progressive vs. backward, good vs. evil, mean-world hypothesis and perceptions of the social 'us' compared to 'others' based on glossing over cultural differences. It thus forecloses possibilities of engaging with the world in complex ways by reducing it to simplistic universalistic narratives.

It is not only multinational enterprises like Disney that work to create the child as passive, innocent and driven by consumption. Prolific media messages also impact childhood. The media representations today are characterised by depictions of childhood with less play and less unmediated contact with the natural environment, where children are subject to more dangers, including violent crimes, and their roles are increasingly overtly sexualised and commercialised. Such changes

> simultaneously reduce the demands of human agency to the ethos of a facile consumerism. It appears that children's 'civic responsibilities are limited to the act of consuming' (Giroux & Pollock, 2010). Through such media apparatus, the past is filtered through an appeal to cultural homogeneity and historical purity that erases complex issues, cultural differences, and social struggles (Giroux, 2012, p. 91).

Childhood can be seen as a critical site where the effects of political and economic changes are witnessed. Increasing economic inequality is perhaps the most recognisable insignia. Changes in children's everyday lives and routines reveal the increasing presence of media, the internet, and the decline in play and social relationships. Play is a defining aspect of childhood, but due to changes in urban and rural spaces, there has been a decay of play spaces for children. Children's outdoor play is decreasing, and increasingly, children are being relegated to home and indoor spaces, with television or internet for company.

3.8.3 Nature of Play: Cracks and Continuities

Play is a defining feature of childhood. Children's play is spontaneous, joyous and creative. Children indulge in play for its own sake. Given any opportunity, they convert their routine activities to play, like opening a door, helping with cooking, sorting bottle caps, plastic bags, a piece of cloth and pebbles. They modify and adapt their everyday lives to play, transforming a stick into a riding broom or an electricity pole, paper into planes and boats, parked cars and scooters as hiding spaces, buttons into marbles and handkerchiefs into a magician's wand. The nature of play is creative and spontaneous, universal and can be seen across social-cultural contexts. The child who works for money spontaneously swings on a gate or jumps over bricks at the first opportunity. Children have always drawn and modified materials from their immediate context in their play.

A point of significance is that with gradual urbanisation in the past century, the cities witnessed denser population, increased ghettoisation and slum dwellings, expansion in the construction of housing and commercial complexes and high-rise buildings, and heavier road traffic – all of which led to a slow decay of play environments for children. Play spaces started disappearing to make way for parking lots, ornamental gardens, gated communities, markets and commercial spaces. Children started playing indoors, in small yard spaces and on terraces. Coupled with the crowding and lack of space, concerns for the child's safety in unsupervised, open environments also led to a decline in urban children's play.

Despite these drawbacks, however, children find spaces and materials to play. They can be seen playing in corners of busy streets, lanes around their homes and abandoned parks. Outdoor play can also be seen in cement pipes awaiting use in construction, railway tracks, etc. Children constantly improvise their play by modifying games and materials. The pretend play of *ghar-ghar*(house-house) 'doctor-doctor' is now modified into reality television programmes which have wide viewership, like *Indian Idol* (a singing contest) and *Kaun Banega Crorepati* (a quiz show with huge monetary rewards). Their play now includes unused cable wires, refuse tetra packs, bottle caps, cardboard and fabric pieces – all modified for unique ways to play. Though children across all socio-economic groups engage in creative play, it appears that children from 'disadvantaged' socio-economic often use materials not designed for play, bringing imagination, novelty and richness to their play. Observations in population-dense environments, like the crowded Khidki Pur extension in Delhi or Dharavi in Mumbai, show how children create their play zones and games.

At the same time, there is an increasing awareness of the need for play spaces in urban environments. This has led to the mushrooming of 'play-zones', some of which are driven by commercial interests. Such zones can be seen in all malls in urban India, with plastic materials, toys, swings and play mats. Small spaces are cordoned off, and children are permitted to enter under adult supervision. These spaces are accessible to children from middle- and higher-income families. Children in urban spaces can also be seen playing in areas meant for parking, terraces, etc. This aspect may be another universal feature of play; children across social class(es) structure their own spaces for playing and modify their materials and games based on their cultural milieu.

3.8.4 Children's Participation in Work

In different communities across the Indian subcontinent, children have been involved in work. They contribute to the subsistence and cash-oriented activities of their families. Through their work participation, they learn about farming, animal husbandry and the use of local environmental resources (Froerer, 2011). However, the scenario is changing with the seeping of ideas about 'modern' childhoods, policy stipulations and laws for their protection. The value of education and the importance of certification are being realised.

Another growing phenomenon is the rise in urban migration from rural areas in search of employment that emanates from industrialisation and trade. This has created overcrowded urban centres. A direct consequence of this is the increase in 'street children'. The needs of street children are unique, as they are constantly on the move, very vulnerable and susceptible to abuse/substance use, and there is a complete absence of any support system. They are often pushed into begging, rag-picking and other revenue-generating activities. There is thus very early adultification in their childhood.

Conclusively, it may be said that as the welfare state gradually gets replaced by a managerial state, the linkages of the state to the private sector become stronger. These changes significantly impact educational policies, education's purpose, and schooling practices. The past decade has witnessed a deliberate positive affirmative policy of children's school enrolment. The right to education has been guaranteed to every child between six and fourteen (Right to Education Act, 2009). At the same time, a different trend is also being witnessed in education. It appears that enrolments are increasing, and there are more choices in schooling. However, the availability of choice has increased social divisions rather than reduced them. In effect, the market mechanisms operate in ways that offer upper- and middle-class parents different opportunities for an 'advantaged' education for their children. Newer and progressive avenues for schooling open up for children from such social classes.

On the other hand, many families from lower social and economic classes send their children to low-fee-paying private schools (Kabeer, Nambissan & Subramanium, 2003; Nambissan & Ball, 2010). Such choices are parents' responses to the increasing demand for an English-speaking workforce in the market, with skills that can be adapted to service providers that fuel the global economy. These trends increasingly characterise how childhoods become more diverse and stratified. Such segregation deepens social and economic inequalities. The reality is that multiple childhoods are lived and experienced in India.

Bibliography

Allami, A. F. (2006). *The Ain - a - Akbari (Vol.-III)* (H. S. Jarrett, Trans.). New Delhi: Low Price Publications. (Original work published 1894)

Anandalakshmy, S. (2010). *Through the Lens of Culture: Centuries of Childhood and Education in India.* Monographs. Chennai: Bala Mandir Research Foundation.

Anandalakshmy, S., & Bajaj, M. (1981). Childhood in the Weaver's Community in Varanasi: Socialization for Adult Roles. In D. Sinha (Ed.), *Socialization of the Indian Child.* New Delhi: Concept Publishing Company.

Appadurai, A. (1996a). *Modernity at Large.* Minnesota, MA: University of Minnesota Press

Appadurai, A. (1996b). *Global Ethnoscapes: Notes and Queries for a Transnational Anthropology.*

Aries, P. (1962). *Centuries of Childhood: A Social History of Family Life.* London: Harmondsworth.

Balagopalan, S. (2011). Introduction: Children's Lives and the Indian Context. *Childhood*, 18(3), 291–297.

Balagopalan, S. (2014). *Inhabiting "Childhood": Children, Labour, and Schooling in Postcolonial India.* New York, NY: Palgrave Macmillan.

Batra, P. (2015). *Quality of Education and the Poor: Constraints on Learning* (TRG Working Paper Series). New Delhi: Max Weber Stiftung.

Bissell, S. (2003). The Social Construction of Childhood: A Perspective from Bangladesh. In N. Kabeer, G. Nambissan, & R. Subrahmanian (Eds.), *Child Labour and the Right to Education in South Asia: Needs Versus Rights* (pp. 47–72). London: Sage Publications.

Butalia, U. (1998). *The Other Side of Silence: Voices from the Partition of India.* Delhi: Penguin.

Carstairs, G. M. (1958). *The Twice-Born; A Study of a Community of High-Caste Hindus.* Bloomington, IN: Indiana University Press.

Chaudhary, N. (2004). *Listening to Culture: Constructing Reality from Everyday Talk.* New Delhi: Sage.

Chowdhury, A., Muni, A. K., Rath, A., & Pati, C. (1996). Assessing Social Support Network among the Socio-Culturally Disadvantaged Children in India. *Early Child Development and Care*, 12(1), 37–47.

Das, V. (1995). *Critical Events: An Anthropological Perspective on Contemporary India.* Delhi: Oxford University Press.

Dube, L. (2001). *Anthropological Explorations in Gender: Intersecting Fields.* Delhi: Sage Publications Pvt. Limited.

Froerer, P. (2011). Children's Moral Reasoning about Illness in Chhattisgarh, Central India. *Childhood, 18*(367), 367–383.
Giroux, H. A. (2012). *Fugitive Cultures: Race, Violence, and Youth*. London: Routledge.
Giroux, H. A., & Pollock, G. (2010). *The Mouse That Roared: Disney and the End of Innocence*. Lanham, MA: Rowman & Littlefield Publishers.
Gold, A. G. (2010). New Light in the House: Schooling Girls in North India. In D. P. Mines & S. E. Lamb (Eds.), *Everyday Life in South Asia*. Bloomington: Indiana University Press
Harvey, D. (1985). *Consciousness and the Urban Experience*. Baltimore, MD: John Hopkins University Press.
Harvey, D. (2005). *A Brief History of Neoliberalism*. Oxford: Oxford University Press.
Kabeer, N., Nambissan, G., & Subrahmanian, R. (Eds.). (2003). *Child Labour and the Right to Education in South Asia: Needs Versus Rights?* New Delhi: SAGE.
Kakar, S. (1981). *Inner World: A Psychoanalytic Study of Childhood and Society in India*. New Delhi: Oxford India Paperbacks.
Kumar, K. (2005). *Political Agenda of Education*. New Delhi: Sage Publications.
Madan, T. N. (1962). The Hindu Joint Family. *Man*, 62, 88–89.
Mandelbaum, D. G. (1970/2016). *Society in India*. Thousand Oaks, California, CA: Sage.
Menon, R., & Bhasin, K. (1998). *Borders and Boundaries: Women in India's Partition*. Delhi: Rutgers University Press.
Minturn, L., & Hitchcock, J. T. (1963). The Rajputs of Khalapur, India. In B. Whiting (Ed.), *Six Cultures: Studies of Child Rearing*. Oxford: Wiley.
Misri, U. (1985). Child and Childhood: A Conceptual Construction. *Contributions to Indian Sociology*, 19(1), 115–132.
Murali, M. K. (2012). Pedagogic Practice and the Violence Against Dalits in Schooling. In C. Sleeter, S. B. Upadhyay, A. Mishra, & S. Kumar (Ed.), *School Education, Pluralism and Marginality — Comparative Perspectives*. New Delhi: Orient Blackswan.
Nambissan, G. B. (2010). The Indian Middle Classes and Educational Advantage. In M. W. Apple, S. J. Ball, & L. A. Gandin (Eds.), *The Routledge International Handbook of the Sociology of Education* (p. 285, 1st ed.). Londaon: Routledge.
Nambissan, G. B., & Ball, S. J. (2010). Advocacy networks, choice and private schooling of the poor in India. *Global Networks*, 10(3), 324–343.
Nandy, A. (1987/2011). Reconstructing Childhood. In A. Nandy (Ed.), *Traditions, Tyrannies, Utopias: Essays in the Politics of Awareness*. New Delhi: Oxford University Press.
Nieuwenhuys, O. (2005). *Children's Lifeworlds: Gender, Welfare and Labour in the Developing World*. London: Routledge.
Pande, I. (2013). Sorting Boys and Men: Unlawful Intercourse, Boy-Protection, and the Child Marriage Restraint Act in Colonial India. *The Journal of the History of Childhood and Youth*, 6(2), 332–358.
Pandey, G. (2001). *Remembering Partition: Violence, Nationalism and History in India*. Delhi: Cambridge University Press.
Parry, J. (2005). Changing Childhoods in Industrial Chhattisgarh. In R. Chopra & J. Patricia (Eds.), *Educational Regimes in Contemporary India*. (pp. 276–298). New Delhi: Sage Publications.
Roland, A. (1989). *In search of Self in India and Japan*. Princeton, NJ: Princeton University Press.
Saraswathi, T. S. (1999). Adult-Child Continuity in India: Is Adolescence a Myth or an Emerging Reality? In T. S. Saraswathi (Ed.), *Culture, Socialization and*

Human Development: Theory, Research and Applications in India (pp. 213–232). New Delhi: Sage Publications.

Saraswathi, T. S., Menon, S., & Madan, A. (Eds.). (2017). *Childhoods in India: Traditions, Trends and Transformations*. New Delhi: Taylor & Francis.

Saraswathi, T. S., & Dutta, A. (1987). *Developmental Psychology in India, 1975–1986: An Annotated Bibliography*. New Delhi: Sage Publications.

Sen, S. (2005). *Colonial Childhoods: The Juvenile Periphery of India*, 1850–1945. New York, NY: Anthem Press.

Seymour, S. (1999). *Women, Family and Childcare in India*. New York, NY: Cambridge University Press.

Sachar, R. (2005. The Sachar Committee report.. Government of India. https://www.minorityaffairs.gov.in/WriteReadData/RTF1984/7830578798.pdf

Sharma, D. (1996). *Child Care, Family, and Culture: Lessons from India* (Unpublished Doctoral Dissertation). Cambridge, MA: Harvard University, Department of Human Development and Psychology.

Sharma, D. (2003). *Childhood, Family, and Sociocultural Change in India: Reinterpreting the Inner World*. New York, NY: Oxford University Press.

Sini, M. (2011). *Matri-patri Continuum and the Societies in Chirakkal* (Unpublished Doctoral Dissertation). Delhi: University of Delhi.

Swaminathan, R. (2008). Bhima Sangha: The Strength of the Little Ones. In R. Swaminathan (Ed.), *Small Hands, Big Deeds: New Forms of Labour Mobilization* (pp. 215–282). New Delhi: Samskriti.

Uberoi, P. (2009). 'Baby' Icons: Forms and Figures of a New Generation. In P. Uberoi (Ed.), *Freedom and Destiny: Gender, Family and Popular Culture in India*. New Delhi; New York, NY: Oxford University Press.

Valmiki, O. P. (2003/2007). *Jhoothan* (A. P. Mukherjee, Trans.). New York: Columbia Publications.

Vanina, E. (2012). *Medieval Indian Mindscapes*. New Delhi: Primus Books.

Vasantha, D. (2004). Childhood, Work and Schooling: Some Reflections. *Contemporary Education Dialogue*, 2(1), 5–29.

Wadley, S. (2010). One Straw from a Broom Cannot Sweep: The Ideology and Practice of the Joint Family in Rural North India. In D. P. Mines & S. E. Lamb (Eds.), *Everyday Life in South Asia* (2nd ed.). Bloomington: Indiana University Press.

Walsh, J. (2003). English Education and Indian Childhood during the Raj, 1850–1947. *Contemporary Education Dialogue*, 1(1), 35–75.

Weiner, M. (1995). *The Child and the State in India: Child Labour and Education Policies in Comparative Perspective*. New Delhi: Oxford University Press.

Reports and Acts

Public report on basic education in India. (1999). New Delhi: Oxford University Press.

Sachar Committee Report. (2006). Ministry of Minority Affairs, Government of India.

National Curriculum Framework. (2005). National Council of Educational Research and Training. New Delhi.

Right of Children to Free and Compulsory Education (RTE) Act. 2009.

4

THE ADOLESCENT WORLD

Theories and Debates

Vishakha Kumar

This chapter explores various contours of adolescent development. It begins by presenting an overview of classical theories that laid the foundations of adolescent research. It also offers contemporary research trends in this area. Adolescence was predominantly viewed as a universal category by early researchers. A methodological concern was that studies conducted on a specific population, primarily elite white males in America or Europe, were generalised to the entire human species. Subsequent research raised their voice against this methodological oversight. The second part of the chapter looks at these voices, which raised concerns and debates in adolescent research. These researches have greatly enriched our understanding of the world of adolescence.

4.1 Popular Depiction of Adolescence: Intersections with Research Findings

The popular conception of adolescence in media draws heavily from the urban scenario, which portrays adolescence as a stage of transition, experimentation, rebellion, desire for autonomy and self-assertion. It is also romanticised as a stage where one looks for anchorage in some form of ideology or where one seeks attention, especially from the opposite sex or when one dreams of a Utopian world. If these images are extended to varied sections of Indian society, we may discover some glaring contrasts. Suppose we were to think that India has a predominantly collectivist culture. In that case, self-assertion and autonomy may be less celebrated than compliance with the elders' wishes in the family. Similarly, social class, gender, caste, region,

DOI: 10.4324/9781003505501-4

urban and rural settings and religion may impact the expression of social adolescence.

Theories of personality in Psychology, like those of Sigmund Freud (1949), Erik Erikson (1968), Peter Blos (1967), Margaret Mahler (1972) and Kroger (1998), among others, saw adolescence as a universal experience. However, the cross-cultural perspective in Psychology, influenced by studies in Sociology and Anthropology, challenged the universalistic theories of development (Saraswathi, 1999, 2002).

Psychologists and researchers like Nsamenang (2002), Brown, Larson, & Saraswathi; Verma & Saraswathi (2002) have challenged the notion of adolescence as a predominantly Western construct. Nsamenang (2002) has argued that most theories of adolescence are based on American and European teenagers. Saraswathi gives a vivid yet contrasting imagery of people between 12 and 18 years of age in the Indian context. A boy from an upper-class family dressed in designer clothes studies in an elite college against a young girl whose head is covered and holding a small child. Then there are boys working in small roadside restaurants, girls whose parents sell for want of money and other girls who get married at seventeen years of age. This brings out the diversity of contexts and experiences of people from the same age group. Saraswathi (2002) explains adolescence in her poetic words as 'kaleidoscopic images – images of dreams for a rosy future, of dreams that died before they took shape, of privileges and deprivations, of leisure and toils, of hope and despair'. Her research concludes that adolescence in India may or may not exist since the social and demographic variations are very diverse.

4.2 Historical Background of Research in Adolescence

G. Stanley Hall conducted the first systematic research on adolescence in the early twentieth century. His two-volume work *Adolescence* was published in 1904 and remains a landmark in scientific research and development on adolescence. In this work, he outlined adolescence as a phase in which human beings transform from being savage to becoming more civilised beings. He also described various development facets, including physical changes, cognitive development and psychopathology. In his paper on Stanley Hall, Jeffery Jensen Arnett (2006) delineates several similarities and differences between Hall's work and contemporary psychologists. The most contentious aspect of his work is that he draws heavily from Lamarkian theory, which is seen as problematic. Hall is credited and criticised most for his idea that adolescence is a phase when people experience intense storms and stress because of the biological changes in the body. He also saw a high correlation between adolescence and crime rate. The former thesis that storms and stress during adolescence were biological and universal experiences was contested by several psychologists. In her work on Samoans, Margret Mead (1928) argued that adolescence is not just a biological stage; sociocultural factors influence it. Adolescents experience storms and stress because of the cultural context and not due to biological changes.

The work of Sigmund Freud (1949) viewed adolescence as a separate and significant life stage guided by biological forces. He called these stages psychosexual because he theorised that human beings are primarily pleasure-seeking. Erik Erikson (1968) went a step ahead and discussed life stages as psycho-social instead of psychosexual. According to him, the psychological processes are influenced by the social context, and this context helps a person resolve the different 'crises' that he/she faces at different life stages. Erikson attributed the development of identity as the primary developmental task during adolescence. His theory changed the discourse of stages of life altogether. From merely physical transformation, adolescence was now understood from a psycho-social perspective. Later, theorists like Robert Havighurst (1948/1972) and James Marcia (1980) elaborated on different aspects of Erikson's framework.

This universalistic picture of adolescence was challenged from several angles. The historical perspective by Glen Elder and Joseph Kett (1977) pointed out that social, political and economic forces shape adolescent experiences at a given time. Glen Elder, in his book, *Children of the Great Depression*, presented data to argue that historical changes influence every stage of human life. The Great Depression had a profound effect on the behaviour, emotions and relationships of people at different life stages. Another thinker Kett whose treatise 'Rites of Passage: Adolescence in America; 1970 to the Present' (1977) had an impact on the discourse on adolescence was Joseph Kett. He argued that adolescence as a construct was 'conditioned by the social forces'. He also stated that the notion reflected society's demographic and industrial nature. Kett's work was criticised for taking a more upper-middle-class perspective. He did not address women, immigrants and blacks in his study. Despite these reservations, his work challenged the idea that adolescence is a universal experience.

Along similar lines, David Bakan, an American psychologist (Bakan, 1971), said that adolescence was an invention, a social phenomenon. He stated that three social movements in America – Compulsory public education, child labour legislation and special procedures for juveniles – together led to the emergence of the construct of adolescence. The legislation fixed the age of adolescence from pubescence to the period specified by law for compulsory education. Therefore, adolescence is sometimes referred to as an artefact of an industrial society. Before delving into contemporary adolescent debates, we will revisit some of the classical theories related to adolescence in greater detail.

4.3 Classical Theories of Adolescence

4.3.1 Sigmund Freud

The work of Sigmund Freud (1949) can be looked at as a pioneering work that gave a systematic stage-wise study of human development. His revolutionary psychodynamic perspective initiated a whole new body of research that inspires even contemporary theorists like Sudhir Kakar (2009). Psychoanalysis gives exceeding significance to the early years of development. Freud argued that the basic foundation of human personality is laid down by age 5. However, he also suggested the four stages of development through which the child progresses. He/she is born with a libido or sexual energy, and each stage marks the expression of libidinal urges through different parts of the body. Freud called these other parts of the body as erogenous zones. He termed the stages as 'psychosexual', connoting the significance of sexual instincts as they progress from one erogenous zone (like mouth, anus, and genitals) to another throughout a person's life (Hjelle & Zeigler, 1992).

Psychosexual development is an invariant, biologically determined sequence in its order of unfolding and characteristic of all individuals regardless of their cultural heritage. Each stage and its experiences lead to some form of development of attitudes, traits and values (Hjelle & Zeigler, 1992). Although Freud did not explicitly focus on parenting styles, his theory suggests the linkage between child-rearing practices and the growing child's personality. The basis of this was two factors: frustration and overindulgence. When a child's psychosexual needs are inhibited, it leads to a lack of gratification. However, when the mother does not train the child to control his inner functions, it leads to dependence or incompetence (Hjelle& Zeigler, 1992).

Freud's theory was carried forward by the Neo-Freudians who challenged some constructs advanced by him, particularly the emphasis on sexuality and aggression and thus made changes to the basic structure of his theory.

4.3.2 Erik Erikson

Erik Erikson (1968), a scholar and disciple of Freud, differed from his master concerning the overarching emphasis on the id or the irrational, pleasure-seeking and unconscious part of the psyche. Erikson argued that ego processes play a far more significant role than that envisaged by Freud. He highlighted the reciprocal interplay of biological, behavioural, experiential and social factors in development. He extended the framework of development proposed by Freud and named the stages of development as psycho-social instead of psychosexual. The developmental stages given by Erikson extended beyond the genital stage and covered the entire life span. He elaborated on the fifth stage of development, roughly extending from 12

TABLE 4.1 Erikson's Stages of Psycho-Social Development

Erikson's Stages of Psycho-Social Development

Approximate Age	Developmental Crises	Important Event
Birth to 12–18 months	Basic trust versus basic mistrust	Feeding
18 months to 3 years	Autonomy versus shame/doubt	Toilet training
3–6 years	Initiative versus guilt	Independence
6–12 years	Peer relationships	School
Adolescence	Love relationships	Peer relationships
Young adulthood	Parenting	Love relationships
Middle adulthood	Mentoring	Parenting/mentoring
Late adulthood	Reflection and acceptance of one's life	Reflection on and acceptance of one's life

to 19 years, as the stage of adolescence. Hjelle and Zeigler, while discussing Erikson's work (1992), describe adolescence as: 'No longer a child but not yet an adult, the adolescent is confronted with various social demands and role changes that are essential for meeting the challenges of adulthood'. He introduced the concept of search for identity, the achievement of which was the main task of this stage (Table 4.1).

The psycho-social dimension, during this stage, has identity achievement positioned at the positive end and role confusion placed at the negative end. These are two ends of a spectrum, and a person towards the end of adolescence must resolve this search for identity either by attaining a coherent and positive sense of self or they experience a sense of loss. The young, according to Erikson, grapple with abstract questions like

- Who am I?
- What am I doing here?
- What do I want to be?
- These are further answered by what am I? how am I?, what do I want to do with my life? etc.

The answers to these questions can be consolidated from past experiences and ideas about the future, including their future social role. The emphasis is placed on the ego and how it is affected by the context (like peers who take on an overarching role during this stage). Three elements involved in the formation of identity, as given by Erikson, include the following:

- Inner sameness and continuity: The person must form a self-image that considers the past and future.

- The significant others must also perceive a 'sameness and continuity' in the person.
- Feedback from others is the third crucial link to a person's identity development. There should be a one-to-one correspondence between the internal and external lines of continuity, i.e. what an individual thinks about oneself and what others think about them. Thus, interpersonal relationships play an essential role in developing the identity of individuals, for it is in the process of interaction that identities are formed and negotiated.

According to Erikson, adolescents begin to search for an ideology. The word ideology here implies a set of values and assumptions that reflect a culture's religious, scientific and political thought. They try to conceive of ideal situations, institutions and people and then contrast them with existing structures. These concerns are rooted in the social and emotional maturity individuals gain during this time. They seek out 'inspiring unification of ideals'. They re-evaluate what has been passed on to them by parents and schools to search for alternative structures. However, according to Erikson, a person who has not re-evaluated beliefs about self and the world offered by family and society nor has achieved an overall approach to life develops a diffused identity (Hjelle & Ziegler, 1992). Erikson also accords value to the changes in technology, economy and political scenarios that influence the social context of an individual. The rapid social changes create uncertainty and pressure adolescents to search for their value system. Erikson interprets students' protests as the need to commit to some goal and give meaning to life.

The social groups the adolescent belongs to play a noteworthy role during this phase of life. The individual may identify with any hero figure or some cult while exploring his/her own beliefs. Erikson points towards a concern that may originate if an individual submerges his/her identity in any hero figure or cultural group that may not allow his/her personality to develop. Further, an individual's social position also determines how to explore options and develop their independent identity. A woman or a member of a minority group may not get the opportunity to achieve a sense of identity if they are not given the same status as their counterpart.

The picture is dismal and obscure at the other end of the spectrum. Individuals unable to resolve the crisis for any reason may experience a profound sense of futility and aimlessness. They may feel inadequate and alienated. In effect, identity achievement is not an end but a continuous life journey. Erikson firmly stated that life is constantly changing; therefore, identity diffusion does not signify that the person may never be able to resolve the crises.

Erikson's theory of stages considers the industrial set-up that allows the young to have special delays in the assumption of adult roles. He coined the term *moratorium* for adolescents in technologically advanced societies to connote a greater interval between adolescence and adulthood. This phase is institutionalised in the form of higher education that allows young persons to explore professional and social roles.

Finally, like every stage, this stage has a virtue: Fidelity. Fidelity means the ability to commit oneself to a value system despite contradictions. The ability to commit oneself to work and relationships comes from a greater awareness of self. Sigmund Freud defined an adult as capable of productive work and love. Erikson went a step further and said that this must extend beyond geniality so that a person develops the capacity to be concerned for others.

4.3.3 Robert Havighurst (1972)

Robert Havighurst proposed that all individuals from infancy to old age progress through a series of developmental stages, each comprising a developmental task. He was the first to coin the term 'developmental task', and he defined it as a

> task which arises at or about a certain time in the life of an individual, achievement of which leads to his happiness and success with later tasks, while failure leads to unhappiness in life, and disapproval by the society, and difficulty with later life.

He further suggested that all developmental tasks are interrelated, and educators must be aware of these developmental tasks. For adolescents, from twelve to eighteen years old, the developmental tasks include achieving new and more mature relations with age mates from both sexes, achieving masculine and feminine social roles, accepting one's body, achieving emotional independence, preparing for marriage and family life, preparing for an economic career, developing an ethical system that can guide behaviour, developing an ideology and desiring socially responsible behaviour (Manning, 2002). His theory can help teachers and teacher educators plan and implement educational experiences in a manner that can facilitate achievement in age-appropriate developmental tasks.

Havingurst (1972) also defined a critical period as when an individual can especially achieve a specific developmental task. Young adolescents have a critical period for developing skills and concepts such as personal independence, attitudes towards social groups, conscience, morality and values. He also added that the critical period may vary as a function of the diversity of the population. Havighurst did not see diversity as a hurdle; instead, he thought young people could learn from and enrich their experiences by interacting with people from different socio-economic classes and cultures (Manning, 2002).

4.3.4 James Marcia

Building upon Erikson's work, James Marcia (1966, 1980) developed four identity statuses along the continuum of exploration and commitment. Identity statuses are both an outcome of the process of identity formation and structural properties of the personality. Both these portray a dominant mode of experiencing the world. Thus, identity status in late adolescence should affect and shape future identity formation (Patterson, Sochting, & Marcia, 1992).

The four identity statuses are as follows:

- **Identity Diffusion:** Arranged hierarchically, this is the least advanced status. Any status may be an adaptive mode of functioning in a certain condition. This status lacks exploration and commitment to an internal set of values.
- **Identity Foreclosure:** It represents a high level of commitment following little or no exploration. For Marcia, foreclosure represents a less developed state than that of *moratorium* or identity achievement. People whose identities are foreclosed generally follow one set of values, usually those of parents.
- **Moratorium:** It is considered a stage instead of a resolution of identity. Some people may stay in moratorium for many years. According to Marcia, moratorium status refers to the exploration of various available options by an individual before committing to them.
- **Identity Achievement:** It represents identity resolution with the achievement of a sense of commitment.

4.3.5 Jean Piaget

Jean Piaget (1932) developed his theory after detailed observation of infants and children. His primary contribution to the field of child development remains that he tilted the discourse from treating the child as a mini-adult to viewing children's thinking as qualitatively different from that of adults. He stated that children's thinking changes from birth onwards to older age as they strive to make sense of the world around them. Piaget identified four factors – biological maturation, activity, social experiences and equilibration. Maturation refers to the unfolding of biological changes that are genetically programmed. The environment has little impact on this. As children mature, their ability to act on the environment also increases. These acts, such as exploration, testing and observation, may alter the underlying cognitive processes. The third factor facilitating development is interaction with others (Woolfolk, 2004).

Piaget also proposed that people have an inherent ability to organise their thinking in psychological structures called schemes. These structures facilitate our interaction with the world around us. Simple structures combine to make more complex structures. Furthermore, as one's thinking becomes more organised and new schemes develop, behaviour becomes more sophisticated. The mental representation of the objects of the world around us helps us to think about them. Piaget also proposed that innate principles facilitating cognitive processing govern children's cognition. Among them, organisation is foremost, which refers to the predisposition to combine simple mental structures into more complex systems. The second principle of cognitive processing is adaptation. It refers to an individual's tendency to adjust to the demands of the environment. This has two other processes associated with it. When a person confronts new situations, he/she applies the existing schema to fit the characteristics of the situation (assimilation) or modifies the existing schema to fit the characteristics of the situation (accommodation).

Formal Operations

This is the final stage of cognitive development (12 years to adulthood). The first and foremost development of this stage is that the adolescent's mental operations reach a high degree of equilibrium. This indicates that adolescents' thoughts are flexible and effective. They can deal more effectively with complex problems of reasoning. Second, adolescents can also imagine the possibilities inherent in a given situation. They also get involved in hypothetical thinking, 'what if..?' questions, and can form hypotheses and test them through mental experiments (Ginsburg & Opper, 1988). Compared to children in the concrete operational stage, adolescents can solve problems that do not have a physical reality by mentally representing them. They can also review several solutions to the same problem.

Inhelder, Barbel and Piaget (1958) conducted several clinical experiments with adolescents involving scientific concepts. They were given several problems based on physics, chemistry and other disciplines. The adolescents were presented with some apparatus or material and were required to explain how they worked. A detailed record of what they did was maintained. The adolescents could act as scientists. Inhelder, Barbel and Piaget (1958) needed to look for the correct answers. Instead, they focused on the thought process and how adolescents' thinking differed from children's in the concrete operational stage. One such experiment was on Archimedes' law of floating objects; they found that children in their concrete operational stage focus on the observable aspects of the experiment. They focus on various objects that are given to them. They can categorise that heavier objects sink whereas lighter objects float. They cannot imagine that a log of wood larger and heavier may float on water, whereas a small nail made of lead would sink.

In contrast, in the formal operations period, a person can think more freely and think of various options to arrive at the concept of density (Parke, 1999). Other such experiments also indicated that a child during the concrete stage does not consider all possibilities before he/she begins. They concentrate on empirical findings that are perceptible. Children cannot consider possibilities on a theoretical plane during the concrete operational stage. For adolescents, possibilities are at the forefront. When presented with a problem, begin by thinking about possible solutions at a theoretical level. They imagine that the same data can be interpreted in several ways (Ginsburg & Opper, 1988). These experiments conducted by Piaget and Inhelder (1958) used those tasks that children were educationally prepared to engage with. He also pointed out that formal operations can be tested on people according to their cultural context and interests. He also said that you cannot infer a lack of competence from a subject's failure at one task which is not culturally familiar (Ginsburg & Opper, 1988).

The second feature of formal operations is their 'combinatorial' property. When children during the concrete operational stage confront a complex problem where several factors influence the result, they test them isolatedly. They fail to take all of these in combination. On the other hand, a person in the formal operational stage will consider all possible options in an exhaustive way to solve a problem. Their cognitive structures have developed so they can think of various problems and their solutions. They do not have to accommodate their cognitive structures to solve new problems significantly. It does not imply that adolescents do not learn new things, but their ways of thinking are almost fully formed by this time (Ginsburg & Opper, 1988).

Adolescents thus get involved in more abstract thinking and theoretical matters. They can think about political theories and philosophical problems. They can understand the more complex social issues and develop a plan for social change. Piaget also thinks that while engaging in abstract thought, adolescents may sometimes lose their ability to be in touch with reality. They can also direct their emotions to abstract things. They can develop feelings for abstract ideas such as freedom, slavery, hatred, etc. However, it does not mean that all adolescents will think like this. His theory indicates a capability that develops during adolescence. Many adolescents may need to display formal operations. They may use it according to their interests and concerns (Ginsburg & Opper, 1969).

Piaget believed that only some would reach this stage. Studies indicate that only some people attain the ability to think abstractly and develop flexibility in problem-solving. This depends on cultural factors, opportunities to engage with such tasks and other factors. College students and other professions that require abstract thinking may use this ability more than others (Ciccarelli, 2008). Cultural groups that do not emphasise symbolic skills and where such educational opportunities are also limited in the formal operational stage may occur late in development.

4.3.6 Lawrence Kohlberg

An essential part of Kohlberg's (1984) work enquires into theories of significant philosophers like Plato's emphasis on one virtue, Aristotle's virtue ethics, Kant's emphasis on reason and Rawls' deliberation on justice. His empirical work begins with the Piagetian notion of stages. In his over fifteen years of research, he found that the universal invariant stages answer the problem of relativism in philosophy. Each stage is typified by a particular form of reasoning displayed in times of ethical dilemmas.

Kohlberg stated that children's moral reasoning is determined by their cognitive capabilities. This moral development builds on the concepts attained in the previous stages of development. Kohlberg developed his theory by posing moral dilemmas to boys between ages 10 and 16 and asking them to respond to those hypothetical situations. According to Kohlberg, the reasons people give to answer dilemmas may be influenced by cultural context, but the underlying principles remain universal. For example, stage one is marked by an emphasis on the status and physical attributes of the possessor; in stage two, human life is seen as instrumental to the satisfaction of needs and so forth. In these cases, a person could either obey the rules and authority figures or ignore such pressures to respond to the needs and welfare of other people. Based on responses from his sample, he formulated a series of three broad levels of moral development and subdivided them into six stages. Each stage was based on the reasons participants gave and on the basis they justified their choice.

People at stage six answer in moral words such as duty or morally correct and use them to imply universality, ideals and impersonality. It is more of a philosophic and theoretical stage. People rarely reach this stage. This stage indicates the direction in which Kohlberg's theory suggests the direction in which ethical development is heading. Kohlberg called his theory the theory of Moral Reasoning, where the highest level is awarded to universal ethical principles based on universal values. The basis for arriving at this is through reason. Moral philosophers saw a remarkable resemblance between Kohlberg's interpretation of the highest level of reasoning and the Kantian framework of ethics. Reason reigns supreme in their work, and women were found wanting on their ability to employ reason efficiently in situations of moral dilemma.

4.4 A Case against Universalism: Contemporary Research on Adolescence

4.4.1 Carol Gilligan

The alternate perspective is given by Carol Gilligan (1982), who worked as a research assistant with Kohlberg. She questioned Kohlberg's approach to formulating the theory that had taken male life as a norm. Her research questions do not focus on gender differences in the nature-nurture debate or who is better than whom categories. Instead, she tries to study the perception of women. She tries to understand how women speak and listen. She attends to the questions about voice and relationships. She found that men and women have a typical way of speaking. Men's voices ring of disconnection and disassociation, and women repeatedly focus on acting selfless.

Gilligan found that when she asked people how they live in relationships and what they do in states of conflict, she heard a different voice from men and women. The difference lay in the fact that women's voices paid much more heed to maintaining connections at a time when the world around seemed to be centred on separation, autonomy and drawing boundaries. To quote Gilligan, 'Within the U.S. society, the values of separation, independence and autonomy are so historically grounded, so reinforced by waves of immigration, and so deeply rooted in the natural rights tradition that they are often taken as facts' (2000).

She discusses women's relational voice as being against the traditional ways of speaking about self, relationships, and morality. She also discusses how women have been seen as people who cannot achieve independence. Instead, she feels that women struggle to maintain connections. Voice remains at the heart of Gilligan's analysis. She explains voice in the following way;

'To have a voice is to be human. To have something to say is to be a person. However, speaking depends on listening and being heard; it is an intensely relational act'; 'Voice is a powerful psychological instrument and channel, connecting inner and outer worlds'. A lack of voice would mean a lack of resistance, creativity and change (1982).

While analysing her empirical data, she found that women have difficulty distinguishing the socially constructed feminine voice from the voice they hear as their own. She added that the social ideals created in literature as 'ideal mother', 'ideal father' and 'ideal children' affect those who fall from the line. These socially constructed voices, even if they differed from women's experiences, are incorporated into their system (1982).

4.4.2 *Is Early Adolescence Really a Stage of Development?*

This is the title of a famous paper by Hershel D Thornburg in 1983. He developed the concept of pre-adolescence, which earlier psychologists such as Sullivan (1953), Redl (1943), and Blair and Burton (1951) had proposed. They had postulated that something unique happens in the years 9 to 13, which either child development theories or adolescent research could not explain. Thornburg argues that the transition from childhood to adolescence was complex in his work. He argues that most stage theories in developmental psychology describe a stage by describing its psychological characteristics. However, he thought that stage should be described in terms of social change. This is not because psychological criteria are incorrect; instead, he felt they must be completed.

Thornburg (1983) conceptualised three transitional periods. The first is early adolescence between childhood and adolescence, the second is youth between adolescence and adulthood, and the third is transitional adulthood, the period close to retirement. He held that all these are social. During early adolescence, physical and cognitive capabilities are in transition. Socially, too, a person is more curious about the outside world by age ten. Peer groups became more critical, and the impact on parents started reducing. The earlier socialisation may come in conflict with the new socialisation. As a result, they may start questioning authority and display defiant behaviour. Social development, like physical and cognitive development, is also transitioning. He also emphasised the need to develop a theoretical framework to inform further research on early adolescence.

4.4.3 *Emerging Adulthood*

The social and economic changes have also widened the scope of adolescence, especially among the upper and middle classes. People spend more time preparing for adult life. A more recent work on adolescence is by Jeffery Jensen Arnett. Arnett (2000) proposed that adolescence can be divided into two periods: adolescence and emerging adulthood. Emerging adulthood is the last leg of adolescence, typically marked by delays in taking up adult roles. He has delineated a distinct stage of development termed 'emerging adulthood' (2000). Based on his empirical research among college-going American adolescents/adults, he found that significant changes occur in identity exploration, demographic profile and subjective perceptions. He thus draws his theoretical framework from several developmental theories that preceded his work. They include Levinson's concept of the *novice phase* (Levinson et. al, 1978), Erikson's notion of *role experimentation* (1968) and Kenneth Keniston's theory of *youth* (1971) (Arnett, 2000). He contends that none of these frameworks developed an independent paradigm for the age group between 18 and 25 years. Rapid changes in industrialised nations have led to an extended period of moratorium. He argues that the experiences of people in this age category can neither be called adolescents nor have they attained adulthood (2000, 2006). He argues that the 'sweeping demographic changes' have made the time between late teens and early twenties a distinct stage. In his view, this period is not just when one enters a profession and marries. Rather, it is a phase when individuals engage in greater exploration. He found it to be distinct from both adolescence as well as adulthood. Young people in this age group may have attained independence compared to childhood and adolescence but have not yet entered the roles and responsibilities of adulthood. That is why he termed this phase as 'emerging adulthood'. It is a time when several changes in life course are possible, and no commitment has been made. Emerging adulthood gives immense opportunities for identity exploration. Arnett identifies three important identity-related issues for this stage – work, love and worldview.

He further holds that this stage is socially constructed and is not universal. It is a 'period that exists only in cultures that postpone entry into adult roles and responsibilities well past the late teens' (Arnett, 2000). It is more of a cultural phenomenon than a country-wide experience. Social class, ethnicity and regional disparity also influence it. In developing countries, there is a rural-urban divide. These variations reflect the opportunities available to the young for exploration because of the extended education or professional specialisation period.

4.5 Do Men and Women Follow the Same Course of Identity Development?

It was argued that the concept of identity was essentially descriptive of male development, as propounded by Erikson (1968). The primary conflict related to describing the feminine identity was the overarching concern with anatomy. Though Erikson (1968) did not concern himself with penis envy and focused on a more positive description of feminine identity, he argued that women were anatomically destined to be more nurturing and accommodating. For Erikson, interpersonal issues formed the core of a woman's identity instead of vocational and ideological issues. Second, a woman's identity was left open in adolescence, leaving space for further development after she married and had a husband and children. During adolescence, her attractiveness may compose an essential aspect of her identity. Thus, her body was crucial to her identity. Third, the sequence of women's development appeared less stage-specific than that of men. The issues of identity, intimacy and generativity could be resolved almost concurrently rather than in a precise sequential manner (Patterson, Sochting, & Marcia, 1992)

Research indicates that till the 1970s, a neat split existed between male identity issues of occupation, religion and politics and female issues of sexuality and sex roles. This neat split began to break in the 1980s. Gender differences began to be defined in a more complex and different manner. Thorbecke and Grotevant (1982) noted that even though men negotiated occupation and interpersonal concerns as separate and independent identity concerns, it was important for young women to negotiate interpersonal issues for occupational identity formation to proceed. Kroger (1998) further noted that the task of identity achievement for women is more complex than for men since it involves meta-decisions of balancing competing commitments.

Carol Gilligan's (1982) landmark book *In a Different Voice* stated that women in most cultures espouse the ethic of care. They spoke the language of relationships and responsibilities against men who spoke of autonomy. In one of her lectures, she states that how adolescence is conceptualised has to change because there is a change in how childhood is conceptualised. She cited the work of Daniel Stern (1998) and Jerome Kagan (1984), who argued in favour of children's social and interpersonal nature. She held that if a child is seen as socially responsive and has moral concerns, we need to see what happens to this connection since what constitutes attachment during childhood may not hold for adolescence. Adolescents are capable of abstract reasoning and differentiating between true and false relationships. They also develop the capacity to detach themselves from their surroundings. This ability to think critically and the capacity to detach oneself from the surroundings may, on the one hand, help them to see the world in a dispassionate manner and, on the other side, may also make them 'self-centred'. Further, Gilligan (1987) refers to the research findings, which show that while reasoning, a care perspective was exclusively employed by girls. In contrast, most men, few girls, and women focus on a justice perspective.

4.5.1 Emergence of Cross-Cultural and Cultural Perspectives

Cross-cultural psychology emerged as a field of research as a reaction against a tendency in psychology to ignore cultural variations. The classical theories discussed above assume that individuals worldwide experience these stages in the same sequential order. However, Euro-American domination is present in the subtext of these theories. The claim of universalism oversees the cultural factors that play a pivotal role in the development of an individual. Cross-cultural psychology thus emerged as a protest against this tendency of mainstream psychology. Cross-cultural studies are comparative. They test the generality of existing theories and knowledge.

On the other hand, cultural psychology is based on the culturally constructed meaning system. It focuses on the interpretative methodology and emphasises the subjective meaning. It is believed that culture and individual psychological functioning are constitutive and cannot be studied in isolation. Thus, context becomes vital for cultural psychologists.

Cultural psychology uses genetic methods to study. This method can be understood as one that includes the history of the entire human race, the historical development of the individual and the everyday lived experiences of the individual. Michael Cole elaborates that along with the history of life on earth, the history of the human race and the history of the individual, the imagination of the future also influences development. He gives the example of a mother whose interaction with her child depends on what she imagines should be her child's future. Thus, cultural aspects are, in a way, transformed into material aspects through this process (Saraswati, 2003).

I would now like to highlight the significant debates concerning adolescence that are raised by the works of Saraswathi (1999), Verma & Saraswathi (2002), and Saraswathi (2003) and other eminent cultural and cross-cultural psychologists:

1. Adult-child continuity: Is adolescence a myth or an emerging reality?
2. Is adolescence a period of storm and stress or challenge and potential?
3. Is adolescence an essentially urban phenomenon, or does it exist in rural India?
4. Is adolescence a creation or an artifact of industrial society?
5. Is adolescence ascribed and circumscribed, or is it personally constructed?
6. What is the beginning and end of adolescence in chronological terms?

The expressions continuity and discontinuity refer to the intermediary stage of adolescence. Any other distinct stage is absent if there is continuity between childhood and adulthood. Saraswathi's (1999) work has highlighted that social class and gender impact the presence or absence of a distinct stage between childhood and adolescence. To elaborate further on this point, she adds that girls experience greater adult-child continuity in the Indian scenario and in many other developing countries than boys. This, too, cannot be taken as a uniform phenomenon since upper-class girls get greater opportunities to explore and prolong their period of dependency on their parents. They can also delay marriage and explore choices in life. However, Saraswathi (2002) held that an individual from the lower class may not have the luxury to reflect the existential problem of whether life was meaningful.

According to Saraswathi (1999), middle-class adolescents are marked by high parental control and involvement, a highly competitive academic setting and high career aspirations set by their parents. The extent of parental involvement in their children's lives can be understood by the delayed emotional dependence on parents, especially the mother and parental say in mate selection. Her work has tried to compile several studies that study variations across class and gender, dividing them into frames, as listed below:

- Childhood and youth in the lower social class – the girl child and the growing up male in the lower social class
- Growing up in the middle social class
- Childhood and youth in the upper social class

These variations also occur between urban and rural settings. She considers the difference in the family's mood when a girl child is born. According to statistics, only 2% of families celebrate the birth of a girl child. Social class also played a pivotal role in influencing the attitude towards girl children. In the lower social class, when the girl is 8–9, she actively participates in household chores and child care. Schooling for a girl child is a luxury; only if the parents spare the girl from the household chores can she enter school (Sarangapani, 2003). The girl is socialised to be a good wife and daughter-in-law. The prescribed roles take precedence for girls and limit their aspirations. Peers who are supposed to play an essential role during adolescence are nearly absent in the lives of lower-class girls. The values celebrated in this section are selflessness and obedience. A similar life pattern follows even for a lower-class girl in urban India, except in the educational aspirations of the girls and their parents.

Moving from urban to rural settings, adolescence appears, especially in lower-class boys. The postponement of the age of marriage and slightly lengthened period of schooling aid in the appearance of this distinct phase. These boys are constantly aware of their families' sacrifices to educate them and their future responsibilities towards their families. They, however, do enjoy some privileges like freedom from household chores. In rural areas, boys are expected to contribute to their family income by the time they are 13–14 years of age. So, boys in this class do not go through a psycho-social moratorium and search for identity.

In most cases, their schooling ends before puberty, and participation in income generation is initiated soon after or concurrently. The roles are prescribed, and the family makes decisions related to marriage. So, there needs to be more scope for experimentation.

The picture of the middle class is distinct from the lower class, with career aspirations taking the forefront. Education is one of the critical concerns of the middle class, and it is seen as the pathway to success. Other concerns linked with future career roles relate to increased competition, limited seats in desired courses and select professions that promise a desirable future. The impact of gender is more evident in the lower middle class, where the male child holds a more favourable position than the female child. Girls' educational aspirations are often sacrificed for the professional growth of the male child. The psycho-social moratorium is experienced only when the individuals enter some course after school. Saraswathi (1999) found that the opportunity to indulge in the luxury of the psycho-social moratorium is more in liberal arts courses or commerce because they give time to students to think and attend to the developmental task of searching for identity. The role of peers becomes critical during this phase. However, the impact of gender is more evident in the search for identity, where boys get greater opportunities for exploration as compared to girls. Girls are socialised to take on domestic roles even if they prepare for future careers. In many cases, the final mate selection is still decided by parents.

An even more distinct lifestyle can be seen among the upper-class children and youth. Though education remains a priority, upper-class adolescents have greater autonomy, mobility and freedom to explore different roles. Individual space and privacy become essential aspects of their identity. The luxurious aspect of their lifestyle is denoted by their easy access to expensive gadgets and vehicles. Their network of friends plays a vital role in promoting consumerism. This class gives a chance to experience psycho-social moratorium. Thus, the macro-context – social, cultural, temporal and historical – makes it possible for an individual to experience adolescence as a distinct stage of life (Bronfenbrenner, 1986).

Saraswathi (1999) thus concludes that in Indian society, where interdependence instead of autonomy and prescription rather than achieved status is more critical, adolescence as a stage is both gendered and class-based. The macro-context influences childhood adulthood continuity and discontinuity (Bronfenbrenner, 1986). Therefore, adolescence experienced by European and American teenagers is markedly distinct from adolescence experienced by non-Western societies. The negotiation for autonomy, which is vital for European adolescents, is treated as a problem in Indian society (Brown & Larson, 2008). Such variations are studied by researchers in different parts of the world like Kenya, the Philippines, the Middle East, Russia and India. Studying adolescents across different regions of the world brings forth images very different from those evident in twentieth-century Europe and America.

Chaudhary and Sharma (2012), in their perspective paper on Indian adolescents, delineate that the Indian sense of self is closely associated with strong family values and shows a combination of agency and interpersonal relatedness. Since other family members, along with parents, are also actively involved in the child's upbringing, he/she develops a strong sense of belongingness. Adults also demand high commitment from their children (Chaudhary & Kaura, 2001). The idea of an independent self should be promoted among the children. This person's interdependence on others differentiates Indian adolescence from the Western concept. In a comparative study between 100 Indian adolescents and 220 middle-class Europeans, it was found that Indian adolescents spend much more time with their families than their American counterparts. The study found that most Indian adolescents liked spending time with their parents in activities like watching TV, talking or doing homework. They experienced little conflict at home. Similarly, another study found that they preferred compromise even if there was conflict among parents and their teenagers. The fundamental underlying belief was that parents have their best interests in mind (Kapadia & Miller, 1995).

Challenging the universal notion of adolescence is another significant work of Kenneth Gergen (2009), a social constructivist. He has discussed the notion of self in the postmodern era. His work is significant because he delineates a close relationship between self and culture. He cites an instance from Balinese culture of naming their children and contrasts it with the Western system. In Balinese culture, children are not called by their names. They have different names for different age groups, signifying their position in the family and the status associated with it.

On the contrary, individualism is deeply rooted in Western culture. This is evident in the name that each child is given at birth to distinguish him/her as an individual from others. With the help of this example, Gergen indicates how closely the concepts of self and culture are intertwined.

Kenneth Gergen (2009) further argues that the social and cultural changes that emanate from technological changes influence the conception of self. He states that advancement in technology has facilitated networking among people. This has resulted in connecting several people simultaneously, leading to changes in the social fabric. He calls this phenomenon 'social saturation'. According to him, this social saturation has also influenced the conception of self and the patterns of life. He contends that the classical notions of self may not hold well in the present scenario.

He further states that in the present time, both the modern and romanticist view of self may not hold ground. The romanticist view sees the self as individual characteristics that suggest personal depth, such as passion, soul, creativity and moral fibre. In this context, relationships are significant. Modernists see the self in terms of the individual's ability to reason. Because of the social changes, the self has also changed. As we enter postmodernism, there are no essences that describe self. There is no clear-cut vocabulary that defines self. He attributes these to the presence of multiple beliefs and practices in the social context. There cannot be an identifiable self in the presence of a multiplicity of voices contending for power. As teachers, we must divest ourselves of stereotypic images and constructs that bring a single image of adolescence to mind. There exist a variety of images situated in different historical and cultural contexts.

4.5.2 Puberty and Emerging Sexuality

The onset of puberty marks an important biological transition for an individual with social and psychological ramifications and biological changes. The appearance of secondary sexual characters and emerging sexuality initiates a new challenge for individuals. The challenge is not just coping with physical changes; instead, coping is a social phenomenon. Culture and society shape how girls feel and behave during this phase. How girls experience 'growing up' is influenced by culture and social class. Ranganathan (2003), in her study, found that puberty is a social construction. She studied the impact of media on girl's awareness of their bodies and sexuality. The result of her study indicated that when girls were asked about their experience of puberty, they associated it with menstruation; they did not mention the development of secondary sexual characteristics. They had many negative associations with the word puberty. They felt that they did not enjoy the same social position as boys. They were embarrassed about the development of breasts since it affected their day-to-day activities such as jumping, playing, etc. Another finding of the study was that social class had an impact on the experience of puberty. A common feature among all the girls was the growing awareness about their body image. They reported being influenced by media and peers in developing a desirable body image.

4.6 Contexts of Development: Role of Family, Peers, Media, Religion and Caste

4.6.1 Family

Sudhir Kakar's essay on family in his book *The Indians* (2009) etches out the idea of the Indian family, which, according to him, is more of 'a psychic reality independent of its actual occurrence'. Though his essay can be critically examined for elucidating Indians as a unified entity, it is significant because it sheds light on some standard features which may be considered significant for the notion of family among Indians. He goes deeper into the 'joint family' system. According to him, the idea of a joint family includes brothers living together after marriage and their wives in their paternal household. The values of fraternal loyalty and filial obedience guide the conduct of each family member. In practice, this may not be the reality.

Kakar (2009) emphasises the psychological 'jointness' even in a nuclear family set-up. Parents visit their married children and live with them for months, or the elder son sends remittances home even if he has migrated with his wife and children to a different place. This set-up makes uncles, aunts, grandparents and cousins integral to the lives of most Indians. Kakar also links joint family set-up with economic and old age benefits. According to him, in a country like India, there are few options for social security, unemployment compensation and other old age benefits, and the family provides succour. This premise holds, especially for the lower class. Individual success and failure have little or no meaning (2009).

The generational conflict, considered significant for development in the Western context, is contrasted with the lack of any such demand from either parents or children's side in the Indian context. Family thus plays a very central role in the life of an adolescent growing up in an Indian context. Kakar highlights the significance of family by stating that 'the Indian family – animated with a powerful sense of life that separation from it leaves one with a powerful sense of exile' (Kakar, 2009).

Depending on the nature of the family, several studies indicate that it has an important influence on the development of an individual, especially during adolescence. A study found a close relationship between parental presence and educational development. Maternal encouragement plays an essential role in the educational advancement of adolescents (Agarwal, 1998). Another study found that family characteristics and adolescent competence have a close relationship. It was seen that the families of more socially competent adolescents tend to be verbally and emotionally expressive and democratic in terms of discipline and decision-making (Carson, Chowdhury, Perry, & Pati, 1999).

It was also found that parents play a role in the development of prejudice and anxiety (Hassan, 1983; Hassan, Enayatullah, & Khalique, 1977). The study found that students' perceptions differ within different caste groups and socio-economic levels. The students of high socio-economic levels felt that their parents show more nurturance and instrumental companionship, emphasise discipline and predictability of standards, give more achievement rewards and are less protective than parents of other socio-economic levels. Caste and socio-economic status interact in influencing specific parental behaviour. These studies merely indicate the influence of familial context on the individual.

4.6.2 Peers

Peers play an essential role in the development of adolescence. Jean Piaget (1932) was among the first to emphasise the role of peers in the development process. He stated that a relationship with equals facilitates the development of mutuality since peers have no hierarchy. He based his argument on his observations of children at play. Even though peer relationships are, in principle, based on equality and reciprocity, some researchers have observed that one partner or a friend gains greater power than others (Giordano, Longmore, & Manning, 2006). Among friendship groups, too, it was found that some groups gain greater power and exert influence over others. Also, in a group, some people are liked more than others, which affects the development of self (Brown, Von Bank, & Steinberg, 2008).

The transition from childhood to adolescence marks a change in friendship patterns. Adolescents spend more time with their friends than parents. Peer relationships become increasingly complex during this time. With the onset of puberty, adolescents are more likely to explore their sexuality and engage in romantic relationships. Even though romantic relationships are distinct from friendships, there is interdependence amongst both kinds of relationships. Research indicates that peer relationships deeply impact romantic relationships (Connolly, Furman, & Konarski, 2000).

Studies in the Indian context indicate that peers play a vital role in the development of individuals during adolescence. It was found that there was a close relationship between family structure, family processes and the adolescents' peer-related competencies. These competencies include attributes such as cooperativeness, group participation and peer acceptance, influenced by family resources (structural and functional) like the father's occupation, family income, aspirations, interests, wanting and getting help from parents (Chowdhury et. al., 1996). Studies conducted in India indicate that besides family, the individual's social context, including their social class, gender and caste, affects friendship patterns. A study by Verman & Saraswathi (2002) revealed that friendship patterns vary amongst members of different social classes. Another study on Indian adolescents found that in their early years, adolescents comply more with parental wishes, whereas late adolescents subscribe towards peer-view (Arora, Verma, & Agarwal, 1985). The peer group not only acts as a solid support system for adolescents but also becomes a medium for the portrayal of aggression and victimisation. It was found that students from the lower castes were more likely to be rejected and victimised by youth of privileged caste groups.

4.6.3 Media

Studies reveal that media, particularly television and mass media, influence adolescents' development. Television viewing reportedly influences adolescents' attitudes towards socio-political problems, marriage, women and education. One area where research has focused is on the attachment that young people develop towards celebrities. Research conducted on British adolescents indicated that celebrities act as pseudo-friends. These attachments help in making a transition towards greater autonomy from parental control. However, if adolescents focus on just one celebrity, it may have a negative impact (Giles & Maltby, 2004).

The media also influences adolescents' perception of their bodies and what is desirable. The images in media create sociocultural ideals and aspirations for youth. Research on girls found that media creates awareness about dieting and dissatisfaction with their bodies (Dohnt & Tiggemann, 2006). However, this phenomenon is not restricted to girls. Boys also get influenced by media images and desire bodies that are projected by media images.

4.6.4 Religion and Caste

Caste and religion, in the Indian context, play a vital role in the lives of Indians. The Indian population is a mix of Hindus, Muslims and Christians, predominantly. There are other religious groups as well, like Zoroastrians and Jews. A social transformation has resulted in the emergence of religious fundamentalism, especially among Hindus and Muslims, leading to communal clashes among adults and young people. Religion is an integral part of the cultural experience of the youth, even though it may not play such a significant role in day-to-day life. Most homes have a place of worship, and youth worship at home, especially during examinations. Temples, churches and other places of worship are a regular feature of the local scene, and most families offer prayers, especially on important festivals. The public holidays are associated with some important festivals that help as a constant reminder of religious practices. The schools also cater to students from all religious backgrounds, though few schools are exclusively for people from specific religions.

4.6.5 Impact of Disability on Adolescence

With the help of the discussion in the paragraphs above, it may be clear that adolescence as a distinct stage is experienced differently by different individuals depending to a certain extent on the context in which they are situated. However, even within the same context, all individuals may not have similar experiences. How do persons with disabilities experience the physical and psychological changes? Do they also have body image consciousness? Are their challenges the same or different from their abled ones? How do social class, caste, religion and ethnicity interact with disability? These are just some issues that must be researched and reflected upon to understand variations in adolescence as a construct.

Studies on disabled persons have tried to understand the relationship between various disabilities and their impact on variables such as self-concept, personality traits, anxiety, aggression, family interaction, as well as behavioural problems. In a study on learning disability, it was found that there is a strong link between personality and learning disability. It was suggested that it is important to understand the personality factors before planning any intervention for individuals with special needs. The study indicated that students with learning disabilities face problems in facing reality and have low ego strength, self-concept, control and spontaneity. The same research also tried to study the urban/rural difference and found that students with learning disabilities were more excitable, impatient, demanding and overreactive (Ganesan, 1999).

4.7 Conclusion

A review of the literature on adolescence, from classical theories to the latest research on adolescence, raises some debates and concerns related to this stage. Despite cultural variation and contextual influences, we can conclude that adolescence is in some way experienced universally. It is a biological experience and a cognitive and psychological change. Therefore, the context in which a person is situated, which includes socio-economic class, gender and exposure to education, plays a significant role in how this stage is experienced by him/her. Adolescence cannot be taken as a cohort where everyone experiences similar psychological transformation as classical theories describe. Instead, adolescence is experienced differently by different individuals according to their socio-historic-cultural context. Through this chapter, we have tried to present a transition from a universal picture to a more pluralistic image of adolescence.

Bibliography

Agarwal, A. (1998). Motivational and Affective Development. In A. K. Srivastava (Ed.), *Child Development: The Indian Perspective*. New Delhi: NCERT.

Arnett, J. J. (2000). Emerging Adulthood. *American Psychologist*, *55*, 469–480.

Arnett, J. J. (2006). G. Stanley Hall's Adolescence: Brilliance and Nonsense. *History of Psychology*, *9*(3), 186–197.

Arora, M., Verma, R., & Agarwal, P. (1985). Parent and Peer Conformity in Adolescents: An Indian Perspective. *Adolescence*, *20*(78), 467.

Bakan, D. (1971). Adolescence in America: From Idea to Social fact. *Daedalus*, 979-995.

Blair, A. W., & Burton, W. H. (1951). *Growth and development of the preadolescent*. Appleton-Century-Crofts.

Blos, P. (1967). The Second Individuation Process of Adolescence. *Psychoanalytic Study of a Child*, *22*, 162–186.

Bronfenbrenner, U. (1986). Ecology of the Family as a Context of Human Development: Research Perspectives. *Developmental Psychology*, *22*(6), 723–742.

Brown, B. B., Larson, R. W., & Saraswathi, T. S. (Eds.). (2002). *The world's youth: Adolescence in eight regions of the globe*. Cambridge University Press.

Brown, B. B., Von Bank, H., & Steinberg , L. (2008). Smoke in the Looking Glass: Effects of Discordance between Self and Peer Rated Crowd Affiliation on Adolescent Anxiety, Depression and Self-Feeling. *Journal of Youth and Adolescence*, *37*, 1163–1177.

Carson, D., Chowdhury, A., Perry, C., & Pati, C. (1999). Family Characteristics and Adolescent Competence in India: Investigation of Youth in Southern Orissa. *Journal of Youth and Adolescence*, *28*, 211–233.

Chaudhary, N., & Kaura, I. (2001). Approaching Privacy and Selfhood through Narratives. *Psychological Studies*, *43*(3), 132–140.

Chaudhary, N., & Sharma, N. (2012). India. In J. J. Arnett (Ed.), *Adolescent Psychology Around the World*. New York: Psychology Press.

Choudhary, A., Muni, A. K., Rath, A., & Pati, C. (1996). Assessing Social Support Networks Amongst the Socio-Culturally Disadvantaged Children in India. *Early Child Development and Care, 121*, 37–47.

Ciccarelli, S., & White, J. N. (2008). *Psychology*. Boston: Pearson.

Connolly, J., Furman, W., & Konarski, R. (2000). The Role of Peers in the Emergence of Heterosexual Romantic Relationships in Adolescence. *Child Development, 71*, 1395–1408.

Dohnt, H., & Tiggeman, M. (2006). Body Image Concerns in Young Girls: The Role of Peers and Media Prior to Adolescence. *Youth and Adolescence, 35*, 141–151.

Erikson, E. H. (1968). *Identity, Youth and Crisis*. London: W.W. Norton.

Freud, S. (1949). An *Outline of Psychoanalysis*. New York: W.W. Norton.

Ganesan, V. (1999). Personality Traits of Students with and without Learning Disability. *Journal of Educational Research and Extension, 36*, 30–34.

Gergen, K. (2009). *Relational Being Beyond Self and Community*. New York: Oxford University Press.

Giles, D., & Maltby, J. (2004). The Role of Media Figures in Adolescent Development: Relation between Autonomy, Attachment and Interest in Celebrity. Personality and Individual Differences, *36*, 813–822.

Gilligan, C. (1982). *In a Different Voice*. Cambridge, MA: Harvard University Press.

Gilligan, C. (1987). Adolescent development reconsidered. *New directions for child and adolescent development, 1987*(37), 63-92.

Gilligan, C., & Goldberg, M. F. (2000). An Interview with Carol Gilligan: Restoring Lost Voices. *Phi Delta Kappa International, 81*, 701–704.

Ginsburg, H., & Opper, S. (1988). *Piaget's Theory of Intellectual Development*. Englewood Cliffs, NJ: Prentice Hall.

Giordano, P. C., Longmore, M. A., & Manning, W. D. (2006). Gender and the Meanings of Adolescent Romantic Relationships: A Focus on Boys. *American Sociological Review, 71*, 260–287.

Grotevant, H., Thorbecke, W., & Meyer, M. (1982). An Extension of Marcia's Identity Status Interviews into the Interpersonal Domains. *Journal of Youth and Adolescence, 11*(1), 33–37.

Hall, G. S. (1904). *Adolescence: Its Psychology & Its Relation to Physiology, Anthropology, Sociology, Sex, Crime and Religion*. New York: D Appleton and Company.

Haslett, S. J., & Kroger, J. (1988). Seperation-Individuation and Ego Identity Status in Late Adolescence: A Two Year Longitudinal Study. *Journal of Youth and Adolescence, 17*, 59–79.

Hassan, M. (1976). Self-Image, Social Prejudice and Child Rearing Practices. *Asian Journal of Psychology and Education, 1*. 30–37.

Hassan, M., Enayatullah, K., & Khalique, A. (1977). A Study of Anxiety in School Children as Related to Child Rearing Attitudes and Some Personality Traits of Parents. *Indian Journal of Psychiatric Social Work*, *6*, 1–7.

Hassan, M. K. (1983). Parental Influence on Children's Prejudice. *Social change, 13*(2), 40-46.

Havighurst, R. J. (1972). *Developmental Tasks and Education*. Chicago: University of Chicago Press.

Hermans, H. J. (2015). Human Development in Today's Globalising World: Implication for Self and Identity. In L. A. Jensen (Ed.), *The Oxford Handbook of Human Development and Culture*. New York: Oxford University Press.

Hetherington, M. E., & Parke, R. (1999). *Child Psychology*. Boston: McGraw-Hill.

Hjelle, L. A. & Zeigler, D. J. (1992). *Personality Theories*. New Delhi: Mc Graw-Hill.

Inhelder, B., & Piaget, J. (1958). *The Growth of Logical Thinking from Childhood to Adolescence*. New York: Basic Books.

Kagan, J. (1984). *The Nature of the Child*. New York: Basics Books.

Kakar, S. (2009). *The Indians: Portrait of a people*. Penguin Books India.

Kapadia, S., & Miller, J. (1995). Parent-Adolescent Relationships in Context of Interpersonal Disagreements: View from Collectivist Culture. *Psychology and Developing Societies*, *17*, 33–50.

Keniston, K. (1971). Psychological Development and Historical Change. *The Journal of Interdisciplinary History*, *2*(2), 329-345.

Kett, J. F. (1977). *Rites of Passage: Adolescence in America: 1790 to the Present*. New York, Basic Books

Khatri, P., Kupersmidt, J., & Patterson, C. (2000). Aggression and Peer Victimisation as Predictors of Self-Reported Behavioural and Emotional Adjustment. *Aggressive Behaviour, 26*(5), 345–358.

Kohlberg, L. (1981). *The Philosophy of Moral Development*. San Francisco: Harper & Row.

Kohlberg, L. (1984). *The Psychology of Moral Development*. San Francisco: Harper & Row.

Kroger, J. (1998). Adolescence as a Second Separation Individuation Process: Critical Review of an Object Relations Approach. In E. Skoe & A. von der Lippe (Eds.), *Personality Development in Adolescence: A Crossnational and Life Span Perspective* (pp. 172–192). New York: Routledge.

Kumar, V., Sharma, R., Sharma, G., & Sharma, A. (2010, September). *Variations Across Adolescence*. CIE: Unpublished.

Levinson, D. J., Darrow, C. N., Klein, E. B., Levinson, M. H. & McKee, B. (1978). The Seasons of a Man's Life. New York: Knopf.

Mahler, M. (1972). On the First Three Phases of Seperation-Individuation Process. *International Journal of Psychoanalysis, 53*, 333–338.

Manning, L. (2002, November-December). Havighurst's Developmental Tasks, Young Adolescents, and Diversity. *The Clearing House*, 75–78.

Marcia, J. E. (1966). Development and Validation of Ego-identity Status. *Journal of Personality and Social Psychology*, *3*(5), 551.

Marcia, J. E. (1980). Identity in Adolescence. *Handbook of Adolescent Psychology*, *9*(11), 159-187.

Mead, M. (1928). *Coming of Age in Samoa*. New York: William Morrow & Company.

Chowdhury, A., Muni, A. K., Rath, A., & Pati, C. (1996). Assessing Social-support Network Among the Socio-culturally Disadvantaged Children in India. *Early Child Development and Care*, *121*(1), 37–47. https://doi.org/10.1080/0300443961210104

Nsamenang, A. B. (2002). Adolescence in Sub-Saharan Africa: An image constructed from Africa's Triple Inheritance. In B. B. Brown, R. W. Larson, & T. S. Saraswathi (Eds.), *The World's Youth in Eight Regions of the Globe*. Cambridge: Cambridge University Press.

Orlofsky, J. (1978). Identity Formation, nAchievement and Fear of Success in College Men and Women. *Journal of Youth and Adolescence*, *7*, 49–62.

Patterson, S. J., Sochting, I., & Marcia, J. (1992). The Inner Space and Beyond: Women and Identity. In G. R. Adams, G. P. Gullota, & Montemayor (Eds.), *Adolescent Identity Formation*. Newbury Park CA: Sage.

Piaget, J. (1932). The Moral Judgment of the *Child. New York: McGraw-Hill Book Co.*

Ranganathan, N. (2011). Puberty, sexuality and coping: An analysis of the experiences of urban adolescent girls. In A. K. Dalal & G. Misra. (ed.) *New Directions in Health Psychology*, 141-154. Sage Publications

Redl, F. (1943). Group Psychological Elements in Discipline Problems. *American Journal of Orthopsychiatry, 13*(1), 77–81. https://doi.org/10.1111/j.1939-0025.1943.tb05979.x

Sarangapani, P. (2003). *Constructing School Knowledge: An Ēthnography of Learning in a School Village*. New Delhi: Sage.

Saraswathi, T. S. (1999). Adult Child Continuity in India: Is Adolescence a Myth or an Emerging Reality? In T. S. Saraswathi (Ed.), *Culture, Socialisation and Human Development: Theory, Research and Applications in India*. New Delhi: Sage.

Saraswathi, T. S. (Ed.). (2003). *Cross-cultural Perspectives in Human Development: Theory, Research and Applications*. Sage.

Saraswati, S. A. (2003). *Age with Spirit: five Ways to embrace change in your life*. HarperElement.

Schlegel, A., & Barry, H. (2015). Leaving Childhood: The Nature and Meaning of Adolescent Transition Rituals. In L. A. Jensen (Ed.), *The Oxford Handbook of Human Development and Culture*. New York: Oxford University Press.

Stern, D. (1998). *The Interpersonal World of an Infant*. London: Karnac.

Sullivan, H. S. (1953). *Conceptions of Modern Psychiatry*. W. W. Norton, New York,

Thornburg, H. (1983). Is Early Adolescence Really a Stage of Development? *Theory into Practice*, 22(2), 79–84.

Verma, S., & Saraswathi, T. S. (2002). Adolescence in India: Street Urchin or Silicon Valley Millionaires? In B. B. Brown, R. W. Larson, & T. S. Saraswathi (Eds.), *The World's Youth in Eight Regions of the Globe*. Cambridge: Cambridge University Press.

Woolfolk, A.E. (2004) *Educational Psychology*. 3rd Edition, Prentice-Hall, Englewood Cliffs, NJ.

5

CHILDHOOD AND ADOLESCENCE IN A DIGITAL WORLD

Chandan Shrivastava

5.1 Being Digital: The Emerging Scenario and Concerns

The expansion of digital media has been one of the most notable developments of the twenty-first century. It has had a powerful influence on children's lives. Children and adolescents before the emergence of the digital age were never surrounded by so many digital tools. They can easily access television with nonstop channels, computers, the internet, tablets, smartphones, YouTube, Facebook, WhatsApp, video games and many other apps. Consequently, digital media is expanding its role in children's socialisation, often becoming more influential than parents and schools, which were traditionally perceived as the primary agents of socialisation. Let us begin with examples of children's engagement with digital media and see the patterns and trends.

Lisa is just two years old. Whenever she cries, her parents give her a mobile phone to play with, which seems to soothe her. The phone has thus become her favourite toy. No other toys can replace it.

Ali is eight years old and is very passionate about phones. He knows almost all the functions of a mobile phone and operates it much more quickly than his parents. How he learnt this so quickly and without much visible effort surprises his parents.

Television is another favourite gadget for children.

Gagan and Priya spend much time watching their favourite cartoons on TV. They even skip their outdoor games and other recreational activities for watching television. Hamid is fond of superheroes and even tries to imitate their actions. Sometimes, this also leads him to injure himself. By watching

DOI: 10.4324/9781003505501-5

reality shows, eleven-year-old Rubina has become so motivated that she wants to become a singer.

Ms. Sandra is a computer science teacher in a school. Despite issuing multiple warnings, she often finds many students chatting on Facebook or playing online games. Ansar is one of her students, and he is so obsessed with a particular computer game that he plays it all the time. He gets very disturbed if she stops him from playing it.

Anhita is a favourite of her family because she is very techno-friendly. She easily shops online, makes payments, uses internet banking and saves the time of others.

These examples indicate the vast presence of digital media in the lives of children across age groups.

Many studies have reported that over the past ten years, there has been a sharp increase in both the time spent in engagement with media and the number of children who use digital media (Chaudron, 2015). The recent report 'Children in a Digital World' (UNICEF, 2017) has highlighted children, adolescents and youth's perception of digital technology worldwide. The report concludes that the digitalisation process is affecting the lives of children across the world significantly. This is true even for the children of the poorest countries where access to digital technology is minimal. The report also highlights the possibilities of digital technology in empowering children, women and persons with disabilities. Other reports also establish that as children grow older, the impact of digitalisation in shaping their life experiences grows with them. However, the outcomes related to the impact of digitalisation on children's well-being are not universally agreed upon. Now, educationists and developmental psychologists are raising many critical questions about both the potential and detrimental concerns of digital media. This is a significant topic of discussion and public debate among policymakers and parents alike (Selwyn, 2016).

At the same time, it is also true that children of the present generation are the first to grow up in a digital world and forerunners of a technological revolution. For children in developing countries like India, exposure to technology is still a new phenomenon that fascinates them. Adolescents are seen to be the most enthusiastic users of digital technologies. However, it is still somewhat early to reach potent conclusions about the kind of impact that digital technologies have on children in India. Existing research studies indicate both positive and negative attributes and possibilities. Some arguments hold that digital media promotes isolation of the individual and reduces social connectedness, while others, in contrast, suggest that digital media motivates and provides opportunities for play, communication, social support, psychological well-being, and identity development (Allen, 2014). To understand these varying perspectives, there is a need to raise more questions about the role of digital media in children's lives and analyse them contextually. Some of the questions, for instance, can be: Why is digital media so appealing for children? How is it successful in capturing their attention? What are the sources and functions of various digital media commonly accessed by children? In what ways is digital media affecting the natural development of children and their mental well-being? How does the digital world shape the perceptions and behaviour of children? Can we categorically define digital media as 'good' or 'bad'? Why has digital media become such a serious matter of concern for us despite its substantial positive aspects? How is digital media shaping the cognition and learning of children? Is digital media inclusive in nature? How can maximum benefits from digital media be drawn to enhance the quality of children's lives?

This chapter analyses these questions and adds value to their existing explanations and debates. It begins by exploring some critical causes of attraction in children toward digital media. Then, the discussion moves to some popular sources and functions of digital media for a more contemporary understanding. The following section deals with some key perspectives and theories that help us understand the interface between digital media and children. An important focus point is digital media's physical and psychosocial effects on children's identity and personality development. The following section discusses some interesting digital media interventions in children's formal education. This is particularly relevant for teachers and parents. The chapter concludes with a brief discussion on the role of teachers and parents in facilitating children to better use digital media for entertainment and learning. An attempt has been made to present multiple perspectives through relevant references and sources. Some examples and case narratives are used in the chapter to build up a contextual understanding of related issues.

5.2 Why Children Are Attracted towards the Digital World?

Let us begin this section by reading this small case narrative.

Suman is a language teacher in a government school in Delhi. She was facing many difficulties in teaching Hindi to class VIII. Her way of teaching through oral reading interspersed with explanations did not interest her students very much, resulting in inferior achievement. She tried many ways of improving her lesson plans and methods of teaching. Some of her efforts were successful, but she still needed to address all the learning challenges of the classroom. Most of the students still needed help with the basic understanding of the Hindi language. On an experimental basis, Suman included digital media, such as audio and video clips, in her classroom activities to develop some language skills in the students. She found that the class was more attentive and participative when she used digital media in her lessons. She also felt more successful in involving all students in the learning activities. She found that using audio sources through mobile phones was an effective pedagogical tool. In her view, using digital tools can help teach many challenging concepts. Digital tools are also helpful in supporting learning for children with special needs. She wonders why digital media is so attractive for children and reflects on utilising it to enhance learning in her classes.

We see that children spend much time on digital platforms for amusement, communication, interaction and learning. Instead of judging whether it is 'good' or 'bad', we should be more concerned about why they are attracted to digital media. Further, how can the digital world's appeal be utilised positively to improve children's learning environment?

The answer to these questions and points of reflection is hidden in the characteristics of childhood and adolescence. In earlier chapters of this book, some vital developmental theories, such as those of Erikson and Piaget, have been discussed. The stage-specific characteristics specified in these theories can be applied to understanding children's attraction towards the digital world. A small child, for example, likes new, fascinating, colourful, and amusing things to play with. Most young children prefer stories about familiar people, animals and fairy tales. Around the age of six to eight years, children prefer concrete experiences and things to engage with to which they can relate. Fantasy, humour and happy endings are also favourite themes. Older children become more realistic and less fantasy-oriented because of cognitive maturation and experiences at school. By the age of ten to twelve years, their interests include adventure, mystery, exploration, etc. Likewise, adolescents are very curious and have high-risk, adventure, and friendship needs. They also have dreams, ambitions and personal utopias.

The digital world provides excellent stimulus for these stage-specific characteristics. Therefore, children pay attention to it. For instance, in a cartoon series, the videos carry interesting stories which children love to watch. They identify with the heroes; there is thrill, excitement and action. Even on the internet, many shows, films, sites, video clips and music clips act as stimuli for them. What can also be seen is a noticeable shift in children's attention from television to computers, laptops, tablets, smartphones, etc., because they provide a more interactive virtual platform for children to engage with and explore.

YouTube, Facebook, WhatsApp, etc., have become a regular part of adolescents' lives. It can be said that the digital world is like a dreamland for them where there is a lot to explore and learn. Many aspirations they hold that cannot be fulfilled immediately in their real lives often get fulfilled through the digital platform. This provides them immense satisfaction. For example, a child wishing to become a soldier or sportsperson cannot achieve this immediately. However, he or she can choose a character of his/

her choice or a role model in a digital game. Such platforms are thus a vital source of stimulation for children.

Another reason why digital media appeals to children is its easy accessibility. Nowadays, in India, almost every family has multiple digital gadgets at home. It is difficult to imagine life without digital engagement. Every social class invests in digital gadgets, and cell phones are seen in every home. So, being digital-friendly is not a privilege any more but has become an everyday necessity and a reality in children's lives. It is a symbol of modernity for common people. It is geographically as well as socially expanding at a fast pace. It is also true that children can engage with digital media better. In the case of adolescents, digital media is a vital source for building social connections and group belongingness. It is faster, more convenient and provides greater independence than conventional forms.

Now, let us explore some crucial forms, sources and activities of the digital world concerning childhood and adolescence.

5.3 The Digital World: Popular Sources and Platforms

It must be understood that the digital world is not a 'finished' and 'fixed' entity. Instead, it is very dynamic and keeps on evolving. There is a continuously changing media environment concerning children and young people (Livingstone & Bovill, 1999). Innovation and new technological developments are its essential properties. The digital world has an innate capacity to renew itself quickly and provide new materials to address the needs and wishes of children. Therefore, we can see a process of evolution in the digital world. As technology develops, the digital world also grows. We had radio earlier, followed by television, computers, the internet, tablets, phones, etc. The spread of digital media in all spheres of our lives, from entertainment to education, health, employment, agriculture, business and many more, is beyond what could have been imagined.

This section discusses a few popular sources and platforms of the digital world, specifically in the context of children's engagement with them.

5.3.1 New Books in Digital Print

Whenever we talk of digital media in the context of children, we generally skip print media. We may have the impression that it has less influence on the lives of children than the virtual media. While this may be true to some extent, the impact of print media on children cannot be denied. Let us start with children's books. Digital print media has dramatically changed the book's images, colours and texts. They are now designed to interest and attract children. Eye-catching picture stories with colourful images are very popular among children. Digital media has also made explaining complex concepts accessible by depicting them through drawings, schematics and photographs.

Along with this, digital print offers a variety of new materials for children to read and learn from, such as magazines, comics, novels, and newspapers. Many children love to read comic books. There are stories with adventure, romance, mystery and mythological tales. Cartoon pictures in the comics are colourful and simple enough for children to understand. Comics provide an enjoyable reading experience for children. So, comics may be used to motivate them to develop reading skills. Here, children are introduced to many new words, thus expanding their vocabulary. Comic books provide the child with an emotional outlet for pent-up feelings. However, it is also argued that comics distract the child from more worthwhile work and keep them from engaging in other forms of play. Pictures of violence are used very often in comic books, which may encourage children to adopt imitative forms of violence in their everyday lives. Along with these benefits, digital printing has made it possible to develop and make available age-appropriate material everywhere.

5.3.2 Television: The Magic Box

Anthony suddenly jumped up from his study corner at home and ran towards the television. Everyone in the room knew it was time for his favourite serial on a children's channel. Rebecca, his sister, could not understand why he only liked watching cartoons. Her favourites were the popular dance and music programmes. On the other hand, her friend, Shazia, hardly watches dance and music programmes. She prefers to watch science-tech programmes.

Television is one of the most popular forms of digital media for children. Sometimes, adults also plan their evenings around television programmes. So, how can children resist this magic box? Television viewing in many homes is a regular family affair. Watching movies in a movie theatre or on television is one of children's favourite pastimes. It would be interesting to analyse the content of the movies children like. Movies are enjoyable for children as they take them into a new world of people, allowing them to imagine situations and actions they cannot do. In movies, children find an excitement not found in their everyday lives.

Similarly, various channels offer many exciting programmes. Channels such as 'Discovery', 'Animal Planet' and 'History Channel'. provide ample content for helpful learning. Children develop awareness about the world through these channels. However, the virtual experience of television programmes is not just limited to entertainment and learning; they are also vital sources of socialisation. The kind of advertisements, characters and issues shown on television deeply impact the children's thinking and personality.

It is often argued that television targets children and adolescents as consumers and commodifies them for economic gains. We can see that television advertisements play a very influential role in shaping the needs of children.

Similarly, the characters of serials and films shape their behaviour. Due to the emotional impact of a film or serial, many children also engage in activities that may harm them, sometimes even ending their lives. Children try to imitate popular characters. Many advertisements and serials also play a role in the gender socialisation of children. Children learn gender-stereotyped behaviours unconsciously by watching television. It takes a substantial part of the time available to children daily, besides the time spent in school and engagement with other activities.

5.3.3 'All in One' Smart Phones

Just ten to fifteen years ago, phones were rare in a family. Now, we may find one Android phone with almost every family member. This transformation has changed our communication pattern and introduced a new 'toy' in children's hands. For a child, an android mobile or smartphone is a Pandora's Box with innumerable, unimaginable features. Video calling, camera, clock, music player, games, apps, internet surfing, WhatsApp, Facebook, email, etc., all are built into a small-sized gadget. Since mobile is handy and easy to control, it is a friendly digital gadget for children, especially adolescents. It is evident from many recent reports that children spend a substantial amount of time playing digital games, watching videos or chatting and surfing on social sites through smartphones.

It is essential to understand the nature of phones and their power and impact on children and adolescents. At the surface level, it appears that we are controlling our phones, but as we ponder deeper, we find that our phones exert much control in our everyday lives, timetable, likes-dislikes, attitudes, movements, etc. The same is also true for our children. The phones currently in use provide features such as 'The Internet of Things' and 'Artificial Intelligence', which capture the digital activities of the user and use this data to influence the users' future actions by providing specific options as suggestions. This feature makes many things easy for the users but simultaneously gets children hooked onto them because of the flashes and displays the phone keeps making. For example, suppose an adolescent likes a particular kind of music. In that case, the artificial intelligence in his/her smartphone will automatically start displaying it or something similar while opening an app or site. This leads children and adolescents to spend more time on their phones, often to the exclusion of other tasks and activities that they should be doing. Further, the overuse of smartphones by children also affects their psychosocial development. This will be discussed in detail in a subsequent section.

5.3.4 Social Sites and Virtual Identities

In the eyes of peers, it is often a shame for many school-going adolescents if they do not have an account on Facebook, WhatsApp or other popular social networking sites. Sometimes, peer pressure forces many adolescents to open virtual social media accounts. While these sites offer many valuable activities, they are also prone to misuse by children and may become detrimental to them. The nature of social sites is very interactive. They offer both information and opportunities for multiple activities by their users. These social sites may be visualised as the virtual world in which children and adolescents represent themselves. At times, they may induce a false sense of self to develop in them. Children start perceiving themselves in the same way as their virtual identity on social sites conveys. The danger of social sites is always in the news, with various examples of users' private data leakages. Adolescents are easy prey for this. Many social sites have been used as a medium to attract them towards extreme ideologies and terrorism. In a way, these sites are firmly but quietly shaping the behaviour of many children. We will discuss their impact on children more elaborately in the following sections.

5.3.5 SMART Classes and Learning Tabs

Children's formal education has not remained untouched by the impact of digital media. New digital technologies are transforming the learning experiences of children in schools. SMART classrooms, for instance, are familiar to our schooling system. Many schools with smart classrooms regularly use digital boards and tablets in teaching-learning. The availability of SMART Classrooms has become a status symbol for schools in India. SMART boards or Digital Boards are Interactive Whiteboards (IWB) connected to a computer or may have built-in support technology and work by touching the screen. The technology of a digital board is very flexible. Teachers can use it to make the classroom more interactive (Kennewell et al., 2008).

Additionally, using the SMART board has shown several benefits for students with and without disabilities. The ability of the board to provide keyboards in different sizes helps students with special needs to prepare their work more effectively. A SMART board has unique features that help attract students' attention for a long time. Also, it allows teachers to use diverse pedagogical strategies with ease. In addition, the SMART board is essential in supporting visual learners and those with vision-based challenges. Thus, it becomes a more inclusive pedagogic approach.

Tablets have also been introduced as a learning tool in classrooms. A tablet is a mobile computer with a display, circuitry and battery in a single unit. According to Galligan, Loch, McDonald and Taylor (2010), tablet computers started to be available from the beginning of this century. They gained popularity in 2002, and soon after their introduction, they became a widespread tool in the education sector (Garland, 2006). Both teachers as well as students can use tablets. There are many ways in which teachers can use tablets as a teaching tool, such as creating blogs for the class as a part of their learning, making class-specific documents, watching videos, or creating small group activities (Gentile, 2012). Students, in turn, can use tablet computers to take notes during class time, read e-books, share information, draw, listen to music or watch videos. In addition, tablets help them to complete and save their assignments (Hieb & Ralston, 2010).

The above are just a glimpse into the tools and gadgets available in the digital world, which influence childhood and adolescence. It is very difficult to describe the exponential expansion of the digital world. To be better understood, it has to be lived and experienced.

5.4 Engaging with the Digital World: Some Key Perspectives

With the evolution of the digital world, many perspectives have also evolved to explain its interaction with the human mind. In this section, we will discuss some of the key perspectives, particularly those relevant to children.

The technological deterministic view is one of the initial responses towards expanding digital media. The view presents digital media as an innovative force that profoundly influences children and youth. It rests on the assumption that technology generates new patterns of expression, communication and motivation in children. In this view, various terms have been used to define the present generation of youth, such as 'Net-generation' or 'digital natives'. These labels attempt to identify a large group of young adolescents who grew up during the expansion of digital media. They also include the present generation of children growing up in a media-rich environment, using computers, playing online games, and constantly communicating and connecting with their friends through electronic devices.

The term 'Digital Native' was coined by Prensky in 2001. According to him, children today are being socialised vastly differently from their parents (Prensky, 2001). The Digital Native perspective claims that a generation (post-1985) has been born digital. So, this generation innately speaks the language and inhabits the specific cultural frameworks of that digital space. Conversely, those not born to this generation are 'digital immigrants' who can attempt to assimilate aspects of the innate culture but will never master the new digital terrain. So, according to these perspectives, the new generations of learners in our schools are 'digital natives' who have innate cultural capabilities to act in a digital space. However, there are contrasting views that have also been raised. According to Bennett, Maton and Kervin (2008), this thesis may be a form of moral panic that takes no account of geography, class or economy. Digital competence depends more on continuous technological access than on a specific generation. An individual's socio-economic background plays a vital role in shaping his/her access to and use of digital technologies.

Further, technological determinism views digital technology as an independent force that drives social change. This view is only partially accurate. It means that digital technology induces changes in social organisation and culture regardless of the social desirability of the change. This is criticised because every society and culture has its own processes and pace to develop, interact with and assimilate digital technologies. A purely deterministic approach ignores material conditions and the social environment within which and through which these technologies operate.

Another important perspective is that digital media has created a new generation of young people who possess sophisticated knowledge and skills with information technologies. These express values support learning by experience in a digital space and have particular digital preferences (Gaston, 2006). Acting in this media-rich environment, the digital generation manifests different beliefs, attitudes and behaviours than previous generations. They can be characteristically termed as optimistic and team-oriented achievers who are technologically talented. Engagement of young adolescents with digital culture profoundly influences their skills and interests. They think and process information differently from their predecessors and depend on information technologies for experimenting and communicating with others. They show eagerness to acquire digital language and skills needed to interact in the digital world and to construct a digital space. Therefore, this view argues that the digital generation is not merely a consumer of digital media but a creative digital producer. They keep thinking of innovations and experiments through digital forms of representation. Digital literacy thus goes beyond the mere use of digital media.

Growing up of children in a digital world can be understood in the context of theories of socialisation and learning. Bronfenbrenner's ecological model suggests that socialisation occurs in various contexts, and the child is in the centre, not as a passive recipient in this process but active in his interaction with the ecological system. He described various sources of interaction, such as family, school, neighbourhood, local government, and culture, under four concentric circles, i.e., microsystem, mesosystem, exosystem and macrosystem, in which mass media is located within the exosystem. While locating mass media in the exosystem can be debated, the theory advocates that children's interaction with the digital world is contextual. In other words, children's engagement with digital media varies with context. This contextual socialisation of children into the digital culture should not be assumed to be easy. The digital culture may initially pose many challenges to children, and they must work hard to overcome them. It is easier to assimilate digital tools for a child living in a digital environment than for those without access to digital media. Therefore, inclusive digital socialisation becomes more significant for Indian children of diverse backgrounds.

The social learning theory of Albert Bandura holds that knowledge is acquired through observation of models. Here, digital media sources can be understood as an effective observation model for children. According to Bandura, cognition, behaviour and environment influence learning and development and are interdependent and reciprocal. Repeated imprinting of a particular behaviour via observation leads to the viewer assimilating a similar behaviour. Therefore, this theory helps explain the effects of engaging with digital media like television, video games, and social sites. Children who watch violence, for example, are more likely to exhibit it in their behaviour. Erica Weintraub Austin derived the Message Interpretation Process model from Bandura's Social Learning Theory to track digital media effects. Accordingly, an individual's behaviour may be dominated by either logic or liking. The model postulates that digital media messages require in-depth logical analysis and wishful thinking (Arnett, 2007).

The constructivist theory of Vygotsky can describe many dimensions of growing up in a digital world. The theory talks about the role of scaffolding in the learning of children. Digital media can be seen as a scaffolding agent because the children of the digital generation depend on digital gadgets to solve their problems. Digital tools often successfully help children to come up with solutions. However, the role of digital media is broader than just being a scaffold. It should instead be understood as an essential cultural tool through which children make sense of the world. By using the digital space, youth are becoming empowered in different social aspects. First, they can overcome the limitations of geography by reaching out to others according to specific interests. Second, they play an important role in society as co-producers of digital content and reach out with their innovative presentations to large and global audiences.

Some views have also evolved to analyse the interaction between children and the digital world critically. According to the displacement theory, using digital media is a choice. If children spend more time with digital media, they will have less time for engaging in other activities, such as sports, school work and social interaction. The result of this displaced activity is increased physical and psychosocial health risks. This view has also created considerable debate over the view that digital media homogenises young people into a single entity with identical characteristics. According to the social construction approach of technology, it is important to note that social groups differ in the extent to which they can access technology, their skills in using technology and the meanings they associate with it. The same technology can have different meanings for different social groups of users. Technologies can and do have a social impact, but they are simultaneously social products that embody power relationships and social goals and structures. Thus, technological changes are process-centric and do not have a singular aim to homogenise.

Thus, understanding digital media's place in young individuals' lives requires avoiding a purely deterministic interpretation and recognising the constructivist outlook of the social embeddedness of technology and its outcomes. However, we must also ask critical questions. The digital world can be constitutive of new cultural features of a young social life, but the point is, can it also reproduce older conditions? Further, should digital technology be individually controlled or socially controlled? This is another level of debate among lawmakers, governments and societies.

5.5 Effect of Digital Media on Children's Development and Thinking

We have seen that digital media has tremendous appeal. How children use digital media is only sometimes facilitative, particularly concerning the physical and psychosocial development of children and adolescents. Some important questions arise: Could digital media adversely affect children's physical development and health? Do digital media affect the thinking and meaning-making process of a child? Can they affect his/her behaviour, goals and aspirations? While it is difficult to answer such questions with certitude, a few research studies provide valuable insights on some aspects. They are discussed in the subsequent paragraphs.

5.5.1 Hindering Physical Development and Health

The detrimental effects of digital media on the physical development of children have received much attention. Obesity among children and its relation to increased digital media use is arguably one of the most widely researched topics. Many international studies have reported that as digital media use has increased, obesity rates have also increased (Anasuri, 2016). However, the biological explanations for this finding are unclear. Some researchers believe that the cause of a rise in children's obesity is strictly related to the amount of time spent with media.

In contrast, others postulate that it is more related to the messages that digital media conveys to them. Other physical health concerns, such as vision problems, hypertension and sleeplessness, are also blamed on excessive usage of digital media. Children's time with digital media increases passive entertainment, reducing the time for other play activities, especially outdoor exercise, such as sports, physical activity, community service, cultural pursuits and family time. Long periods of inactivity and passive watching of television or playing video games can also affect their overall health.

Thus, the effects of digital media are far-reaching and potentially harmful in influencing the growth and health of children and adolescents.

In the psychological realm, many children and adolescents are not yet mature enough to distinguish between fantasy and reality, mainly when presented as 'real life'. This is particularly true for very young children who revel in fantasy. Adolescent utopias are also not uncorrupted by this. For example, by believing in the advertisement of particular beauty products, adolescents aspire to become more beautiful and may end up struggling with side effects, no effects or compounded body image issues. Some researchers have found that digital media interferes with sleep patterns, especially when there is access to digital media in the child's bedroom. This may lead to attention problems, poor school performance, depression, and other health risks. Attention deficit hyperactivity disorder (ADHD) has also been associated with digital media (Chaelin et al., 2018). However, some studies support digital media usage since children may benefit from honing their motor skills, problem-solving abilities and group cooperation.

5.5.2 Disturbing Psychosocial Development and Mental Well-Being

Can we deduce that many fears, tensions, bad dreams and tendencies towards delinquent behaviour that show up in children's behaviour are the result of regular doses of murder and mystery movies and stories filled with violence, torture and barbaric acts that they watch?

Digital media's impact on children's psychosocial development requires much deeper study and analysis than superficial perceptions. Digital media that children routinely engage with, such as video games, the internet and online programmes, are relatively more recent and have yet to be researched much. Their impact on the psychological development of children needs to be clarified.

It has been observed in some experiments that television programmes and video games that project violence may lead to manifestations of more violent behaviours among certain groups. This is consonant with the social learning theory propounded by Bandura, which was discussed in an earlier section of this chapter. Many television programmes and videos have been associated with inducing fear and anxiety in very young children on account of the visuals, sounds and storylines that they carry. At times, they may even cause psychological disturbances since children often imagine fantasy to be real. The important point is that despite their potential harm and threat to wellness, we hardly have any checks on their development and saleability. Movies that do not depict murders, brutal fights, gory scenes showing torture and other types of violence are much fewer in number than those that do. In India, a UA certification is given by the Censor Board to films which are at the crossroads of the adolescent and adult worlds. These, rather than sounding cautious, induce more curiosity and viewership. While it is too presumptuous to conclude that engagement with digital media alone causes children and adolescents to be aggressive and violent, there is no denying that excessive exposure to movies, comics, radio and television does influence children in different ways, often getting them completely hooked on to them. An interesting viewpoint in this regard, on a more positive note, suggests that some comedy and mystery movies and television thrillers may provide a harmless outlet for aggression in normal children, enabling them to live these experiences vicariously.

5.5.3 Creating Social Isolation

Most texts in Child Development discuss how television watching impacts children's social interaction with their families and peers in a direction that promotes social isolation. This has been the observed trend over the last two decades. There is no wonder that the expanding digital world promotes more self-absorption with gadgets and tools in children and adolescents, often excluding family and friends, leading to an increased risk of social isolation. Another important mental health hazard that emanates from this is that social networking sites build social relationships, often at the cost of real relationships. Adolescents spend a lot more time on these sites building virtual relationships, which they often imagine to be real and take family and peers who are around them for granted. Prolonged engagement with imaginary friends may become an addiction for children. The consequences of such imaginary relationships not living up to expectations in the real world can also cause trauma, which in turn may lead to social isolation.

Interestingly, a trend is also seen that socially integrated children spend less time on digital platforms or watching television. They are happy engaging with family and friends. It may thus be inferred that social isolation may be a cause of excessive digital media usage rather than a consequence. On the other hand, many lonely children may turn to television for entertainment and draw a sense of happiness from it. Many adolescents use digital media to escape the stresses of their lives and meet their social needs. Digital media can also regenerate motivation in children and adolescents when feeling low. We can find many examples of movies which are inspirational, carrying heroic depictions and becoming excellent sources of motivation. Whether media promotes social isolation or better social engagement will thus tend to vary from child to child and the contexts in which they live and grow. There is no denying, for instance, that while television viewing is often perceived as an isolating activity, it frequently occurs in the company of friends and family, leading to feelings of bonding and togetherness. It is thus important to consider the context whenever investigating the relationship between digital media use and behavioural changes in children and not draw generalised conclusions.

5.5.4 Endorsing Early Adultification of Children

One of the severe accusations against digital media is the early adultification of children. This is because digital media carry features and content which are more adult-like. Children engage with these through self-propelling that is seldom regulated. Their curiosity drives them to explore more and more and watch and do what adults do. This often results in their growing up much before time. They start dressing and behaving like mini-adults, losing the naturalness and spontaneity of childhood. Many practicing psychologists attribute this to the early exposure they get through digital media to the experiences of the adult world.

What is more serious, however, is that media is not just a source of such exposure; it acts as a motivator and legitimiser of the early adultification of children. The reality shows on television are living examples of this. Children are encouraged to act as adults for entertainment and fame. Even the adultification of cartoon characters indirectly promotes the same tendencies in children. Commercial advertisements, through their promises, often tend to target the child as an adultified consumer. This is contrary to the principle of natural growth and development in children.

5.5.5 Legitimising Stereotypes

If we analyse the content of our daily television programmes and advertisements, we can locate many gender stereotypes within them. This is true of popular serials, films, cartoons and laughter shows. The dialogues in which the various characters speak, and their dress and demeanour carry many sexist statements that depict gender discriminatory behaviour and attitudes, both visibly and invisibly, which are legitimised in the name of entertainment and fiction. Even in cartoon series, a particular male or female character is promoted. For example, men are portrayed as stronger than women. Women are shown as beautiful with slim waists and figures in flowing dresses and tresses, while men are shown as macho and muscular in most Walt Disney fairy tale productions. Portraying girls and boys in stereotyped feminine and masculine roles is also very common in films. This influences children's attitudes and behaviours towards their own and other genders. Women are generally cast in roles with glamour and superficiality, in the traditional role of a simpleton wife and mother or as the vamp who is wicked and disruptive. Apart from gender stereotypes, social stereotypes are perpetuated by depictions that reproduce compliance with the social order. Virtues and qualities that the characters embody relate to good social adjustment, dutiful citizen and good boy-nice girl. Seldom are there any digressions. While there is nothing wrong in carrying such embodiments, the child or adolescent, with his/her ideas of right and wrong or having agency of his/her own, is given no space or projection. So children end up internalising what they should be uncritically. They may feel the need to redefine some of their childhood learnings later in life. Parents and teachers need to understand that the projection of stereotypes in television programmes, cartoons and films is so strong and fascinating that children inadvertently get affected by them and start believing them.

5.6 Understanding the Role of Digital Media in Children's Learning

In an earlier section, we discussed the adverse effects of digital media on children. Here, we will focus on its more positive attributes, particularly its role in children's learning. In schools, from the admission process to classroom learning, there is a dependence on digital media to smooth things out and deal with numbers and volumes. The entry of digital technology into children's learning zones is one of the most significant educational changes in contemporary times. As has already been discussed, different types of technology have entered classrooms, such as digital boards, tablets, and learning management systems. Given this changing scenario, the question is whether digital classrooms should replace conventional classrooms. Further, how does digital technology change children's styles and efficacy of learning, and how and what do children feel about it?

To begin with, what we need to understand is that digital technology is a relatively new concept in Indian schools. Most school students and teachers are themselves experiencing it for the first time. The access is also restricted to the more elite and financially strong schools. Digital technology has been introduced in some schools by providing and using digital boards and tablets in classrooms. However, at the school policy level, the Central Advisory Board of Education (CABE) has resolved to take steps towards Operation 'Digital Board', on the lines of 'Operation Blackboard', to equip all classrooms with digital learning technologies. This intervention aims to offer new opportunities and ways of teaching and learning by engaging the learner and teacher differently from the earlier conventional approach. Digitalised classrooms are thus likely to be a widespread reality.

According to the National Curriculum Framework (NCF-2005) for School Education, technology should be integrated into the classroom for the larger goals and processes of education rather than viewed in isolation or as an add-on. So, the digitalisation of learning in a classroom should be understood more than just the installation and utilisation of digital technology. Instead, it must be understood contextually with its influence on the fundamental nature of the learner. The National Policy on Information and Communication Technology (ICT) in School Education also reiterates the need for critical evaluation of digital content related to the teaching-learning process.

Currently, classrooms are understood as complex cultural and sociological spaces with a dynamic interface between teachers, learners and the curriculum transaction process. Introducing digital technology like the 'SMART' classroom can redefine these complexities and interfaces. Learners' cognition and their learning abilities, teachers' knowledge and teaching skills, and the curriculum-pedagogy interface would all be influenced by it. Therefore, this process of digitalisation of learning in the form of SMART classrooms is opening new dimensions of studies in the field of Teacher Education aimed at building conceptual and empirical understanding about them. Some researchers have argued that digital technology has shown a positive impact on students, both in and out of the classroom, if it is integrated in meaningful ways (Hicks, 2011). However, contrasting perspectives also say that learners' use of digital technologies should not be confused with deep knowledge and understanding. According to Selwyn (2016), we should not be seduced by the hype and rhetoric often accompanying the introduction of digital technology in schools.

Concerns about the not-so-attractive aspects of introducing digital technology in the education of children centre around fears of loss of uniqueness of each child, making the mind respond to technology-driven stimulation, limited space for out-of-the-box thinking that is expressed as apprehensions by teachers and educators need to be researched. They cannot be dismissed since some adverse effects of children's engagement with digital media have already been recognised. From the lens of educators, the oft-expressed apprehension is that technology should not reduce children to mere consumers of technology. Instead, the use of technology should be consonant with the basic constructivist principles of learning. According to Anna Craft (2012), who wrote from a constructivist and socio-cultural perspective, the narrative surrounding technology use in schools stifles children's creativity as it often overshadows the 'childhood empowered' narrative.

An important standpoint that merits discussion is that technology can benefit the nature and quality of students' learning. The success depends on the choice and use of appropriate tools and applications. The connections between the curriculum and technology should thus be carefully visualised and strengthened since they can play a vital role in enhancing children's learning (International Society for Technology in Education, 2000). Given the diversity that marks our classrooms, the potential to build children's cultural capital must also be visualised. Thus, educators must think and plan effective strategies for integrating technology in classrooms. The success of this can be seen operationally when students can select technology tools to help them obtain information promptly, analyse and synthesise the information, and present it professionally. Some Indian case studies have shown whole-school responses to using technology in the classroom and individual teachers making an effort to make a difference for their learners in a more localised way (Motteram, 2017). Research has also shown that the Indian students have a positive attitude towards technology. They see it as an important means for fulfilling their future career plans. This is good news for digital media. So, what emerges is that there are both advantages and disadvantages. Thus, we need to find ways to optimise the role of digital media in our society, taking advantage of their positive attributes and minimising their negative ones.

In contrast to adults, children and youth constitute a broad and diffuse category. The early years of life are characterised by rapid growth and development. The concerns about digital media vary across and within the developmental life stages of childhood and adolescence. Consequently, debates on current challenges concerning provision, protection, and participation must be addressed in the context in which they are addressed.

There is a need to inculcate an appropriate understanding of digital technology in children for a better future since digital media are now regarded as an integral part of their everyday lives. For children to be acquainted and engaged appropriately, parents and teachers should be aware of the relevance and usefulness of digital media. Maintaining good digital conditions for children requires a coordinated and collective effort from all the relevant stakeholders. Digital safety is another area which needs to be promoted in schools and at home. We also need to address the notion of digital autonomy along with digital safety.

It is a matter of concern that research on digital technology is mainly focused on the technological part of its utility. Researchers need to explore the conceptual and humane aspects of technology. In addition, digital technology is still regarded as an outsider to the educational process with add-on utility. There is a need to change this perception. Teacher Education programmes should adequately address digital education's applications and conceptual dimensions for enhancing learning.

We need to recognise the importance of a teacher's role in guiding children about the meaningful integration of digital media in their lives. A teacher should be professionally prepared to select and use available digital media advantageously for the growth and development of children. A teacher can help build a better taste of digital media in children through classroom activities. Parents and the community should also play an essential role in mediating the impact of digital media on children.

Finally, we need to understand that every civilisation, in the course of development, invented some useful technological tools for its existence. A new technology can add considerable value to the earlier one. Digital media is no exception to this, considering this is the era of Artificial Intelligence.

Bibliography

Allen, K. A., Ryan, T., Gray, D. L., Mcinerney, D. M., & Waters, L. (2014). Social Media Use and Social Connectedness in Adolescents: The Positives and the Potential Pitfalls. *The Australian Educational and Developmental Psychologist, 31*(1), 18–31.

Anasuri, S. (2016). Mass Media Making Its Impact on Overweight and Obesity: A Developmental Overview. *IOSR Journal of Humanities and Social Science, 21*(4), 29–39.

Arnett, J. J. (2007). *Encyclopedia of Children, Adolescents, and the Media.* Thousand Oaks: Sage Publications.

Bennett, S. J., Maton, K. A., & Kervin, L. K. (2008). The 'Digital Natives' Debate: A Critical Review of the Evidence. *British Journal of Educational Technology, 39*(5), 775–786.

Chaelin, K. R., et al. (2018). Association of Digital Media Use with Subsequent Symptoms of Attention-Deficit/Hyperactivity Disorder Among Adolescents. *Journal of American Medical Association (JAMA), 320*(3), 255–263.

Chaudron, S. (2015). *Young Children (0–8) and Digital Technology: A Qualitative Exploratory Study across Seven Countries.* European Commission: Joint Research Centre.

Craft, A. (2012). Childhood in a Digital Age: Creative Challenges for Educational Futures. *London Review of Education, 10*(2), 173–190.

Galligan, L., Loch, B., McDonald, C., & Taylor, J. A. (2010). The Use of Tablet and Related Technologies in Mathematics Teaching. *Australian Senior Mathematics Journal, 24*(1), 38–51.

Garland, V. E. (2006). Digital Literacy and the Use of Wireless Portable Computers, Planners, and Cell Phones for K–12 Education. In L. Hin & R. Subramaniam (Eds.), *Literacy in Technology at the K–12 Level: Issues and Challenges* (pp. 308–321). Hershey, USA: Idea Group Publishing.

Gaston, J. (2006). Reaching and Teaching the Digital Natives. *Library Hi Tech News, 23*(3), 12–13.

Gentile, M. (2012). The Importance of Managing iPads in the Classroom. *Education Digest: Essential Readings Condensed for Quick Review, 78*(3), 11–13.

Government of India. (2012). *National Policy on Information and Communication Technology (ICT) in School Education.* Department of School Education and Literacy, Ministry of Human Resource Development.

Hicks, S. (2011). Technology in Today's Classroom: Are You a Tech-Savvy Teacher? *Clearing House, 84*(5), 188–219.

Hieb, J. L., & Ralston, P. S. (2010). Tablet PCs in Engineering Mathematics Courses at the J.B. Speed School of Engineering. *International Journal of Mathematical Education In Science & Technology, 41*(4), 487–500.

International Society for Technology in Education. (2000). *National Educational Technology Standards for students: Connecting Curriculum and technology.* Eugene, OR: Author. Available: http://cnets.iste.org.

Kennewell, S. S., Tanner, H. H., Jones, S. S., & Beauchamp, G. G. (2008). Analysing the Use of Interactive Technology to Implement Interactive Teaching. *Journal of Computer Assisted Learning, 24*(1), 61–73.

Livingstone, S., & Bovill, M. (1999). *Young People and New Media: Report of the Research Project 'Children, Young People and the Changing Media Environment'*. London: London School of Economics.

Motteram, G. (2017). *Teaching and Technology: Case Studies from India.* New Delhi: British Council.

NCERT. (2005). *National Curriculum Framework*. New Delhi: NCERT.
Prensky, M. (2001). Digital Natives, Digital Immigrants. *On the Horizon*, *9*(5), 1–6.
Selwyn, N. (2006). Exploring the 'Digital Disconnect' between Net-Savvy Students and Their Schools. *Learning, Media and Technology*, *31*(1), 5–17.
Selwyn, N. (2016). *Is Technology Good for Education?* Toronto, ON: John Wiley & Sons.
UNICEF. (2017). *The State of the World's Children: Children in a Digital World*. New YorK: UNICEF.
Woolfolk, A. (2004). *Educational Psychology*. New Delhi: Pearson.

6

PEER ENGAGEMENT IN CHILDHOOD AND ADOLESCENCE

Rashi Mukhopadhayay

6.1 Introduction

The development of children refers to the processes of change that take place in them, which are both biological and psychological. The biological changes are often more visible as they get reflected in the changing contours of the growing child's body. The psychological changes, which include the development of the intellect, emotions, language abilities, social skills, social relationships and morality, can also be seen in how the child behaves and responds in different social situations. All development takes place in relation to society. Children go through various stages of childhood as they grow up, namely infancy, early childhood, middle childhood, late childhood and adolescence. During this period, they move from dependency to increasing autonomy. The circles of influence on them also keep expanding as they grow. For instance, initially, the family is the child's only universe. However, as the child grows, friends, peers, community, and neighbourhood are significant components. Each of them provides a set of social relations and a set of meaningful experiences to the child. It is thus important to study the nature and form that social relations take during childhood and adolescence with all their nuances and complexities that include all the circles of influence in the child's life.

This chapter attempts to describe and analyse the nature and forms of interpersonal relations of children and adolescents. It also explores different perspectives that explain the development of friendships during childhood and adolescence and the factors influencing the same. The first section of the chapter focuses on the theoretical perspectives on friendships. A discussion

DOI: 10.4324/9781003505501-6

on the emergence and importance of friendships follows in the second section. The third section presents the factors affecting friendships.

6.2 Perspectives on Children's Friendships

In this section, the theoretical approaches of three psychologists have been discussed: Gesell, who presented the normative developmental approach to understanding the development of friendships; Sullivan, whose focus was on understanding interpersonal relations across the developmental stages; and Selman's developmental stage-focused approach.

6.2.1 Arnold Gesell: The Normative Developmental Approach

Gesell conceptualised a comprehensive approach, stressing development as a gradual patterning of processes, with each succeeding year bringing forth characteristic behaviours and trends. At the core of Gesell's theory were his concepts of 'reciprocal intervening' (the unevenness of development as counterbalanced systems fluctuate ascendancy, alternatively achieving dominance during ontogenesis) and 'spiral reincorporation' (early developmental patterns partly occur within subsequent developmental periods, although at higher levels of organisation) (Gesell, Ilg, & Ames, 1956; cited in Foot, Chapman, & Smith, 1980).

According to Gesell (1956), the development of friendships follows the same ontogenetic course as other behaviours. Thus, there are periods of equilibrium and disequilibrium; the child fluctuates between unstable relationships with many children and more intimate attachment to close friends. Nevertheless, with increasing age, children's friendships progress towards greater maturity as mutuality and reciprocity, the keystones of friendship, become more evident.

He theorised that at every age level, characteristic friendship patterns emerge. So, a 3-year-old demonstrates a preference for one companion, irrespective of gender, and begins to use the word 'friend', though a 4-year-old often chooses a same-sex friend. In this period, friendships are not stable. They easily break during play due to the egocentric nature of preschoolers' interactions. By 6 years of age, children enjoy being with friends and spending time with them. However, friendships are still fragile. Gesell found that 'best-friend' relationships appear at around 8 or 9 years of age. At this stage, friendships are more stable and do not break for insignificant reasons. There is greater mutuality and reciprocity; children can maintain friendships despite conflicts.

At around 10–11 years of age, children have many friends who are adapted to specific occasions, such as a best friend to play with, work with, talk to and so on. Preadolescent friendships are characterised by greater emotional involvement, stability, and tolerance for conflicts compared to earlier stages.

6.2.2 Harry Stack Sullivan: A Clinician's View of Friendship

Sullivan (1953) postulated that throughout the development sequence, children need interpersonal relationships. During childhood (2–4 years), the child is not ready to engage in peer relationships outside the family.

Further, due to feelings of hopelessness and general anxiety, the young child is heavily preoccupied with building self-dynamism, which broadly evolves from experiences of approbation and/or disapproval from parents. The self, therefore, grows and resembles the valuations of the child made by the significant others. He theorised that the juvenile era occurs between 4 and 9 years of age and is uniquely characterised by a need for playmates. The cooperation and conformity that emerge are self-motivated as the child attempts to achieve greater personal prestige in the eyes of peers. The development of social accommodation is the positive outcome of the juvenile era. By social accommodation, he meant the child's ability to learn and grasp slight differences in interpersonal style and cognitive perspectives. This developmental advance results from reduced egocentrism and increased peer interaction.

Sullivan (1953) hypothesised that a need for interpersonal intimacy develops through maturation and experiences. Specifically, a new type of interest evolves in which members of the same sex become 'chums' or close friends. Within this relationship, the preadolescent develops a genuine sensitivity to the individual concerns of his chum, not a self-centred sensitivity but a sincere interest in the welfare of other human beings (Morgan, 2014).

6.2.3 Psychological Understanding of Children's Friendships

Children's ideas about friendship unravel through a sequence of stages. Each new stage represents a restructuring of children's understanding of what it means to be a friend. This is reflective of their development in cognitive abilities.

In the process of developing friendships, children pass through the following four stages (cited in Rice, 1992):

1) Autosociality (infancy and toddler stage): Children want to be in the company of other children and play, but they play alongside other children and not with them.
2) Childhood heterosociality (2–7 years): Children in this stage seek the companionship of other children regardless of gender.
3) Homosociality (8–12 years): In this stage, children prefer to play with children of the same gender.

4) Adolescent heterosociality (13 years and above): In this stage, children's interests, happiness and friendships are found with those of both genders.

Selman (1981) proposed that the development of children's conceptions of friendship would relate closely to their development of social understanding. He gave a stage-wise description of developmental trends in children's friendships.

1) Level 0: Egocentric and undifferentiated perspectives (0–6 years)

At this age, friends are viewed as momentary playmates. The basic idea of friendship is all about having fun. Children's friends will be those who are conveniently available, may be due to distance from their home, parents' peer group or same activity group, and who engage in the same activity or game. Therefore, our understanding of friendship relationships relies heavily on the concept of proximity. A close friend is someone with whom children are regularly playing at that point in time. Egocentricism prevents children from acknowledging that other children may have a different perspective. They may thus keep or terminate friendships on a day-to-day basis as well. A child at this stage fights over specific toys or spaces rather than conflicts which involve personal feelings or interpersonal affection. Despite such variations, it is also found that children tend to maintain friendships and, over some time, show preferences for the same set of peers.

2) Level 1: Subjective or differentiated perspectives (6–8 years)

In this level of friendship, children recognise that friendship goes beyond engaging in an activity together but continue thinking in practical terms. Their idea of friends is those children who are kind towards them – such as sharing toffees, saving them a seat in the classroom or on the school bus, giving gifts or learning a new play game together. However, children often do not know how they contribute to the friendship. The value of friendships for children at this level is evident in the display of emotions when it comes to friends and talking about their friends, such as happiness (my friend gave me an eraser today), sorrow (he did not come today to school), astonishment (she sat beside me in the school bus) and pride (she talks and plays with only me). Children can reflect on their thoughts and feelings from others' perspectives.

3) Level 2: Self-reflective thinking or reciprocal perspective-taking (9–15 years)

At this stage, children are aware of interpersonal perspectives as reciprocal. Friendship is no longer just a matter of engaging in the same activities. Instead, it is a mutually agreed-upon relationship in which children like each other's personal qualities and respond to one another's needs and desires. At this age, they can consider their friend's perspective and their own. It thus leads to the awareness of the mutuality of human perspective and, hence, a self-other relationship. So, children expect that if they do something good for a friend, that friend will return the favour at the next opportunity. It is also seen that children tend to be critical of themselves and others at this stage. They may also have their own 'groups' or 'clubs' that involve elaborate rules and discussion regarding who can be included as a member and who cannot.

4) Level 3: Third-person or mutual perspective-taking (8–15 years)

At this level, there is an awareness of the continuity of relationships and adequate bonding between close friends. Friendship is seen as a means of developing mutual intimacy and support. Children view friendship as an ongoing, systematic, committed relationship involving more than doing things for each other. They demand the exclusivity of their friends and thus are possessive about them. At this stage, friends are seen to help each other solve problems and confide thoughts and feelings that they do not share with anyone else. They know how to compromise and are kind towards each other without expecting anything in return because they genuinely care about each other's happiness. This is also the 'Joined at the Hip' stage for some children. Girls, more often than boys, may be best friends and expect each other to do everything together. They feel deeply betrayed if a best friend chooses to be with someone else.

5) Level 4: In-depth and social perspective-taking (adolescence to adulthood)

Adolescents respect their friends' needs for both dependency and autonomy. Dependence reflects the awareness that friends must rely on each other for psychological support and to gain a sense of self-identification (Foot, Chapman & Smith, 1980).

Children's understanding of friendship and their expectations from their friends changes as they grow older. They have certain expectations about relationships with friends that appear across different peer groups. These expectations seem to progress in three stages (Bigelow, 1977; Bigelow & LaGaipa, 1975, cited in Hetherington & Parke, 1993). The first, reward cost stage (2-3 years), is characterised by similar expectations, everyday activities and proximity. Next, similar values and attitudes towards rules and sanctions appear at the normative stage (4–5 years). Following this, at the empathetic stage (6–7 years), self-disclosures, understanding and shared interests occur.

William Damon (1977) collated the works of various researchers into a three-stage sequence of how children's friendships evolve over a period. He found that friendships in children begin from a concrete relationship (based on pleasurable activity) and evolve into more abstract relationships (based on mutual considerations and psychological satisfaction). The three-stage sequence (Berk, 1994) is discussed below.

1) Level 1: Friendship as a handy playmate (4–7 years)

Children at this age know a friend as someone they spend time with while engaging in various activities, such as playing and sharing toys and other materials. Friendship begins quickly as saying 'Hello' to children in their neighbourhood. As quickly as the friendship starts, it dissolves easily as well, for one or another reason, like a child refusing to play, refusing to share, hit another child or not being available to play.

2) Level 2: Friendship as mutual trust and assistance (8–10 years)

Children's concept of friendship becomes more complex and moves towards becoming a more committed relationship during middle childhood. There is mutual agreement to be friends. Children begin to appreciate each other for their personal qualities. They also now respond to their friend's needs and desires. Phrases like – 'she cares for me, she shares with me, helps me with my work' are common. When friendship breaks, the reasons given are violations of trust, not helping when help is required, breaking promises and the like.

3) Level 3: Friendship as intimacy and loyalty (11–15 years and older)

The meaning of friendship becomes deeper at this level. It is defined as intimacy (seeking psychological closeness and mutual understanding) and loyalty (giving or showing firm and constant support or allegiance). Friendship is regarded as a relationship that has evolved, become stronger over a period of time and also stayed firm for a longer duration.

6.3 Emergence of Friendship

During childhood and adolescence, peers assume special significance since the child spends enormous amounts of time with them at school and often in the neighbourhood and community. A peer can be understood as an individual of similar age, status and interests. Friends are a subset of peers who engage in mutual companionship. A friend is often defined as a person with whom one has a bond of mutual affection. In an individual's life, friendship is an inevitable bond. It is of even more importance in the lives of children and adolescents. The social relations of children and adolescents are centred on their families and friends. Their relationships with their peers influence their lives and overall development from birth through adolescence. Many of their choices, beliefs, ideas, dreams and aspirations can be traced back to emergence in the peer group.

In contemporary times, an exciting trend seen in urban locations is that most children, from a very early age, are educated in the company of their peers. What is commonly observed is that children enter play schools as early as 2 years of age and spend a substantial part of the day with their peers. Even after school hours, they spend time with peers through informal arrangements made by their parents and through various activity classes, including hobby and tuition classes that they attend after school hours. From among their peers, they usually bond more closely with a select few. These select few become their friends with whom they remain more involved. In subsequent paragraphs, we will explore how patterns of friendship emerge across developmental stages.

Friendship is regarded as an important human relationship. The emergence of friendship necessitates a child's ability to relate to other children of his/her age. A newborn's interactions with other newborns start as soon as they are born. However, not all such interactions develop into friendships, as interactions with some peers may be more frequent and long-lasting. The peer group is the child's social world, with its language, mode of interaction, values and acceptable forms of behaviour (Ladd, 2005).

The peer group of children, at first, comprises children of family members and friends of their parents. Peer relationships emerge as early as 6 months and become increasingly important as children grow into adolescence. Infants start communicating with others around 6 months of age, smiling, touching and babbling. Later on, as most infants and toddlers meet their peers regularly, there is an increased interaction with them. This increased interaction amongst peers may be due to the child starting with an early care centre, such as a crèche, play school, day care, or even parents organising peer group activities such as play dates. Children have been observed in nurseries and day-care centres to have definite preferences for certain peers.

In India, children often grow up in joint families, typically comprising grandparents, uncles, aunts and cousins. Parenting becomes a shared responsibility, and there is likely to be at least one more child of the same age. Thus, growing up together often results in strong bonds with cousins. In urban spaces, where joint families are shrinking, parents often take infants on walks or to the park regularly to ensure engagement with the neighbourhood. It is not uncommon for strangers to interact with infants and children. In upper-middle-class households, interaction patterns have become more structured. Parents, mostly mothers, organise 'play dates' with other children of the same age group to foster interactions between peers they approve of.

Several factors may promote early peer relations and their sustenance during the first 2 years of a child's life. These factors include their ability to maintain joint attention with others, regulate their emotions, imitate the actions of others and also the degree of their linguistic competence. It is also seen that preschoolers' engagement with friends differs from their engagement with neutral associates or children they do not like. For instance, a common observation is that children have more cooperative exchanges and differences with children who are their friends than those who are not. Further, relationships at this stage may also suggest the template for future friendships. In effect, while new relationships are never exact copies of old ones, the organisation of behaviour in relationships generalises from old ones to new ones (Killen & Smetana, 1999).

Moving away from the small world of the family to the engrossing world of one's fellow mates is usually underway before the child turns 4. Peer interactions have been mainly seen to be dyadic. Children's friendships, likewise, are always seen to occur at a dyadic level (Gifford-Smith & Brownell, 2003). Children become familiar with the concept of 'friend' by 3 or 4 years old. Each child's friendship varies in form and nature, characterised by intimacy, shared activities, and conflicts. Young children are likelier to imitate positive social interactions, often accompanied by appropriate emotional responses such as smiling and laughter. They also show independence from their parents and enjoy interacting with their peers (Dwaretzky, 1981). For preschoolers, the way to form friendships is to play with another child. Some researchers have argued that the development of peer relationships during the first year or two may pass through three distinct phases:

- The first stage, which is the object-centred stage, starts when children occasionally interact with one another, but most of their attention is focused on objects or toys that they engage with.
- During the second stage, also called the simple interactive stage, infants respond to one another and prefer to engage in social play over solitary play.
- During the third stage, by the age of 2, the child enters the complementary interactive stage, where many complex social exchanges occur between children.

At this age, children tend to form friendships based on proximity. Thus, schools and neighbourhoods emerge as significant places for developing friendships as children can spend extended time with each other. While gender does not play an important role in friendships at an early age, as children move towards late childhood, same-sex friendships are preferred. In a typical Indian school, it is not uncommon to see children segregating into gender-based groups during free time or in sports classes. This is often true even in the absence of instructions. However, it is not uncommon for parents and teachers to restrict children from interacting with or developing friendships with children of the opposite gender. This is more prominent in rural and lower-middle-class households in urban spaces.

Friendship bonds at this stage extend beyond playing together. Children become each other's confidantes. Relationships are based on mutual trust and accompanied by high expectations. Thus, close friends may isolate one group member at the whim of a single child who becomes the group leader for that time. However, this allegiance is highly volatile. Leaders of a group change quickly and are often based on appearances, distributing or sharing chocolates, being academically bright, being quick-witted or anything else that the group assigns value. Children like to develop 'gangs' and refer to each other with code names and converse in a secret language or through code words that only the 'in-group' understands. These 'gangs' hold significance in providing a sense of belongingness and shared experiences of activities that involve breaking rules and social norms. Activities include climbing trees, jumping over walls, staying out too late, cycling to forbidden places, exploring haunted houses, collecting stamps, stones or sometimes even dead animals! 'Flower Power', 'Wicked Boyz', 'Rockin' Kidz', and similar names are decided upon, and hand-made badges or bandanas are chosen as identity markers. Many of these groups or gangs are based on the socio-economic backgrounds of children. Children with similar access to resources tend to study in the same schools and visit similar places. They are also encouraged by parents to spend time together. This makes friendships during late childhood coloured by gender, class and sometimes religious and caste markers.

However, these groups only last for a while. Sometimes, they disappear altogether; at other times, they are replaced by more personalised friendships between two to four children as they grow up.

An adolescent's understanding of a friend is very different from a child's understanding. If asked to define who a friend is, both may answer 'someone close to you', but the meaning implied by them would differ considerably. The idea of being 'close' for a child could be someone who lives nearby with whom he/she plays, but an adolescent would not necessarily include space in his/her conceptualisation. Instead, he/she would likely include many psychological dimensions in the definition of a friend. These may relate to shared values and interests and the idea that a friend is someone to be trusted with very personal information (Dacey & Kenny, 1997). Older children view friendship as more complicated and the development of friendships as a gradual process. Friendships are seen to become more intense as children gain insights into each other's traits, interests and values.

Friendship patterns during adolescence tend to become very pronounced. These friendships are relatively stable and easily recognisable by teachers and parents. The impact of friendships during adolescence is evident through the oft-expressed disapproval by parents and teachers about the 'bad company' of their adolescent children or students. Poor academic performance or experimentation with clothes, hairstyles or lifestyle choices are often blamed on friends by parents. Conversely, adolescents tend to stick to those friendships despite their parents' disapproval. This contrasts friendships during childhood, where parents' approval holds value. Adolescents view friends as crucial for sharing their secrets, thoughts, ideas, aspirations and dreams. Often, friends tend to know about each other's states of mind and secrets. With the influx of technology, it is not uncommon for children in this life stage to have their smartphones and thus stay in close touch with friends over social media platforms.

Gender roles also influence friendships at this stage. Young boys and girls are vastly influenced by media-projected and socially sanctioned stereotypes of 'popular' masculine and feminine ideals. These are reinforced by peers and sometimes by schools and families. The Eriksonian quest to find one's identity is further accentuated by peer pressure for conformity. Experimentation, rebellion, academic pressure of the much-dreaded school leaving board examinations, choosing a career path, coping with bodily changes and discovering one's sexuality are some of the concerns that adolescents need support with. Parents are sometimes busy and sometimes too conservative to share the concerns of adolescents. Friends, thus, provide much-needed support and even advice that may not be forthcoming from other sources. This has substantial implications for the tightrope caregivers must walk on in engaging with adolescents.

6.4 Importance of Peer Relationships

A child's relationship with peers differs from that with his/her parents or other adults. An adult–child relationship is usually complementary, but a child–child relationship is based on reciprocity. Making friends is not an easy process as individuals require various skills such as socio-emotional and socio-cognitive skills, like perspective-taking, empathy (recognising emotions and feelings of others), self-disclosure and good communication skills for making friends and keeping them (Blair, Perry, O'Brien, Calkins, Keane, & Shanahan, 2013; Rubin et al., 2011). Friendship is a unique relationship that differs from others as it has functionality and significance. Hartup (1978) believed that friendships provide children with a context of skill learning, emotional and cognitive resources and models for later relationships.

Children may engage in various activities with friends, such as playing, studying or attending hobby and activity classes. Engaging in such activities can result in friendship. Interaction with peers provides the child a platform to experiment with various social behaviours, including prosocial and aggressive behaviour, leadership bids and sex roles, negotiation, persuasion, cooperation, compromise, emotional control and conflict resolution (Smart & Smart, 1982).

Further, friendships serve as socialisation agents that help to mould children's behaviours and beliefs. Children choose how to spend their leisure time, like sitting together to study, playing video games or going to the market to buy things for school/home. Peers offer new ideas and points of view. They also serve as role models that provide benchmarks for acceptable behaviour, demonstrating what is possible and admirable. In addition, peers act as reinforcers for each other. They act in ways considered appropriate for their age, gender or ethnic group, thus supporting each other in reaffirming their choices. Ridiculing each other in jest, gossiping about others, teasing, being accepted or being ostracised are various ways peers sanction each other's behaviours and habits.

Adolescents may experience (a) ostracism, defined as intentional ignoring and exclusion of an individual by a group or an individual, e.g., receiving the silent treatment and being intentionally left out of a game (Williams, 2007); (b) peer neglect, like being overlooked and forgotten in the peer group; (c) peer exclusion through actively being left out of group activities; and (d) relational victimisation, which involves hurtful manipulation of or damage to peer relationships, manifested as deliberate exclusion, friendship withdrawal and intentional ignoring (Crick & Bigbee, 1998).

The discussion above highlights the central role that friendships play in the lives of children and adolescents. The following paragraphs illustrate the significance of peer relationships in their lives.

6.4.1 Developing Social Relations

During early adolescence, peer activities revolve around cliques, which consist of small groups of peers, usually of the same sex, that interact frequently. Simultaneously, adolescents may also belong to crowds and large peer groups that share related activities and values. They often choose friends based on their parents' behaviour and rules. Adolescent peer groups may thus end up reinforcing behaviours that tend to be approved by the parents. A somewhat universal trend related to social relations seen in almost all adolescents is that they spend more time interacting with peers than with family members.

This is possibly one of the reasons why peers grow to have such a significant influence on adolescent development.

6.4.2 Socialisation

As peer groups evolve from childhood into adolescence, they will likely become an increasingly powerful socialising influence. Across developmental stages, the most socially accepted or popular individuals are likely to be most attuned to and skillful at meeting the norms within their peer groups. Although popularity may be a marker of levels of adaptation in adolescents, it also appears likely to expose them to the socialisation influences of their peers over time. During adolescence, peer socialisation influences may be particularly strong, but unlike in childhood and adulthood, the norms of peers in adolescence may not be entirely positive.

6.4.3 Developing Life Skills

Friendship is considered to be a mark of positive mental health. According to Newcomb and Bagwell (1995), friends and non-friends differ in four broad aspects. These are 'positive engagement', 'conflict management', 'task activity' and 'relationship properties' (cited in Rubin, Bukowski, & Laursen, 2011). Friends resolve conflicts by greater use of negotiation against power assertion that suits both friends and is mutually agreed on. Friends can resolve their conflicts more quickly and amicably and continue their engagement with each other even after disputes and their resolution (Hartup, Burkowsum & Newcomb, 1996).

Playing together, arriving at decisions about activities to pursue, expanding their circle of friends and sharing possessions are part of everyday negotiations that children engage in with each other. These are valuable lessons in developing life skills of decision-making, assertiveness and confidence building.

6.4.4 Emotional Development

An essential feature of a friendship is that it is a voluntary relationship. One has a choice in initiating, maintaining and ending a friendship. Friendship not only ascertains intimacy and affection for an individual; it also provides children with an environment of warmth, trust, empathy and a platform for self-disclosure. As emotional resources, friendships give the children a secure base, unlike how caregivers serve as a secure base for young children to explore their surroundings, enter new territory, meet new people, tackle new problems and have fun.

6.4.5 Cooperative Learning

Children teach one another in many situations and are generally effective. Peer tutoring occurs during interaction with friends, where information gets transmitted from one child to another. Friendship also provides space and opportunities for cooperative learning, allowing children to combine problem-solving abilities and share rewards. Peer collaborations, in contrast, occur when novices work together on tasks that neither can do separately. Friendships enhance social skills since cooperation and conflict occur more readily in friendships than in other relations, and children learn how to deal with them.

6.4.6 Finding One's Support System

An essential aspect of friendships is that they help buffer against any negative impact a child may experience in family circumstances. They also provide considerable moral and emotional support, allowing children to nurture positive feelings in themselves and feel more cheerful and confident. In the preschool years, children see their friends as age-mates who are primary sources of recreation. As they grow older, however, they experience comfort and safety in the company of their friends. Simple actions like eating lunch together in the recess, playing together and sitting together constitute the basis of their friendships. During late childhood, in addition to enjoying tasks and activities together, they seek emotional support from their friends, especially if they get into trouble. This is more so in cases where their homes lack affection or are too regimented. During adolescence, friends become the primary reference group. They are considered much more important than family. Adolescents feel very comfortable revealing their innermost thoughts and feelings to their friends (Levitt et al., 1993; Patrick et al., 2002; Rose, 2002; cited in Sathappan & Sathappan (2017).

School teachers tend to recognise these patterns of peer group interactions early. Children choose to sit with the same friends on bus rides and in classrooms. A change in friendship or being isolated is thus most quickly noticed by school teachers.

6.4.7 Developing Identity and Positive Self-esteem

Erikson (1950) highlighted that adolescence allows finding answers to the question 'Who am I?' Adolescents are ambivalent about their relationships with parents. Although parents are undoubtedly of primary importance in shaping children's lives, friends become increasingly more important during adolescence. Adolescents spend much of their time with their friends and are more likely to share and confide their feelings and personal decisions, seek opinions and address problems with peers rather than their parents.

They have more intimate and supportive friendships and tend to engage in intimate self-disclosure by discussing their worries and fears with their best friends. The quality of their friendships is also related to the psychological adjustments of children and adolescents. Adolescents with supportive friendships have high self-esteem, tend not to be lonely or isolated and enjoy a good reputation with peers.

There are at least two reasons why being ignored by peers might be uniquely associated with adolescents' psychological well-being: First, individuals' perceptions of themselves and their social worlds are primarily determined by the feedback that they receive from significant people in their lives (Harter, 1998); and second, being ignored and receiving little attention from peers sends a strong and negative message to adolescents about their sense of self-worth. When being ignored repeatedly by many peers whose attention matters, it is plausible that adolescents begin to believe that they do not deserve peer attention and may question their 'right to exist' and feel disconnected from or invisible among peers.

Peers can also be socialising agents who support challenging adult rules and norms and, at the same time, reinforce the need to question what is expected by parents. Adolescents often begin to look outside the family for new ideas, associations, and activities, exploring new avenues and taking risks. These new ideas, beliefs and values may agree with or contradict values and beliefs attained at home, school and community. The growing influence of peers may also present a challenge to the family. It is observed that children in urban settings increasingly spend time away from family with school and social activities that parents themselves have enrolled their children in. This leads to further extension of the peer group.

6.5 Factors Affecting the Development of Peer Relationships

Friendships and peer relationships do not function in isolation from the rest of the social world. They are linked to or even embedded in other relationship systems. First among these interdependencies are the connections between family relationships and friendships.

Children are born into a set of circumstances that are beyond their control. Aspects such as class, caste, gender, family background and social context are deterministic factors that influence childhood and adolescent experiences. The subsequent paragraphs discuss the factors affecting interpersonal relationships of children and adolescents.

6.5.1 Family

Parents are the primary caregivers and the first socialising agents in a child's life. Their attitudes, values and beliefs partially define the strength of the parent–child attachment. However, as the child grows and develops, there is a visible change in parents' expectations. They begin to push their children towards fulfilling ambitions and goals that they often set. These can reflect the unfulfilled desires of parents or their aspirations for their children. The child's academic achievement is seen as the achievement of the family.

Although the socialisation of Indian children is a collective responsibility of the whole family, parents play a highly influential role. In particular, the mother can be seen to be much involved in parenting. Baumrind (1971), in her seminal work on parenting, classified parenting styles into authoritarian, authoritative and laissez-faire. Authoritarian parents are high on control and low on warmth, implying that they provide little rationale for the demands they make upon their children. Authoritative parents are high on warmth and control, meaning they regularly explain their demands and limits to the children. Laissez-faire parents tend to ignore children's demands and let them do as they please as long as they do not harm themselves. Researchers have found that children of authoritative parents tend to show more autonomy and independence. Children of these parents also show greater confidence and have healthier self-concepts. More recent ethno-theories of parenting emphasise that parents tend to follow the same practices used for parenting them. This indicates the influence of culture on parenting styles. Parenting in Asian countries is seen to be more controlling and dominating than in Europe and America. A collectivist culture often also results in greater dependence on parents for decision-making.

6.5.2 Socio-Economic Background

Families from higher socio-economic backgrounds have more liberty in choosing the day-care centre or school they will send their children to, as well as their preschool children's social interaction patterns and, thereby, their friends. They have the economic, intellectual, emotional and social resources to fully help their children develop their characteristics. Children growing up in families that are marked by violence and aggression tend to accept it as the norm. The impact of patriarchy is visible on the behaviour and thought patterns of children. They observe and learn social roles of masculinity and femininity from their fathers and mothers. This is reflected in the division of household chores assigned to growing boys and girls, dress code norms and freedom enjoyed outside the home. Often, this is an extension of the level of respect and participation in decision-making between parents. This, in turn, impacts the expectations of children from peers of the same and opposite gender. Digression from stereotypes invites ridicule and often social isolation.

Similarly, where conflict resolution at home is through verbal and physical aggression at home, children learn to adopt the same model with peers. Thus, fighting and winning become central to maintaining peer relationships.

Families, therefore, have the potential to lead children to adopt violence and delinquent behaviour. Coupled with adolescent rebellion, this encourages challenging the law. In some upper-class families, children have access to guns and weapons that enhance their sense of entitlement emanating from the social status they enjoy because of being from high-income families. While cases of misuse of firearms by minors have been more prominent in the Western world, the culture is slowly finding its way into certain sections of Indian society as well. Fights between peers are becoming increasingly violent. This indicates that economic background tends to colour the nature of children's peer relationships.

6.5.3 Gender

As has been discussed earlier, gender plays a vital role in friendship. Friends, in turn, tend to influence gender role socialisation strongly. Children tend to prefer friends of the same or opposite gender at various developmental stages. This has already been discussed at length earlier in the chapter. Children typically grow up trying to fit into the gender roles of the culture and community in which they are born. Peers tend to play a significant role in developing masculine and feminine behaviour. Children, under the influence of peers, sometimes make choices that they are expected to make as girls and boys rather than the choices that they want to make. Thus, girls invariably choose bags, stationery and accessories with female figures of Power Puff Girls, Barbie or other fairy tale princesses. Boys, on the other hand, select masculine superheroes like Ben 10 and Superman.

In many societies, heterosexual friendships are not accepted as a regular part of growing up. While this pattern is slowly changing in upper- and middle-class households in urban spaces, the social structure prevents open interaction between same-age children and adolescents of the opposite gender. This typically begins with admissions into single-gender schools. Even in co-education schools, teachers, encouraged by school administration and parents, segregate spaces for students along gender lines, reducing chances of intermingling. Heterosexual friendships are thus rare and are often frowned upon. In such a hugely structured space, it is therefore not surprising that there is no documentation of the friendship patterns of transgender people or their experiences with peers.

To begin with, the number of transgender people in schools is negligible. Adolescents who challenge the heteronormativity of sexuality are often at the receiving end of jokes. Often turning into social isolates, children breaking accepted gender norms are most hit by peer pressure.

6.5.4 Religion

In a religiously diverse society, children in various parts of the world are not insulated from the impact of religious backgrounds. They do not choose the religion that they are born into. However, not just their religion but also their perception of other religions significantly impact the peer relationships they develop. Living spaces, particularly in rural areas, are usually organised around religious lines. Even in urban spaces, it is not uncommon to find ghettos of religious minorities. This means that children typically grow up in neighbourhoods with other children of the same religion. There is some possibility of coming across heterogeneity of religious background in schools, but interaction patterns are also often restricted. Parents sometimes go to the extent of forbidding children from forging friendships with children of other religions. This is most starkly visible in the case of Hindus and Muslims. Children are expressly prohibited from sharing food or visiting each other's homes. Heterosexual and inter-religious friendships are a total taboo. Such restrictions prevent children from growing up together and learning from each other's culture. Instead, they breed a culture of intolerance and perpetuate a sense of the 'other' as the archetypal enemy. In contrast, where families and schools are open and liberal, children grow up with liberal attitudes and mindsets that can look beyond personal choices and lifestyles to develop lasting friendships based on trust and understanding.

6.5.5 Caste

As stark as religious divides are the divisive lines of caste; caste is also an ascribed identity. In India, children grow up with caste markers and are sometimes referred to by their castes in schools and neighbourhoods. Often, these are derogatory names assigned to them based on their castes. Children are aware of the caste backgrounds of their classmates and use them to tease and sometimes bully each other. State-sponsored provisions supporting the education of children from Scheduled Castes make the caste backgrounds of children a part of everyday school functioning. Like religious backgrounds, parents often encourage children to stay friends with other children of their respective caste groups. Experiences in and outside schools for children from Dalit backgrounds are often marked by discrimination and alienation. Shared stigmatisation and marginalisation also lead to familiarity and a sense of togetherness. Children thus end up forming caste-based friendships.

6.5.6 School

The discussions in the earlier paragraphs have repeatedly referred to schools as important spaces for developing friendships. The impact of class, gender, religion and caste is also visible in peer relationships in school settings. In addition, some schools also practice ability grouping, often based on students' academic performance. This means that children tend to spend more time with children performing similarly in academics. This, in turn, influences their self-image and sometimes even aspiration structures. Schools are also spaces where children form their identities and discover themselves. Children gain acceptance from their peer groups through their identity assertion as the class clown, studious, prankster, teacher's pet or something else. Acceptance by peers and close friends helps children choose their sense of self. Schools thus turn out to be important spaces for developing social ties.

As is apparent in the discussion above, each factor works together to synergistically influence the nature and pattern of peer relationships during childhood and adolescence. This multitude of factors also means that each friendship is unique and holds different meanings for children and adolescents. The strength of the influence lies in the uniqueness provided by a mix of these individual factors.

6.6 Conclusion

Peers play important roles in children's lives at much earlier points in development than is commonly believed. Experiences in the first 2 or 3 years of life affect children's acceptance by their classmates in nursery school and the later school years. Children who are competent with peers at an early age and those who show prosocial behaviour are particularly likely to be accepted by their peers. Aggressive children are often rejected by their peers, although aggression does not always preclude peer acceptance. The risk for children with early behavioural and emotional problems is exacerbated by peer rejection that they might experience.

Conversely, early friendships and positive relations with peer groups appear to protect children against later psychological problems. While, at one time, we might have thought that peers begin to influence children during primary school and adolescence, very early interactions with peers at home and in child-care settings could set the stage for later problems. Because peer acceptance is associated with better psychological adjustment and educational achievement, programmes that support early competence with peers will have educational and mental-health policy implications. In many or most cultures, peers, compared to adults, play even more prominent roles in socialisation as children leave behind early childhood and move into middle childhood and adolescence. Peers are important influences on children in their socialisation process, whereby they influence the directions and outcomes of their development through selective observation, imitation, and choosing to engage in particular activities and modalities of interaction that may reinforce expected roles and responsibilities.

Activity settings are routine everyday experiences that provide children opportunities to learn and develop through modelling and interacting with others. They are the instantiation of ecological and cultural systems surrounding the child and family and how institutions and prevailing cultural norms make themselves felt in the lives of children and influence their development.

Guided participation can be defined as the process by which children become actively involved in progressively more advanced activities and skills. For example, by engaging with peers more competent than themselves, children can learn to structure their tasks, actions and experiences, shaping the direction and outcomes of learning and development.

Children's experiences with their peers are significant for developing their understanding of others. It is evident from various research that when children conflict with peers and siblings, learning from these situations may foster cognitive and moral development. The actions and reasons children give in a conflicting situation reveal what they understand about social rules and other people's feelings and intentions.

The idea that interaction between peers can be intellectually important has led to a focus on learning from peers in educational contexts – through peer tutoring, peer cooperative learning and peer collaboration (consisting of two novices working together on a problem in which neither takes the lead).

The link between family relationships and children's relationships with peers has been a keen area of interest for researchers, where the focus has been on understanding attachment. It is suggested that children who are insecure about their parents as toddlers are at higher risk of difficulties with aggressive and antisocial behaviour and with their peers later on. Links between other aspects of children's family lives, such as discipline, parental mental health, complex marital relations and family disruption, and other adverse life events, have all been linked to children's difficulties in peer relationships. However, there is still a need to explore the links between parent–child relationships and close friendships.

In India, childhood experiences may vary depending on various factors such as socio-economic status, caste, class, gender and languages spoken at home. The importance of peers and the development of peer relations in the lives of children and adolescents is pertinent to policymakers and service providers in the educational, social-service and mental-health sectors. When a child joins school, there is a change in routine, and the child learns to manage the biological clock accordingly. The school becomes an important place where the child learns to interact socially with elders and peers. It is where friendships are forged and broken, and the child learns the rules governing relationships with peers and elders. School needs to build upon the child's skills, such as listening and speaking, and teach new skills, such as reading and writing. Instead of knowing what the parents demand or aspire for their child, schools should focus on their strengths and abilities and hone them by encouraging positive peer relationships. The beginning of school brings new opportunities and challenges for children. Supporting and enhancing the child's self-esteem and self-confidence is critical during this period, and teachers can play a vital role here. It is important to have good mental health so the child can enter adulthood as a healthy human being.

Children participate as active partners in several diverse relationships, yet each relationship traverses, in one way or another, with the others. This is true for family relationships and friendships emerging within larger peer social groups. In different relationships, children act differently and evoke different reactions from their various social partners, peers or parents.

Bibliography

Bagwell, C. L., & Schmidt, M. E. (2013). *Friendships in childhood and adolescence*. London: The Guilford Press.

Baumrind, D. (1971). Current patterns of Parental Authority. *Developmental Psychology Monograph*, *4*(1, Pt. 2), 1-103.

Berk, L. E. (1994). *Child development* (3rd ed.). New Delhi: Prentice Hall of India.

Bigelow, B. J. (1977). Children's friendship expectations: A cognitive-developmental study. *Child development*, 246-253.

Bigelow, B. J. & LaGaipa, J. J. (1980). Friendship and social relations. In H. C. Foot, A. J. Chapman, & J. R. Smith (Eds.), *The development of friendship values and choices* (pp. 15–37). New York: John Wiley and Sons. Ltd.

Blair, B. L., Perry, N. B., O'Brien, M., Calkins, S. D., Keane, S. P. & Shanahan, L. (2014). The indirect effects of maternal emotion socialization on friendship quality in middle childhood. *Developmental Psychology*, 50(2), 566–576.

Blair, B. L., Perry, N. B., O'Brien, M., Calkins, S. D., Keane, S. P. & Shanahan, L. (2013). The indirect effects of maternal emotion socialization on friendship quality in middle childhood. *Developmental Psychology*, 50(2), 566–576. Published online 2013 June 24.

Child Care and Children's Peer Interaction at 24 and 36 Months: The NICHD Study of Early Child Care. *Child development*, 72(5), September/ October, 1478–1500.

Crick, N. R., & Bigbee, M. A. (1998). Relational and overt forms of peer victimization: A multi-informant approach. Journal of Consulting and Clinical Psychology, 66, 337-347

Dacey, J., & Kenny, M. (1997). Adolescent development (2nd ed.). Boston: WCB/ McGraw-Hill.

Damon, W. (1977). The social world of the child. San Francisco: Jossey-Bass.

Dwaretzky, J. P. (1981). *Introduction to child development*. New York: West Publishing Company.

Erikson, E. H. (1950). Childhood and Society. New York: Norton.

Foot, H. C., Chapman, A. J. & Smith, J. R. (Eds.). (1980). *Friendship and social relations in children*. London: Wiley.

Gesell, A. (1956). *Youth: The years from Ten to Sixteen*. New York: Harper and Brothers, Publishers.

Gifford-Smith, M. E., & Brownell, C. A. (2003). Childhood peer relationships: Social acceptance, friendships, and peer networks. *Journal of School Psychology*, *41*, 235–284.

Harter, S. (1998). The development of self-representations. In W. Damon (Editor-in-Chief) & N. Eisenberg (Vol. Ed.), *Handbook of Child Psychology (Vol. 3). Social, Emotional, and Personality Development* (5th ed.), pp. 553–617. New York: Wiley.

Hartup, W. W. (1978). Children and their friends. In H. Mcgurk (Ed.), *Issues in childhood social development* (pp. 130–163). Cambridge: Cambridge University Press.

Hartup, W. H., Bukowski, W. M., & Newcomb, A. F. (1996). *The company they keep: Friendships in childhood and adolescence.* Cambridge: Cambridge University Press.

Hetherington, E. M. & Parke, R. D. (1993). *Child psychology- a contemporary viewpoint* (4th ed.). New York: McGraw Hill.

Hopkins, B. (2005). *The Cambridge encyclopedia of child development.* Cambridge: Cambridge University Press.

Killen, M., & Smetana, J.G. (1999). Social interactions in preschool classrooms and the development of young children's conceptions of the personal. *Child Development, 70,* 486-501.

Ladd, G. (2005). *Children's peer relations and social competence: A century of progress.* London: Yale University Press.

Morgan, J. H. (2014). The interpersonal psychotherapy of Harry Stack Sullivan: Remembering the legacy. *Journal of Psychology & Psychotherapy*, 4, 6. https://doi.org/10.4172/2161-0487.1000162

Newcomb, A. F., & Bagwell, C. L. (1995). Children's friendship relations: A meta-analytic review. *Psychological bulletin*, *117*(2), 306-347.

Ormrod, J. E. (2018). *Development of peer relationships and interpersonal understandings.* Retrieved October 10, 2018, from https://www.education.com/download-pdf/reference/22985/

Rice, F. P. (1992). *Human development* (3rd ed.). London: Prentice Hall.

Rubin, K. H., Bukowski, W. M. & Laursen, B. (2011). *Handbook of peer interactions, relationships, and groups.* New York: The Guilford Press.

Sathappan, R. & Sathappan, M. (2017). The effects of technology on peer relationships and interpersonal understanding: A case study at a teacher education institute in Malaysia. *Journal of Social Science Research,* 11(1), 2257–2267.

Selman, R. L. (1981). The child as friendship philosopher. In S. R. Asher & J. M. Gottman (Eds.), *The development of children's friendships* (pp. 242–272). Cambridge: Cambridge University Press. Retrieved November 18, 2018, from https://www.psychologytoday.com/us/blog/growing-friendships/201202/childrens-growing-friendships

Smart, M.S. & Smart, R.C. 1982. Children. Development and Relationships. 4th ed.. New York: Macmillan.

Sullivan, H. S. (1953). *Conceptions of Modern Psychiatry.* W. W. Norton, New York.

Williams, K. D. (2007). Ostracism. *Annual Review of Psychology, 58*(1), 425–452. https://doi.org/10.1146/annurev.psych.58.110405.085641

Yu, J. J., Tepper, K. H. & Russell, S. T. (2009). *Peer relationships and friendships.* Building Partnerships for Youth. National 4H Council and the University of Arizona. Retrieved September 25, 2018, from http://performwell.org/index.php/identify-outcomes/relationships/10-indicators/229-close-friendships

7

DECONSTRUCTING GENDER

Basic Concepts and Ideas

Neema Chaurasiya

7.1 Introduction

This chapter addresses the key concepts and ideas that help us to develop an understanding of gender. Although gender is pervasive and affects every individual, its influence on the development of self is often ignored. Many of our experiences, beliefs and practices are coloured by gender. However, socialisation practices often make these gendered processes go unnoticed and unquestioned. Further, since gender is assumed to be biologically determined, it is usually taken for granted and not questioned by individuals or the society surrounding them. It is important to highlight that gender is an important dimension in identity development. It affects our viewpoint towards the world – how we perceive ourselves and others, our choices, actions and our understanding of things and ideas. The role of gender in all these processes is crucial but often not explicit. This implicit process becomes all the more crucial for practitioners in education, given that education plays a significant role in gender socialisation. Students and teachers bring to the learning contexts the gender identity they relate to. This defines not only who they see themselves as but also determines their social behaviour in educational contexts and society at large. If education is seen as a process that can change thoughts and behaviour, it is all the more important to know 'who' learners identify themselves to be.

'Gender', as we will see further in the discussion, is not given but created in an individual's mind. It is carefully imbued and maintained for material and non-material benefits. The power and existence of ideas surrounding gender lie in societal acceptance. This chapter begins with a discussion on gender, sex, and sexuality. It moves on to discuss the means through which

DOI: 10.4324/9781003505501-7

gender concepts are constructed, the factors that contribute to their development, the interface of the factors with gender per se and how they influence an individual's identity. One section of the chapter attempts to touch upon the relationship of gender with education and also throws some light on the dynamic, two-way relationship between them.

7.2 Gender, Sex and Sexuality

There have been various formulations regarding the differences between the terms 'sex' and 'gender'. Most of the practitioners in the fields of academics, research, teaching and feminist writing discern between the two terms 'sex' and 'gender' based on their emergence from the fields of Biology and Sociology, respectively. The former is determined by birth and based on bodily or physiological features; social structures ascribe the latter. In common everyday contexts, 'gender' and 'sex' are usually used and understood to be synonymous. Gender differences between men and women have been projected as a natural part of human behaviour and identity. One primary reason why it is difficult for people to differentiate between gender and sex is due to the 'everydayness of gender' (Sreenivas, 2015, p. 269). In other words, gender has penetrated our day-to-day actions, choices, notions and behaviour so much that it is never questioned. We need to examine this distinction between sex and gender, as this will help us to build perspective and apply concepts related to gender in schooling practices.

'Sex' is broadly defined as the bodily or physical distinctions that exist between the male and female members of a species. So, a human infant is labelled a 'girl' or a 'boy' based on the genital differences between them at birth. Based on this distinction, specific characteristic roles are expected out of them; for instance, the male child is expected to exhibit masculine traits while the female child is similarly expected to display feminine traits of behaviour. These differences in expected behaviour are assumed to be based on the biological differences between them at birth. Over the years, various gender theorists, feminist writers and philosophers have pointed out the fallacy of this expectation. They claim that the human child being born, regardless of his/her sex, does not naturally incline towards masculine or feminine traits. The male child learns to take upon masculine traits through socialisation, and the female child similarly acquires feminine traits. The socialisation process is complex, multi-layered and, at many stages, very well institutionalised. With time, the acquired traits become the individual's second nature, a part of his/her self-perception and identity. They are projected as naturally ordained gender.

One, however, needs to examine this claim of gender differences being 'natural' critically. For argument's sake, if we assume that gender differences are natural, they should be the same throughout the world or universal in their features, like other laws ordained by nature. The first premise, however, does not hold since the norms and behaviours associated with masculinity or femininity differ worldwide. The concepts of masculinity and femininity will be discussed in detail in the subsequent sections. Still, it is necessary to highlight that the traits associated with both change from society to society. For instance, in tribal or agricultural societies, physical strength and power are considered to be the epitome of 'maleness', while in urban societies, to provide for a family, one has to 'earn a living' that requires professional skills rather than physical prowess. Some social classes even view 'masculinity' as the ability to exercise control (ideological or physical) over people of the other sex. In some societies, masculinity may also be equated with the ability to produce children. A combination of these or some other qualities may define masculinity in different cultures. Similarly, the qualities associated with and expected from girls and women under femininity differ from society to society and culture to culture.

Feminists make use of this idea to argue that since gender is not universal, it is not naturally pre-ordained but socially constructed. Simone de Beauvoir, in her book *The Second Sex*, explains it as – 'one is not born a woman but becomes one' (1973, p. 301). Of course, the focus for feminist writers was to oppose the unjust, discriminatory practices against women based on gender roles that are projected as a by-product of natural biological differences between men and women, as we will see in the sections that follow that 'the sex-gender system is the institutionalised system which allots resources, property and privileges to persons according to culturally defined gender roles' (Roy, 2007). This system is more discriminatory towards certain genders as compared to the others. The subjugated ones thus struggle for their rights. This brings us to our second premise: if gender roles are assumed to be natural, they should remain constant over time, like other natural laws. The feminist movement over the years has struggled to liberate women's gender roles out of the limitations of home and family towards new roles of work, education, jobs and leadership. Since the 1960s, there has been a significant shift in women's position and roles in society, which shows that the idea of femininity and associated roles are flexible. Two centuries earlier, women were seen only as mothers, wives and nurturers. Even if they worked, they were limited to the so-called feminine professions such as nursing, stitching, teaching, home management and child-rearing.

In contrast, now they are professionals, innovators, scientists, political leaders and business personnel. These new roles for women prove that, unlike natural laws, gender roles can be altered and adjusted. Gender, thus, is a 'set of culturally accepted norms of behaviour that are seen as appropriate for the sexes in a given society at a given time' (Roy, 2007). One can easily surmise that there are no universals regarding gender.

For both men and women, gender differences represent differences in identities that the society prescribes through its various institutions; they are projected as natural and thus upheld. Any questioning and disturbing of the established notions or roles associated with being a man or a woman is seen as tampering with the 'normal' order of nature, a deviation from the norm.

Gender philosopher Judith Butler takes the notion even further and argues that the normative differences between these identities of gender that one internalises over time make us neglect the fact that 'sex' itself is a socially constructed idea and not naturally ordained (1988). Many feminists disagree with this position of sex and see it as a fundamental biological difference between the male and female bodies.

Butler argues that sex differentiation is decided through certain physiological features at birth, but human bodies can be differentiated through various physical features. Out of these, we use only the ones dealing with procreation to divide people into male and female sexes. How did we decide upon these as defining factors for differentiation? Any other features can replace these as an equally valid basis for differentiation of humans, e.g. tall and short people, black or white people, or people with blue and black eyes. The differentiation into male and female sexes based on genitalia at birth is as random a distinction as any. Then, we expect gender traits to follow based on such a random distinction and believe the differences between sexes to be naturally intended when there are so many other differences in physical features at birth.

The physical features for 'sex determination' are prescribed by a discipline – Biology, which, like other disciplines, is a part of a gendered system. In simpler words, the ones who pick out physical features of human bodies as a differentiation basis for 'sex' are themselves socialised into gender. Thus, when Biology specifies that 'male' and 'female' are naturally different, it specifies just one of the many ways of differentiation between human bodies. Based on a randomly selected differentiation, rules are framed to standardise the behaviour of men and women. Sex differentiation is not naturally occurring, but like gender, it is socially determined. However, they still are distinct from each other, as gender is all-encompassing as a social construct under which bodies are gendered as different sexes.

Butler's conception of 'Sex' being socially constructed is a powerful argument since it points us towards the multi-layered identities in terms of gender. Before further exploring this, let us first delve into another marker of gender identity – sexuality.

It is commonly believed that human sexuality follows the so-called biological 'sex' differences. So usually, an individual's sexual orientation is expected to be (1) heterosexual, (2) conform to the sex he or she is assigned at birth, and (3) remain constant throughout their existence. However, as we have seen above, sex differences are socially determined. Also, there has been no consensus in research on how the so-called 'biological sex' influences sexual orientation or sexuality. Sexuality is not even clearly divided into heterosexual and homosexual categories. Sigmund Freud introduced the term 'innate bisexuality', according to which humans by birth are predisposed to be bisexual in orientation, and heterosexuality thus is normative. Sexuality has no natural affiliation to a person's ascribed 'sex' or 'gender'. Sometimes, an individual chooses not to subscribe to sexuality and views themselves as asexual. Sexuality, therefore, is not static or delineated. It is fluid and defined as per the individual's perception of self.

7.3 Gender Identities

The process of development of gender identities majorly comprises three markers: (1) the physical differences defined by biology referred to as natural differences of 'sex'; (2) the feminine or masculine traits ascribed based on these differences referred to as 'gender'; and (3) the sexuality that is attributed according to the biological features.

These three are supposed to be naturally consistent with each other and together form a normative masculine or feminine gender identity, which in turn supplies one with gendered personality, beliefs, attitudes and gender roles. However, these are not able to explain the other variants of identities in terms of gender, such as transvestites, bisexuals, transsexuals, transgender and so on.

When we look at the approach of Butler, Beauvoir and other Feminist writers and philosophers, who profess gender, sexuality or sex differentiation to be social concepts, as discussed in the previous section, we realise that the three markers of gender identity are not necessarily consistent with each other as per nature but only expected to be congruent as per the social system. The two categories of masculine and feminine are ascribed to make them manageable in the social context, in harmony with social beliefs, rules and expectations.

This makes one question the way we understand gender identity. If an individual is not confined by one sex, one gender and one sexuality, and these are not naturally consistent with each other, then they may or may not identify with neat binaries of male and female gender identity.

The vast variety offered by different combinations of these three markers and the fact that they can be fluid and flexible gives us the potential for an assortment of gender identities. This clarifies the basis for Lesbian, Gay, Bisexual, Asexual and Transgender identities, which are not 'non-natural' but a part of this fluid continuum of gender identities, where the bodily features, the ascribed gender traits and sexuality are not in sync with the binaries of masculine and feminine gender identities.

These gender identities other than masculine and feminine have so far been commonly viewed as unnatural or abnormal, and the individuals who identify with them are not accepted within the social system. This is despite the legal recognition and status accorded to them. The socially sanctioned binaries of masculine and feminine are so deeply rooted that even the individuals who identify with any other gender begin to question themselves.

7.4 Gender Performance and Power

From the discussion so far, it might appear as if 'gender identity' is imposed by society upon the individual. However, while understanding gender, one should not forget that an individual actively builds upon a gender identity. So, the individual has agency in developing one's gender identity.

The question then arises as to why an individual with an agency would succumb to the social constraints of gender that limit or contradict one's natural inclinations.

'Gender' is not forced upon individuals. They are active in identity development, albeit in an unconscious way. This agency is not denied or suppressed. It is just not part of conscious awareness. Butler's idea of gender performativity throws further light on this. She propounds that masculinity and femininity are performances enacted in front of a social audience. Through this performance arises a gender identity.

Whether consciously or unconsciously, all humans create and strengthen the gender roles that are expected by society through gender performance. Being social creatures, humans observe and enact actions for learning. Young children, through observation, learn the different behavioural norms of the masculine and feminine genders. They imitate these to gain social acceptance and form a sense of belongingness to a category, contributing to their sense of self. So when women and men behave or act according to the prescribed notions of gender for feminine and masculine, respectively, they unconsciously follow a script in their minds. This script of how a woman or a man 'should be' is acquired over time. The domination is symbolic and is exercised through the unconscious performance of roles; gender is thus internalised. The body, hence, becomes gendered through performed gender behaviours, and the gender division is viewed as natural or innate. It is a continuing cycle of observation, reproduction and consolidation of gender performance.

When Butler propounds that the performance of gender creates gender, she means that this performance of being a man or woman establishes the gender identity not only in front of the social audience but also strengthens the notion of their ascribed gender in the individual's mind. The performance of gender also acts as a model for the younger generation to imitate, thereby transmitting it from generation to generation. For Butler, sex and sexuality in the vein in which they conform or are expected to conform to a common axis are also performances, like gender.

The performance of gender is closely related to power in the social context. When individuals conform to the conventional gender expectations, they are sanctioned power by the system to promote the reinforcement of their performance. For instance, women who perform the typical gender roles through marriage and child-rearing are given access to assets and social respect, which are denied to the ones who do not. They also get to enjoy the privileges and power that come with the class and caste of the men they associate with. Even when we see women in positions of political, economic or social power and authority exercising the privileges and control that come with those positions, they have to conform to the gender norms, without which the position or the associated power would not be theirs to command. One can witness this in the family and work or public spheres. It is not just the denial of resources that women non-conforming to gender roles face; it is often a violent backlash. The same also occurs when men flout the expected gender performance, as displayed through the example in the previous box. This power operating underhand within the system, enabling or disabling one, depending on an individual's conformity to gender performance, is oppressive as it confines the expression of a person's choices in life. The manifestation of this power is multifarious and will be detailed in the following sections.

The performance of gender within the social discourse of power often becomes so normalised that it takes place almost involuntarily. So, individuals perform it without question, although they do possess the ability to question. With this conception, gender does not remain an imposition exercised on the individual by society nor is it chosen actively by the individual exercising agency, whether consciously or unconsciously; it thus comes across as a dynamic interaction whereby the individuals participate in the social process of the construction of gender.

7.5 Masculinity, Femininity and Gender Stereotypes

In the previous sections, we discussed how gender binaries are shown to be formed based on biological determinism, while in practice, they are socially constructed together by the individual and the society. The normalisation process into gender binaries begins from birth itself. Masculinity puts forth the social definition of what it means 'to be a man' while femininity defines what it means 'to be a woman'. These narrow categorisations are oppressive and profoundly affect an individual's identity and self-concept.

Femininity is supposed to be the performance of gender by women; it is associated with notions of nurturing, dependence, weakness and docility and ideas of appearance dealing with beauty, daintiness, elegance and grace. Over the years, especially with the rise of the feminist movement, the ideas of femininity – the norms, roles and expectations – have undergone considerable changes. They have now come to include various kinds of women – the ones who do not conform to the established notions of female appearance, the lesbian or bisexual women flouting the norms of stereotypical feminine sexuality, the racially or culturally different women, working women and homemakers and so on. Earlier, homemakers were the ideals of femininity; now, the beautiful-looking working woman who believes in feminism and manages the home and the work front has become the ideal to vie for. Thus, the idea of femininity changes from context to context, but what remains constant is that society and not the women define it. So, though the idea is demonstrated to be flexible by the efforts of the women's movement, the female body and identity are still marked deeply by social influences.

Masculinity, on the other hand, is always portrayed in terms of the idea of a macho man, strong, tough and virile. It has to do with physical appearance as much as femininity. So, both body and behaviour are imbued with the concept of masculinity through sociocultural ideas, which are portrayed to be natural features of the biological male. Some people thus argue that men are naturally prone towards behaviours such as aggression and violence. However, as we have discussed before, natural biological differences do not fix one's orientation towards any gender or the conduct associated with them. Therefore, behaviours associated with and displayed by men, such as violence, must have other reasons. Roy (2007) opines that the gendering process has something which makes men take risks and choose the path of violence to deal with conflicts. The ideas of masculinity which are fed into young boys by society are the driving force behind behaviours such as violence and misogyny. The anxiety of the performance of the masculine – powerful, violent, silent, independent and strong – is also one of the reasons for this insecurity since the ideal that they vie for is unattainable and unnatural. Masculinity is socially constructed and not a fact. Therefore, it has to be constantly defended; the aggression portrayed as a feature of masculinity is this defence of the idea of masculinity. Constant assurance is required through the performance of masculinity so that the belief in that fragile idea can be upheld. Domestic violence, gender violence and backlash against women on the web are all examples of this assertion of the idea of masculinity, which feels threatened and has to be defended.

Masculinity also is not a uniform idea. Throughout, there are different forms of masculinity. They are sometimes in contrast to each other or dominate each other. Men, though more powerful in a patriarchal society than women, do not hold an equal share of that power. Several factors, such as age, wealth, social status, caste and occupation, play a significant role in maintaining hierarchies of masculinity.

'Hegemonic Masculinity' is the most common and visible form; it dominates all other kinds of masculinity. It is usually constructed and portrayed through popular media as 'the alpha male', the ideal that all other men aspire to be. This idea is so deeply rooted in our minds that it is not questioned. The more powerful and privileged a man is, the more he is unaware of the constructed nature of his masculinity, which lends him that power. He is ignorant of other forms and kinds of masculinity and the domination exercised on them. This lack of awareness contributes to its perpetuation. Since individuals are unaware of social forces that influence the idea, they cannot question its power and authority. Roy (2007) argues that this lack of awareness and reflection is what resists change.

There are studies, ideas and voices regarding the notions of femininity. The women's movement has struggled to bring these issues to the fore for decades. Comparatively, there is still plenty of work required to see the effects of masculinity on the male identity and behaviours since 'men do not talk about what it means to be a man' (Roy, 2007).

This kind of conceptualisation of gender binaries in terms of identity had paid little or no attention to the systemic oppression exercised on individuals and the immense exclusion and marginalisation experienced by homosexual, queer, transgender and inter-sexed people. With the growing awareness and dialogue on the issue of gender identities as a result of the 'neo-liberal celebration of difference' (Nagalia, 2018, p. 85), the spotlight is shifting slowly from 'women's studies' towards 'gender studies' in academic discourse now.

7.6 Gender Stereotypes

Gender stereotypes are the expected norms of behaviour for both sexes. Individuals identify themselves as masculine and feminine in their minds and thus are under self-sanction for the performance of their gender identity. Unlike this, gender stereotypes are usually society's expectations of the individual based on their gender identity. Stereotypes lead to gender bias, and they also contribute significantly to establishing gender identities. Any deviations from the norms earn societal backlash.

Gender Stereotypes are expressed through various indicators. Some of these are discussed in the subsequent paragraphs.

7.6.1 Appearance and Body Language

Stereotypes regarding appearance for women are contextual but mainly include – rules on what to wear – unattainable body standards and looking young, beautiful and presentable all the time. The body language is expected to be graceful, poised and not in the way of others, particularly men; women are supposed to be as invisible as possible, especially in public domains. Body language stereotypes for women do not have as detailed rules as appearance. However, they are conveyed more through what is unacceptable, i.e. taking up too much space in the social sphere, behaving in an uninhibited manner, or talking or laughing too loudly.

Men's appearance and body language, according to stereotypes, have to be macho, conveying strength and power. Lack of facial hair, skinny or graceful men are not considered manly enough according to stereotypes.

7.6.2 Physical Spaces and Language

The physical spaces available to men and women, according to stereotypes, are different. A man in the kitchen or a woman in the office boardroom are not anomalies today, but these are not viewed as their natural spaces. Women unaccompanied by men in several public spaces are vulnerable due to gender stereotypes, as they are seen as transgressing the physical spaces available to them.

The language acceptable for both sexes does not limit itself to the use or avoidance of swear words. There are sanctions on the topics that are acceptable, e.g. talking about sex in social contexts for women or talking about menstrual issues in the presence of men is taboo. The stereotypes regarding how things are said also differ. Men are expected to be assertive and aggressive, while women are passive and polite. The time duration given to women in family or workplaces for speaking and the attention or audience provided to them are lesser as compared to men, based on the regressive gender stereotypes.

7.6.3 Profession and Career Roles

Stereotypical career expectations for both sexes are restrictive and oppressive. The choice of career to opt for, the duration of time to be devoted to study and the access to education itself is dictated by gender stereotypes.

Occupational identities such as farmer and scientist have largely been inaccessible for women. Men as dancers and homemakers have been looked down upon in social contexts.

Women are believed to lack the educational capabilities or calibre for fields relating to computational, analytical or logical calculations; they are therefore not encouraged or supported for such subjects, professions or projects. This leads to even fewer women in these fields, giving the impression that the stereotypes are true.

For men, the stereotypical notion of being seen as the primary breadwinner is a source of tremendous pressure. Failing to provide for a family also causes ego issues or mental trauma for them.

7.6.4 Emotions

Aggression and endurance are considered acceptable emotions to be displayed by men and sentimentality, kindness and nurturance for women. Any deviation is highly criticised. 'Men do not cry' is the most common outcry one hears that reflects the sanctions on human behaviour by gender stereotyping. It results in very trying psychological issues for both sexes – dealing with suppressed emotions that are considered unacceptable by the standards of their respective gender.

7.6.5 Behaviour

Behavioural norms for both sexes on a day-to-day basis, including their choice of peer group, sexuality, likes, dislikes and preferences, are closely regulated by gender stereotypes. While young girls and boys are expected to have friends of the same sex through adolescence, as one grows up, normative heterosexuality becomes the call according to stereotypes.

From aspirations for adults to choosing playthings for children, all behaviours are expected to be in line with the stereotypical depictions relating to gender. No matter how young or old, women are not supposed to be very ambitious. Men who are not aspirational are seen as lacking in something essential to be displayed in men's behaviour.

These stereotypes are so deeply entrenched that the individuals question themselves if there is something wrong with them if they do not fit into these gender identities and stereotypes. Such is the trauma of isolation, criticism and other forms of backlash which come with being non-conformist to gender stereotypes that it becomes a source of mental suffering and bitterness against society for the individual. Due to societal isolation, they are also alone in this suffering, which deepens the anguish. There are no spaces or language even to counter the established discourse of gender stereotypes on a day-to-day basis.

Gender stereotypes are internalised over the years by observational learning and socialisation. In the following sections, we will discuss how these stereotypical conceptions are normalised through socialisation.

7.6.6 Gender Socialisation

Socialisation is the process through which the individual internalises the norms and ideologies of society. The stereotypes and the notions of femininity and masculinity are thus passed on to future generations through gender socialisation. It is a complex, multi-layered process that can happen in apparent and non-apparent ways.

Gender socialisation does not reproduce gender as it is; an individual's agency plays a role in the process. Gender roles, therefore, do evolve and alter over time, but the core condition remains the same; that is, assigning roles based on gender still continues.

Socialisation occurs through various agencies and social institutions such as family, kinship, school, peers, religion, media, and education. We will examine below the roles that some of these play in the process of gender socialisation.

7.6.7 Family and Kinship

Children learn the behavioural norms and gender identities ascribed to males and females early on through observation in the family and the immediate social circle. The everyday conduct of parents, siblings, kin and elders in the family acts as models for the young ones to imitate in terms of gender roles, e.g. they notice the duties and responsibilities of mother and father, the way siblings of different genders dress, the language (both verbal and body language) which the elders use according to their position and hierarchy in the family based on their gender and so on.

They also notice relatives, neighbours and peers visiting the house and discern the acceptable and non-acceptable behaviours for both sexes by replicating them and observing the patterns of positive or negative reinforcement. They act out as parents of the same sex or different professions; they witness being gender appropriate through play as well.

The family thus acts as a critical institution of gender socialisation – transmitting the roles, hierarchies and norms of gender to the younger generation.

7.6.8 School and Peer Interaction

As children grow up and start going to school, they develop another group of gender role models in the shape of teachers and peers. Peer interaction also acts as a check on deviant gender behaviour; through isolation, criticism and humiliation, any child who does not conform is singled out. Education and schooling are crucial socialisation tools, which will be discussed in detail in the next section.

7.6.9 Social and Religious practices

Social and religious institutions lay down rules for gender roles, norms and values. Marriage as a social institution has defined roles for men and women, which the child observes and internalises in the family. The celebrations and grandeur surrounding weddings in India are another way of gender socialisation due to the statuses of the girl's family and the groom's. Women in social customs are seen as valuable gifts, always to be 'owned', so they are 'given away' at the time of marriage. They are expected to be meek and dependent on familial connections, while men are supposed to care for them and provide for the family. Religious taboos on menstruation and widowhood also limit women's status. All of these contribute to the image of women as passive, obedient, weak and dependent, while men are projected to be strong and able; observing such social and religious customs acts as a gender socialisation process for young girls as well as boys.

7.6.10 Mass Media and Popular Culture

Gender socialisation takes place through the stereotypical representation of genders in popular culture and media. Both print and electronic media forms accessible to young children and teenagers play an essential part in their identification with gender roles.

Mass media projects images of how men and women are supposed to appear, behave and be like. Magazines and video games are targeted at specific genders; likewise, the content varies according to gender stereotypes. Other media sources, such as television commercials, ads in print media, TV programmes, movie songs, and books, mainly propagate gendered representations of delicate and dainty women with unattainable and unhealthy beauty standards and over-masculinised images of macho men. For the young generation, gender stereotypes are normalised mainly in social context through their depiction in movies, songs and social media, which become idolised in their minds. The Internet is a widely available platform that reinstates the gender rules prevalent in the social set-up. For instance, the vehement backlash against the voices and opinions of women on social media plays a role in strengthening the stereotypical gender norms. The cultural context to which an individual belongs provides for literature, myths, folk songs and folklore depicting stereotypes of males and females, which also act as socialisation, especially for children.

7.7 Education and Gender

Education and gender share a dynamic two-way relationship. Though their association differs from context to context, it can broadly be characterised into two parts.

- Education as a tool of socialisation: This works for both men and women, where education is a tool for socialising them into gendered roles and identities.
- Education as a resource: Due to its capacity to offer socio-economic mobility, spaces of dissent, and power, which come with knowledge and awareness, education acts as a resource and has historically been denied to the oppressed genders.

These roles will be dealt with in detail in the subsequent sections.

7.7.1 Education's Role in Gender Socialisation

Education acts as a significant tool for reinforcing the gender stereotypes upheld by society. Schools and educational institutions assist in the formation of gender identities. One of the ways this is achieved is by supplying gendered models to imitate in the form of teachers, peers, curriculum and texts, which are internalised by young girls and boys. The gender 'normalisation' process works underhand as well as on the surface in our classrooms, curriculum and daily outside class activities. From the uniforms that the students are made to wear differing according to their assigned genders to the expected norms of behaviour for 'good boy' and 'nice girl' to gender segregated seating, single-sex educational institutions, modelled gender behaviour and attitudes of teaching faculty, glorified masculine and feminine figures in textbooks. The language of the educational discourse reinforces gender stereotypes. The subject disciplines that the students learn in educational institutions are not only considered suited to a particular gender but the career choices arising out of them are also regarded as appropriate according to gender binaries. For example, home science is as inaccessible for a boy as Natural Sciences is for a girl. This bias becomes a basis for the young learners' stream selection in high school.

Inside the classroom, the representation of stereotypes in textbooks (both in the written word and illustrations) is not very difficult to notice; despite policies to root out the gendered representation, these persist. In the books, one can see the depiction of male and female stereotypes in the representation of professions, daily responsibilities, dress codes and moral and ethical norms considered 'respectable'. The student–teacher interactions and even the language used in the classroom incorporate structures of gender hierarchies.

Behaviour is closely regulated in terms of gender; any deviation from the norm leads to ridicule; a 'tomboy' girl or a 'sissy' boy is not only mocked by peers, they are even singled out by the teachers or the school authorities as anomalies, and often pressurised to conform to established gender, sometimes even by dragging the parents of the children in for the 'reform'. Silence on issues also works to reinstate gender stereotypes; for instance, aggressive behaviour, being loud, breaking of rules or mutual fights by boys will be ignored more readily or go unnoticed by teachers, being excused as typical masculine behaviour. Similarly, non-participation in sports, poor performance in disciplines such as maths or science or being quiet, socially withdrawn or passive in the classroom will not earn ire from female students by the same standards of being labelled as feminine attributes. The logically proven basis for such attribution does not exist, as we have witnessed. In this case, the silence of the teachers, whether in classroom processes or outside of it, on such behaviour is deeply problematic. Let us assume a reversal in the exemplified characteristics above for both genders, i.e. a loud, aggressive, prone to fighting girl or a very quiet, not inclined towards sports boy. The institution can now easily label the children in question as 'problem-child'. The lack of questioning by educators over such everyday gendered practices is what makes educational discourse so profoundly gendered.

The educational institutions thus mirror the existing ideas of gender disparities in society and help their continuation by transmitting them through generations.

It is also important to note that this is not a deliberate process. Every educational institution is based in the context and deeply set in social practices, and it cannot be completely rid of the unequal gender relations, the language of the gender discourse or the power hierarchies of gender norms. The central struggle here is to become conscious of the gender socialisation process of education and help the learners be aware of the same.

7.7.2 Education as a Resource

Education has the potential to challenge the existing gender hierarchies by offering spaces for awareness and critical questioning. It provides access to economic independence and social and political power positions and opens avenues for more inclusive set-up and positive social change. For this very reason, historically, education has been denied to the oppressed genders, especially to women, for limiting their critical reflection on their conditions.

The fight for equal educational access for other genders has been raised recently. Historically, the feminist movement brought up the issue of the inaccessibility of education for women and stressed its importance for the larger question of social justice. Women all over the world fought for the right to education. The barriers to access are multiple. In patriarchal contexts and developing countries, sociocultural gender roles restrict girls from physically stepping out of the house as their sphere of activity is defined mostly within the home walls. Household chores, taking care of younger siblings, cooking, cleaning, etc., claim a considerable share of a girl's time compared to boys. Religious rules also play a significant role, with 'purdah' being a defining feature of femininity for some. Even without it, the severe curtailment of women's sexuality in the form of limited mobility, restrictions on dress and social interactions with other genders, especially after puberty, also contribute towards the female dropout rates in schools. The public spaces a girl has to negotiate to reach school are male-dominated. These and other out-of-school factors impact a girl's educational performance, competence and presence in the educational sphere.

Schools also play a role in curtailing girls' access to education by being insensitive towards these out-of-school factors. The fundamental problems, such as lack of toilets, sanitation issues, and lack of commute facilities, become more challenging for girls post-puberty, leading to dropouts. So does the lack of female teachers, not only in terms of the dearth of educated role models but also making school a male-dominated sphere, similar to the one the women negotiate outside while reaching schools. The sociocultural restrictions on their nature and behaviour, attributing passivity and submissiveness as feminine traits, lead them to be restrained and unable to reach their potential in the classroom. Schools act as instruments for gender socialisation, as discussed in the previous section.

The factors limiting women's participation in education thus do not work in isolation; they combine and interact to form a complex matrix of opposition. Consequently, there is a much greater struggle for women, not only in terms of enrolment or retention in school but also in terms of educational performance and day-to-day negotiation within the male-dominated domains.

These imbalances hinder women from reaching their educational potential, benefitting from their educational qualifications and actualising their prospects.

Limiting educational access or regulating the quantity, quality or subject matter of education for women has far-reaching consequences on their self-identity and how they view themselves. Having no sense of significance for their own identities, they unquestioningly accept the gender disparities meted out. Their disregard for self-worth is reflected in their daily choices, behaviour and devotion towards submissive roles.

The educated women, on the other hand, feel burdened to compensate for the opportunity for educational access by proving their 'worth', lest the argument of women not being worthy of equal education wins.

In both these scenarios, there is tremendous pressure upon gender to prove itself worthy of equality and equal educational resources, even when there is no question of inequality of genders in the first place, if not for gendered social disparities.

7.8 Patriarchy

Several conceptualisations have been employed to understand what is at the basis of the subordination of women under patriarchy. Feminist writers have pointed out the argument of biological determinism, which is used to make a case against women's equality; it claims that biological differences also cause differences in mental capability and physical capacities, which result in women being inferior to men. As discussed earlier, these projected differences are not biological but socially constructed. Subsequently, these differences are used to establish the superiority of men over women in the patriarchal society.

Simone de Beauvoir also points out that gender differences, which assign men the role of breadwinner in a family, give them a position of power as they control the resources (1973). This sets the sexes into a hierarchical opposition against each other, whereby women's position is projected to be subordinate and a man's to be superior. These positions are projected onto the institutional, social, political and economic contexts, and thus, society turns masculine to its core; women are the outsiders, the 'other', consistently marginalised.

These two assumptions of women being biologically inferior and men being the breadwinners for the family and controllers of resources form the core of the patriarchal system of women's oppression. Let us try to understand what patriarchy means and how it plays out.

Over the years, patriarchy has been defined and understood in several ways, while earlier, it only meant the rule of the eldest male member of a household, who was termed the patriarch. It has evolved over the years and now defines a whole gamut of male domination over any sphere, home, work, social, political, economic or even virtual spaces. Any discrimination based on gender resulting in the devaluation of women, either in public or private spaces, can be termed as patriarchy. It is a system of discrimination, which enforces roles and codes of behaviour on women which devalue them. These roles limit their potential, choices and possibilities in life.

Now, to address the second concern of how patriarchy plays out in society.

Various agencies and institutions exercise power or control over women in several ways. These include religion, kinship, caste, tradition and culture. Legal and political authority is derived based on these, as are economic sanctions to relegate women to the margins. Men have dominated and controlled. These institutions and systems have not changed much over the years.

Patriarchy manifests itself in the form of control, neglect, disregard and abuse of women in various setups. So, women have to struggle for equal rights in education, property ownership, decision-making, and other aspects of day-to-day life. In contrast, these rights are readily available and unquestioningly provided for men. Various examples can be drawn from daily life discourse – the burden of household work on girls and women, lack of educational opportunities, denial of freedom of expression and mobility, lack of control over fertility and reproduction, body and sexuality and so on.

Apart from the denial of equal rights, the patriarchal system works on the twin aspects of rewards and punishments. It constructs the 'ideals' of womanhood – norms, definitions and roles that restrict a woman's potential or capabilities. It limits their roles to mothers, wives, sisters and homemakers and rewards the ones who passively conform to these roles. These are not randomly designated work division roles; they devalue the labour that goes into nurturing and label it as a woman's natural duties. They offer no real power in decision-making or resource management, even inside the household. The 'ideal' wife or mother is put up on a pedestal in the patriarchal system and granted social sanctions. They are celebrated through literature, festivals and religious rituals. So, women strive to achieve this ideal and, in the process, actively participate in upholding the social roles that subjugate them. Women are expected to develop a sense of self or identity in relation to others. They are barely respected as individuals in a social context; this view unconsciously shadows their choices and attitudes in life. The society also views them according to their eventual marital exchange, which becomes a consideration in bringing up girls in conformance to the marriage ideal – nurturing, passive, meek and dependent.

This has a keen effect not only on the socio-economic position of the women in terms of lack of resources but also on the way they view themselves. They have no sense of self-worth, being demeaned and devalued all their lives. They face pressure to be 'useful to men'; otherwise, they would be discarded or devoid of protection and consequently have no social significance or economic support. Such a self-perception becomes the basis for their further devaluation. The whole cycle thus relegates them to the margins with constrained access to resources, limitations on life choices and daily routines designed to support the men they are associated with. It leaves them with a very unjust setting to perform and prove themselves at par with men in education, career, politics or economy.

The women who refuse the roles of wife or mother, deny following the traditional rules of wifehood or motherhood, or transgress the acceptable gender norms in any other manner are projected to be against their nature or unnatural in their ambitions, non-conforming to their basic biology. There are visible changing trends in some countries and cultures that are more gender equitable in their attitudes and spirits, but the numbers are still relatively low.

It is essential to point out that experiences of patriarchy differ according to culture, religion, age, education, caste, class and region. Further, since patriarchy doles out differential treatment for men and women, usually denying women access to resources and power in the private sphere, it leads to them being in a disadvantaged position in the public sphere as well.

Interestingly, patriarchy is not only unfair to women; it makes undue demands over the dominant gender, too. Since men have their roles defined by the patriarchal system, they have an image or an ideal to match as well. With strict demands of conduct expected of them to earn a living and provide for the family, any failure results in social ridicule, self-doubt and frustration. Patriarchal oppression exists, therefore, for both women and men, though it is more repressive for women than men.

7.8.1 Resources and Opportunities

The power of gender most visibly manifests itself in the form of control over resources. We have already discussed education as a resource denied based on gender and its consequences. The other resources bestowed and denied based on gender are discussed below; some are tangible, some are non-tangible, but all offer power over those genders who are denied a share in these resources. For convenience purposes, they are discussed in points. However, one should remember that these are not neatly divided categories in practice; they overlap and influence one another in several ways.

7.8.1.1 Property and Financial Resources

According to sociocultural norms, property and economic resources are controlled mainly by men and are passed on from generation to generation amongst the male members of the family. Even by law, men are assumed to be the head of the household in terms of property ownership. Recently, through changes in inheritance laws, legal rights have been granted to daughters for a share in paternal property. However, these are not exercised due to varying factors – family and social prohibitions along with the emotional pressures they levy, customary and traditional practices held in place through generations, religious rules and sometimes purely by violence. So, though women contribute to the largest share of household chores, they control income and property ownership the least.

Women are commonly viewed as burdens, not seen as native to either their father's or husband's home. In her father's home, a girl is viewed as a 'guest' or a 'gift' to be 'given away' during marriage. At the husband's place, she is almost an outsider with a lower social position in the family hierarchy. The condition of widows is also seen to be pitiable. Mostly, they survive on the charitable efforts and benevolence of their families. Women seldom hold property or economic resources which they can call their own.

Property and money are powerful resources on their own; they also have a massive influence over subtle powers at work; for instance, they affect decision-making abilities and sway over spaces of expression. Power thus begets power to those who hold control over these economic resources.

7.8.1.2 Laws and Legal Rights

The legal system and rights are an individual's point of access to social justice. Therefore, we consciously view the right to law or legal justice as a resource here. There are several ways in which women are denied access to legal resources.

Most of the laws dealing with economic and social resources are patriarchal to the core, either in their framing or in their interpretation. One of the reasons for this is that the people operating in the field of law, including judges, lawyers and lawmakers, are principally men from the bourgeois class. Their construction, interpretation and implementation of laws are laden with gender bias. For instance, the non-recognition of marital rape in the legal framework due to the social, cultural and religious sanctity of marriage as an institution in India is an excellent example of laws mirroring and upholding the oppressive patriarchal set-up.

Religion's sway over framing and upholding laws in a secular country like India is also remarkable. It influences laws on marriage, divorce, inheritance and various other issues. As mentioned earlier, it is one of the institutions asserting the norms of a patriarchal system. Religion uses different standards of morality for men and women, which subjugate women; this is reflected in the legal system as well. The practice of 'triple talaq' (unilateral instant divorce by husband) is recently being debated. In contrast, the system of polygyny (the practice of a man having more than one wife) continues under Islamic law. These subordination practices against women are recognised under the legal system of the country.

With the perspective shift in legal provisions, such as the altered right to inheritance and the strengthened laws against rape, it would seem on the surface that the conditions are changing for the better. However, access to such laws for women remains a huge issue. There are physical hurdles in access to police stations or courthouses due to restrictions on mobility or the intimidation that comes with these being majorly male-dominated spheres.

Then, there are constraints over legal narratives, which are highly patronised in the patriarchal system. In simple words, this means that women are often pressured into altering statements in various legal cases, resulting in a lack of agency or voice. This results from a lack of agency in other spheres – family, marriage or kinship. It may also occur due to poor knowledge of legal procedures, partially due to education being denied to women.

7.8.1.3 Sexuality and Mobility

Under the patriarchal system, severe restrictions are placed on women's bodies and sexuality. Women's sexuality is seen as being passed on from the patronage of father/brother to husband, always under an owner. It is also related to the notions of family honour and shame. The linkages between a woman's sexuality and a family's honour are never questioned; on the flip side, men's promiscuity does not affect the family's honour in the social context at all. For women, chastity till marriage is not only desired, it is enforced. 'The expectation that a woman cannot or should not willingly engage in premarital sex is rooted in the mores of a conservative society and patriarchal notions of chastity and virginity' (Vishwanath, 2018, p. 20).

After marriage, women are expected to provide sexual services to their spouses according to their needs. The lack of laws regarding marital rape, quoted in the previous point, is an example of this. Another example can be seen as the difference in the legal age of consensual sex for an unmarried girl and a wife in child marriage.

Women's sexuality is also controlled by restrictions on dressing, including the idea of 'purdah' or 'hijab', limiting interaction with the other gender and laying down acceptable and non-acceptable behaviour norms. Family members, society and religion closely monitor compliance with norms. There are also moral, legal, sociocultural and religious restrictions to limit a woman's mobility and sexuality, e.g. menstrual taboos limiting access to religious places.

Control of women's sexuality thus becomes a tool for limiting their mobility and life choices. Girls dropping out of schools at higher secondary levels due to the onset of puberty or the distance of high schools from home can be explained by these restrictions on sexuality and mobility.

These restrictions are carried forth through violent means as well for women who transgress the norms. Violence against women is almost systemic in its form; access to the law has hurdles, as discussed before, and the state refuses to intervene except in exceptional cases, thereby legitimising it through silence. Physical or sexual violence and harassment in the private or public sphere are all blatant examples of the same. So are rapes or rape threats that are attempts to limit a woman's sexuality. The very idea that the body of a woman can be violated and made 'impure' is a classic example of the psychological control exercised over women's sexuality.

The sense of psychological insecurity instilled through violence, whether threatened or manifested, limits women from actualising their potential or even realising it. It profoundly affects their belief and confidence in themselves, hence moulding their identities towards the submissive feminine ideal that they are forced to follow. There is also a deep relation between violence against women and economic exploitation of women since the former restricts their mobility and thus limits their career and educational choices.

7.8.1.4 Health and Reproductive Rights

Men control women's health and reproductive lives in various ways. Largely, women have no say over fertility rights – the number of children, when to have children, the use of contraceptives, termination of pregnancy, etc. These are dictated directly or through societal pressure by the in-laws or the husband – the rules dealing with reproductive capabilities, whether by legality or religion, are laid down by men. Politically as well as socially, the state programmes regarding family planning put limitations on a woman's reproductive rights. Apart from the lack of reproductive rights, issues regarding dwindling sex ratio due to female infanticide or female foeticide are widely known problems. Because of the laws against female foeticide, illegal abortions pose a threat to a woman's health and life, and mostly, she has no say in it. The availability, use and quality of contraceptive methods are also questionable.

In addition, the idealisation of motherhood in a patriarchal set-up makes nurturing children intensely demanding, solely assigned to being a woman's job. Together with reproduction, the bringing up of children makes a very high demand on a woman's health, body and time. It forms one of the bases of women's oppression, both physically and psychologically – limiting her physical mobility and potential and building up an intense psychological pressure to conform to the high ideals of motherhood.

The health conditions and facilities for women, especially in rural and semi-urban spaces, are deplorable. One of the reasons for this is the low value women place on their self-significance due to patriarchal oppression. The absolute submission and devotion expected of them make them neglect their selves. As a result, their nutrition intake, health conditions and life expectancy are way lower than men's. The daily life choices which women make due to psychological pressures or the ones that are enforced upon them both result in them being devoid of health and reproductive rights.

7.8.1.5 Technological Advancements and Progress

A share in technological advancements is a prerequisite for progress in our world today. Various patriarchal arguments and attempts have been made to deny women access to the virtual space and the potential that it offers.

A vehement backlash is triggered in online spaces when a woman does not conform to the established gender norms; having an opinion and voicing it in the public domain is itself seen as an act of rebellion. It results in threats, criticism, and hatred against them. The Internet is a vast and anonymously accessible space, and controlling such hazards is a huge problem despite the laws that prevent them. This limits women's presence, visibility and right to expression in the virtual world.

Physical access to information technology is also controlled by denying them mobile phones or computers, especially in rural contexts. The reason cited for this is that their minds will be corrupted by technology. The real fear remains the liberation of female sexuality and identity in the virtual world, leading to the rejection of gendered identities and rules imposed over them by patriarchal society.

Since technology provides alternates for social spaces and promotes networking beyond the immediate environment, it is highly dreaded by the patriarchal system as a source of female liberation. Movements like '#MeToo' against sexual harassment have indeed realised these fears to some extent. Another example can be found in rural India, where mobile phones act as a means for women to network without moving out of the physical private spaces that they are confined to, thus bringing the 'outer world into the women's spaces' (Tenhunen, 2015, p. 41). It also gives them better access to information, educational resources, and visibility in the socio-economic sphere. This is why such restrictions are imposed on the possession of mobile phones, especially for young girls.

7.8.1.6 Economic Productivity

Women's productivity is controlled by the male domination over economic institutions that define the idea of labour and productivity. So, household chores, such as rearing and nurturing children, caring for the family elders, cooking, cleaning, women's agricultural labour support in rural households, etc., are seen as non-productive labour. At the same time, these tasks leave men free to pursue their occupations, which are defined to have economic value. The social image is then constructed of a woman being financially dependent on the male members while she contributes equally or more than them in terms of labour.

Male family members dictate women's careers and job choices; sometimes, even the decision of whether a girl or a woman will work outside the home is taken by the father or the husband. Male members of the family often also have a say in the expenditure of women's earnings. They are simultaneously expected to look after the household work, increasing their jobs twofold. In almost every industry, there is a gendered pay gap, i.e., women are paid less for an equal amount of work done. Some of the higher-paying fields or jobs are dominated by men only, with women having limited or no access to them.

The work done by women thus is unrecognised, unpaid or paid less compared to their male counterparts, resulting in women losing out on economic resources. Patriarchy, hence, has direct economic and material gains for men.

7.8.1.7 Representation, Education and Career Opportunities

Representation is a powerful resource as it makes one's voice and experience heard. It gives expression, visibility and validation, and offers spaces for ideas and social change. Women's representation in spheres of power is limited by the patriarchal set-up – law, education, politics, etc., are all male-dominated domains. Various factors contribute to this, including restrictions on women's mobility and access. Educational experiences, as discussed earlier, are laden with bias in terms of access and gender socialisation.

Women's career options limitations are not just related to educational expenditure. The prejudices against women pursuing specific disciplines or fields as careers are deeply set in patriarchal norms, e.g. sports or sciences are not usually considered to be career options for women. Women are thus curtailed from representation, careers and educational resources, which limits their potential.

7.9 Intersections of Gender

Gender norms and expectations, as expressed earlier, are not universal. We discussed how feminists use the argument of changing gender roles to challenge the assumption that gender roles are naturally ordained. However, time is not the only factor which affects gender. Different experiences of gender exist simultaneously, as gender does not exist in isolation. It interacts with various socio-political and economic entities that make it a very subjective experience; when gender intersects contextual factors such as age, education and disability, its experience for the individual changes considerably.

The term 'intersectionality', coined by Crenshaw (1989), aptly describes the cross-section of social stratification, whose relationships affect the experience of various kinds of social inequalities and injustices. For instance, caste and class are two different forms of social hierarchies, but when they meet together, they amplify the oppression caused by the dominated. The differences between people are thus translated as the differences in experiences of marginalisation. When viewed in terms of gender, intersectionality opens up a whole gamut of subjective marginalisation experiences. So, though all women face marginalisation based on gender, their issues are not the same; some are more marginalised than others. For example, in the West, the experiences of white middle-class women were very different from the women belonging to lower classes and of African-American descent; they were doubly marginalised for being women and for being black. Similarly, in the Indian context, factors like caste, class, region and religion interact with gender to form a stratified web of marginalisation.

Class in itself is a factor that amplifies the experience of oppression for women. The poorer a woman is, the less right over her future and body she has. Women from slums work as daily wage labourers, where they are paid much less than their male counterparts, or they work as maids in households where there are no minimum wage limits and their services are underpaid. They are also at risk of sexual exploitation. Their day-to-day issues in work environments are very different from those of working women in the middle or upper class. At home, girls from poorer backgrounds face problems like child abuse, prostitution, poor health care facilities and child marriage due to ignorance or to get rid of one more person to feed. Early marriages result in early pregnancies and worsened health conditions or a large number of children due to lack of knowledge or unavailability of contraception. With limited resources, the children are again devoid of education and other resources. Thus, the cycle of social differences and gender oppression continues. Male children in poor families have a better chance of receiving food, healthcare and education since they are seen as the family's hope for economic benefit. Women and girls belonging to lower economic classes thus are in a way more perilous position than boys. Apart from caste and class, the geographical region also affects women's marginalisation; the differences in available resources in urban and rural areas are pretty apparent. The problems of women belonging to minorities, such as tribal groups and areas, or the ones caught in conflict zones, barely even come to the fore.

7.10 Inclusion/Exclusion Based on Gender

The problem of resources being allotted and domination being exercised based on socially ascribed gender identities contradicts the basic arguments of social justice and inclusion. These are projected to be the tenets of any nation's democratic system. The issue of gender identity, when combined with marginalisation based on it, then expands from an individual issue to a social one, as it challenges the concepts of equity and equality in the system.

The solutions suggested, e.g. women's reservation in politics and education. They have not garnered much effect since most of the reserved positions still go vacant or are filled by people conforming to the prescribed gender norms as per the 'performance' of gender or by the comparatively privileged sections of women. Reservation for women seems to be an inadequate solution, therefore, to the more significant problem of discrimination based on gender in the first place. It also does not solve the problem of vulnerability faced by other subjugated genders.

As evidenced by constitutional support for minorities and backward classes, identity should not cause exclusion in a democratic set-up. However, gender identities are not even acknowledged as bases for exclusion despite causing immense marginalisation for the oppressed genders.

7.11 Conclusion

With or without conscious thought, in a variety of apparent and non-apparent ways, gender is rooted in almost all aspects of our society, including education. Its roots go deep into the socialisation and derived identities we call our own. The effects range from thinking patterns to behaviour to the transmission of stereotypes, and hence, the circle of gender domination continues. The only way out is to recognise the ideas and concepts associated with gender that influence identity formation and become aware of the process of normalisation of gender identities, which are projected as natural or given but are very carefully constructed by social institutions.

The awareness of gender hierarchies should also take into account the unawareness of the oppressors, i.e. the ignorance of the people who hold and exercise the power derived from gender. The violence exercised in terms of gender identities through ideas associated with gender does not discriminate between the oppressed and the oppressors; it affects both, just not equally or in a similar manner. The deprivations and restrictions experienced by and imposed on women are more apparent and intense, whereas the confines placed upon men are more subtle and yet to be explored fully, even in research. At the same time, those experienced by people of other genders are slowly finding their voice.

The twin roles education plays in this regard are to be emphasised here. Education does help in the perpetuation and normalisation of gender identities, but at the same time, it is a resource that offers spaces for reflection and retaliation. This resource will be utilised to counter the established, unquestioned and essentially oppressive gendered ideas and concepts.

Bibliography

Beauvoir, S. de. (1973). *The second sex 1973*. New York: Vintage Books.

Bem, S. L. (1981). Gender Schema Theory: A Cognitive Account of Sex Typing. *Psychological Review*, 88(4), 354–364. Retrieved from https://www.ahcafr.com/wp-content/uploads/2015/07/gender_schema_theory.pdf

Butler, J. (1988). Performative Acts and Gender Constitution: An Essay in Phenomenology and Feminist Theory. *Theatre Journal*, 40(4), 519–531.

Chopra, R., Osella, C., & Osella, F. (2004). Introduction: Towards a more nuanced approach to masculinity, towards a richer understanding of South Asian Men. In R. Chopra, C. Osella, & F. Osella (Eds.), *South Asian Masculinities: context of change, sites of continuity* (pp. 1–32). New Delhi: Women Unlimited, an Associate of Kali for Women.

Crenshaw, K. (1989). Demarginalizing the Intersection of Race and Sex: A Black Feminist Critique of Antidiscrimination Doctrine, Feminist Theory, and Antiracist Politics. *University of Chicago Legal Forum*, 1, 139–167.

Dahat P. (2016, January, 23). Eight tribal women allege gang-rape by security forces. *The Hindu*. Retrieved from https://www.thehindu.com/todays-paper/tp-national/Eight-tribal-women-allege-gang-rape-by-security-forces/article14015652.ece

Freud, S. (1962). *Three essays on the theory of sexuality* (J. Strachey, trans.). New York: Basic Books.

India Times. (2016, March 17). More than 150 women were killed across India in 2014 because they were thought to be witches. *India Times*. Retrieved from https://www.indiatimes.com/news/india/more-than-150-woman-were-killed-across-india-in-2014-because-they-were-thought-to-be-witches-252138.html

Jeffries, A. (2018, July 22). Why women don't make science videos? *The Times of India*. Print.

Josselson, R. (1987). Conclusion: Reflections on female identity. In R. Josselson (Eds.), *Finding herself: Pathways to identity development in women* (pp. 168–191). San Francisco: Jossey Bass.

Koechlin, K. (Presenter). (2018, August 9). Episode 1: Dancing to his own beat [Audio podcast]. In BBC World Service (Ed.), *Kalki presents: My Indian life*. Retrieved from https://www.bbc.co.uk/programmes/p06gxt5c

Nagalia, S. (2018). Conceptualising Gender Studies: Curriculum and Pedagogy. *Indian Journal of Gender Studies*, 25(1), 79–107.

Nigam, N. (2018, July 23). CBSE UGC NET: Female aspirant faces harassment for wearing jumpsuit, refused entry. *The Indian Express*. Retrieved from https://indianexpress.com/article/education/cbse-ugc-net-female-aspirant-faces-harassment-for-wearing-jumpsuit-refused-entry-5268972/

PTI. (2018, July 30). Stopped from entering temple, say Dalit women. *The Hindu*. Print.

Rajagopal, K. (2018, July 25). Ban on entry of women in Sabarimala is patriarchal: SC. *The Hindu*. Retrieved from https://www.thehindu.com/todays-paper/tp-national/ban-on-entry-of-women-in-sabarimala-is-patriarchal-sc/article24507566.ece

Roy, R. (2007). *A little book on men*. New Delhi: Yoda Press.

Sreenivas, D. (2015). Between politics and discipline: Gender studies in an institutional setting. *Indian Journal of Gender Studies*, 22(2), 265–281.

Tenhunen, S. (2015). Gender, intersectionality and smartphones in Rural West Bengal. In K. B. Nielsen & A. Waldrop (Eds.), *Women, gender and everyday social transformation in India* (pp. 33–45). New Delhi: Anthem Press.

Vishwanath, N. (2018). The shifting shape of rape discussion. *Indian Journal of Gender Studies*, 25(1), 1–25.

8

CONCEPTUALISING DIVERSITY AND INCLUSION IN CONTEMPORARY TIMES

Yukti Sharma

8.1 Introduction

Inclusion has become one of the most crucial contemporary issues in education. It is closely associated with other constructs like disability, gender, caste, diversity, disadvantaged groups, discrimination, marginalisation and exclusion. A contextualised understanding of these constructs is a prerequisite for appreciating the need for inclusion. Diversity and inclusion are the key catchwords in school education and find articulation in all contemporary national and international programmes and policies worldwide. The need for a comprehensive conceptual understanding of them, drawn from theoretical ideas and ground realities in the field, is thus critical. An attempt is made to achieve this in the present chapter.

The chapter begins with a discussion on diversity amongst learners in classrooms, understood from different lenses. It then explains how marginalisation and exclusion occur in classroom and school contexts, both intentionally and unintentionally. The focus then shifts to describing the emergence of special education, the subsequent paradigm shifts in the field, and explaining how they lay the ground for inclusion. The chapter ends with a discussion of the idea of 'inclusive pedagogy'.

8.2 Understanding Diversity

There is no better arena than school classrooms to understand the construct of diversity and its challenges. Let us begin by documenting responses likely to be obtained while engaging in a discussion with school teachers about

DOI: 10.4324/9781003505501-8

what they understand about diversity based on their everyday experiences in the classroom.

Response One: Diversity is generally visible in learners' mental or cognitive abilities. It may be seen as children having different intellectual levels, so some are bright and some are dull. Alternatively, there could be differences in their educational achievement; some are consistently high achievers, while others are low achievers. Diversity may also be seen in their understanding levels, learning capabilities and preferred learning styles.

Response Two: Diversity is represented by variations in students' family background, caste, religion, culture and socioeconomic status. There are differences between girls and boys, too. Some children are first-generation learners and do not have resources at home to support their education. Some girls come from communities where education for girls is not valued or encouraged. Some children may be bright but do not do well since they speak their local language and struggle with the vocabulary of formal standard language used in education. These are some ways in which diversity shows up.

Response Three: There are a few children with disabilities in every class. The disabilities may be visual, orthopaedic or related to difficulties in reading and writing. The styles of learning of each of these children are very different. They need different methods of teaching and a lot of individualised supervision. This is what creates diversity in the class.

As visible in the three sets of responses drawn from teachers' narratives, the first response looks at diversity more from an academic standpoint, focusing on the learners' cognitive capacities, understanding levels, learning capabilities and learning styles. In contrast, the second response locates diversity in a sociocultural context, highlighting differences emerging from how society is stratified and structured. The third response looks at diversity from a disability perspective. It is essential to understand that although each of the three responses highlights distinct features, what unifies them is that they present classroom scenarios that are real. Each of them thus requires detailed discussion. The following section takes up a more detailed discussion of each of the three responses in terms of the theories, issues and debates they reflect.

8.2.1 Diversity Stemming from the Social Background of the Learner

8.2.1.1 Learners from Diverse Cultural and Linguistic Backgrounds

Several studies have provided evidence to show that students from culturally and linguistically diverse backgrounds experience lesser educational outcomes than their peers (Bennett et al., 2004; Conchas & Noguera, 2004). This is because our societies are ethnocentric, and the dominant culture occupies the central position that positions various other cultures and linguistic groups in the periphery. All the norms and values followed during interactions among students in a classroom are mainly of the dominant cultural or linguistic group. Thus, a child from a different cultural or linguistic background is, by default, at a 'disadvantage'. Also, in the past, the 'deficit theories' blamed individuals for their conditions, labelled them as at risk, disadvantaged and poor, and often promoted various stereotypes associated with them, such as being violent, illiterate, etc. It is essential to remember that the child has been socialised to follow the norms and values of their native culture, which they bring to the classroom. However, since the system is biased towards the predominant culture, the child faces cultural conflicts and feels alienated from the school. The child's diversity becomes a disadvantage for them and gradually renders them a disadvantaged or marginalised entity in the classroom. It is thus essential to recognise learner diversity concerning cultural and linguistic background factors. For teachers, it becomes necessary to value each culture and include the prior experiences and knowledge that children bring from their respective cultures and linguistic backgrounds in the classroom dynamics and teaching-learning process.

8.2.1.2 Learners from Low-Income Families

Children from low-income families live in familial contexts that differ significantly from their peers from middle- and high-income families. They are generally helping hands for their parents in terms of labour and economic utility and spend most of their time assisting them in their occupations or doing household chores, especially for girls. This often leads to their coming late to school or attending school irregularly, which adversely impacts their learning and achievement in formal education. Schools treat them as similar to other students, having universal expectations from them without crediting to their unique needs emanating from their difficult life circumstances.

8.2.2 Gender and Diversity

Differential treatment of boys and girls and stereotyped gender-centric expectations from them are not new to classroom discourses. They have their roots in the traditional division of labour and roles ascribed to men and women in patriarchal societies, leading to the development of feminine and masculine personalities, respectively. Some common examples are getting boys to hang nails, move furniture around, perform experiments in the science laboratory, etc. At the same time, girls are asked to tidy and decorate the class, ensure cleanliness, and order, record and organise the data related to scientific experiments. The concepts selectively presented in science textbooks are also gender-biased and present boys to be more powerful than girls. At times, teachers are not aware of their own gendered biases. Hence, their expectations, assessment and feedback are not for the individual but for gender groups. A widespread perception that teachers hold is that boys are more intelligent than girls and boys are thus more risk-taking and creative, whereas girls are more conformist but more sincere towards work. Sex differences are often confused with gender differences. In either case, 'diversity', which should ideally place boys and girls at par with each other, plays out as difference or the domination of one gender over the other.

8.2.3 Diversity Stemming from One's Regional Background

Some children belong to varied geographical regions, such as hilly areas, seashores and deserts, where living conditions vary greatly. These children may have to walk long distances or travel in inclement weather conditions to reach their schools. The more remote a geographical location is from the centre of development, the more likely it is to pose severe challenges for children. For children from such habitations, standardised curricula and pedagogy need to be revised since they seldom reflect the everyday lived realities of the children. Children cannot relate to them and find it challenging to make the necessary adjustments. This becomes all the more critical when a child has to shift from their native region to a new place that requires them to adjust to the new circumstances.

8.2.4 Diversity Stemming from Disability

Children with disabilities are generally looked upon as less capable of accomplishing tasks that their non-disabled peers can achieve. The lens is one of viewing them as deficient and thus incapable of achieving normative standards. Simply put, they are seen as lacking the capacity to fulfil the norms and expectations that any system holds for them. This view is referred to as the 'medical model of disability'. It is still a dominant way of perceiving persons with disabilities. In this view, the individual is seen as a pathological or abnormal case in which the central focus is their impairment or medical condition. Such a view presupposes that a 'normal' body is free of problems and challenges. Historically speaking, in the medical model, children with disabilities were treated with a charitable attitude, were often kept in segregated settings and were labelled as sick, mad or insane without giving any thought or focus to their other abilities. This model was strongly critiqued on the following grounds:

- It treated the individual as a physio-pathological object and reduced them to a non-social entity.

- It categorised persons as sick or insane and justified their being treated as 'abnormal' and inferior.
- It gave a scientific basis for segregating them from society and excluding them socially.

The reductionist paradigm of the medical model was challenged by disability rights activists who questioned the objectification of the body of an individual. They strongly condemned the significant assumptions that were inherent in the model. Although the activist movement started in the 1960s, it was in 1975 that the UK-based organisation called the Union of Physically Impaired Against Segregation (UPIAS) very strongly emphasised that it was the society that disabled individuals with impairment by isolating them and excluding them from participating as fully functioning persons within its ambit. In its manifesto, UPIAS asserted that disability was a manifestation of social discrimination against persons with impairment. This was the origin of the 'social model of disability', a phrase coined by Michael Oliver in 1983, one of the strongest proponents of this school of thought. The social model proposed the following:

- 'Disability' is a social construction and was imposed on people with impairments externally.
- The disabling environment around the individual prevents them from fully functioning in society.

Oliver (1990) distinguished between the terms 'impairment' and 'disability'. In his view, impairment refers to the lack of a particular body part, defect or mechanism. In contrast, disability is the disadvantage or discrimination imposed on the individual with impairment. The blame was thus placed on society and its ways of looking at persons with disabilities. The social model brought about a radical change in the way persons with disabilities were perceived and understood. Instead of merely focusing on the individuals' deficits, the focus shifted to identifying and removing social barriers and attempting to create enabling environments. The social model of disability thus shares its epistemological basis with theories of gender and race (Reddy, 2011), where the focus is on how social identity gets constructed in society for certain groups of people who have been treated unequally and excluded or marginalised. In the context of persons with impairment, Goffman (1963) theorises the process of exclusionary practices. He explains that social identity takes two forms. One is the 'virtual social identity' that refers to the demands made 'in effect' by a person. The other is the 'actual social identity' that refers to attributes the person possesses. Thus, a person is perceived mainly based on their virtual social identity, which is laden with 'stigma' as explained by Goffman and with various stereotypes that society associates with the group to which the person belongs. These stigmas and stereotypes are the value judgements made by the dominant groups of society on the groups not in majority or power to represent their differences as the diversity of the human race rather than being seen as deviations from the so-called 'normal' or the dominant groups. Including such groups in society requires them to be free and liberated from the stigmas and stereotypes imposed on them. This entails questioning the stereotypes influencing people's thinking by creating undue biases for certain groups in society. At this point, we need to discuss practices propagating exclusion and marginalisation for these groups before discussing the need for inclusion in society and education.

Two ways of understanding exclusion that paved the way for the emergence of inclusion are functionalism and reproduction. They are discussed below.

- **Functionalism** presumes that social reality is objective and perceives any problem in functioning that belies the norm or standard of expectation as pathological (Skritic, 1991). Such persons face threats of exclusion in different ways. To illustrate with an example, any problem of school failure is explained by finding inabilities or defects in children. Such a view presupposes that school as an institution is highly structured, and children who fail or cannot attend school or demonstrate low academic achievement are misfits for school. One contradictory example in this context relates to the rigidity of school timings, as depicted in the story by Mahasweta Devi Verma called *Why, Why Girl*. Here, a tribal girl who is triple disadvantaged is not able to attend school, as during school time, she has to work with her mother. The girl in the story questions the teacher about the fixed timings of the school and makes an effort to change the timings but is unable to accomplish her goal. She finally has to give up and exit from the system. This clearly shows how, on account of structural and functional rigidities in the system, many individuals get excluded as they cannot meet the system's inflexible requirements.
- **Reproduction**: A critical notion related to reproduction has been drawn from Bourdieu's idea of 'cultural capital'. He explains that in industrialised societies, success in educational institutions depends on possessing cultural capital, which, according to him, is being familiar with the dominant culture and being able to use and comprehend appropriate 'educated language'. According to him, this leads to the reproduction of the same dominant culture as cultural capital supports only students from the dominant class. Children from lower classes and other communities are at a disadvantage in the education system as neither can they relate to the dominant culture nor to the curriculum and classroom discussions based on it. This creates social inequalities and legitimises

> these inequalities by keeping children from specific communities, classes and cultures out of the system. The entire system of education, including teachers and the knowledge being transacted, becomes a part of this exclusionary process. This is considered an intentional process that the hegemonic groups of any society deliberately practice.

Tomlinson (1987) critiques special education on the same lines and refers to critical theorists to question the role of professionals in the social and cultural reproduction of a particular class in any given society. She presents her theoretical position and that of other critical theorists in the text below, where she expounds on how the dominant classes socially create and reproduce various ideas related to education. Hence, the meaning and consequences of 'disability' may differ for children belonging to different groups.

> Critical theorists have suggested that the answers to questions about why children fail might lie as much in a society's social, economic and political structures as in anything intrinsic to children or 'lacking' in a child. From a critical theorist's viewpoint, it becomes easier to question the deficit model of children, which assumes that negative properties intrinsic to children – low IQ, disability, inability – are wholly responsible for the child's educational failure. Examining the social processes by which 'achievement' is defined becomes easier. Who, for example, decides what achievement means in a society where the highest achievers are almost always white, upper- or middle-class males? Why does being a poor reader and working class seem to have much more serious and long-term social consequences than being a poor reader and upper or middle class?
> *(Tomlinson, 1987, p. 34).*

8.3 Journey from Special Education to Inclusion: The Backdrop

Inclusion has grown as an idea from being an approach to becoming a reform movement that focuses on establishing practices and processes in society and its institutions that respect diversity and variations in caste, social class, religion, region, linguistic background, gender, disabilities/impairments and all other dimensions without any discrimination. In effect, to include means to create spaces for all and accept all with dignity. It implies accepting all without imposing conditions of worth or normative standards. It is not easy to trace the origin of the idea of inclusion or even track its growth. However, reflections of commitment to inclusion are now visible in the various national policies and acts, theoretical formulations, research and educational practices. In the field of education, inclusion as an idea emerged when the shift from segregation to integration took place concerning the education of children with disabilities. At the same time, there is no denying that it has roots in special education. Special education offered a parallel or need-based alternative to those who could not fit into the 'mainstream' education system. Special schools offered education to those children who had been excluded from the regular system of schooling on account of their inability to adapt to the pre-decided normative structures and expectations of outcomes. However, over the years, with the emergence of the human rights perspective and the social model of disability, the focus has shifted from the individual to the preparedness of society and its various institutions. This takes on the form of inclusive education, and in society, it relates to the social inclusion of all. The special school has begun to pave the way for a 'general' or inclusive school in schooling practices. In this context, a breakthrough took place in 1997 when the International Standards Classification of Education replaced the phrase 'special education' with 'special needs education' to detach it from the connotation that it is an education that takes place only in special schools. Thus, special education is now called *special needs education (SEN)*. It is an 'educational intervention and support designed to address special educational needs' (Florian, 2014). With this definition, a common understanding is that SEN involves 'something' in addition to what is offered in general schools. This seems to be based on the notion that regular schools would meet the needs of most children. However, not all, particularly those few generally at the tail end of the normal probability curve, require additional support or interventions. This is the group that requires SEN. SEN thus gets positioned at the periphery of the education system, offering provisions to children at the extremities of the bell curve. It also reinforces the idea that learners' ability/performance in a class can be distributed through a bell curve. However, at the same time, the concept of SEN is broader than special education in the sense that it focuses on the needs of children emerging from diverse contexts and circumstances. It thus encompasses 'all' children with special needs, other than children with disabilities. The concept of SEN has, however, been critiqued on the following grounds:

I. In SEN, identifying and classifying groups of children as the only ones needing something 'additional' may prove discriminatory for them as they may not be treated at par with their peers and may get marginalised within the education system. Further, although the language in special education that is used to address various groups of people with impairments underwent various changes, such as from blind to visually impaired to visually challenged, this does not necessarily resolve issues of discrimination and labelling. This is mainly because overemphasising their unique needs has led to overlooking their other needs.
II. Teachers have the closest engagement with learners in the classroom. Although there is no denying that most teachers reach out to all learners

and address diversity issues through pedagogy and classroom management, their understanding of diversity may focus more on learners in the 'normative centre'. There is a possibility that those at the margins may not become part of this diversity.

III. A key idea associated with SEN was that it only referred to interventions specific to a particular group and required specialised training. This created another level of discrimination for children with special needs as they were not considered the responsibility of a general teacher as s/he was not trained for it. While this was not purely intentional, it was an outcome of the idea that it was highly specialised.

IV. Furthermore, although SEN has expanded to include diverse groups of children with special needs other than those with disabilities, the question that is often raised relates to how it can offer educational provisions for all children.

Another significant issue is that although SEN/special education has been seen as a strategy to achieve educational rights for children with special needs by provisioning and making various resources accessible to them, a matter of concern is that teachers may lower their expectations from children with special needs. Most teachers address their needs and acknowledge their differences during their engagement with children, but they do this for children in the class. Labelling and classification as children with special needs excludes them from the class, not physically but from being a part of the learning opportunities planned for most other children in the class. Recognising this incongruence, SEN has been criticised for reinforcing the inequities in the classroom.

Both SEN and special education have been considered specialised responses to an individual's unique needs that work by providing appropriate strategies or devices for matching a specific difficulty in learning rather than a universal, beneficial or effective approach for all. They should be aligned with the primary goal of general education and should be seen as extending the learning experiences from what is generally available for everyone in the classroom. This requires a shift in attitude where learning is considered a collaborative process for everyone, including children with special needs. Special education should then be seen as enriching learning opportunities created in the classroom for all learners so that each can participate. It requires strategies, approaches and practices that have not been used in a general classroom as they were meant only for 'some'. For example, writing in large letters is not only meant for a child who is partially blind but equally for any child who has difficulty seeing, whether it is due to their sitting position in the class or due to them having less familiarity with the standard language. In this process, as we detach these approaches from a specific group of learners, we automatically do not consider categorising or labelling the learners. Instead, our focus is on offering varied opportunities that are universal and provide a choice/ option for learning to each learner. This is the inclusion of diversity among learners rather than all learners!

8.4 Towards Inclusion

In the section above, we discussed the emergence of inclusion from special education and, at the same time, how special education was expected to be seen as an integral part of the quest for inclusion. We saw how special education and regular mainstream education have challenged each other on issues of exclusion, inequality/equality and marginalisation. This makes it clear that inclusion is not simply about including children with disabilities or children with special needs in regular classrooms. It is a response to the diversity in the human race, of which individuals with disabilities and other disadvantaged groups are an integral part. As also stated above, it is based on human rights and education being a fundamental right. Thus, inclusion acknowledges and conserves diversity by making it a structural and functional part of society. It requires acceptance of every individual of the society with their originality in terms of culture, language, values, abilities, traditional /folk knowledge, food habits, etc. This means that it cannot be the mere inclusion of an individual or a community we are talking about but the inclusion of different cultures, languages, values, communities, folk knowledge, etc. Diversity in all these aspects that make the background and identity of an individual or a community must find a place in society where stereotypes and prejudices associated with each of these are questioned. It goes beyond mere acceptance. It values cultures and recognises differences by establishing their relevance in society through our knowledge systems, media disseminating this knowledge and institutions engaging with these knowledge systems. Schools create a micro-society through their culture and ethos, largely a reflection of the outside world. Whether schools have been influencing society or not, society and its hegemonic groups have been controlling schools and using them as their agents for the reproduction and sustenance of the dominant culture. Also, school is the first formal institution in an individual's life. Hence, inclusion in schools can be the first step towards inclusion in society. Inclusive education in school should aim at eliminating the discriminatory and exclusionary practices that may be a result of an attitude or mindset towards a particular diverse group, whether it is based on caste, class, culture, race, ethnicity, gender or disability. It requires a radical approach where there is a shift from constructing explanations of educational failure that focus on the characteristics of individual children and their background towards an analysis that tries to understand that the difficulties that children face are due to the barriers to participation and learning experienced by children in the school system due to the way it is organised (Booth & Ainscow, 2011) This shift in thinking has been referred to as an 'organisational paradigm' (Dyson & Millward, 2000). The other shift in thinking is how diversity is viewed in schools. Schools have to be prepared to respond positively to diversity among learners by not looking at it as a problem but as seeing their differences as opportunities for enriching the learning process (Ainscow 2013). A new culture has to be established in schools where there is acceptance and appreciation for each other's differences, where children begin to learn collaboratively and give space for teachers to reflect (Ainscow, 2014). Special education needs to contribute by realigning its strategies and approaches for developing inclusive schools and making them responsive towards all children. The role of special educators, other school personnel and parents has to be redefined to work in collaboration with the teacher. Inclusion is an ever-evolving process and should be strategised through inclusive education that encourages teachers to engage with classroom realities and diversities rather than focusing on predetermined experiences for learners.

8.4.1 Understanding Inclusive Pedagogy

Is there something called inclusive pedagogy? Inclusion is based on the fact that education is a fundamental right. This implies that every child has a right to education in a regular school. Being a right, it puts the onus on the state to provide free and compulsory education to all children, irrespective of their condition or life situation. This suggests that every child has an equal right to opportunities to learn in a regular school. It locates every learner in a classroom that has no 'normative centre' but where diversity among learners is acknowledged, and each learner is seen to be 'unique' in their way. It requires a universal and comprehensive pedagogy to address each learner's diverse yet unique needs. Where integration has put the onus on the child to prepare themselves to fit the rigidly structured expectations of schools, inclusion accepts the diversity and uniqueness of each child as it is without requiring them to change.

On the contrary, it expects society and its institutions to modify their structures and functions from standardised expectations to a 'universal' form that provides opportunities for the participation of all. In the school context, this primarily means that teachers should believe in inclusive pedagogy and practices wherein they respond to individual needs within the classroom as they emerge. The focus has to be on all children learning together. In effect, this would mean providing choices and options for the learners amidst various activities and experiences based on various interests, needs, abilities and diversity of learners' backgrounds. Instead of predetermining learners' needs, the teacher discovers the learning needs and contexts in real classroom situations. This is in tandem with the universal design of learning (UDL), which is so broad in its approach that it can include and address the needs of each learner in the classroom. In this approach, the teacher does not invest in classifying or categorising the learners in class. Instead, they prepare to make the classroom experiences more holistic by encouraging children to share and learn from each other's experiences. It involves using strategies and approaches that are generally not used in schools. Thus, inclusive pedagogy involves extending the idea of teaching and evolving to a level that questions and challenges the idea of school as a normative centre that has been established and followed for years. In this framework, learners can exercise choice and are involved in planning for their learning. Their participation increases in terms of making choices and making decisions for themselves. This ensures the participation of all children.

8.5 The Indian Context

We understand that India is a multicultural society with its citizens practising different religions, dwelling in topographically varied regions, speaking different languages and dialects within a region, and belonging to different castes and communities (Misra, 2008). Thus, apart from the population of persons with disabilities, there exist many other groups that have been discriminated against and/or marginalised in terms of access, availability of resources and opportunities for education. With the processes of modernisation and social mobility, diversity has become more complex. Although the various constitutional provisions, policies, commissions and legal provisions have been aligned towards equal treatment of all communities in every respect, the understanding they embody has varied. Hence, as we explore some of these provisions and acts, three significant drifts can be seen as follows:

- The paradigmatic change in thinking from impairment (as in the medical /deficit model) to recognising the development of provisions for persons with disabilities (Bhattacharya, 2010).
- There was an increase in the types of disability notified in various schemes and acts, where the number of disabilities was six in DPEP, seven in the PWD Act (1995) and rose to 21 in the RPWD Act (2016), showing thereby that the idea of disability has become broader and more inclusive. The RPWD Act also includes people suffering from diseases like thalassemia and haemophilia, as these have been found to affect normal bodily, cognitive and physical functions. It includes persons who have suffered acid attacks, too, for similar reasons.
- The expansion in the idea of children with special needs being referred to as 'children belonging to disadvantaged groups' is inclusive of all

children who are marginalised on account of their disability and/or their social context/conditions of living.

In its Preamble, the Constitution of India (GoI, 1949) ensures the right to equality of status and opportunity, equality before the law, non-discrimination and the right to life and liberty through Articles 14, 15, 19 and 21. Although these articles are generic in the sense that they do not specifically talk about disabled or marginalised groups, the assumption is that they cover the entire population, which includes persons with disabilities and other forms of social disadvantage. Further, Article 45 of the Constitution commits to providing free and compulsory education for children through a Directive principle. It states: The State shall endeavour to provide, within a period of 10 years from the commencement of this Constitution, for free and compulsory education for all children until they complete the age of 14 years. As a Directive Principle of State Policy, provision was made, but ensuring that every child indeed became a beneficiary was not covered during the implementation of the principle. Somewhere, there was an assumption that providing access was an end in itself. Recognising this gap, the parliament enacted the 86th Amendment to the Constitution in 2002, making education a fundamental right for all children from 6 to 14 years. The legal provisions covered under The Right of Children to Free and Compulsory Education (RTE Act, 2009) provide for the right to free and compulsory education to children of the age group of 6–14 years, including children with special needs. In the case of children with disabilities, under Clause (i) of Section 2 of the Persons with Disabilities (Equal Opportunities, Protection and Full Participation) Act, 1995, s/he has the right to pursue free and compulsory elementary education by provisions spelt out in Chapter V of the PWD Act (1995). The Act clearly defines a child belonging to a disadvantaged group as 'one belonging to a scheduled caste, scheduled tribe, socially and educationally backward class or such other group facing disadvantage owing to social, cultural, economic, geographical, linguistic, gender or other similar factors" (Chapter 1, Article 2, Subsection d), to which children with disabilities were added through its amendment in 2012. This amendment made two more provisions for children with disabilities, considering that their educational progression is slower and therefore recognising that they may take more years to complete their school education. It also recognised that children with severe disabilities may not be medically advised to attend school. The two specific provisions in this regard are:

(i) Children with disabilities (including children with cerebral palsy, mental retardation, autism and multiple disabilities) shall have the right to pursue free and compulsory education per Chapter V of the PWD Act (1995) till 18 years of age.

(ii) Children with 'multiple disabilities' and 'severe disabilities' will have the right to opt for home-based education.

Sections 8 and 9 of the third chapter of the Act further ensure that children belonging to disadvantaged groups are not discriminated against or prevented from pursuing and completing elementary education on any grounds. Duties have been duly assigned to the appropriate government and local authorities to facilitate this. Section 4 of the Act provides the right to get admission to an age-appropriate class for all children, including those who were never admitted or had dropped out before completion of elementary education. What is observed is that the out-of-school children who are early dropouts or never enrolled belong mainly to the disadvantaged and marginalised communities, or are children with special needs, or those living in difficult circumstances. Thus, the Act not only allows them to get included in the school system at any stage of their lives, it also gives them the right to study in an age-appropriate class, saving them from the humiliation of sitting with younger children. It also recommends special training for such children to bring them on par with the other children in the class, including accelerated learning if required, considering their varied life experiences and acknowledging their mental capabilities to be higher than other children at the same level. Hence, the act not only provides excluded children entry to the school but makes provision to engage them appropriately. Section 6 of the Act provides access to schools in the neighbourhood based on the premise that the schooling facilities should be within the reach of all children. If the schools are not available at a reasonable distance, it may prevent children from attending school regularly, which is a case of functional exclusion. Also, the Act does not specify the distance for determining the neighbourhood idea and leaves it to the respective states to decide as per their context. However, it draws attention to meeting the needs of the diverse geographical locations and situations in India. Section 10 of the Act casts a duty on the appropriate government bodies to ensure the admission, attendance and completion of elementary education by even persuading the parents, if required, that they send their wards regularly to school, particularly for older girls. It provides 25% reservation to children from disadvantaged groups and economically weaker sections in private unaided institutions and special category schools.

Thus, the Act is based on the idea that a just and humane society can be created by the values of equality, social justice and democracy, which can be achieved only by providing inclusive education for all. The implicit belief underlying this is that schools should act as a means of social cohesion and promote inclusion in society. This was also suggested by the Kothari Commission (1964–1966) through its ideas of 'common' and 'neighbourhood' schooling. As quoted in the act, diversity enhances learning and development, while segregation impoverishes the classroom environment of all schools, private or government. The act acknowledges that other children would learn from interacting with children from disadvantaged and weaker sections rich in knowledge systems associated with trade, craft, farming, etc. These children ought to be treated as sources of knowledge so that they get treated equally. Also, the act challenges the notion of ability as it states that no school should subject children to any screening procedure and treat them equally.

Further, it ensures that the diversity that characterises Indian society finds due representation in every classroom, making it a more inclusive universe by providing equal opportunities and spaces to all children, irrespective of their social and economic backgrounds. The idea is aptly embodied in the quote that follows: 'The guidelines also refer to the importance of moving towards composite classrooms with children from diverse backgrounds, rather than homogenous and exclusivist schools: heterogeneity and diversity in classrooms lead to greater inter-learning, respect for differences, tolerance and creativity' (Section 13).

Tracing back the national policies and other acts, we find that although the New Education Policy of 1986 had as one of the objectives to integrate the physically and mentally disabled in the general community as equal partners, it supported an integrated model where the 'handicapped' children had to be prepared to study in the mainstream regular schools. Also, the term 'handicapped children' was used, which indicates that the focus was on the impairment of the child rather than on the child itself. The idea of special schools with hostel facilities was also floated without much clarity about its relevance. Emphasis on vocational training programmes to make children with disabilities more self-reliant and self-sufficient showed that not much was expected from them. No strategies were proposed to nurture them to realise their full potential through curricular modifications or pedagogical flexibility. Following this, the Plan of Action, which came in 1992, also proceeded along the same lines and focussed on mainstreaming the children with disabilities. The assumption implicit in this was that the children would have to learn to fit into the mainstream. The Plan of Action, however, made one significant recommendation: That children with special needs should be educated only in regular schools and not in special schools. The catch was that special schools were visualised as bridge schools to prepare children with disabilities for regular mainstream schools. The message that was drawn from such a supposition implied that there were no explicit expectations from regular mainstream schools to prepare themselves for the inclusion of children with disabilities. Furthermore, the children who belonged to disadvantaged groups other than children with disabilities were not included in the zone of consideration. In 1992, the Rehabilitation Council of India was established by an act of parliament. It became the vision-building and regulatory body for monitoring and standardising courses for training professionals required in special education and rehabilitation of persons with disabilities in no less than 16 categories. The setting up of the Rehabilitation Council of India signified that persons with disabilities were not yet included in regular institutions; instead, they required rehabilitation. A fillip to provisions for people with disabilities came with the National Trust Act (1999), in which the government recommended programmes that created barrier-free environments and opportunities for capacity development of persons with disabilities. It ensured the protection of the rights of persons who were marginalised within the disability section, such as persons with autism, cerebral palsy, mental retardation and multiple disabilities. The District Primary Education Programme (DPEP;1994), a scheme launched by the Government of India, supported an integrated model in the form of a programme called Integrated Education of the Disabled, for which all kinds of support were provided to the states and Union Territories which included aids, resources, incentives and specially trained teachers. In 2000, the Government of India launched the Sarva Shiksha Abhiyan (SSA), which, among its other aims, directly focussed on inclusion. It provided Rs. 3000 per child to schools for the inclusion of disabled children. It also made monetary provisions for the engagement of resource teachers (Mondal & Mete, 2012). Other measures subsumed in SSA were early identification, educational placement, individual education plans (IEPs), parental training, community mobilisation and removal of architectural barriers. Its 'zero rejection policy' states that no child shall be denied admission in any school of their preference based on caste, creed, gender, economic status and/or disability. Thus, SSA first reflected inclusion by providing an equal platform to all children apart from children with disabilities. It focussed on children with special needs, including children from disadvantaged sections, and acknowledged most of the factors that excluded them from formal school set-ups. SSA also emphasises preparing schools by providing resources, teacher preparation programmes and creating conditions that provide opportunities to all children from the disadvantaged sections of society. After this was the Right to Education Act (2009), which has been discussed above. The recent addition was the Revised Persons with Disabilities Act (2016), which expanded the list of disabilities to 17. It also helped to define disability as an evolving and dynamic concept, which is in tandem with the idea that UNESCO propounds.

8.6 Looking Ahead: Planning Educational Experiences

Inclusive pedagogy is an evolving idea that requires the participation of all stakeholders, including the children themselves (Pearson, 2016). This participation should be in the process of making decisions from their admission in the system to the expectations carved out for them and, of course, the nature of systemic engagement provided to them. This requires constant interaction between the teachers, parents and special educators, along with the children themselves, to inform any planning for each child rather than deciding what they should study based on a set of predetermined assumptions.

8.6.1 The Use of Terminologies

The fields of inclusive education and special education have been inundated with the use of different terminologies with predetermined connotations built into them. Such terminologies often constrain dialogue or discussion about what should be done for children with special needs. The connotations carry imperatives that give direction to the action to be taken. Farrell (2009), for instance, discusses that the term 'inclusion' has a positive connotation that influences most debates in school education. In this line of thought, mainstreaming as a strategy can be justified as being better than special schools as a step towards inclusion. At the same time, we know that mainstreaming propagates the hidden inequalities in the education system by its prefix 'main' and considers other education set-ups as less critical.

Similarly, when an inclusive school is compared to a special school, the terms impose an unquestioned understanding that the former school would be better. It is assumed that the former has inclusive practices, whereas the latter is based on exclusionary ideas. Not only is the purpose of a 'special school' being overlooked in doing so, but the inclusive school has begun to be considered utopian since it is based on ideas of equality and social justice. This may constrain setting up practices and systems that make a school inclusive. It may perpetuate the belief in special schools.

Barrier, another related term that gets significance through the social model of disability, presumes that some barriers are created in society that lead to disability. The implication is that removing barriers or working towards a 'barrier-free environment' leads to inclusion. One contention related to this is how the notion of barrier is understood. It must go beyond physical barriers and include in its spectrum of concerns other barriers created due to rigidity in the education system and other biases and prejudices that penetrate it. This is because barriers may vary with context and require a comprehensive analysis before they can be addressed and/or removed.

8.6.1.1 The Idea of 'Need'

The idea of need in educational contexts can be understood in relation to making provisions that include curriculum planning, pedagogical approaches, assessment strategies, resources and other initiatives. If making provisions has to be child-centred, it becomes essential to understand their unique needs. Needs may be looked at in various ways. Farrell (2009) refers to primarily two kinds of needs. He refers to one as goal-directed needs necessary for achieving a particular goal. For instance, a child with a visual impairment may need braille to learn to read, or a child who is deaf may require assistive devices to communicate effectively in the class. However, sometimes, the child's needs may not be very explicit as the context of the child may be very different.

An illustrative example is that a child having difficulty understanding what is being taught in the class can face this for several reasons, and it may be difficult to pin it down to one or two causative factors. In such a case, the teacher must take pre-emptive steps to facilitate the child's education. Such needs that may not have a specific goal are called unconditional needs. Identification of unconditional needs requires the joint participation of parents, teachers, special educators and other school personnel. In the case of goal-directed needs, the goals need to be decided from the particular child's perspective rather than merely based on the group to which the child belongs. The human rights perspective places the child before their group or the label given to the child. Hence, the labelling game has been strongly questioned for reducing the child and their needs to a mere label. Based on the discussion above, viewing needs in terms of the classification given by Lewis and Norwich (2005) may be worthwhile.

- Needs common to all children
- Needs specific to a particular group
- Needs unique to an individual child

They categorise the group-specific needs as a '*general difference position*' and the unique needs of children as a '*unique difference position*'. They emphasise the 'unique difference position', which focuses on the unique differences among the learners and rejects the group's specific needs. According to them, group-specific needs have limited usefulness in planning for curricular experiences or any other kind of provisioning. Hence, it may be easy to address the generic group-specific needs of all individuals, but it disproves their differences. Also, too much emphasis on group-specific needs may lead to ignoring the children's other needs. The discussion above shows that the deliberations on the idea of 'need' favour the child's unique needs, implying that the child needs to be understood in the classroom without making a prior explicit attempt to label or place them in a group. However, at the same time, the diversity in their needs has to be acknowledged, which requires that the curricular experiences and classroom environment be flexible enough to include all children, irrespective of their different contexts.

8.6.1.2 Universal Designs of Learning

Universal designs of learning (UDL) is one of the approaches that advocate a flexible learning environment in terms of creating curricular materials, pedagogic strategies and other resources that offer alternatives considering the unique needs of each child in an inclusive classroom. It provides numerous ways of representation, expression and engagement in the classroom so that each child can function in their way and meaningfully relate to the classroom experiences.

- Representation refers to designing instructional materials in multiple ways to make the content accessible to the most significant number of diverse learners. Also, the multiple representations of a concept enable access for a broad range of learners and provide them with the opportunity for in-depth engagement with the concept (Courey et. al., 2013).
- Expression refers to alternative means of expressing or communicating learners' learning or ideas. This includes assessing learners' understanding using various alternative assessment forms, such as interviews, interaction with the learners, and creating stories, poems, drawings, etc. This allows all learners to make choices on their own from the given alternatives, which, in a way, helps them have a positive experience.
- Engagement is making an instructional plan that stimulates students' interest and motivation by incorporating their choices. This may involve hands-on activities, creative experiences, projects, etc.

Thus, one of the main ideas behind UDL is to meet the needs of all children and not just children with special needs. It suggests pre-emptive instruction planning, designed to encompass the differences among learners rather than retrofit the lesson plan that initially fails some learners (Casper & Leuichovius, 2005, as quoted in Courey et. al, 2013). Hence, UDL is in tandem with the philosophy of inclusion, where diversity is the norm rather than the exception (Bouck et al., 2009). It is a whole class approach, so the teacher does not need to differentiate as per the needs of only a few learners. The accommodations are done in the beginning, keeping in mind the learning processes for all children, irrespective of their special needs. As it involves making choices by the learners, it is genuinely child-centric. Thus, UDL scaffolds experience for the benefit of all learners, recognising the existing diversity.

8.7 Concluding Note

The idea of diversity discussed in this chapter shows that there can be several ways in which it can be perceived. Also, diversity within a classroom cannot be presumed before having an experience with the learners. That is, it is to be discovered with the learners gradually in continuous interaction with them. This not only requires teachers to be sensitive and empathetic towards their learners, but the teachers should also understand the various perspectives related to diversity, some of which have been referred to in this chapter. Also, processes of exclusion prove how, historically speaking, human diversity did not get acknowledged. Instead, the differences among communities or groups of people perpetuated the prejudices and stereotypes that specific communities hold to exercise domination and control. People with disabilities were one such group that were initially identified only through their impairments. More recently, their identities have been socially constructed. The journey in the field continues, looking for new strides and commitments.

Bibliography

Ainscow, M. (2013). *From exclusion to inclusion: Ways of responding in schools to students with special educational needs.* Centre for Equity in Education, University of Manchester. https://files.eric.ed.gov/fulltext/ED546818.pdf

Ainscow, M. (2014). From special education to effective schools for all: Widening the agenda. In L. Florian (Ed.), *The Sage handbook of special education* (2nd ed., Vol. 2, pp. 171–185). Sage Publication.

Bennett, A., Bridglall, B.L., Cauce, A.M., Everson, H.T., Gordon, E.W., Lee, C.D., Mendoza-Denton, R., Renzulli, J.S., & Stewart, J.K. (2004). *All students reaching the top: Strategies for closing academic achievement gap.* Naperville, IL: North Central Regional Educational Laboratory.

Bhattacharya, T. (2010). Re-examining issue of inclusion in education. *Economic and Political Weekly*, 18-25.

Booth, T., & Ainscow, M. (2011). *Index for inclusion; Developing learning and participation in schools.* Bristol: Centre for Studies on Inclusive Education.

Bouck, E. C., Courtad, C. A., Heutsche, A., Okolo, C. M., & Englert, C. S. (2009). The virtual history museum: A universally designed approach to social studies instruction. *Teaching Exceptional Children*, *42*(2), 14-20.

Casper, B., & Leuichovius, D. (2005). Universal design for learning and the transition to a more challenging academic curriculum: Making it in middle school and beyond (NCSET Report). Retrieved from http://eric.ed.gov/ERICWeb-Portal/detail?accno=ED495873

Conchas, G.Q., & Noguera, P.A. (2004). Understanding the exceptions: How small schools support the achievement of academically successful black boys. In N. Way & J.Y. Chu (Eds.), *Adolescent boys: Exploring diverse cultures of boyhood* (pp. 317–337). New York: New York University Press.

Courey, S.J., Tappe, P., Siker, J., y LePage, P. (2013). Improved lesson planning with Universal Design for Learning (UDL). Teacher education and special education, 36(1), 7-27. https://doi.org/10.1177/0888406412446178

Dyson, A., & Millward, A. (2000). *Schools and special needs: Issues of innovation and inclusion.* Paul Chapman.

Farrell, M. (2009). *Foundations of special education: An introduction.* Wiley-Blackwell.

Florian, L. (2014). Reimagining special education: Why new approaches are needed. In L. Florian (Ed.), *The Sage handbook of special education* (2nd ed., Vol. 1, pp. 9–22). Sage Publication.

Goffman, E. (1963). *Stigma: Some notes on the management of spoiled identity.* Prentice-Hall.

GoI. (1949). The Constitution of India. Government of India.

Lewis, A., & Norwich, B. (Eds.). (2005). *Special teaching for special children? Pedagogies for inclusion.* UK Open University Press.

Misra, C.R. (2008). Education for tribal children in India. In R.P. Dasen & A. Akkari. (Eds.), *Educational theories and practices from the majority world* (pp. 145–167). New Delhi: Sage Publication.

Mondal, A., & Mete, J. (2012). ICT in higher education: opportunities and challenges. *Institutions*, *21*(60), 4.

Oliver, M. (1990) The Politics of Disablement, Basingstoke: Macmillan and St Martins Press.

Pearson, S. (2016). *Rethinking children and inclusive education- opportunities and complexities.* Bloomsbury Academic.

Reddy, C.R. (2011). From impairment to disability and beyond: Critical explorations in disability studies. *Sociological Bulletin*, *60*(2), 287–306. Indian Sociological Society.

Skrtic, T. (1991). *Behind special education: A critical analysis of professional culture and school organization.* Love Publishing Co.

Tomlinson, S. (1987). Critical theory and special education. *CASTME Journal*, 7(2), 33–41.

9

FROM IQ TO MULTIPLE INTELLIGENCES

Tracing the Journey

Charu Sharma

This chapter describes the pluralistic and wide range of intelligences inherent in children and adolescents, locating the same in the historical backdrop of perspectives on intelligence. It traces the evolution of the construct of intelligence from its origins in the psychometric tradition to more recent conceptualisations in contemporary discourse. Accordingly, the chapter presents a comprehensive discussion of the major theories and perspectives on intelligence. A critical discussion of issues that underlie the dominant understanding of intelligence is also presented. A significant component of the chapter focuses on the theoretical formulations of multiple intelligences, which revolutionised the field of intelligence. The basic supposition in the theory of multiple intelligences holds that children possess a wide variety of intelligences – linguistic, logico-mathematical, spatial, bodily-kinesthetic, musical, interpersonal, intrapersonal and naturalistic intelligences. Such a view posits a critical reflection of existing school systems and necessitates the formulation of a radically different approach for the organisation of curriculum, pedagogy and assessment in schools. One section of the chapter has been devoted to this.

9.1 Introduction to the Construct of Intelligence

The construct of Intelligence has been conceptualised in varied ways by different psychologists. Some dominant formulations explain intelligence as an individual's capacity to understand the world, memory, communication ability, creativity, logical thinking and abstract thinking, self-awareness and problem-solving. As is evident from the various formulations, Intelligence has been conceptualised on many different parameters, which include

DOI: 10.4324/9781003505501-9

cognitive abilities, individual attributes, traits and skills. The fields of educational psychology and developmental psychology have long been exploring ideas and theories that examine the construct of intelligence, drawing from research on children and adolescents. Let us examine some of these.

Intelligence has been defined by a renowned psychologist, Weschler (1958), as the global capacity of a person to think rationally, act purposefully, and deal with his/her environment. Most contemporary psychology textbooks accept a working definition of intelligence as the general ability to perform cognitive tasks. Some books support a more behaviourally inclined definition, such as the capacity to learn from one's experience or adapt to the environment efficiently. Sternberg (1985) integrated these two aspects of intelligence and held that intelligence is the cognitive capacity of an individual to learn from experience, remember important information, reason well and cope with the demands of everyday life.

Robert Sternberg (1985), Howard Gardner (1993) and David Perkins (1995) are some of the most influential theorists of intelligence in contemporary times. Drawing from their writings and the work of earlier theorists, intelligence may be best understood as a combination of the abilities to learn, pose and solve problems. The ability to learn includes all types of formal and informal learning with the help of any combination of education, training and experience. The ability to pose problems includes recognising problem situations and transforming them into more clearly defined problems. The ability to solve problems includes achieving tests and undertaking complex activities regularly. This conceptualisation of intelligence, however, may be too optimistic since it implies that each individual has the potential to become more intelligent over time. Individuals can evolve to become more intelligent through constant learning, practice and experience by developing appropriate tools and making more effective use of these tools (Perkins, 1995).

Arriving at a satisfactory understanding of the construct of intelligence has been the quest of many persons who have worked with children for several decades. These include psychologists, parents, teachers and philosophers. They have liberated several notions and ideas. A dominant idea relates to the measurement of intelligence. A strong view in this regard is the utilitarian value to measure intelligence because it is considered to be a good indicator of an individual's performance at school, in his/her profession and in many other aspects that define success in his/her life (Gottfredson, 2004; Herrnstein & Murray, 1994).

Notwithstanding this, measuring intelligence with the help of intelligence tests is one of the most controversial areas in psychology. Critics suggest that there is a tendency of researchers and educational practitioners to misuse the scores on tests of intelligence. There cannot be a single test to measure the complexity of human intelligence, and all such tests are often loaded with cultural biases. They also label persons with unchangeable scores and make comments about their intellectual status.

9.2 The Concept of Intelligence Quotient

The measurement of intelligence using various tests has been a significant area of research and practice for nearly a century. The intelligence quotient (IQ), which is the measure of intelligence, is a complex concept. There is no clear agreement as to what constitutes IQ or how to measure it, and yet there is an extensive and continually growing collection of research papers on the topic. IQ has been conventionally measured as the ratio of an individual's cognitive or mental age and chronological age, which are calculated using specific tests designed for the purpose.

There are many different types of IQ tests using a wide variety of activities, tasks and items. Many IQ tests consist of single types of items, but other tests tend to have a broad collection of tasks with different contents (numerical, verbal and visual-spatial). Such tests focus on different cognitive processes, such as verbal comprehension, reasoning, rapid decisions, memory, spatial imagery, visual comparisons and retrieval of general knowledge. There is, however, immense controversy surrounding the use of IQ as a measure of intelligence. At the same time, IQ remains a dominant basis for screening and diagnosing persons with intellectual challenges.

Another construct of intelligence, also a matter of debate, relates to describing intelligence in terms of a single factor called the general factor of intelligence (g). General intelligence refers to the speed at which the human mind processes information. The uni-factor or one-factor theory of intelligence considers intelligence as an individual's single attribute or common knowledge capacity. Various theories attempt to accommodate the relationship between general intelligence and more specific abilities, each testing their theories by trying to explain 'exceptions' to normal intellectual development. IQ appears to have a reliable genetic component, but ongoing controversy exists regarding the relationship between race, genes and intelligence. It continues to be a significant debate in intelligence.

Opposing the single-factor theory of intelligence, some theorists and psychologists proposed a two-factor theory. In their view, intellectual abilities consist of two factors: The general ability, known as the 'g' factor, and the second, referring to a group of specific abilities, known as the 's' factor. The 'g' factor is the universal inborn ability, so the greater the 'g' in an individual, the greater the success will be. The 's' factor is acquired from the environment. The 's' factor may thus vary from one aspect to another in the same individual.

There are many differences in the rate at which children and adolescents progress from one level of cognition to another. This is reflected in their school performances. At one extreme, there are a few children who face difficulties in cognition and everyday activities, while at the other end of the spectrum, there are some children who are exceptional, gifted and tend to excel at various tasks. Historically, the g and s factor theories of intelligence and IQ tests have been patronised widely for selection and measuring progress of individuals in a range of aspects, such as school performance, performance in higher education, access to an occupation and as a measure of success in individuals' professional and personal lives.

More recently, the shift to recognition of diverse abilities in children and adolescents, which manifest as achievements in various academic, scholastic and co-curricular aspects, led to questioning IQ and other psychometric measures as adequate representations of an individual's intelligence. The focus became considering intelligence as a multi-dimensional construct. Humans, thus, have multiple intelligences and not unitary intelligence. In the multiple intelligences approach, intelligence is seen as pluralistic rather than unitary. It believes that there are different types of intelligence, which find representation in individuals in different ways. This is a significant departure from the psychometric theories of intelligence.

The theory of multiple intelligences emerged in the 1980s. Its uniqueness came from the belief that cognitive competence had more than one dimension, including a set of talents, abilities and mental skills that may be referred to as intelligences (Gardner, 2011). It also brought to the fore that only two intelligences – linguistic and logical-mathematical – were overemphasised in the traditional theories and approaches to human intelligence. These, in turn, influenced the teaching and curriculum design in schools.

9.3 Theoretical Frameworks on Intelligence

In this section, intelligence has been traced historically from its conceptualisation in traditional psychometric theories to more recent ones. Many debates have been raised, alternating the accurate conceptualisation of intelligence to measuring the intelligence of individuals. These also find discussion. During the era of behaviourism and psychometrics, intelligence was thought to be an inherited, general, single entity which could be measured with the help of Intelligence tests. Psychometrics was the first scientific approach to studying and defining intelligence, and it is still the primary lens through which intelligence is measured (Anderson, 1999). The first set of intelligence tests in the psychometric tradition emerged from the work of Francis Galton (1906) during the late 19th century. According to Galton (1906), the measurement of intelligence should be a direct measure of a person's underlying intelligence, and so he suggested reaction time as a feasible approach and developed different sensorimotor measurements for quantifying intelligence.

A more comprehensive framework in the psychometric tradition has been credited to French psychologist Alfred Binet (1908), celebrated in history as the man who created the first 'intelligence test'. Different versions of this test exist even today. The French Ministry of Education deputed Binet (1908) in the early 1900s to develop an intelligence test that could help identify children at risk for school failure. Binet and his colleague, Theodore Simon (1916), developed an intelligence test known as the Binet-Simon Intelligence Scale – the first test that effectively measured intelligence (Binet & Simon, 1916). The scale included items on numerical reasoning, logical sequences, verbal reasoning and memory, and it was initially designed to measure the intellectual performance of children with learning difficulties at school, but later versions of the test were also developed for the so-called 'normal' school-going children. It brought about a major turning point in psychology as the average level of performance was the criteria for assessing intelligence. Binet and Simon revised the test in 1908 and then again in 1911, serving as the model for many subsequent intelligence tests.

A German psychologist, Stern (1985), devised the notion of IQ, which represents the ratio of one's mental age to chronological age, as measured by some intelligence tests. Lewis Terman (1916) of Stanford University is also credited for popularising IQ tests in the United States during the 1920s. Terman (1916) adapted and developed an English version of Binet-Simon's Intelligence Scale since the age norms for American children did not correspond well with the French children. He revised Binet's test in various ways, specifically by increasing the upper age limit and developing the first paper-and-pencil, group-administered versions of the intelligence test, which resulted in the now famous Stanford-Binet test (Terman & Merrill, 1950). The intelligence tests gradually became a standardised norm in the American educational system because of Terman's efforts. Moreover, his work played a significant role in promoting the belief that intelligence is inherited and unchanging.

Another eminent psychologist, David Wechsler (1958), argued through his work that the original Binet-Simon intelligence tests were heavily loaded on assessing verbal abilities and were not appropriate for measuring other kinds of intelligence. He proposed that intelligence tests should combine verbal and non-verbal components to test intelligence in different age groups of individuals, including children (Weschler, 1958). He later suggested that a profile of intelligence should be developed which can predict the performance of the individual on various abilities using a range of sub-tests for specific age groups, apart from an overall IQ score. Wechsler's tests (1958) became the standard and continued to be widely respected.

9.4 'Two-Factor' Theory of Intelligence

A fascinating approach to understanding intelligence, which involved analysis of the relations among experimental intelligence tests using the factor analysis technique, was initiated by Charles Spearman (1927). He proposed a 'two-factor' theory of intelligence. Spearman (1927) was one of the first psychologists to suggest a factor analytic approach to measuring intelligence. The theory considers that there is one general factor (g) and two or more specific factor(s) that account for individuals' performance on intelligence tests. Spearman conceptualised the g factor as general mental ability. The 'g' factor is involved in deductive reasoning and is linked to the 'skill, speed, intensity, and extent of intellectual output' (Sattler & Ryan, 2001).

In the second decade of the 20th century, Spearman (1927) conducted the first official factor analysis of correlations among IQ test variables. He found that a single common factor explained the positive correlations among tests. He named it g for 'general intelligence factor'. He interpreted it as the core of human intelligence that, to a larger or smaller degree, influences success in all cognitive tasks and creates a positive manifold. This interpretation of 'g' as a common cause of test performance is still dominant in psychometrics. Spearman believed that individuals who perform well on intelligence tests also tend to do well on various intellectual tasks, such as vocabulary, mathematical and spatial abilities. Based on his observations of correlations among performance on various intellectual tasks and factor analysis of data collected on intelligence tests, he proposed that intelligence consists of two underlying factors: 'g' and 's'. The first 'g' factor consists of all the general abilities and skills that all individuals possess. The second 's' factor includes specific skills and talents required to perform certain tasks. The main thrust of Spearman's analysis was the 'g' factor or general intellectual capacity, which formed a major theoretical platform for many subsequent approaches to intelligence. Spearman believed that general mental ability represented the 'inventive' aspect to mental ability rather than the 'reproductive' aspect. The cognitive abilities associated with general mental ability might include describing how two concepts are related or finding a second idea that is related to one that has already been proposed. Tests with high g loading are complex and include tasks that involve reasoning and hypothesis testing. Tests with low g loadings are less complex and include tasks that involve recognition, recall and speed (Sattler & Ryan, 2001).

9.5 Multi-Factor Analysis Approach to Intelligence

Yet another psychologist who applied the factor analysis approach to intelligence was Loius Thurstone (1938). He proposed the first multi-factor approach to intelligence and argued that the core of intelligence lies in seven primary mental abilities or basic interrelated factors rather than one general factor. According to him, the primary mental abilities are verbal comprehension, word fluency, number facility, spatial visualisation, associative memory, perceptual speed and inductive reasoning. He argued that the general factor 'g' is a second-order ability that arises only because the primary or 'first-order' factors are related. Thurstone held that intelligence is better described by considering distinct primary mental abilities rather than a single factor 'g', which does not provide significant details about specific intelligences in the individuals.

The theory further argues that intelligence is the expression primarily of specific mental abilities or factors that include an individual's cognitive abilities. Thurstone believed that intelligence is not an expression primarily of a general 'g' factor that pervades all mental activities nor is it the expression of innumerable highly specific 's' factors. However, there are 'certain' mental operations which have a common 'primary' ability which gives them psychological and functional unity and further differentiates them from other primary mental operations. These mental operations then constitute a group. In other words, there are many groups of mental abilities, each of which has its own primary factor, giving the group functional unity and cohesiveness. These primary factors are said to be relatively independent of the others. Thurstone proposed the following seven primary mental abilities visible in humans: Number ability, which refers to the ability to do numerical calculations rapidly and accurately; verbal ability, which is measured with the help of tests involving verbal comprehension; spatial ability, which can be seen in any task in which the subject is free to manipulate the imaginary object in space; memory ability which involves the ability to memorise quickly; word fluency or the ability to think about isolated words at a rapid rate; Numerical facility, which refers to the ability to engage with numbers logically and rationally, and reasoning ability which is found in tasks that require a subject to discover a rule or principle involved in a series or groups of letters. Based on these primary mental abilities, he constructed a test of intelligence named The Test of Primary Mental Abilities.

Theorists following modern factor analysis introduced hierarchical patterns of group factors, with the 'g' factor still explaining part of the variance in all the tests. J.P. Guilford (1967, 1988) proposed a three-dimensional structure of the human intellect model. Guilford (1988) refused to accept the existence of a general factor and claimed up to 150 elementary factors (which he later extended to 180 factors) in his 'Structure of Intelligence' Model. According to Guilford, every intellectual activity can be classified based on its content, mental operations and the resultant products derived from contents and operations. This model of intelligence describes human intellectual functioning in terms of elementary factors or abilities, which are made up of a combination of three main dimensions with certain types: Operations (six types), Contents (six types) and Products (six types). The contents were categorised into five types: Visual, auditory, symbolic, semantic and behavioural. Operations were classified into five types: Cognition, memory retention, memory recording, divergent production, convergent production and evaluation. The products were categorised into six types: Units, classes, relations, systems, transformations and implications. He proposed that each combination of a specific operation, a specific content and a specific product defines a unique type of intelligence, leading to 180 types of intelligences in individuals. The consequent type of intelligence by processing information can be described in terms of forms such as units, classes, relations or implications. This approach to intelligence seeks to quantify the concept of intelligence and is considered very measurement-oriented.

Raymond Cattell (1971) conceptualised two kinds of intelligence, fluid and crystallised, which he hypothesised are typically present in all individuals. Fluid intelligence was described as the ability to develop techniques for solving problems that are new, creative and novel from the perspective of the person, based on spatial and visual imagery. Crystallised intelligence, in contrast, refers to the ability to bring previously acquired, often culturally defined, problem-solving methods to bear on the current problem based on reasoning, problem-solving and verbal skills.

Later, other psychologists – Vernon (1983), along with Cattell, Horn and Carroll (1978) – proposed a hierarchical theory of intelligence with the 'g' factor at the top, followed by sub-factors at the middle and lower levels (Deary, 2001). An interesting study by Raymond Cattell and John Horn (1978) reflects a factor analytic approach to intelligence. The Cattell-Horn Fluid-Crystallised Intelligence Theory considers that there are two major types of intelligence: Crystallised intelligence and fluid intelligence. Crystallised intelligence implies the knowledge and acquired skills possessed by an individual. This type of intelligence involves well-established and overlearnt cognitive functions related to mental products and achievements (Sattler & Ryan, 2001). Crystallised intelligence tends to be strongly influenced by formal and informal education and is thought to increase at least until middle adulthood. Crystallised intelligence is dependent on being exposed to culture and is not culture-free. For example, the activities that cover crystallised intelligence include general information and vocabulary.

Fluid intelligence is the ability to reason and comprehend non-verbal (culturally free) information. Fluid intelligence is thought to increase during childhood gradually, and it peaks in adolescence. After peaking, fluid intelligence is thought to gradually decrease over the rest of an individual's life due to the degeneration of physiological brain structures. For example, the activities that tap into fluid intelligence might include figure classifications and matrices.

After this original two-factor conceptualisation of intelligence, Cattell, Horn and Carroll (1978) proposed that more than two specific abilities underlie learning. They proposed nine different 'broad' intelligence classifications and developed the Cattell-Horn-Carroll theory of cognitive abilities. Visual processing is the ability to accurately perceive/interpret spatial information and visually and mentally manipulate figures. Auditory processing refers to listening and responding appropriately to auditory information. Short-term memory refers to immediate awareness, alertness and retrieval of recently learnt information. Long-term storage and retrieval refers to retrieving information from long-term storage. Processing speed is the ability to quickly and efficiently respond to simple tasks. Decision speed refers to the ability to respond quickly to tasks of slight or moderate difficulty. Quantitative knowledge refers to the ability to understand and apply mathematical concepts.

9.6 Triarchic Theory of Intelligence

The triarchic theory of intelligence was developed by Robert Sternberg (1985), who considered general intelligence 'g' and earlier componential theory as significant and subsumed them under a larger framework. He believed intelligence comprises three separate, though interrelated, abilities: Analytical, creative, and practical intelligences. He hypothesised that intelligence relates to and is demonstrated in three aspects: The internal world of information processing, experience and past learning, and the external world of adapting to, shaping and selecting real-world environments. The intelligence components describe the structure of cognitive processes used to adapt to, shape or select real-world environments.

Sternberg (2000) proposed that the three facets of intelligence are analytical, creative and practical intelligences. Analytical intelligence is similar to the standard psychometric definition of intelligence and corresponds to his earlier componential intelligence, measured by analogies. Creative intelligence refers to the ability to react to novel stimuli or situations, which refers to the experiential aspect of intelligence. Practical intelligence involves grasping, understanding and solving real-life problems in the everyday web of life, which is the contextual aspect of intelligence. He hypothesised that intelligences relates to three different yet related aspects of the human mind. The first aspect is the internal world of information processing; the second level refers to learning based on past experiences; and the third aspect refers to the adaptation to the external and real-world environments. Sternberg strongly believes that rigorous efforts and practice can increase intelligence.

In 2011, he consolidated his work and proposed the triarchic theory of intelligence to provide a more comprehensive description of intellectual competence than traditional differential or cognitive theories of human ability. The triarchic theory describes three fundamental aspects of intelligence. It does not argue against the validity of a general intelligence factor; instead, the theory posits that general intelligence is part of analytic intelligence, and only by considering all three aspects of intelligence can the full range of intellectual functioning be fully understood.

Sternberg's three types of intelligence, called the triarchic theory, are:

1. *Analytical or Componential Intelligence:* This type of intelligence allows one to process information effectively and think abstractly. Most tests measure this type of intelligence. Analytical intelligence is what we generally think of as academic ability. It enables us to solve problems and to acquire new knowledge. Problem-solving skills include encoding information, combining and comparing pieces of information and generating a solution. Componential intelligence is the ability to process information effectively. This includes meta-cognitive, executive, performance and knowledge-acquisition components that help to steer cognitive processes. Analytical intelligence measures one's ability to solve academic problems, such as analogies and puzzles. It is seen as a reflection of how the individual relates to one's internal world.

2. *Creative or Experiential Intelligence:* This type of intelligence allows a person to develop new ideas. People high in creative intelligence can find connections between different and distinct concepts. It is defined by the ability to cope with novel situations and to profit from experience. The ability to quickly relate novel situations to familiar situations (that is, to perceive similarities and differences) fosters adaptation. Moreover, based on experience, we can solve problems more rapidly. Experiential intelligence refers to the ability to deal with novel situations, effectively automating ways of dealing with situations so they are easily handled in the future, and the ability to think in novel ways. Creative intelligence reflects an individual's ability to connect their internal world to their external reality. It includes one's ability to use prior knowledge in new or innovative ways in different circumstances, such as finding a new approach to a problem. In this way, creative intelligence encompasses creative thinking.

3. *Practical or Contextual Intelligence:* Practical intelligence involves one's ability to understand and effectively deal with everyday tasks. It is reflective of how the individual relates to the external world. This type of intelligence allows a person to find practical solutions to real problems. People with this type of intelligence are often considered 'street smart'. Practical intelligence, or 'street smarts', enables people to adapt to the demands of their environment. For example, keeping a job by adapting one's behaviour to the employer's requirements is adaptive. But if the employer is making unreasonable demands, reshaping the environment (by changing the employer's attitudes) or selecting an alternate environment (by finding a more suitable job) is also adaptive. Practical intelligence is the ability to do well in informal and formal educational settings, adapting to and shaping one's environment as being 'street smart'.

Most individuals will score higher in one of the three areas of intelligence. Sternberg provides examples of people who are quite talented in one of these areas but not so talented in the other two. In that sense, his approach to the field of intelligence is like Howard Gardner's (2008). However, Sternberg does not focus on specific intelligence components aligned with various academic disciplines. He is more concerned with helping people develop components of intelligence that will help them perform well in whatever they choose.

Further, he strongly believes that studying and practice can increase intelligence. Quite a bit of his research focuses on such endeavours. Some of his work focuses specifically on 'street smarts' versus 'school smarts'. He notes that some people are particularly talented in one of these two areas rather than in the other. This observation is consistent with the work of Lev Vygotsky (1978), who argues that the type of learning that goes on outside of school distinctly differs from that in school. While some students are talented in both informal and formal education, others are much more successful in one rather than the other type of education.

In recent years, the triarchic theory has been updated and renamed the Theory of Successful Intelligence by Sternberg (2011). Intelligence is defined as an individual's assessment of success in life by the individual's own (idiographic) standards and within the individual's socio-cultural context. Success is achieved through combinations of analytical, creative and practical intelligence. The three aspects of intelligence are referred to as processing skills. The processing skills are applied to the pursuit of success through the three elements of practical intelligence: Adapting to, shaping and selecting one's environments. The mechanisms that employ the processing skills to achieve success include utilising one's strengths and compensating or correcting for one's weaknesses. Sternberg's theories and research on intelligence remain contentious within the scientific community. He believes that intelligence has less to do with success in the classroom and more with success in the real world. He refers to the ability to succeed in life as 'successful intelligence'. He holds that people have three types of intelligence and that 'successfully intelligent' people learn to balance the three types of intelligence effectively.

According to Sternberg (2011), people do not need to be high in all three types of intelligence to be 'successfully intelligent'. Instead, they must determine their strengths and weaknesses and use both effectively. If they are strong in a certain area, they must build on that strength. If they are weak in an area, they need to improve or find a way to compensate for the weakness. He believes that all three types of intelligence can be developed. He also believes that students learn better if how they are taught matches their learning ability. This means teaching and testing students in ways that use all three types of intelligence: analytical, creative and practical.

9.7 Emotional Intelligence or Emotional Quotient

More recently, two other kinds of intelligences: Emotional intelligence and social intelligence have also received international attention. Social intelligence refers to the ability to understand other people with reference to factors affecting social group formation, motivation and cooperation with others. Social intelligence may be perceived as related to interpersonal intelligence. It is a cumulative measure of an individual's self, evolved social beliefs, behaviours, attitudes, social awareness and capacity to manage complex social changes.

Daniel Goleman (1995) advanced the concept of emotional intelligence. Emotional intelligence is a specific type of social intelligence that involves the ability to regulate one's and others' emotions, discriminate among them and use the information to guide one's thinking and actions.

Emerging from the concept of emotional intelligence is its operational contour, called the emotional quotient (EQ). EQ is becoming an increasingly valued area of psychological research due to its adaptive properties for individuals and society. Although experts tend to differ somewhat in their definition of emotional intelligence and the standards for its empirical assessment, most of them agree that individuals having high EQ scores possess character traits that foster strong interpersonal skills, excellent coping strategies and decision-making abilities that lead to positive outcomes. Theories and applications of emotional intelligence aim to improve the individual's quality of life by helping her/him to achieve goals, form satisfying relationships, find meaningful work and attain personal and professional success. An understanding of emotional intelligence is therefore not only conducive to intellectual growth, it holds a significant role in individual happiness.

Emotional intelligence, in effect, may be considered a type of social intelligence that involves the ability to monitor one's and others' emotions, discriminate among them and use the information to guide one's thinking and actions. All meaningful relationships, including parent–child, teacher–student, between colleagues at work and other similar relationships, which are generally cherished and perceived as strengths, are based on dimensions of emotional intelligence. It involves abilities that may be categorised into five domains: Self-awareness, managing emotions, motivating oneself, empathy and handling relationships.

- Self-awareness refers to observing oneself and recognising a feeling as it happens.
- Managing emotions involves handling feelings so they are appropriate, realising what is behind a feeling and finding ways to handle fears and anxieties, anger and sadness.
- Motivating oneself or channelling emotions to realise a goal involves emotional self-control, delaying gratification and stifling one's impulses.

- Empathy involves being sensitive to others' feelings and concerns, taking their perspective, and appreciating the differences in how people feel about things.
- Handling relationships or managing emotions in others is about social competence and social skills.

Historically speaking, it was not until 1990 that the term 'emotional intelligence' was first used when Mayer and Salovey (1993) formulated their original hierarchical model of EQ. They defined emotional intelligence as 'the ability to monitor one's own and other's feelings and emotions, to discriminate among them and to use this information to guide one's thinking and actions' (Mayer & Salovey, 1993). Borrowing from Mayer and Salovey's theory, Daniel Goleman (1995) published his path-breaking work, *Emotional Intelligence*. His theory, derived from work on brain research, sought to prove that emotional stability, or EQ, is more important than IQ in determining one's success.

Englund and collaborators (2004) proved that low measures of emotional intelligence and social competence are found to correlate to feelings of negativity, hostility, aggression and/or frustration towards others. In group settings, individuals with low EQ scores fail to participate in group tasks and do not contribute to discussions; they display little consideration towards others and their opinions and are uninterested in group activities. With this knowledge, the world began to recognise the value of hiring emotionally intelligent individuals for their skills in social competence. Highly emotionally intelligent individuals are desirable job candidates for their traits, such as the ability to function well within a group, work cooperatively towards group goals and strive towards attaining positive outcomes of problem-solving tasks. Further, emotionally intelligent individuals are respected and wield influence in group dynamics. These individuals can guide discussions, promote participation by others and often make final decisions that others adhere to. They are confident, believe in their abilities and expect success for their effort.

However, the growing popularity of emotional intelligence has not been without criticism. A critique of empirical research on emotional intelligence points to the problem of self-reporting findings. Research that resulted in the development of the various EQ scales may represent or be vulnerable to subject bias. It is possible that subjects responded to self-report studies by portraying themselves more positively and/or by providing answers they wished the investigators/researchers to read/observe. Applied studies may also be vulnerable to subject-bias effects.

In his book *Smart Schools*, David Perkins (1992) analyses many different educational theories and approaches to education. His analysis is strongly supportive of Gardner's theory of multiple intelligences. Perkins' book contains extensive research-based evidence that education can be considerably improved by more explicit and appropriate teaching for transfer, focusing on higher-order cognitive skills and project-based learning. Perkins (1995) examines a large number of research studies on the measurement of IQ and of programmes of study designed to increase IQ. He presents detailed arguments that IQ has three major components or dimensions. Neural intelligence refers to the efficiency and precision of one's neurological system. Experiential intelligence refers to one's accumulated knowledge and experience in different areas. It can be thought of as accumulating all of one's expertise. Reflective intelligence refers to one's broad-based strategies for attacking problems, learning and approaching intellectually challenging tasks. It includes attitudes that support persistence, systematisation and imagination. It includes self-monitoring and self-management.

Experiential intelligence is based on years and years of accumulating knowledge and experience in informal and formal learning environments. Such knowledge and experience can lead to higher expertise in one or more fields. People who live in 'rich' learning environments have a significant intelligence advantage over people who grow up in less stimulating environments. Experiential intelligence can be increased in such environments. Reflexive intelligence can be thought of as a control system that helps to make effective use of neural intelligence and experiential intelligence. A person can learn strategies that help make more effective use of neural and experiential intelligence. The habits of mind included under reflexive intelligence can be learnt and improved. Metacognition and other approaches to reflecting on one's cognitive processes can help.

9.8 Evolution of the Perspective of Multiple Intelligences

The perspective of multiple intelligences is a more recent conceptualisation of intelligence. According to the American psychologist Howard Gardner (1983), a unitary, general factor of intelligence cannot adequately represent a human's complex and diverse capabilities. Therefore, he evolved a theory of multiple intelligences against the backdrop of the traditional and widely held view of intelligence as a unitary trait that can be adequately measured by intelligence tests (Gardner, 1999). In his research work in neuropsychology and developmental psychology, Gardner (2008) began to question the traditional view of intelligence during the 1970s and onwards. He derived his theory from extensive brain research, which included interviews, tests and research on hundreds of individuals. He studied the cognitive profiles of stroke and accident victims, prodigies, autistic individuals, those with learning disabilities, savants and people from diverse cultures. Gardner (1999) found that the traditional psychometric theories of intelligence focused only on problem-solving strategies and ignored the creation of products. The psychometric theories also assumed that their notion of intelligence is universal, regardless of cultural contexts and values.

Gardner (2008) describes intelligence as the bio-psychological potential to process information that can be activated in a cultural setting to solve a problem or fashion a product valued in one or more community or cultural settings. This conceptualisation locates intelligence in what people can do and the products they can create *in the real world*, in contrast to the implied intelligence indicated by a test. It suggests a qualitative expression, a description of an individual's collection of intelligences, rather than a single quantitative expression of a set of narrowly defined paper-and-pencil tasks. His research suggested that intelligence is centred in different areas of the brain, which are interconnected, rely upon one another, can work independently if needed and can be developed with the right environmental conditions (Chen & Gardner, 2005).

Multiple intelligences refer to a group of eight intelligences. Gardner (1983) originally identified seven components of intelligence – linguistic, logical-mathematical, spatial, musical, bodily-kinesthetic, intrapersonal and interpersonal – but later, in 1999, he added one more intelligence, namely naturalistic, to his list. A brief description of each of these multiple intelligences (Moran, Kornhaber, & Gardner, 2006) is provided below:

1. *Linguistic Intelligence*: The ability to understand and use spoken and written communication.
2. *Logical-Mathematical Intelligence*: The ability to understand and use logic, numerical symbols and operations.
3. *Musical Intelligence*: The ability to understand and use such concepts as rhythm, pitch, melody and harmony.
4. *Visual-Spatial Intelligence*: The ability to orient and manipulate three-dimensional space.
5. *Bodily-kinaesthetic Intelligence*: The ability to coordinate physical movement.
6. *Interpersonal Intelligence*: The ability to understand and interact well with other people.
7. *Intrapersonal Intelligence*: The ability to understand and use one's thoughts, feelings, preferences and interests.
8. *Naturalistic Intelligence*: The ability to distinguish and categorise objects or phenomena in nature.

Gardner (2011) argues that these intelligences are relatively distinct from each other and that each person has some level of each of these eight intelligences. He later speculated about existential intelligence, which reflects an individual's capacity to consider 'big questions' about life, death, love, and being. However, neither existential intelligence nor any other proposed intelligence sufficiently meets the criteria for identification as a unique form of intelligence. Instead of relying primarily on traditional factor analytic analyses, Gardner based his theory on analysing the research literature using eight criteria by drawing upon findings from evolutionary biology, anthropology, developmental and cognitive psychology, neuropsychology and psychometrics.

9.9 Implications of the Different Perspectives on Intelligence

The different perspectives on intelligence suggest that every child possesses intelligence, which may manifest differently. In the traditional theories of intelligence, where intelligence is measured as a status of capacity, the school curriculum, pedagogy and subsequent assessment practices tend to focus largely on students' academic achievement. One important critique of this emanates from the multiple intelligences perspective, which emphasises that schools should consider individual differences among students as being immensely significant. The focus should thus be on nurturing the diverse abilities, skills and talents of students at different grades. They should promote the development of many talents, skills and abilities by inculcating and nurturing multiple intelligences through different aspects of life at school. Some implications of different aspects of life at school, such as curriculum, classroom pedagogy, teachers and assessment, are listed in the following section.

9.9.1 For Schools

- It is suggested that schools should encourage the development of multiple intelligences in regular classroom teaching and assessment.
- The teaching-learning environment of the school should try to encourage the development of all kinds of intelligences in children and adolescents.
- The schools should refer to educational objectives propagated by the multiple intelligences perspective for systematic implementation at grade and classroom levels.
- The school administration should provide full support and guidance to the teachers who utilise multiple intelligences theory in their classroom teaching and assessments (Hoerr, 2000).
- Teachers' implementation of multiple intelligences in classroom activities and assessments needs support from stakeholders in all domains.

9.9.2 For Curriculum

- The school curriculum should have spaces for addressing all eight kinds of multiple intelligences.

- Schools should go beyond traditional visualisation and inputs in linguistic and logico-mathematics-based subjects.
- Likewise, the school curriculum should promote the development of a multi-dimensional range of intellectual abilities rather than focusing on traditional reading, writing, and mathematics or related disciplines of mathematics, sciences and languages.
- The syllabus and textbooks should be designed to integrate all aspects of intelligence.

9.9.3 For Teachers

- Teachers should provide optimum teaching-learning experiences and nurture the development of multiple intelligences in different grades at school.
- Teachers should maintain everyday logs of the progress and achievements of students with observations and written records.
- This can help to assess each student's manifestations of intelligence and serve to strategise their teaching approach.
- There are many pedagogical methods that the theory of multiple intelligences supports. The curriculum should ensure space for these.

9.9.4 For Assessment

- The assessment system based on the perspective of multiple intelligences should be broad-based and provide for the evaluation of different kinds of intelligence.
- Teachers should adopt different assessment methods, such as hands-on activities, group or individual projects, and presentations in both academic disciplines and co-curricular activities.
- Assessment should involve continuous and formative methods of evaluation, which may also involve a few innovative ways, such as self-assessment or peer review, for a more comprehensive assessment of students at schools.

9.10 Concluding Remarks

In this chapter, different theorists' psychometric conceptualisations of intelligence were traced historically, along with their critique by more recent perspectives. The evolution of the theory of multiple intelligences and its relevance to school education was presented. A discussion on the educational implications of this perspective followed this.

The theory of multiple intelligences critiqued the traditional psychometric theories by highlighting that they had largely focused on the measurement aspect of intelligence and had ignored explaining the development of intelligence. Their conception of intelligence was thus unitary or factor-centric. In fact, the conception of intelligence as multiple rather than singular forms the primary distinction between the theory of multiple intelligences and the conception of intelligence that dominated Western psychological theories and much of common discourse. The critics of psychometric intelligences further argue that no single intelligence test can apprehend the complicated nature of human intelligence, and no single measure is completely free from cultural biases. The theory of multiple intelligences sought to broaden the scope of human potential beyond the confines of the traditional notions of intelligence (Anderson, 1999). The theory's overarching principle suggests that intelligence is better conceived of as multiple and content-specific rather than unitary and general.

The theory of multiple intelligences has been highly influential, especially among educators and school planners. Gardner (2008) pointed out that standardised intelligence tests assess multiple intelligences in a strikingly decontextualised manner. He argued that intelligence had more to do with the capacity for solving problems and fashioning products in a context-rich and naturalistic setting.

It should be noted that the multiple intelligences perspective does not belong exclusively to Gardner (2011). He advanced the original theory, but several other researchers and scholars also applied its basic principles to educational settings in their respective countries. The educational implications of the theory and its impact on education have been extensive and wide-reaching. Several research studies have been conducted, and their results underlined that the approach of multiple intelligences has immense advantages in different educational settings. The significant contributions in this regard have been to various educational domains, such as learning, achievements, attitudes, motivational levels of students and the satisfaction of teachers. Some schools worldwide have incorporated the principles of multiple intelligences into their school's vision, curriculum and pedagogy. Moreover, several books have been written on the relevance of the theory of multiple intelligences for schools, teachers and communities (as cited in Chen, Moran, & Gardner, 2009). The chapter ends by raising a few research questions for reflection, furthering knowledge building and directing future research endeavours.

- How can multiple intelligences be identified in children and adolescents across various age groups?
- What are the different ways of promoting multiple intelligences in children and adolescents?
- How can we develop age-appropriate activities to nurture multiple intelligences in children?
- What should be the role of different aspects and parameters in developing multiple intelligences at school?

- How can teachers help promote multiple intelligences at school?
- Are there more intelligences that can be identified in children apart from the theory of multiple intelligences, especially in the socio-cultural context?
- In what ways can we promote the development of intelligences through various factors of socialisation, particularly parents, friends, community and different sources of media?

Bibliography

Anderson, M. (Ed.). (1999). *The development of intelligence*. Hove: Psychology Press.

Armstrong, T. (2009). *Multiple intelligences in the classroom*. Alexandria: ASCD.

Binet, A. (1908). *A method of measuring the development of the intelligence of young children*. London: Courier.

Binet, A., & Simon, T. (1916). *The development of intelligence in children: The Binet-Simon Scale* (E. S. Kite, trans.). Baltimore: Williams & Wilkins.

Cantor, N., & Kihlstrom, J. F. (1987). *Personality and social intelligence*. Englewood Cliffs: Pearson College Division.

Cattell, R. B. (1971). *Abilities: Their structure, growth and action*. Boston, MA: Houghton Mifflin.

Cattell, R. B., Horn, J. L., & Carroll, J. B. (1978). A check on the theory of fluid and crystallized intelligence with description of new subtest designs. *Journal of Educational Measurement*, *15*(3), 139–164.

Chen, J., & Gardner, H. (2005). Multiple intelligences: Assessment based on multiple intelligence theory. In D. Flanagan & P. Harrison (Eds.), *Contemporary intellectual assessment: Theories, tests and issues*. New York: Guilford Press.

Chen, J., Moran, S., & Gardner, H. (2009). *Multiple intelligences around the world*. New York, NY: Jossey-Bass.

Deary, I. J. (2001). *Intelligence: A very short introduction*. Oxford, UK: Oxford University Press.

Englund, M. M., Luckner, A. E., Whaley, G. J., & Egeland, B. (2004). Children's achievement in early elementary school: Longitudinal effects of parental involvement, expectations, and quality of assistance. *Journal of Educational Psychology*, *96*(4), 723.

Galton, F. (1906). *Noteworthy families*. London: J. Murray.

Gardner, H. (1983). *Frames of mind: The theory of multiple intelligences*. New York, NY: Basic Books.

Gardner, H. (1999). *The disciplined mind: What all students should understand*. New York: Simon & Schuster.

Gardner, H. (2000). *Intelligence reframed: Multiple intelligences for the 21st century*. London: Hachette UK.

Gardner, H. (2008). *Multiple intelligences: New horizons in theory and practice*. New York: Basic Books.

Gardner, H. (2011). *The unschooled mind: How children think and how schools should teach*. New York: Basic Books.

Gardner, H. (2011). *Frames of mind: The theory of multiple intelligences*. London: Hachette UK.

Goleman, D. P. (1995). *Emotional intelligence: Why it can matter more than IQ for character, health and lifelong achievement*. New York: Bantam Books.

Gottfredson, L. S. (2004). Intelligence: Is it the epidemiologists' elusive "fundamental cause" of social class inequalities in health? *Journal of Personality and Social Psychology*, *86*(1), 174.

Guilford, J. P. (1967). *The nature of human intelligence*. New York: Guilford Press.

Guilford, J. P. (1988). Some changes in the structure-or-intellect model. *Educational and Psychological Measurement*, *48*, 1–4.

Herrnstein, R. J., & Murray, C. (1994). *The bell curve: The reshaping of American life by differences in intelligence*. New York: Free Press.

Hoerr, T. R. (2000). *Becoming a multiple intelligences school*. Alexandria, USA: VA Association.

Horn, J. L., & Cattell, R. B. (1967). Age differences in fluid and crystallized intelligence. *Acta Psychologica*, *26*, 107–129.

Mayer, J. D., & Salovey, P. (1993). *The intelligence of emotional intelligence*. New York: Free Press.

Mayer, J. D., Salovey, P., Caruso, D. R., & Sitarenios, G. (2001). *Emotional intelligence as a standard intelligence*. New York: Free Press.

McKenzie, W. (1999). Multiple Intelligences (MI) inventory. Retrieved from http://surfaquarium.com/MI/index.htm.

Moran, S., Kornhaber, M., & Gardner, H. (2006). Orchestrating multiple intelligences. *Educational Leadership*, *64*(1), 22–27.

Perkins, D. N., Crismond, D., Simmons, R., & Unger, C. (1995). Inside understanding. In D. N. Perkins, J. L. Schwartz, M. M. West, & M. S. Wiske (Eds.), *Software goes to school: Teaching for understanding with new technologies* (pp. 70–87). New York, NY: Oxford University Press.

Perkins, D. N. (1992). Smart schools: From training memories to educating minds. Free Press.

Perkins, D. N., & Grotzer, T. A. (1997). Teaching intelligence. *American Psychologist*, *52*(10), 1125.

Sattler, J. M., & Ryan, J. J. (2001). Wechsler Adult Intelligence Scale-III (WAIS-III): Description. In J. M. Sattler (Ed.), *Assessment of children: Cognitive applications* (p. 412). San Diego: Jerome M. Sattler.

Sattler, J. M., & Saklofske, D. H. (2001). Wechsler Intelligence Scale for Children-III (WISC III): Description. In J. M. Sattler (Ed.), *Assessment of children: Cognitive applications* (pp. 220–265). San Diego: Jerome M. Sattler.

Spearman, C. (1927). *The nature of intelligence and the principles of cognition*. London, UK: Macmillan.

Stern, D. N. (1985). *The interpersonal world of the infant: A view from psychoanalysis and developmental psychology*. London: Karnac Books.

Sternberg, R. J. (1985). *Beyond IQ: A triarchic theory of human intelligence*. New York: Cambridge University Press.

Sternberg, R. J. (2000). *Handbook of intelligence*. New York: Cambridge University Press.

Sternberg, R. J. (2011). The theory of successful intelligence. In R. Sternberg & S. B. Kauffman (Eds.), *Cambridge handbook of intelligence*. New York: Cambridge University Press.

Sternberg, R. J., Forsythe, G. B., Hedlund, J., Wagner, R. K., Horvath, J. A., Williams, W. M., & Grigorenko, E. (2000). *Practical intelligence in everyday life*. Cambridge: Cambridge University Press.

Terman, L. M. (1916). *The measurement of intelligence*. Boston, MA: Houghton Mifflin.

Terman, L. M., & Merrill, M. A. (1950). *The Stanford-Binet Intelligence Scale*. Boston: Houghton Mifflin.

Thurstone, L. L. (1938). *Primary mental abilities*. Chicago, IL: University of Chicago Press.

Vernon, P. A. (1983). Speed of information processing and general intelligence. *Intelligence*, 7(1), 53–70.

Vygotsky, L. (1978). Interaction between learning and development. *Readings on the -Development of Children*, 23(3), 34–41.

Wechsler, D. (1958). *The measurement and appraisal of adult intelligence*. Baltimore: Williams & Wilkinds.

10

BEYOND THE GENDER BINARY

Understanding the Gender-Diverse Child

Shivani Arora

10.1 Introduction

Gender-diverse persons face a lot of psychological, social and economic hardships. They are often discriminated against and may even be denied their basic fundamental rights. Disowned by family and rejected by mainstream society, transgender individuals are prone to high-risk behaviour. However, this scenario is changing globally and in India too. Many recent legislations have been introduced to give it recognition and focus. The attempt is clearly to restructure the conventional attitudes and beliefs that prevail in society about gender orientation so that there is wider acceptance of persons outside of the accepted gender binary of male and female.

Jasmine (name changed), 19 years old, recounts her first memory as an intense like for a white pearl necklace belonging to her mother. She wore it whenever she got a chance. She also loved to wear colourful bangles, paint her nails and wear red lipstick. She always felt like a girl and immensely enjoyed it when her mother would paint her toes just like she painted hers. She liked to play with dolls at home but never had any since boys do not play with dolls. By the age of 5–6 years, when other boys in their housing colony played together, she played with the girls – the only 'boy' in a group of girls. One distinct memory of Jasmine's childhood is wrapping a towel around her head and pretending to have long, flowing hair. She would often pluck flowers from roadside plants and wear them in her hair. She also liked to drape her mother's clothes and jewellery.

By the time she was in class six and aged 12, everyone in her school and neighbourhood started teasing her. Unknowingly, her walk, talk and behaviour had acquired feminine undertones, making everyone notice and

DOI: 10.4324/9781003505501-10

ridicule her. Slowly, the number of friends she had also declined. Even the teachers in her school made fun of her. They would laugh at the jokes made by her classmates about her. As a result, the classmates felt encouraged to tease her even more. For one school function, she was chosen by the dance teacher as a lead dancer in the annual day fisherman dance to be performed by girls. She was trying to make fun of her and was supported by other teachers and students. She was happy to be selected, unsuspecting of the teacher's motives. Her parents, however, disapproved of it. Her father, who was out of town for some work, was quite angry with the idea of a boy dressing up as a girl when he heard about it on his return. On the said day, Jasmine wore the designated costume and makeup. She could not stop looking at herself in the mirror and admiring herself, and she performed with complete devotion. She dressed in all her finery, a bright red sari, long earrings, flowers in her hair and makeup; Jasmine knew this was what she was meant to be, her true inner self uninterrupted. While the dance was highly appreciated, a boy dressed as a girl soon became the talk of the town and somehow gave everyone a legitimised right to humiliate and tease her. She was called by different names, and given titles like chhakka, gay, etc. This did not disturb her anymore. She did not get affected by the nasty comments of her peers, although she did feel sad at times because no one understood her predicament. This incident proved to be a turning point in Jasmine's life. The more she re-lived herself in the dancer's attire, the more contented and happy she became. It was clear in her mind that she was a girl from within. A declaration of the fact that her feelings, emotions and preferences were those of a female while her body was assigned a male sex by birth.

10.2 Adolescence and Youth

Now that Jasmine was aware that her inner feelings reflected those of a woman, she developed a strong dislike for her body, which was attaining puberty and thus displayed male characteristics like facial hair, Adam's apple, skin hardening, etc. She felt that her body defined her boundaries. She felt caged inside a body which did not belong to her. This body forced her to conform to the societal standards against her wishes and, at the same time, gave others the right to humiliate and reject her. The difference between her mental orientation and physical structure made her depressed and anguished. There was no one to share her trauma with, no one who understood her, making her more vulnerable and lonely. All her preferences indicated that she was a woman, but her body did not confirm that. Whenever she looked at her body, she was filled with feelings of self-loathing and disgust. She hated the body she was born with and felt extremely helpless. How she wished she could change it! She withdrew from social interactions and spent most of her time listening to music (sad songs) or imagining how life would be as a woman. She started staying indoors, especially in her room, where the mirror was her best friend. In private moments, she would dress up as a woman, trying on different looks, in a sari or wearing a salwar-kameez, putting on eyeliner and lipstick, and stealing earrings she could wear. She also tried to play different feminine character roles: she was a wife on one day, a mother or a girlfriend on another day. Whenever she was alone at home, she felt happiest. She felt free and independent. She had no fear of being found out and could be herself.

In the year 2003 came a Hindi movie called Jism (body), starring John Abraham, and with this release came the realisation that Jasmine liked boys and not girls. She was instantly attracted to John's masculine body and fell in love with it. At the age when heterosexual relationships develop, Jasmine was interested in people of the same sex. At an age when boys around her were talking about girls and how they would even bunk a class to see a particular girl, she discovered that she liked boys and was drawn to them. In class nine, Jasmine developed strong feelings for a boy in class eleven of the same school. She would try to meet him at every opportunity, touch him and generally blush in his presence, but he never paid any attention to her. She secretly would conjure up scenarios where she was a pretty woman, and he was her love interest. One day, she was put on the same basketball team as that boy and was pleased to hear this. She could not control her happiness and ended up confiding in her closest friend, a girl who lived near her house. However, this turned out to be a big mistake. Her friend did not keep her secret and told everyone about her infatuation. It brought Jasmine into the limelight. Everyone in their colony got to know that Jasmine liked boys. Now, the boys looked at her like she was diseased (the disgust and hatred in their eyes was almost palpable), and all the girls made fun of her. Her family was distraught at the news; their only son was gay. What had they done to earn the wrath of god? Her mother nearly broke down, and her father beat her with a belt till she almost fainted. This was followed by a round of friendly and sympathetic advice from friends and relatives. Some suggested going to a doctor, while others felt Jasmine could be 'cured' only by priests or mystics, leading to endless rounds at both agencies. After wasting time, energy and money, they realised this was futile. Their only son was gay, and they could not do anything about it.

Jasmine, on the other hand, was full of shame and guilt. The infamy she had inflicted upon her family was killing her inside. She was so embarrassed that whenever she went out and saw a group of men or women conversing, she was sure they were talking about her. She checked the meaning of the word 'gay' many times in the dictionary but was still not convinced that it described her. Her liking had changed in favour of boys, which confirmed her sexuality as a girl, and this scared her all the more. She knew she was not gay, but then who was she? This was a question that constantly hounded her. She developed strong feelings of self-doubt. This was all too confusing for her. There was nobody she could talk to or discuss her inner feelings with. Her parents looked at her like she was a repulsive, mentally sick person whom they were forced to live with. Although she was reluctant to accept that she was gay, she gave in.

Jasmine became quiet. She withdrew from all relationships and spoke very little to her parents. The fact that she had let her parents down was eating her up. She was tired of being talked about by all but stopped reacting to their scorn for her. She felt that nobody cared whether she was dead or alive. She had become a social isolate. She did not want to live like that.

The case given above describes the trauma and abuse experienced by a transgender person simply because he did not subscribe to the normative gender divide. A transgender person identifies with a gender other than the one assigned to him/her at birth. Such an individual may be born as a male but identify and express himself as a female, as in the case of Jasmine, or vice versa.

10.3 Understanding the Gender-Diverse Individual

From the moment that we are born or even earlier, at the prenatal stage, our world is categorised into the binary configuration of gender. Once labelled, a child is either a girl or a boy and must act according to the behaviours constructed and approved by mainstream society. The predominant heteronormative culture of the civilised world maintains that there are only two genders, namely male and female, which are acceptable (Kitzenger, 2005). This binary that prevails in the construction of gender is challenged by individuals who identify as transgender. The next question that comes to mind is, who is a transgender person?

Transgender is generally described as an 'umbrella' term for persons whose gender identity (the gender with which they identify) and gender expression (an individual's outward gender presentation like clothing, body language, or hairstyle) do not conform to the sex (gender) assigned at birth. For example, a person born with male genitalia and therefore set to be a male may harbour feelings of intense femininity and look upon himself or perceive himself as a woman rather than a man (gender identity). He may also prefer to dress like a woman, have long hair and pierced ears (gender expression) and engage in behaviours stereotypically associated with women, like body language, softness, etc., and may also come across as a woman. He may seek medical and sometimes surgical intervention to 'correct' or 'align' his biologically given sex with his perceived and preferred gender identity. Thus, we may say that transgender is an adjective which includes but is not limited to men and women born with a biological sex which contradicts their perceived or felt gender. It consists of the following:

(a) Transsexuals are individuals who have had hormonal or surgical interventions to align their bodies with their perceived gender identity.
(b) Eunuchs/Hijra individuals who do not identify as male or female and thus call themselves the third gender (Supreme Court of India, 2013). They may be emasculated (nirvana), non-emasculated (akka/akva), and intersex (born with mixed genitalia).
(c) Transvestites are those who are born male but have feminine sexual orientation and tend to cross-dress, using clothing of the opposite gender.

What emerges then is that transgender is a general, inclusive term which takes into its ambit all individuals who fall outside the customary binary construction of gender and challenge the stereotypical dichotomous gender roles. It refers to all gender-variant individuals with different identities and experiences. It includes preoperative, post-operative and non-operative transsexual people who strongly identify with the gender opposite to their biological sex: male and female. The term transgender is relatively new, originating in the late 1980s and used in its contemporary popular sense (Boswell, 1991). According to the Harry Benjamin Gender Dysphoria Association,

> the term transsexual emerged into the professional and public usage in the 1950s as a means of designating a person who aspired to or lived in, the anatomically contrary gender role, whether or not hormones had been administered or surgery had been performed
>
> *(Benjamin 1966).*

10.4 The Queer Iceberg

Our society tends to look at transgender persons as superficial and illegitimate. They are not only stigmatised for being different but also excluded. They face a lot of humiliation, rejection, mistreatment, psychosocial and emotional abuse and an invalidation of their true authentic self. The gender-diverse child who is considered abnormal and a natural disaster ends up leading a traumatic, harrowing life due to his/her gender incongruence that takes the form of an asynchronous relationship between his/her biological sex and perceived gender orientation. Such a child experiences a harsh invalidation of his/her gender expression. There is tremendous pressure on him to conform to the traditional gender structure, leading to inner turmoil, which often leads the child to resort to escape mechanisms, seek gender-affirming communities and engage in high-risk-taking behaviour. Research indicates that rejection from the family is the most significant cause of depression, hopelessness and suicidal tendencies. Support from even one close family member or parent can help buffer the effects of stigma (Koken et al., 2009) and is related to healthier sexual behaviour (Wilson et al., 2012). Social support is related to feelings of acceptance (Koken et al., 2009), positive emotions (Budge et al., 2013) and decreased psychological distress in trans individuals (Davey et al., 2014; Moody & Smith, 2013; Nuttbrock et al., 2002; Rotondi et al., 2011).

Conversely, a lack of social support for trans-individuals is associated with emotional hardship (Budge et al., 2013; Moody & Smith, 2013) and risky sexual behaviour (Pinto et al., 2008; Wilson et al., 2012). The representation of sheer fear, angst and revulsion from the parent who himself is coming to terms with this revelation adds to this ostracism. The school is yet another place where the transgender individual is subjected to much discrimination, even during the elementary school years (Gay, Lesbian, and Straight Education Network, 2012). Beginning in middle school, lesbian, gay, bisexual and transgender (LGBT) youth are at an increased risk for suicidal ideation and attempts, depression, anxiety, non-suicidal self-injury and being victimised by peers in person or online (McGuire et al., 2010). Lack of response or redressal from the concerned authority communicates a message of approval of harassment of LGBT youth and promotes an unsafe environment for transgender students (Bagley & D'Augelli, 2000). All these factors significantly contribute to a high dropout rate, burnout or indulgence in high-risk behaviours.

10.5 The Myths and Misconceptions Surrounding Gender-Diverse Persons

10.5.1 Myth 1: All Trans Persons Are Born Like That

According to a demographic study conducted by Blackless et al. (2000) and Fausto-Sterling (2000), very few individuals are born with ambiguous genitalia or reproductive organs, including chromosomes and hormones, commonly known as intersex. Only 1.7% of human births can be categorised as *intersex,* that is, individuals born with mixed genitalia (male external genitals and female internal genitals or vice versa). The difference between intersex individuals and transgender persons is that a transgender experiences incongruence between the gender assigned to them at birth and the gender perceived by them. For instance, an individual may be born (unambiguously) male but may think and feel like a female. In contrast, an intersex individual is born with anatomical anomalies which need medical attention or correction.

The only similarity between the two is the requirement for corrective surgery. The intersex individual undergoes surgery due to physiological and anatomical rectification, while a transgender person does so to align their body with the perceived gender.

10.5.2 Myth 2: Transgenders and Eunuchs are the same

Most people mistake transgender people to be the same as 'hijras' or eunuchs. Hijra is a South Asian term from the *hijr* (Arabic), meaning leaving one's tribe. A hijra is a male at birth (and sometimes an intersex person) who goes through a process of *nirvana* to remove his genitals and is initiated into a well-structured group with a guru at the top of the hierarchy. It is a social group with *philosophical, religious and social beliefs, and customs. At the same time,* a transgender person can be a male or a female, preoperative, post-operative or non-transitioning individual who feels significant distress by being born with a particular sex and identifying with another. Transgender is an all-encompassing '*umbrella term*' which includes the eunuch.

10.5.3 Myth 3: Transgender Persons Only Beg, Steal or Are Commercial Sex Workers

Our society is extremely unkind and unaccommodating of transgender persons. They are discriminated against, disowned by families and even abused and violated. The transphobic mindset of the society at large forces them to beg, steal or even become commercial sex workers to feed themselves. Everyone wants to live a life of dignity, but when marginalised and excluded from all avenues of respectful living, one is pushed to beg or steal. Most uneducated or unskilled people fail to find a decent means of living.

10.5.4 Myth 4: All Transgender Persons Undergo Sex Reassignment Surgery

However, another popular myth is that all transgender persons undergo sex reassignment surgery (SRS) to realign their bodies with their felt gender identity. While most of them do seek transition, they may do so at a social level by coming out of the closet in the quest for an open validation of their true selves or even at a medical level, which involves hormonal therapy at the primary stage, followed by corrective surgery at the final stage; how an individual's transition is entirely at the discretion and personal choice of the individual. That said, regardless of the method of transition chosen, a person who experiences significant stress due to being born in the 'wrong body' qualifies as a transgender person.

10.6 Analysing (Trans) Gender Identity: Perspectives and Approaches

Before we embark upon any theoretical analyses, we must understand the difference between gender and sex. Sex is a species' biological and physiological categorisation into male and female. At the same time, gender is socially constructed and refers to the behaviours, roles and attributes the society assigns to the male and female sexes.

Our gender identity, however, is an amalgamation of different factors such as the sex assigned at birth, social roles, sexual orientation and identity.

An interaction of these factors can generate our sense of how we truly conceptualise and envision ourselves.

The different perspectives which highlight the various conceptualisations on this issue are as follows.

10.6.1 The Traditional Approach

The traditional approach endorses the essentialist notion of gender, which takes gender identity to be sacrosanct with the gender assigned at birth. A man, by virtue of being a male, is supposed to act masculine and be attracted to women, while a woman is feminine by being born as a female and should be attracted to men. We are initiated into a social structure which labels a child as early as a foetus and labels it as a boy or a girl. This very first compulsory and institutionalised system supports gender hetero-normativity. This school of thought emphasises the normative binary gender structure and rejects departure from it.

10.6.2 The Social Constructivist Approach

This approach, as the term suggests, views gender to be socially constructed and not innate. It challenges the essentialist concept of gender and asserts that trans-identity can also be socially constructed, as much as the male and female identities. How gender identities are perceived is socially situated, culturally determined and approved. An extension of the Social Constructivist Theory is the performative theory, which reiterates that gender is a 'performance' that people undertake daily. Butler (1990) put forth the view that gender identity was a result of repeated performances of the behaviour that is socially approved and expected of one's sex. 'Gender is a repeated stylisation of the body, a set of repeated activities within a highly regulatory frame that congeal over time to produce the appearance of a substance, of a natural sort of a thing' (Butler, 1990). The important point is that since the social constructivist view deems gender to be a prescribed role, any deviation from it is looked down upon as 'not normal'.

10.6.3 The Postmodern Approach

The postmodern approach rejects the earlier discussed notions of gender diversity and describes it as a more fluid construct to be represented along a continuum instead of discrete categories. It looks upon gender identity as phenomenological and context-specific and encourages the narratives of transgender persons in its quest to celebrate diversity and pluralism. The lived experiences of the gender diverse offer an insight into a new world order where patriarchal and misogynistic notions of gender are challenged.

10.6.4 The Transgender Theory

It emphasises that gender identity emerges as a result of an amalgamation of or an intersection of the lived experiences of the trans-individual and the physical embodiment of that gender. This combination transcends both empirical essentialism and the social constructivist approach. According to Nagoshi (2010), transgender theory integrates this embodiment with the self and socially constructed aspects of identity through the lived experiences of those with intersecting identities. Thus, it provides a theoretical basis for reconciling feminist and queer theories with social work, practice and advocacy about not only issues of working with transgender but more significant issues of social oppression and authoritarian control.

10.6.5 The Medical Model

With the recent publication of *DSM V* and *ICD 11*, gender diversity has come a long way from being seen as an established disorder in the earlier versions of *DSM III and IV* and *ICD 10* called Gender Identity Disorder. This pathologises the gender-anatomical discord, referring to it as a psycho-pathological disorder, explicitly stating that there is only one average gender identity and all other ways of expressing it are flawed and deficient. These diagnoses then further lead to oppressive social policies and an unfair judicial system while continuing to support the traditional gender-based hegemony.

A more expansive term has replaced this erstwhile model of psychopathology, Gender Dysphoria in *DSM V* and *ICD 11*, describing acute distress resulting from the felt incongruence between the mind and the body. This not only reflects a paradigm shift in medicine but also de-pathologises transgenderism by shifting the onus from disease to discomfort.

10.6.6 The Genetic Model

Recent genetics research has pointed towards many factors associated with the development of mind-body gender incongruence. Some of these factors include the following.

10.6.6.1 Androgen Insensitivity Syndrome and CAH

Androgen insensitivity syndrome (AIS) is when a genetically male person has X and Y chromosomes and is resistant to male hormones called androgens. As a result, he may have some or all of the physical traits of a woman but genetically be a male.

10.6.6.2 Congenital Adrenal Hyperplasia

This is an inherited disorder typically characterised by excessive production of androgen and virilisation of the female external genitalia, among others.

The constant tussle leading up to an existential crisis between the mind and the body, owing to different factors (social construction, genetic reasons, normative gender structures, etc.) as explained by the above-described models, manages to sustain a social as well as psychological imbalance within the individual, causing much social, psychological and emotional stress. One's subjective sense of self and identity feels violated.

All this is done to synchronise the mind with the body, to end the intrapersonal conflicts and hopefully reduce the exclusion, discrimination and humiliation that come with the territory.

10.7 Challenges Faced by Transgender Youth

This section explores the different challenges experienced by gender-diverse individuals. These have been classified as follows:

(a) Psychological challenges
(b) Social challenges
(c) Economic hardships

10.7.1 Psychological Challenges

Research (Liu and Mustanski, 2012) has found that depression, bullying and harassment, personal rejection and abuse, and lack of legal protection are the stressors associated with a higher rate of mental disturbance in LGBTQ individuals. They are subjected to interpersonal violence, rejection by the family and large-scale discrimination by mainstream society. Lack of support from the family is known to encourage suicidal ideation and high-risk behaviours. Research indicates that support from even one close family member or parent is known to help buffer the effects of stigma (Koken et al., 2009) and is related to healthier sexual behaviour (Wilson et al., 2012).

According to the Minority Stress Model (Meyers, 1995), social scientists have empirically stated that minority groups suffer from considerable mental and physical health issues as compared to the majority by belonging to a sexual (or racial) minority group, which is stigmatised.

The gender non-conforming are frequently harassed, discriminated and marginalised. They are even denied their fundamental human rights, leading to increased vulnerability and exclusion.

10.7.2 Social Challenges

The gender-diverse youth face a series of social challenges ranging from inequality to discrimination to social exclusion. They have no access to education and are usually denied medical and healthcare benefits. Due to a lack of educational or vocational guidance and skills, transgender persons do not have jobs or a dignified source of income, forcing them to indulge in activities which are bereft of human dignity, like sex work, human trafficking and begging. Their families disown them, and they are humiliated and constantly subjected to sexual abuse and hate crimes. The revulsion of social agencies, including the family, induces feelings of isolation and abandonment, leading to a negative self-concept and poor self-esteem. Society looks down upon them and treats them as unwanted elements. They are not only treated in subhuman ways, they often become victims of physical abuse.

10.7.3 Economic Hardships

Lack of social support, rejection by the family, and psychosocial abuse cause gender non-conforming children to discontinue education (Grossman & D'Augelli, 2006). This leads to a limited array of vocational and employment opportunities for them. They are often disowned by their family and thus cannot provide for themselves. Such adverse conditions force them to indulge in highly risky and less than respectful activities to earn their livelihood, like sex work and begging.

The variety of challenges faced by the transgender youth represent a complex chain of events which tend to reinforce each other, thereby creating a vicious cycle, as has been shown in Figure 10.1.

10.8 Coping Mechanisms

We all respond to challenging situations and events with a psychological or behavioural intervention to contain or minimise the stress that is caused. This individual response to a stressor is known as coping. According to Lazarus and Folkman (1984), 'Coping is the constantly changing cognitive and behavioural efforts to manage external and internal demands that are appraised as taxing or exceeding the resources of the person'. Most gender-diverse individuals tend to focus on passive coping mechanisms (Zeidner & Endler, 1996), like withdrawal, substance abuse, social isolation, etc., instead of using active coping mechanisms like problem-solving, seeking psychological help, etc. Transgender persons who are severely discriminated against, harassed and almost disowned by family indulge in emotion-focused coping. Their ability to respond and recover from the stress is acutely compromised, making them vulnerable to high-risk behaviours such as suicide, substance abuse, self-harm and commercial sex work.

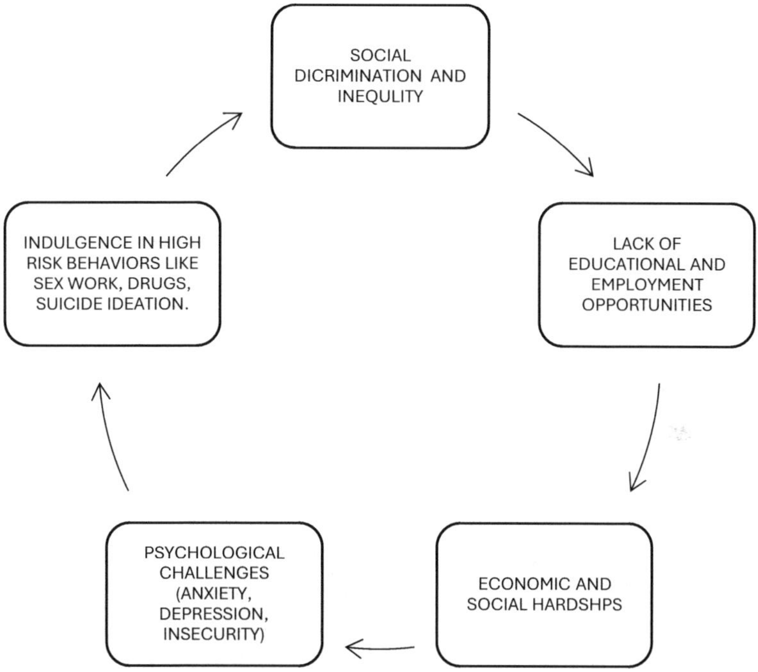

FIGURE 10.1 The Intertwining of Social and Psychological Factors Responsible for the Marginalisation and Exclusion of Transgender Persons

Source: Developed by the Author

10.9 Strategies for the Inclusion of the Gender-Diverse Youth

10.9.1 Recognition and Acceptance of Gender Diversity

Transgender individuals are subjected to extreme violence, discrimination and stigma all because they do not subscribe to the heteronormative gender structure. They feel excluded and are invisible to the mainstream society. Both the state and the society have an obligation and a commitment to protect and promote the interests of minorities. An inability to do so reflects a social and moral failure on the part of society.

We should strive to create a more tolerant and accepting society which recognises and appreciates gender diversity and not a society which challenges their existence. Validation and acknowledgement of diverse gender expressions by sensitisation and incorporating awareness in the general population will promote a stronger engagement from the community and encourage them to contribute as productive citizens. There should be the development of more pro-transgender legislation which incorporates the unique needs and perspective of the LGBTQ community into the external policies.

Transgender inclusion is the responsibility of not just a few but of each person to ensure greater visibility, representation and destigmatisation of the gender diverse. All this can only be achieved by understanding and empathising with them and accepting them with unquestioning positive regard and openness.

10.9.2 Facilitating a Gender-Diverse Environment at Home

In an online research conducted by Durwood et al. in 2017, the aim was to study the *mental health and self-worth of socially transitioned transgender youth*. It was found that parental acceptance and unconditional positive regard at home create an atmosphere of recognition and inclusion, responsible for making these children mentally healthy with a sense of positive self-esteem. Social support for transgender individuals is associated with less distress and higher psychosocial well-being (Budge et al., 2013; Davey et al., 2014; Erich et al., 2008; Moody & Smith, 2013).

Acceptance and support extended by parents and family results in greater resilience and self-esteem in gender-diverse individuals, while rejection and dismissal lead to greater anxiety, depression and other psychological issues. The parent's primary responsibility is to accept their children as they are and nurture them in the best way possible.

10.9.3 Freedom of Expression to the Felt Gender

A gender-diverse individual goes through an intense conflict between the sex assigned to him/her at birth and his/her innate gender. This gender dysphoria tends to be psychologically and emotionally a very stifling experience. Thus, everyone must enjoy the fundamental human right of being accepted for who he/she is. For the gender-diverse person, the experience of being part of an inclusive society would require freedom to be seen and heard without the fear of being intimidated or oppressed.

10.9.4 Early Intervention and Support by Professional Experts

To understand that gender is fluid rather than dichotomous is an urgent matter that merits attention. Parents often lack the necessary awareness to formulate an informed opinion. The role of gender specialists is thus to help both the gender-diverse child and his/her family to deal with the trials and tribulations that he/she might face and also find appropriate channels and outlets to express his/her unique needs. The specialist also helps to build up resilience in the child and family members to societal stressors and discrimination that may occur.

10.9.4.1 Creation of a Safe and Accepting Environment

A recent study by Gordon et al. (2018) indicates that most gender non-conforming young adults between the ages of 13 and 18 years reported feeling more unsafe on the school premises and facing more harassment and bullying than their cisgender counterparts. They were also more likely to miss school or drop out because they felt threatened. Thus, it is imperative to encourage the development of environments which make gender-diverse youth feel safe and wanted.

10.9.4.2 Organise Sensitisation and Awareness Programmes

Teachers, faculty members and school staff need to comprehend that in the contemporary, diverse classroom, the gender binary is replaced by a gender spectrum wherein understanding the gender non-conforming students by being sensitive to their unique needs is of paramount importance. This can be achieved by creating an accommodating, non-harassing environment that encourages openness in communication and expression.

10.9.4.3 Screen Films that Teach Children About Gender Diversity and Gender Equality

Media often encourages and is responsible for sustaining gender stereotypes. It can play a critical role in creating awareness about gender-diverse persons and building a case for their inclusion in mainstream society. Building sensitivity and awareness about gender diversity can also be achieved.

10.9.4.4 Role of a Teacher

The teacher should engage in an empathetic relationship with his/her gender-diverse learners. A non-judgemental attitude towards them and special care and attention to their specific needs, difficulties and lived experiences can go a long way in normalising their inclusion in the classroom. The onus for this rests with the teacher, particularly the class teacher.

10.9.4.5 Use of Trans-Friendly Textbooks

To facilitate an inclusive classroom, a curriculum where gender-diverse voices find representation and expression can go a long way in shaping public attitudes.

10.9.5 Changing Global Scenario

In the last ten years, much has begun to change for transgender persons. They are beginning to gain more visibility and social support. Social networking and social media have emerged as valuable interaction and communication channels to mobilise support for their issues and concerns. According to a statistical report by the Department of Culture, Media and Sport in England (2016), 89.5% of the gender diverse used social media outlets compared to 70.1% of the general non-LGBTQ population. It facilitates interpersonal interaction and ensures privacy and anonymity if so desired. A significant body of research indicates that LGBTQ people use social networking sites to deal with the various social challenges and daily life issues concerning them, like finding a partner or dealing with social isolation (Hillier & Harrison, 2007; Hillier, 2001). More and more gender-diverse individuals use social media to come out of the closet or publicly disclose their gender orientation. Since gender-diverse are marginalised and stigmatised, online avenues offer greater visibility, which in turn helps in combating prejudices and stereotypical notions and moving towards more equality.

In the Indian context, a landmark judgement by The Supreme Court of India (judgement no. 604/2013) in 2013 proved to be a significant milestone which guaranteed the right to a quality life, equality, non-discrimination, access to education and healthcare to the transgender community. It also accorded the status of 'third gender' to them. It entitled them to certain reservations in educational and employment opportunities. While this was indeed a very revolutionary judgement, its repercussions were many. To begin with, the cultural resistance that society held towards gender-diverse could not be dealt with on the ground just by a declared judgement. It required much more work in positing attitude change and societal preparedness before anything could be achieved. To strengthen the cause further, The Transgender (Protection of Rights) Bill (2016) was introduced. The bill provides for the full inclusion and participation of transgender people in society through government measures that ensure their rehabilitation, vocational training and self-employment. It prohibits discrimination against a transgender person to education, healthcare, access to goods, services, facilities and opportunities available to the public; right to movement; the right to reside, rent, own or occupy the properties; opportunity to hold public or private office and access to government or private establishments.

More recently, in a historic verdict (2018), the Supreme Court of India decriminalised consensual same-sex relationships by overturning a 158-year-old colonial provision that previously existed. This verdict recognises the fundamental right under Article 21 of the Constitution, which guarantees the fundamental right to life and dignity of life. The verdict further holds that society has no right to impose morality upon any individual. Bodily autonomy is individualistic and a matter of personal choice. So, the LGBTQ should be allowed to make their own choices without facing discrimination.

All pro-transgender legislations made have been an indication that we are ready to embark upon a new social order which recognises and appreciates gender diversity.

10.10 Conclusion

To conclude the discussion of the above sections, I would like to begin with a quotation by Martin Luther King Junior, which very aptly summarises the predicament of transgender persons. 'Injustice anywhere is a threat to Justice everywhere'.

The principle of social justice may be drawn from this, which at a conceptual level implies equal opportunities to all citizens with no discrimination on any socio-demographic variable. It means that rights and resources are for all. However, what is seen is that gender non-conforming individuals are pushed to the margins and are denied almost all of their fundamental human rights just because they do not adhere to the normative structure of gender. The identity realisation process for the gender diverse thus becomes more challenging. The neglect and stigmatisation meted out to them further compound this process.

Taking cognisance of this, we must all strive to create a society which is open to the recognition and acceptance of different gender identities and is liberal enough to end discrimination and embrace a pluralistic model of gender. It is only then that gender will be looked at as a flexible and fluid variable spread across a continuum instead of being relegated to the binary of being either male or female.

Bibliography

"2016 Hate Crime Statistics". *FBI*. Retrieved 14 November 2017.

Allport, G. W. (1979 [1954]). *The Nature of Prejudice*. Cambridge, MA: Addison-Wesley.

American Psychiatric Association. (1987). *Diagnostic and Statistical Manual of Mental Disorders* (3rd ed., TR). Washington, DC: Author.

American Psychiatric Association. (2013). *Diagnostic and Statistical Manual of Mental Disorders* (5th ed.). Washington, DC: Author.

Bagley, C., & D'Augelli, A. (2000). Gay, Lesbian and Bisexual Youth Have Elevated Rates of Suicidal Behaviour: An International Problem Associated with Homophobia and Homophobic Legislation. *British Medical Journal, 320*, 1617–1618. https://doi.org/10.1136/bmj.320.7250.1617

Benjamin, H. (1966). *The Transsexual Phenomenon*. New York: Julian Press.

Blackless, M., Charuvastra, A., Derryck, A., et al. (2000). How Sexually Dimorphic Are We? Review and Synthesis. *American Journal of Human Biology, 12*(2), 151–166.

Boswell, H. (1991). The Transgender Alternative. *Chrysallis Quarterly, 1*(2), 29–31.

Budge, S. L., Adelson, J. L., & Howard, K. A. S. (2013). Anxiety and Depression in Transgender Individuals: The Roles of Transition Status, Loss, Social Support, and Coping. *Journal of Consulting and Clinical Psychology, 41*, 601–647. doi:10.1037/a0031774

Butler, J. (1990). *Gender Trouble: Feminism and the Subversion of Identity*. New York: Routledge.

Davey, A., Bouman, W. P., Arcelus, J., & Meyer, C. (2014). Social Support and Psychological Well-Being in Gender Dysphoria: A Comparison of Patients with Matched Controls. *International Society for Sexual Medicine, 11*, 2976–2985. doi:10.1111/jsm.12681

Durwood, L., McLaughlin, K. A., & Olson, K. R. (2017). Mental health and self-worth in socially transitioned transgender youth. *Journal of the American Academy of Child & Adolescent Psychiatry*, *56*(2), 116-123.

Erich, S., Tittsworth, J., Dykes, J., & Cabuses, C. (2008). Family Relationships and Their 190 Correlations with Transsexual Well-Being. *Journal of GLBT Family Studies, 4*, 419–432. doi:10.1080/15504280802126141

Fausto-Sterling, A. (2000). *Sexing the Body: Gender Politics and the Construction of Sexuality*. New York: Basic Books.

Goldblum, P., Testa, R. J., Pflum, S., Hendricks, M., Bradford, J., & Bongar, B. (2012). In-School Gender-Based Victimization and Suicide Attempts in Transgender Individuals. *Professional Psychology: Research and Practice, 43*, 468–475. doi:10.1037/a0029605

Gordon, A. R., Conron, K. J., Calzo, J. P., White, M. T., Reisner, S. L., & Austin, S. B. (2018). Gender Expression, Violence and Bullying Victimisation Findings from Probability Samples of High School Students in 4 US School Districts. *Journal of School Health*, *88*(4), 306–314. doi:10.1111/josh.12606

Grant, J. (2017). Injustice at Every Turn: A Report of the National Transgender Discrimination Survey. http://www.thetaskforce.org/static_html/downloads/reports/reports/ntds_full.pdf

Greytak, E., Kosciw, J., & Diaz, E. (2009). *Harsh Realities: The Experiences of Transgender Youth in Our Nation's Schools*. GLSEN Research. Retrieved 12 October 2015.

Grossman, A. H., & D'Augelli, A. R. (2006). Transgender Youth: Invisible and Vulnerable. *Journal of Homosexuality, 51*(1), 111–128. doi:10.1300/J082v51n01_06

Hillier, L. (2001) I'm wasting away on unrequited love: gendering same-sex attracted young women's love sex and desire. *Hecate*, 27(1), 119-127.

Hillier, L., & Harrison, L. (2007). Building Realities Less Limited Than Their Own: Young People Practising Same-Sex Attraction on the Internet. *Sexualities, 10*(1), 82–100. doi:10.1177/1363460707072956

Kitzinger, C. (2005). Heteronormativity in Āction: Reproducing the Heterosexual Nuclear Family in After-Hours Medical Calls. Social Problems, 52(4), 477–498.

Koken, J. A., Bimbi, D. S., & Parsons, J. T. (2009). Experiences of familial acceptance-rejection among transwomen of color. *Journal of Family Psychology, 23*, 853–880. doi:10.1037/a0017198

Lazarus, R. S., & Folkman, S. (1984). *Stress, Appraisal, and Coping*. New York: Springer.

Liu, R. T., & Mustanski, B. (2012). Suicidal ideation and self-harm in lesbian, gay, bisexual, and transgender youth. *American journal of preventive medicine*, *42*(3), 221-228.

McGuire, J. K., Anderson, C. R., Toomey, R. B., & Russell, S. T. (2010). School Climate for Transgender Youth: A Mixed Method Investigation of Student Experiences and School Responses. *Journal of Youth and Adolescence, 39*(10), 1175–1188. https://doi.org/10.1007/s10964-010-9540-7

Meyer, I. H. (1995). Minority stress and mental health in gay men. *Journal of health and social behavior*, 38-56.

Moody, C., & Smith, N. G. (2013). Suicide Protective Factors among Trans Adults. *Archives of Sexual Behavior, 42*, 739–752. doi:10.1007/s10508-013-0099-8

Nagoshi, J. L., & Brzuzy, S. (2010). Transgender Theory: Embodying Research and Practice. *Affilia: Journal of Women & Social Work, 25*(4), 431–443.

Nuttbrock, L., Rosenblum, A., & Blumenstein, R. (2002). Transgender identity affirmation and mental health. *International Journal of Transgenderism.*

Nuttbrock, L., Hwahng, S., Bockting, W., Rosenblum, A., Mason, M., Macri, M., & Becker, J. (2010). Psychiatric Impact of Gender-Related Abuse Across the Life Course of Male-to-Female Transgender Persons. *Journal of Sex Research, 47*, 12–23. doi:10.1080/00224490903062258

Pinto, R. M., Melendez, R., & Spector, A. (2008). Male-to--Female Transgender 201 Individuals: Building Social Support and Capital from within a Gender-Focused Network. *Journal of Gay and Lesbian Social Services, 20*, 203–220. doi:10.1080/10538720802235179

Radhakrishnan, J. (2013). In the Supreme Court of India Civil Original Jurisdiction Writ Petition (Civil) No. 400 of 2012 National Legal Service Authority Judgment. https://www.humandignitytrust.org/wp-content/uploads/resources/NALSA_v._UoI.pdf

Rotondi, N. K., Bauer, G. R., Travers, R., Travers, A., Scanlon, K., & Kaay, M. (2011). 202 Depression in Male-to-Female Transgender Ontarians: Results from the Trans PULSE Project. *Canadian Journal of Community Mental Health, 30*(2), 113–133.

Transforming our World: The 2030 Agenda for Sustainable Development. *United Nations – Sustainable Development Knowledge Platform.* Retrieved 23 August 2015.

Wilson, E. C., Iverson, E., Garofalo, R., & Belzer, M. (2012). Parental Support and Condom Use Among Transgender Female Youth. *Journal of the Association of Nurses in AIDS Care, 23*, 306–317. doi:10.1016/j.jana.2011.09.001

World Bank. (2013). *World Development Indicators 2013.* Washington, DC. © World Bank. https://openknowledge.worldbank.org/handle/10986/13191 License: CC BY 3.0 IGO.

World Health Organization. (1992). *The ICD-10 Classification of Mental and Behavioural Disorders: Clinical Descriptions and Diagnostic Guidelines.* Geneva: World Health Organization.

World Health Organization. (2017). *The ICD-11 Classification of Mental and Behavioural Disorders: Clinical Descriptions and Diagnostic Guidelines.* Geneva: World Health Organization.

Zeidner, M., & Endler, N. S. (1996). *Handbook of Coping: Theory, Research, Application.* New York: John Wiley & Son Publisher.

11

DECONSTRUCTING THE NOTIONS OF SELF AND IDENTITY

Toolika Wadhwa

11.1 Introduction

The terms 'self' and 'identity' are often used interchangeably. 'Identity' has recently found its place in everyday discourse with the permeation of technology in human lives. 'Social networking identity', 'identity theft', 'proof of identity', etc., are some ways we are routinely reminded of the 'value of our identities'. As teachers, practitioners and scholars, we come across literature addressing the theme of self and identity across the disciplines of Psychology and Sociology. Despite the wealth of literature on identity, there is little clarity on how it should be understood. In this chapter, the focus is on demystifying these constructs.

The chapter begins by discussing the overlaps in self and identity. This is followed by a discussion of the various approaches to understanding identity. A brief overview of the works of classical and contemporary theorists in the area follows. This forms the base for raising the field's key issues and debates. Towards the end of the chapter, the abstract and esoteric ideas related to self and identity are provided, grounding by situating them in concerns relevant to present-day school systems and society.

11.2 Deconstructing Self and Identity

Let us begin by taking a minute to think about our primary school experiences. Most of us would have undergone the experience of writing sentences in the language class on 'Myself'. Most children write their full names, parents' names and occupations, and where they live and study. As we grow up, the essays expand to include intangible aspects of our

DOI: 10.4324/9781003505501-11

nature, interests, aspirations and the like. This indicates that our understanding of ourselves grows with cognitive development and the expanse of life experiences.

Unfortunately, there is no clear answer to the question above. Recognising this, the present section has been titled *Deconstruction Self and Identity*. In the following paragraphs, the notions of self, identity and related constructs will be discussed in detail. The purpose is to clarify our understanding of these notions based on existing research literature and theories. It would be prudent to begin by tracing out the history of the study of 'self'.

Academic writing on 'self' can be traced back to the works of Plato in Western philosophy and the Upanishads and Tao te Ching in Eastern thought. Each of their writings addresses questions about self and identity in the context of consciousness and reflexivity. Reflexivity refers to examining one's feelings and thoughts when thinking about one's actions. In the classical view, this was central to understanding the self. For nearly 2000 years, the discussions on 'self' remained a part of religious and theological discourse.

In Psychology, the first discussion on 'self' started in 1890, when William James emphasised the importance of studying the self to understand human emotions. James was one of the first psychologists who attempted to integrate cognition, emotions and physiological responses in defining identity. He felt that the consistency of one's feelings and things that otherwise differed constituted identity (Hammack, 2015, p.13). Most psychologists, however, did not elaborate on James' conceptualisation. Two strands in the study of Psychology emerged. One emphasised studying human behaviour. This strand, known broadly as behaviourism, aligned with the larger trend in academics of scientific experimentation. The works of Allport and Catell in studying personality and developing measurable constructs are significant here. Their works focused on identifying factors that contribute to personality types and traits. Building on their work, many studies concentrated on finding correlations with self-esteem, attitudes, group behaviour and the like (Leary and Tangney, 2012, p. 5). The other strand focussed on intangible psychological processes that contribute towards understanding the 'self'. This was led by Freudian psychoanalytic thought and was furthered by Adler, Horney and Sullivan in the realms of ego psychology, self-psychology and object relations theory (Table 11.1).

Academic writing in the 1970s addressed several themes related to self. These included self-awareness, self-esteem, identity, self-concept and so on. We will revisit these themes a little later. Baumeister (1998) concluded that given the vast spectrum of writings in the area, the self may be seen as an aggregate of all related subtopics. It has since been argued that self-reflection is central to all of these. It is a reflection of our 'selves' that differentiates us from animals (Figure 11.1).

TABLE 11.1 Different Theoretical Perspectives on Self

Ego Psychology *relies upon the structural model of personality proposed by Freud and studies an individual's interaction with the external world and one's inner forces. Thus, Freudian concepts of id, ego and superego form the basis of this approach.*
In *Self-Psychology*, the focus is on understanding individuals from their subjective, experiential world view. Thus, therapists tend to rely on empathetic relations with clients to develop a deeper understanding of them. This strand is often considered the beginning of the relational approach to psychodynamic therapy.
In *Object Relations Theory*, the process of development of self in relation to others is considered significant. The theory emphasises that our relations with others around us in adult life are based on our experiences during childhood.
If you would like to read more about each of these theories, you may explore the works of Anna Freud, Hartman and Rapaport for Ego Psychology; Heinz Kohut for Self-Psychology; and Ronald Fairbairn's work for Object Relations Theory.

In a subsequent section, we will discuss the theories propounded by a few psychologists under each of the approaches mentioned above. Let us first look at the various constructs of self and identity.

11.3 Self and Identity

James (1890) studied how people view themselves and how their perceptions of self affect their well-being and interpersonal relationships. Subsequent theorists have studied the differences and overlaps in self and identity (Roeser et al., 2006; Côté & Levine, 2002). Contemporary psychologists believe that both 'self' and 'identity' are 'part of the process of developing a sense of who one is' (Schwartz et al., 2010). Identity is a search for and deciding on a set of commitments. Self is the view that developments form and influence the commitments made.

Self-concept is seen to emerge during infancy, whereas the development of identity is seen as unique to adolescence. It is believed that the development of cognitive abilities facilitates identity development. Greater choices than responsibilities also mark adolescence compared to later life stages. Further, accumulated life experiences also support identity development during adolescence.

Theorists also argue that self and identity differ in the relative emphasis placed on the reference to a person's inner world and the external social world. Identity is seen to focus more on the sameness and differences that link the internal world of subjective, psychological experiences with the outer world. The self, in turn, refers to how one perceives one's inner world.

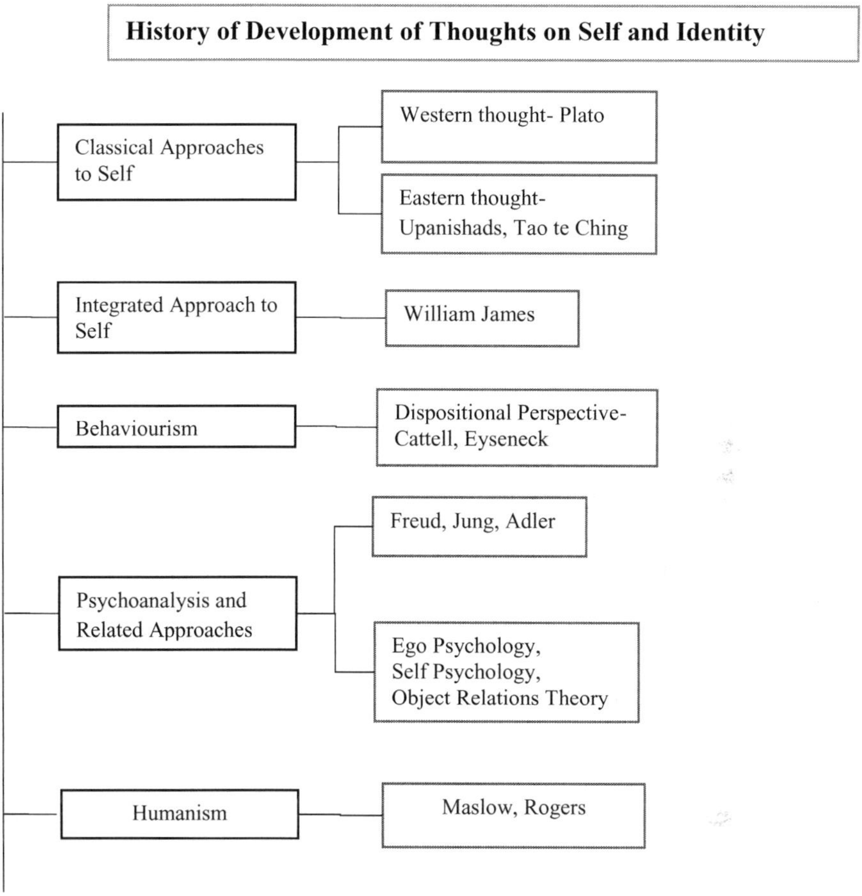

FIGURE 11.1 Developments in the Study of Self and Identity

Source: Author

In simpler words, the self is an individual, psychological process; identity serves as a tool to present the self to the social and relational world.

11.4 Self-Concept

Self-concept is the total organisation of beliefs about self in various domains. This organisation or schema (in Piagetian terms) also provides the framework within which we operate. We tend to protect ourselves from any inconsistencies that might arise that threaten our understanding of ourselves.

Self-concept is the holistic view of oneself. This spreads across all domains – abilities, intelligence, interests, and the like. Greater surety and consistency

Negative Self Esteem
teem

Positive Self Esteem

FIGURE 11.2 Continuum of Self-Esteem

in how one views himself/herself represents clarity of self-concept. This clarity, in turn, influences self-esteem.

11.5 Self-Esteem

Self-esteem refers to the sense of worth one attaches to one's self-concept. In developing self-concept, we tend to attach a value to the image we form. In doing so, we develop emotional, subjective responses to the qualities we ascribe to ourselves. If more positive feelings are attached, it implies that we have a positive sense of self or positive self-esteem. A feeling of worthlessness will lead to the development of negative self-esteem.

Keep in mind that self-esteem is not static. It is a dynamic process of continually valuing ourselves and changing our perceptions of worthiness. Thus, we all keep travelling along the continuum of self-esteem (Figure 11.2).

This also brings forth an important dimension of hope. Through proper guidance and direction, a person with negative self-esteem can be helped to develop positive self-esteem. For children and adolescents, good and bad behaviour, academic performance, particularly in examinations, friendship bonds and acceptance, and body image are essential dimensions to which they attach value to themselves.

The case above highlights the critical role of society in developing positive self-esteem. Being accepted by others holds a significant influence not just during adolescence but also in subsequent life stages. Further, we tend to base our self-esteem on how others perceive us. Thus, our sense of self is inextricably intertwined with what others think about us.

11.6 Approaches to Understanding Self and Identity

In the first section, we saw a long history of studying self and identity. Psychologists and theorists have used different approaches to studying self and identity. Some of these will be discussed in this section.

11.6.1 Developmental Approach

The developmental approach to understanding self and identity draws upon growth and development across various life stages. The domain of self and identity expands from childhood to adolescence and beyond. The approach thus tends to focus on the content of self and identity in its expanse from tangible, concrete aspects, such as where one lives, to abstract aspects related to one's beliefs and worldview. Key psychologists who have worked with this approach are Freud and Erikson. Kohlberg also studied the development of self but focussed only on the dimension of morality.

11.6.2 Narrative Approach

In this approach, a greater focus is on developing an integrated perspective of one's self and identity. Proponents of this approach believe that everyone tries to form a sense of one's past experiences, present life and the possible future that can create an integrated whole. The result is a narrative or story with characters, episodes and settings. This approach develops the story of one's life that tends to revolve around a few central themes. This narrative or story is a dynamic conceptualisation that is ever-evolving. Some of the theorists who have worked on the narrative approach to identity development are Cohler and Freeman.

11.6.3 Sociocultural Approach

We had earlier discussed that self and identity are social processes. The developmental and narrative approaches acknowledge that self and identity develop within social contexts. However, the sociocultural approach brings the role of context in the development of self and identity to the centre stage. The approach draws upon the works of Lev Vygotsky. Although Vygotsky put forth his theory in the 1930s, it has only been in the past two decades that the approach has been used to study the development of identity. Contemporary psychologists draw upon the disciplines of sociology and anthropology to understand identity. Simply put, our identities are based on the groups we belong to. Two processes significant to developing social identities are acceptance by others and differentiating from 'others'. Proponents of social identity and ethnic identity believe that sociocultural factors are paramount in our identities. The works of Jenkins (2008), Tajfel & Turner (1979) and Phinney & Rosenthal (1992) are significant in this area.

11.7 Classical and Contemporary Conceptualisations

11.7.1 Dispositional Perspective

Disposition refers to a person's inherent characteristics. It may also refer to tendencies to behave and think in particular ways. The 'trait' approach most popularly defines the dispositional perspective. Trait theories of personality emphasise that personality has biological underpinnings. This is in comparison to 'state' theories that focus on nurturance or the role of environment in personality development.

The trait approach assumes that behaviour is determined by 'traits' that are relatively stable over time. Traits, thus, are the fundamental units of personality. Let us deconstruct the meaning of traits. We can infer that:

- Traits predispose a person to act in specific predefined ways.
- The tendency to act in this predefined way will be independent of the situation. In other words, traits remain consistent across situations.
- Traits remain consistent over time.
- Traits vary across individuals.
- Traits differ across individuals due to genetic differences.

Given the above characteristics of traits, psychologists have tended to measure traits in quantitative variables. A person is given a numeric score that indicates *how much* of a trait that person possesses. For instance, through a standardised test, it may be inferred that a person is 70–80% impulsive. Trait theories are considered part of the psychometric approach because of the tendency to ascribe quantitative variables to personality.

11.7.1.1 Hans Eysenck (1916–1997)

Eysenck proposed a theory of personality based on biological factors. He argued that the genetic traits that a person inherits affect his ability to adapt to the environment around him. Eysenck's initial work was with soldiers, where he developed a battery of questions about their behaviour. The soldiers were being treated for neurotic disorders. He found that the answers to these questions showed internal consistency. Each soldier's responses revealed a set of personality traits that could be associated with that soldier. He called these 'first-order personality traits'. Using the statistical factor analysis technique, he reduced the study of behaviour to many dimensions. In other words, factors clubbed together to form dimensions. The dimensions, or what he called 'second-order personality traits', were identified as

1. Introversion/extraversion
2. Neuroticism/stability

He viewed personality as dependent on the balance between the processes of excitation and inhibition. He also traced back these dimensions of personality to their biological roots.

Let us look at these dimensions more closely.

11.7.1.1.1 Extraversion/Introversion

Contrary to popular perceptions, extroverts are more than just people who are more talkative and expressive. They are more social and tend to want excitement and change. They are often impulsive and carefree, thus more willing to undertake unknown tasks and adventures. Eysenck argued that their nervous system is 'under aroused' and craves stimulation.

In contrast, introverts are quieter and reserved. They tend to be in control of their emotions and wish to plan their actions. They are least likely to get up on the spur of the moment for an outstation adventure trip. They tend to be serious and reliable. Eysenck said this is because their nervous system is 'over aroused' and needs to be calmed to balance out.

Remember that extraversion and introversion are two extremes. In reality, the two lie on a continuum, and people can be more or less introverted or extroverted. A third category is ambiverts, referring to people who lie in the centre of the extraversion/introversion continuum.

11.7.1.1.2 Neuroticism/Stability

Neuroticism is the tendency for a person to be in a state of anxiety or negative emotional state. It refers to the reactivity of their sympathetic nervous system. A stable person is likely less reactive, even in stressful situations. They are likely to maintain a calm and level head. Someone high on the continuum of neuroticism is likely to be unstable and prone to impulsivity, anger or fear. They respond quickly to stressful situations.

At a later stage in his career, Eysenck added a third dimension – psychoticism/normality.

11.7.1.1.3 Psychoticism/Normality

Psychoticism refers to the tendency to be aggressive, causing trouble, lacking empathy and even being cruel. **Eysenck linked psychoticism to high levels of testosterone. Psychoticism has also been used to refer to the tendency towards anti-social and criminal activities. A low level of testosterone refers to normal behaviour.**

11.7.1.2 Raymond Cattell (1905–1998)

Cattell disagreed with Eysenck's view that personality can be understood in only two or three dimensions of behaviour. He argued that it is necessary to look at several traits to understand the individual's personality as a whole. To study personality, Cattell collected data from primarily three sources:

1. L-Data: This comprised life records such as academic achievement, regularity at work, etc.

2. Q-Data: This comprised a questionnaire he developed to rate an individual's personality. This is the now famous 16 PF (personality factor) scale.
3. OT-Data: This is the data gathered from objective tests revealing the individual's personality.

Like Eysenck, Cattell also used factor analysis to identify behaviours that can be grouped in the same people. This helped him to identify 16 personality traits that are common to all. He divided traits into source and surface categories. **Surface Traits** refer to those traits that are easily identified by others and are overtly visible in behaviour. **Source Traits** are not easily visible. They underlie the various aspects of behaviour. Cattell considered source traits more important in describing personality than surface traits.

11.7.2 Psychodynamic Perspective

The psychodynamic perspective shifted the focus from studying behaviour to internal psychological processes. Originating from the works of Sigmund Freud, this perspective emphasises the unconscious processes and childhood experiences of individuals in shaping personality. Unconscious processes are seen to have a bearing on our thoughts and behaviours. For instance, we may not fully know our emotions or unexpressed wishes, but these will guide our behaviour. This will be discussed in greater detail through the work of Freud and Jung.

11.7.2.1 Sigmund Freud (1856–1939)

Freud, known as the father of psychoanalysis, propounded a theory of personality that systematically studies unconscious psychological processes that influence an individual's functioning. He believed that childhood experiences are the most significant influence in shaping the personality of adults. A common example of this is that traumatic experiences during childhood may lead to a neurotic personality in adulthood. Neurosis refers to feelings of stress and anxiety leading to less than optimum functioning. It is to be remembered that these feelings of anxiety or the associated childhood trauma will not be in the conscious awareness of the individual. In other words, the individual will continue to feel stress and anxiety without being aware of the cause. Freud undertook detailed case-based clinical work, documenting his therapeutic processes with his patients. This led to the development of his theory of personality. The paragraphs that follow present the structure of personality in his theory.

11.7.2.1.1 Structure of Personality

Freud divided personality into conscious and unconscious realms, giving more importance to the unconscious mind over conscious processes. In his topographical model, he used the analogy of an iceberg. Like the tip of the iceberg visible over the surface of the water, we are aware of only a tiny portion of our mental activity. Most of our psychological processes lie below the surface. He divided these hidden processes into subconscious and unconscious processes. The subconscious are things we are unaware of but can become aware of if we choose to. The unconscious contains aspects that we are not and cannot become aware of. This unconscious is a repository of all wishes and impulses that we do not acknowledge in our conscious but have a bearing on our behaviour. Some thoughts and desires may be too painful to be brought to the conscious mind and thus are *repressed* or locked into the unconscious. Given the importance of the unconscious mind, the critical aim of psychoanalysis is to make the unconscious conscious.

In addition to the conscious-unconscious divide, Freud provided a structural personality model. He divided the mind into id, ego and superego. These are not physical divisions in the brain but hypothetical conceptualisations of how the mind functions.

Freud believed that the id operates entirely at the unconscious level. Id works on the pleasure principle. In other words, it seeks instant gratification for desires and basic instincts. When a child is born, id is the most dominant. As the child grows, the ego develops from the id. The ego operates on the reality principle. It works with the goal of satisfying the demands of the id in socially acceptable ways. The ego functions in both the conscious and unconscious mind. Subsequently, during early childhood, the child grows up to understand the moral standards followed in the social world around him/her. The superego develops at this stage. Working on the morality principle, the superego motivates individuals to behave responsibly.

The id and superego, thus, are in a constant tussle between fulfilling desires and behaving morally. The ego works towards resolving these internal conflicts. Acting immorally and fulfilling desires all the time will lead to feelings of guilt. In contrast, always behaving morally will lead to many unfulfilled desires. Either of these states will lead to unhealthy functioning. A healthy individual is thus one who is ego-dominated and able to balance between id and superego.

11.7.2.1.2 Psychosexual Stages

Another key aspect of the personality theory propounded by Freud is the five psychosexual stages of development. He divided the development of human beings into oral, anal, phallic, latency and genital. The stages are named after the dominant erogenous zones at that particular time. Freud believed that children are born with an urge to gratify themselves sexually. This sexual energy was termed libido. At the oral stage, the mouth is the predominant erogenous zone. Activities of feeding and sucking thus pleasure the child. At the anal stage, the anus serves as the erogenous zone. Toilet training and controlling bowel movements are the dominant activities. At the phallic stage, the sexual organs become the erogenous zone, and pleasure is derived from stimulating these organs. This is followed by a latency stage where libidinal energy is diminished. At the onset of adolescence, the genital stage sets in, which is marked by the need for sexual intercourse. Overstimulation or understimulation at these stages can lead to unhealthy personality development.

Freud's emphasis on understanding children as sexual beings was and is still widely criticised. If you wish to read further on his work, you may want to search about Oedipus and Electra complexes, defence mechanisms and dream analysis.

11.7.2.1.3 Critical Evaluation

While Freud's theory explains human behaviour, generalisable, empirical evidence does not support it. It is also not good at predicting behaviour. It is thus often criticised for being unscientific. Since his work was based on casework, all the limitations of working with individuals from a particular sociocultural background apply to it, thus limiting its scope of application in other settings. However, his work was revolutionary in its time and focused on the qualitative understanding of individuals rather than arriving at generalisability. Much of the works of later psychologists have supported or refuted his work.

11.7.2.2 Carl Jung (1875–1961)

Carl Jung supported Freud and shared his interest in studying the unconscious. However, he did not support Freud's view of libidinal energy as being only sexual. He believed that libido is psychic energy that motivates and guides us in spiritual, intellectual and creative pursuits. Jung also differed from Freud's belief that the unconscious mind contains repressed memories that are collective of our ancestral past and not just of the individual. Further, Jung believed that not just our past experiences but also our future aspirations influence our behaviour.

11.7.2.2.1 Theory of the Unconscious

Like Freud, Jung regarded the psyche to be made up of conscious and unconscious processes. The conscious mind comprises the ego, and the unconscious contains the personal and collective unconscious. The ego consists of thoughts, memories, and emotions in awareness.

The unconscious is divided into two layers. The **personal unconscious** is the first layer, similar to Freud's unconscious. It comprises the information and memories that are repressed or forgotten. The personal unconscious contains complexes, a collection of thoughts, memories and feelings associated with a single concept. A more significant association with a particular concept would lead to a more elaborate complex and thus, a greater chance of influencing behaviour. The second layer of the unconscious is the **collective (or transpersonal) unconscious**. Jung believed that all members of the human species share this. This comprises memories from our evolutionary history. Certain characteristics, such as fear of the dark, snakes, etc., are imprinted upon us due to our shared evolution. Some of these shared tendencies collectively form archetypes.

Archetypes are thought systems that have the same meaning across cultures. These appear in various art forms, such as music and literature. Symbols across cultures are similar because they have emerged from the shared archetypes across the human race, e.g. the image of the mother or nature gods. Four of his archetypes that are important are as follows:

1. Persona: Persona or mask is the external face presented to the world. The persona conceals the individual's true self and presents the socially acceptable image to the world.
2. Anima/Animus: It is the image of the opposite sex. In other words, it is the unconscious feminine side in males and the masculine tendencies in women.
3. Shadow: It is the instinctive, animal side of our personality. It is similar to the id in Freud's theory. It has both creative and destructive energies.
4. Self: It is the true image of the individual. The total of unified experiences leads one to discover one's fullest potential and capabilities.

11.7.2.2.2 Critical Evaluation

Jung's theory did not enjoy the same popularity as Freud's. It is not as structured and contains many abstract ideas. His theory is also seen as more mystical and obscure. Like Freud, his theory is also criticised for being unscientific and speculative. However, Jung's theory also alluded to the introversion-extroversion personality orientations. In addition, he believed that people function on the thinking, feeling, sensing and intuiting dimensions. These, along with the personality orientations, lead to understanding personality types.

11.7.3 Humanistic Perspective

The limitations of the dispositional and psychoanalytical perspectives led to the rise of the humanistic perspective in psychology in the mid-twentieth century. This is also known as the third force in psychology, with behaviourism and psychoanalysis representing the first two forces. The humanistic perspective focuses on the inner potential of individuals and their striving towards maximising their capabilities. In this section, we will study the work of Maslow and Rogers.

11.7.3.1 Abraham Maslow (1908–1970)

Maslow presented a personality theory based on human needs and motivation. He believed that human behaviour is directed towards fulfilling our needs. This is what motivates us to work and develop.

In sharp contrast to Freud, who studied unwell people, Maslow chose to study healthy individuals to put forth his theory of human motivation. He wanted to study people in optimum psychological health. His theory is most famous for presenting a hierarchy of needs that motivates individuals to work. He also gave the notion of 'peak experiences'.

11.7.3.1.1 Hierarchy of Needs

Maslow described human needs as arising in a particular order. He said that a lower-order need must be at least partly satisfied before a higher-order need develops. The pyramidal structure in which his hierarchy is often presented was, in fact, not developed by him. The structure gives the impression that the need hierarchy is rigid. Maslow had always argued that needs are fluid and multiple needs exist simultaneously. The hierarchy of needs that he suggests is as follows:

1. Deficit Needs: These are needs that lead to a deficiency in life if they remain unfulfilled.
    a. Physiological needs such as food, water, sleep, etc.
    b. Safety needs include physical and psychological safety.
    c. Social needs include love, family, friendship and acceptance from others.
2. Being Needs: These are those needs that lead to leading a fuller life when they are fulfilled.
    a. Esteem needs include being valued by others and by oneself.
    b. Self-actualisation needs include performing to the best of one's ability and potential.

Going by the hierarchy of needs, it can be inferred that people would work towards fulfilling their needs and achieving self-actualisation. At this final stage, Maslow said that people would be able to become what they are truly capable of.

11.7.3.1.2 Peak Experiences

Maslow propounded that actualised people often have what he termed peak experiences. These are moments of extraordinary experiences during which a person feels alive and self-sufficient while being more a part of the larger world. Some psychologists have attributed a mystical and spiritual quality to such peak experiences. Self-actualised people are likely to have peak experiences more frequently, but almost everyone is likely to have peak experiences at some point.

11.7.3.1.3 Critical Evaluation

Maslow's theory is criticised for lacking scientific evidence. The theory also does not present a cause-and-effect relationship between needs and behaviour and is challenging to apply and test. Nevertheless, it was the first theory to present a positive view of human nature.

11.7.3.2 Carl Rogers (1902–1987)

Rogers agreed with Maslow's assumptions about human nature. He added that people need a nurturing environment to grow further. He propounded that openness, acceptance and an empathetic understanding are key to a person's healthy growth and development. Additionally, he believed everyone works towards achieving their goals and fulfilling their desires.

11.7.3.2.1 Self-Concept

Rogers viewed the self as the organised set of perceptions and beliefs about oneself. Self is influenced by the experiences a person has and how they interpret their experiences. He agreed with Freud on the influence of childhood experiences on self-development. However, he did not believe in the deterministic nature of these experiences. He also believed that the environment in later life influenced the development of the self.

The way an individual perceives himself or herself is the self-image. One's real self, in effect, is the self-image and the perceptions others hold about the individual. The ideal self represents what we would like to be. Incongruence between the real and ideal self leads to discontentment and lower self-worth.

Since our sense of self-worth is based on how others perceive us, Rogers propounded the notion of positive regard. Interactions and experiences with signification others are central to developing positive self-worth. If a person feels valued and loved, he is likelier to attach value to himself. This is called positive regard. Parents, teachers and caregivers tend to attach conditions in valuing children. For example, you will be given a bicycle if you achieve good marks. This is known as conditional positive regard. Over time, people learn to assign conditions to themselves or develop conditional positive self-regard. Thus, they value themselves only when they feel they have behaved in certain ways or achieved something. This, in turn, leads to negative self-esteem or low self-worth.

In contrast to this is the concept of unconditional positive regard. Caregivers and significant others view, accept and love the person for what he or she is. Love and acceptance are not withdrawn if the person makes a mistake or does something wrong. This encourages children, adolescents and adults to try new things without fearing mistakes. People who receive unconditional positive regard are more likely to self-actualise. In contrast, persons who have received conditional positive regard as children are likely to seek approval from others in adult life.

11.7.3.2.2 Self-Actualisation

Actualisation is the tendency of individuals to strive towards 'maintaining and enhancing their experience'. In rejecting the deterministic nature of psychoanalysis and behaviourism, Rogers propounded that human behaviour is based on their perception of the situations in which they are. Perceptions of the world around us and the basic tendency to actualise together determine behaviour. The right environment contributes towards promoting the creative potential and goodness that are inherent in everyone. Since each individual is unique, the development will be different for everyone. In explaining destructive behaviour, he said individuals develop a poor self-concept when external factors inhibit self-evaluation.

11.7.3.2.3 Congruence

The self-actualisation process necessitates achieving congruence between the ideal and the real self. Every individual continually strives towards becoming his or her ideal self. When the real self moves closer to the ideal self, a greater sense of satisfaction and an enhanced sense of self-worth result; thus, a person who has achieved congruence between the real and ideal self will have a positive sense of self-worth. Such a person would be an actualising person.

11.7.3.2.4 Fully Functioning Person

A fully functioning person is actualising. He gave five key characteristics of a fully functioning person:

1. Openness to Experience: Rogers believed fully functioning people are more accepting of their emotions. Negative emotions are also embraced as part of the experience, thus allowing them to be honest towards themselves.

2. Existential Living: Fully functioning people are aware of the world around them. They live in the present and are not prejudiced by past and future experiences.
3. Organismic Trust: Fully functioning persons trust their feelings and instincts. Their decisions are based on rational choices and what they think is the right thing to do.
4. Creativity: Rogers believed that fully functioning persons are not afraid of thinking outside the box. They continue taking risks and trying new and different experiences.
5. Fulfilled Life: They are happy and satisfied and live freely. They seek out new experiences and challenges to continually grow and evolve.

Rogers believed that fully functioning persons are happy and often high achievers. Although he gave a set of characteristics, he also posited that becoming a fully functioning person is a goal that only some would achieve. This is also because our real and ideal self is continually changing. It is thus a process towards fully functioning that helps us grow.

11.7.3.3 Self in Society

In the theories discussed above, the focus was on discussing personality and its development. This section will look at classical and contemporary conceptualisations of self and identity. In an earlier section, we have already discussed that the line between self and identity is quite blurred. In this section, theories and perspectives on both self and identity have been presented.

11.7.3.4 Urie Bronfenbrenner (1917–2005)

American psychologist Urie Bronfenbrenner developed the ecological systems theory. He used his theory to explain that the child and the environment within which he/she lives interact to influence his/her growth and development. The ecosystem comprises multiple layers ranging from the child's immediate environment to the more extensive political and economic system within which he/she lives. Each of these ecosystems interacts with each other. The model is typically depicted as a set of concentric circles (Figure 11.3).

The first and the most immediate environment around the child comprises the home, school and peers. This exists in the larger community in which the child lives. This is referred to as the microsystem. The interaction within the microsystem is two-way – the environment influences the child. In contrast, the child reacts to this environment, influencing how the systems treat the child.

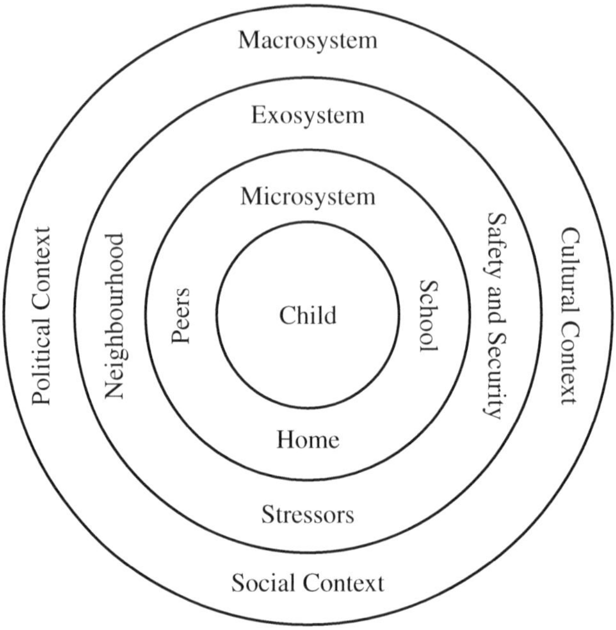

FIGURE 11.3 Adaptation of Bronfenbrenners' Concentric Circles Model

Source: Author

The interaction between the different microsystems, such as the school, the home and the peer group, is called the mesosystem. The influence on the child thus needs to be understood in the complex interplay of the various processes and systems.

The next layer is the exosystem. This represents those influences with which the child may not directly interact. For instance, the larger neighbourhood presents a sense of safety and security. The stressors and tensions the parents experience will also influence how the child experiences the home environment. All these indirect influences hold significance on the child's development.

The macrosystem represents the next layer of the concentric circles model. The cultural experiences of the social and political system in which the child grows up will hold significance in this stage. An example is the variation in everyday experiences of a child growing up in Delhi and those of one growing up in conflict-ridden Kashmir.

The entire ecological model needs to be understood in the context of time. This refers to change concerning the immediate environment in terms of family income, family structure, schooling experiences, and in the context of larger societal changes such as wars and economic cycles. This is referred to as the chronosystem.

It is important to understand each of these systems in their complex interplay to understand a child's development. Further, the child must be looked at in each context to be understood as a whole.

11.7.3.5 Erik Erikson (1902–1994)

Erikson's work is one of the most accepted theories in identity development. Based on Freudian psychoanalytic tradition, Erikson (1963) proposed an eight-stage theory of psychosocial development. He differed from Freud in two significant ways. First, Erikson gave credence to the role of social influences in developing identity. This was in contrast to the Freudian emphasis on libidinal energy. Second, while Freud's stage theory ends at adolescence, prioritising childhood experiences, Erikson's work presented a lifespan approach from infancy to old age. At each stage, the individual is seen to face a psychosocial crisis. The ability or inability to resolve this crisis significantly affects the individual's identity development. Like Freud, Erikson also believed in an epigenetic approach to personality. In other words, the effect of one life stage extends to subsequent life stages.

Two key aspects of Erikson's stage theory are conflict resolution and the stage of adolescence. Erikson believed that development occurs in the face of conflict between the individual's psychological needs and society's social needs. This is why his theory is referred to as the psychosocial theory. At each stage, in the face of this conflict or crisis, the individual learns to accept the difficulties and resolve the crisis. Second, Erikson gave primacy to experiences during adolescence. He believed this life stage is crucial to developing a sense of identity.

The eight stages of Erikson's theory are briefly discussed here.

Stage 1: Basic Trust Vs. Mistrust

At the infancy stage of 0 to 1½ years, the infant views the world uncertainly. The experiences at this stage help the child to develop trust if the primary caregiver can provide stability and consistency in meeting the child's needs. The inability to build trust will lead to mistrust and a lack of healthy relationships later in life. This is generally seen if experiences during infancy are marked by caregiving, which is harsh, unpredictable and uncertain. The inability to develop trust at this stage can lead to anxieties and suspicions about the world around them. These can percolate well into adulthood. Successful conflict resolution at this stage leads to developing a sense of hope in the goodness of other people and the support that can be derived from them.

Stage 2: Autonomy Vs. Shame and Doubt

This stage occurs during early childhood from 1½ to 3 years of age. Children at this age begin to behave more independently as they can move around and make choices in food, toys and the like. New skills are developed in managing everyday tasks. These are essential in becoming more autonomous, such as controlling one's bowel movements, wearing clothes on one's own, learning to bicycle, picking up toys on one's own, etc.

At this stage, if the child is criticised for being unable to complete tasks or perform efficiently, the child is likely to develop doubt in one's abilities. This will lead to a lower sense of self-esteem. The child needs to develop a positive belief in his or her abilities. This can develop only with the help of a parent who supports the child's trials and errors.

Stage 3: Initiative Vs. Guilt

This stage extends from 3 to 5 years. In this stage, the child begins interacting with other children and is marked by opportunities to explore the world through their interpersonal skills. At this stage, the child needs to be encouraged to develop friendships, ask curiosity-based questions and not be reprimanded for initiatives undertaken by the child. The child may sometimes overstep boundaries, so the caregiver must balance guiding and criticising. The child should not feel guilty for asking too many questions or taking too much initiative. Some guilt will be necessary for the child to develop a sense of self-control.

Stage 4: Industry Vs. Inferiority

In this stage of 5 to 12 years, children become more active in school. They begin to learn reading, writing and arithmetic. Teachers play a crucial role at this stage in helping children develop basic skills and master tasks relevant to their age. Peers also play an important role. Competences developed and mastered through industry will be showcased to the social world. Appreciation received will develop a sense of pride in the child, whereas being ridiculed and rebuked can lead to embarrassment and inferiority compared to other children of their age.

Stage 5: Identity Vs. Role Confusion

During adolescence, the individual faces the crisis of developing a sense of identity or facing role confusion. This stage extends from 12 to 18 years of age. At this stage, exploring personal values and beliefs leads to developing a sense of self. At this stage, the child begins to transition towards adulthood by exploring one's goals and deciding about the roles one wants to adopt in the future.

Erikson propounded that the individual faces the typical questions – Who am I? What am I? Where am I going? What am I going to become? – at this stage. Finding answers to these questions may lead to experimenting with different roles before arriving at a final set of principles one wishes to live by. This is known as the stage of moratorium. Failure to find answers to these questions can lead to an identity crisis.

James Macia (1966) extended Erikson's work to present four possible outcomes of the experience of a moratorium. These are referred to as identity statuses.

Identity foreclosure is reached when one has arrived at a sense of identity without adequate exploration of alternatives.

Identity diffusion is when the person neither attempts to explore alternatives nor has arrived at a sense of identity.

Psychosocial moratorium is when the person is still exploring alternatives and has not reached a sense of identity. The exploration may continue for several years before arriving at what one firmly believes.

Identity achievement is reached after having successfully arrived at one's beliefs and commitments after exploring various alternatives.

Stage 6: Intimacy Vs. Isolation

The stage of identity development is followed by young adulthood, where developing intimate relationships with others is paramount. This stage lasts from 18 to 40 years, in which forming long-term commitments with a partner is important. The inability to form long-term commitment during this stage can be because of a fear of commitment, which can lead to isolation and feelings of loneliness and depression.

Stage 7: Generativity Vs. Stagnation

Middle adulthood, 40 to 65 years, is marked by the need to settle down. At this stage, individuals typically view themselves within the larger social context. Giving something back to the society is also significant. Thus, raising children, becoming productive at work and becoming involved in community activities are also important.

Stage 8: Ego Integrity Vs. Despair

Senior citizens above the age of 65 often take retirement from the life of work and contemplate their accomplishments. They develop a sense of integrity if they see themselves as having led a successful life. A sense of despair can develop if one feels dissatisfied with one's accomplishments.

Erikson's theory is appreciated because many people can connect with the life stages propounded by him. However, the theory fails to give any universal conflict resolution mechanism at each stage. In other words, it does not describe the nature of experiences one should have to move from one stage to another successfully.

11.8 Key Issues and Debates

The discussion in the preceding section has focused on the theoretical conceptualisations of self and identity, both explicitly and implicitly. Psychologists have evolved these theories in response to changes in our understanding of the world around us. However, these theories are not comprehensive, either individually or collectively. Certain issues and debates have continued to remain unresolved. Some of these are discussed in this section.

11.8.1 Commitment Vs. Exploration

The identity status theory has been critiqued for being narrow in its approach. The approach also lays little emphasis on social and contextual factors affecting identity development. The key foci of exploration and commitment are more focused on personal experiences. These often need to be contextualised in the social situations in which they are experienced. Contemporary conceptualisations focus on a more socially contextualised way of understanding identity.

It is also argued that individuals may explore different avenues all their lives rather than commit to a particular set of ideas or goals. Any commitment is thus seen as temporary stability before the process of evolution resumes. Some psychologists feel that brief periods of stability are a cause for worry if the process of identity development is continuous and gradual (Kunnen and Metz, 2015).

11.8.2 Assigned and Chosen Identities

Another way to understand identities is to look at assigned and chosen components of identity. As mentioned earlier, identity is understood within the social context in which one lives. Thus, developing a sense of identity fits the various dimensions of one's personality to arrive at internal coherence and a sense of relatedness to the social world (Josselson, 1987). The dimensions thus range across personal and contextual domains.

Research literature based on Erikson's work has focussed on understanding how individuals develop a sense of identity by exploring many choices and opportunities. Occupational identity is one of the most studied domains of exploration. In addition, the domains of religious beliefs and values are also studied (Grotevant, 1992). Phinney and Rosenthal (1992) have explored how assigned components of identity, such as ethnicity, interplay with their choices. Grotevant (1992), using a case of adopted individuals, also studied the interplay between assigned and chosen components of one's identity. He also argues for a lifespan approach to understanding the process of identity development. Other constructions, such as gender and social class, may sometimes act as assigned components around which one must navigate other aspects of identity. Josselson (1987) asserts that before adolescence, most of the dimensions of identity are ascribed to us. These include social class and religious domains, which one lives with and the school one attends. Towards the end of adolescence, one carves out an identity for oneself through the choices made.

It is important to note that assigned and chosen dimensions may not be mutually exclusive. On the contrary, assigned components of identity tend to provide the context within which choices are made, e.g. the religion, class, caste and gender, that one is born in act as assigned components of identity. These can place real or perceived constraints on the opportunities and choices available to the individual. Grotevant (1992) raises an important concern about how society perceives certain choices.

> Are the individuals' characteristics in the assigned domain undervalued by society? When assigned characteristics are undervalued by society, both psychological and societal processes can inhibit identity development. Because of a history of prejudice or discrimination, individual adolescents might develop feelings of inferiority, low self-esteem, and external locus of control, which might in turn decrease their likelihood of self-directed identity exploration in other domains
>
> *(Grotevant, 1992, 83-84).*

11.8.3 Individual and Collective Identities

Most of the theories discussed above focus on the development of self. Many of these theories have evolved in Western contexts where individualism is valued. Achieving one's potential, for example, may not be given as much importance in a collectivist society as would be subordinating individual interests for collective interests. While Grotevant (1992) and Arnett and Jensen (2002) assert that adolescents in America understand religion as a chosen component of identity, this may not be true in other cultures. Arnett and Jensen (2002) write that in the individualistic culture of America, adolescents prefer to form their own religious beliefs with little influence of religious institutions or parents' religious beliefs and their own childhood experiences. However, in a collectivist culture in India and other Asian countries, religion may not be a chosen but an assigned domain of identity. Thus, the struggle to find individual and collective identities will likely vary across social and cultural contexts. In a collectivist culture, making choices towards developing an individual identity would not just be marked by conflict with the outside world of home and the larger community but also internal conflict in making personal choices at the cost of a collective one. Even in collectivist cultures, we see adolescents and young adults striving towards making a mark for themselves. Is this divide between individual and collectivist identities thus only theoretical?

11.8.4 Contextual and Constitutional Dimensions

From the dispositional perspective, we read how personality is seen to tend to have certain traits. Later theorists, including psychoanalysts and humanists, have also given importance to the social environment. Yet we often see people around us with the same traits, likes, habits and preferences as their parents. Is this only an influence of socialisation within the family? The genetic causes of inheriting physical features are no longer debatable.

Individual contexts and constitutional dimensions both impact personality. Psychiatric disorders such as depression, bipolar disorder and schizophrenia are also sometimes genetic. This indicates that thought processes are also marked by heredity or constitutional backgrounds. Nevertheless, the role of context must be supported. Growing up in a conservative or liberal country, being a religious minority or majority group, belonging to a particular caste, class or gender background, being accepted for one's sexual preference, etc., are all social dimensions that are likely to impact one's identity development strongly. The debate between identity as contextual or constitutional thus continues.

11.9 Contemporary Concerns

The discussion in this chapter has provided a bird's eye view of how theorists perceive self and identity. However, self and identity are not esoteric concepts that remain distant from the real world. They are relevant not only to theorists, researchers and practitioners in psychology, education, management and the like but also to people in all domains and age groups. In the discussion earlier, we established how contemporary conceptualisations view identity development as a process that takes place within the sociocultural context. To understand self and identity today, we must thus look at them in today's world's social, cultural and temporal context. In this section, we shall discuss the concerns that have emerged with recent developments in Psychology and the world around us.

11.9.1 Revisiting Developmental Milestones

In the chapter on adolescence, you would have already read how the stage has been argued to have emerged as an artefact of an industrial society. To briefly reiterate, adolescence emerged because engagement in industrial processes eliminated the need for children to work along with their parents. This prolonged the time they could spend in the care of their parents. Over the last few decades, with greater access to higher education, technological advancement and changing work patterns, young adults have had greater lengths of time available to them to explore. While Erikson propounded that adolescents engage in a quest for identity, the world around us witnesses this quest to continue during adulthood. Young adulthood, typically characterised by settling into professional responsibilities and committing to intimate relationships, has emerged as a continuation of adolescent exploration. Pasupathi and Hoyt (2009) said that late adolescence *and* early adulthood are significant periods for consolidating autobiographical memories, which contribute to the development of self. Arnett (2000) coined emerging adulthood to describe this life stage. He visualises this as a developmental life sage influenced by social class and cultural contexts. He argues,

> Sweeping demographic shifts have taken place over the past half-century that have made the late teens and early twenties not simply a brief period of transition into adult roles but a distinct period of the life course, characterised by change and exploration of possible life directions
>
> *(Arnett, 2000, p. 469).*

He posits that emerging adulthood is a distinct life stage from adolescence to full-fledged adulthood in that emerging adults are relatively more independent in their social roles since they are no longer expected to behave as dependent children or adolescents. At the same time, they do not have to shoulder home and family responsibilities. His proposition warrants attention in the context of social trends worldwide. However, his work has not yet been studied in the context of rural and collectivist societies.

11.9.2 Identity in Minority and Majority Contexts

Perhaps more than any other century in the history of human evolution, the last century has witnessed migration across regional boundaries. This cross-border migration for study, work or in search of better opportunities has led to the development of multicultural societies. Cross-border migration may be across the boundaries of states, nations or continents. Melting pot or salad bowl are common phrases used to describe multicultural societies. A melting pot is where people from different regional, linguistic, ethnic or racial backgrounds come together to form a common culture that bears only faint traces of their backgrounds. In the salad bowl theory, the different cultures are more likely to retain their original identity and develop a common one. In a multicultural society, people migrating are likely to form a minority. If they retain their original identities, it is seen as a threat to integrated identities. In contrast, they may lose their distinctiveness if they merge into the common majority culture. This is true for the larger social contexts and schools where students from different backgrounds come together to study.

11.9.3 Developing Fluid Identities

In a multicultural context, we see people trying to find a place for themselves in the intersection of diverse and sometimes conflicting experiences. It was traditionally believed that what emerges is a unified whole impacted by individuals' various experiences. As adolescents and youth struggle to make sense of increasingly pluralistic societies, they develop the ability to have multiple identities. They continue to exist in multiple worlds, often donning the persona of the space they are in at the time. This does not indicate fractured or hypocritical personalities. Instead, they develop multiple identities that suit the various contexts in which they simultaneously exist. It is like wearing clothes that are representative of different cultures in different social contexts. The fluidity stems from this multiplicity where people smoothly transition from being loving parents to strong leaders to being quiet readers to playing in a rock band. Schachter (2004) supported this view as more relevant to the twentieth century.

> These conceptions of self, rather than suggesting an innate striving towards a unified identity, suggest that the more natural psychological state is one of contradictory tendencies (Gordon and Gergen, 1968) and 'multiple' selves (Markus & Wurf, 1987). These conceptions suggest that the contemporary sociocultural context, rather than promoting identity synthesis, requires that the individual manage different self-concepts flexibly
>
> *(Schachter, 2004, p. 169).*

11.9.4 Identity in the Digital Age

The digital age is considered to have begun in the 1970s. Since the first advent of computers, society has evolved phenomenally. Initially, the digital age was characterised by access to information. Access to information changed the way individuals perceive knowledge processes and increased the pace of knowledge generation. This has led to different stressors on what individuals need to know and skills that they need to develop to survive in a changing world. With easy access to technology, social media presence has enabled connecting to a larger world. At the same time, networking websites and apps such as Facebook, Snapchat, Twitter and WhatsApp, among others, have made it important for adolescents, and even children, to make their online presence felt. Psychologists have reported children coming to them with problems of internet addiction, cyberbullying, fear of missing out

(FOMO) and the like. These are indications of the immense challenges that children and adolescents face today. Social identities sometimes overtake real identities, leading to a false sense of self, relying only on online friendships, delusions of fame and acceptance. This book's chapter on social media engagement has already addressed these issues in great detail. At present, it would suffice to say that the digital era has added another dimension to exploring identity. For further engagement, you may read Manago (2015).

11.9.5 Changing Family Dynamics

We have recognised family as the primary agent of socialisation for children. We have also recognised that family dynamics can play a significant role in identity development by providing unconditional positive regard. With industrialisation, migration of families and changing job structure, family structures have also changed. Kakar (2007) contests the popular notion that the traditional joint family system is withering away. He argues that with both parents working, grandparents look after children.

Nonetheless, the dynamics within the joint family are changing, particularly in urban spaces, with more individualism being seen. It may be inferred that a joint family is like a set of nuclear families living together under the same roof, with space for nuclear families and some shared activities. Kakar termed this the 'psychological nuclearisation' of families, leading to greater individualisation of children. The traditional role of fathers has also been replaced by greater participation in the parenting process. The stereotypical roles of fathers and mothers have been replaced by more fused roles marked by mutual respect and sharing of family responsibilities. All of this is likely to impact childhood experiences and identity development.

11.9.6 Navigating School Experiences

Besides family, schools are primary socialising agencies for developing self and identity. The role of the school and the various actors in the institutions, such as teachers and peers, play a significant role in the lives of children. In addition, the school as an institution itself plays a key role. Besides setting the norms and standards of behaviour for children, the school provides children with a sense of belonging. Focus on achievement and rewards presents a system of conditional positive regard for children. Teachers set standards of behaviour, academics and performance that children strive to meet. Repeated focus on failure lowers the sense of self-worth for children. In contrast, when teachers encourage children and help them develop faith in their abilities, unconditional positive regard and self-esteem result. It is also the place where the first peer group develops for children. Peers play an important role in making children feel wanted and accepted for who they are. Constant bullying and teasing can lead children to lose confidence in their abilities. The school environment and teachers can be important in building a sense of self and identity. School uniforms help in building a sense of community identity. Assemblies, house activities and the prefectorial system provide opportunities for leadership and expression. Academic and non-academic activities provide space for discovery and enjoyment. After home, school is likely to be the place where students feel most safe. Yet recent events of harassment, corporal punishment and sexual misconduct have indicated the need to revisit school spaces and tap into their potential to nurture children.

11.10 Concluding Remarks

This chapter presented an overview of theories in self and identity. There are no clear-cut definitions of self and identity. The terms have evolved with developments in the field of Psychology. Understanding that self and identity do not develop in a vacuum and are social processes is important. Thus, contemporary concerns and issues further evolve our understanding of self and identity.

Bibliography

Arnett, J. J. (2000). Emerging Adulthood: A Theory of Development from Late Teens Through the Twenties. *American Psychologist, 55*(5), 469–480.

Arnett, J. J., & Jensen, L. A. (2002). A Congregation of One: Individualised Religious Beliefs Among Emerging Adults. *Journal of Adolescent Research,* 17(5), 451–467.

Baumeister, R. F. (1998). The Self. In D. Gilbert, S. T. Fiske, & G. Lindzey (Eds.) *The Handbook of Social Psychology* (pp. 68–740). New York: OUP.

Berk, L. E. (2007). *Development through the Life Span* (3rd ed.). New Delhi: Pearson Education.

Bronfenbrenner, U. (1990). Alienation and the Four Worlds of Childhood. In R. E. Muuss (Ed.), *Adolescent Behaviour and Society* (4th ed.). New York: McGraw Hill.

Côté, J. E., & Levine, C. G. (2002). *Identity Formation, Agency, and Culture: A Social Psychological Synthesis*. Mahwah, NJ: Lawrence Erlbaum Associates.

Erikson, E. (1963). *Childhood and Society* (2nd ed.). New York: Norton.

Gordon, C., & Gergen, K. J. (1968). The self in social interaction: I. Classic & contemporary perspectives. John Wiley & Sons.

Grotevant, H. D. (1992). Assigned and Chosen Identity Components: A Process Perspective on their Integration. In G. R. Adams, T. P. Gullotta, & R. Montemayor (Eds.), *Adolescent Identity Formation, Vol. 4: Advances in Adolescent Development* (pp. 73–90). New Delhi: Sage.

Hammack, P. L. (2015). Theoretical Foundations of Identity Development. In K. C. McLean & M. U. Syed (Eds.), *The Oxford Handbook of Identity Development* (pp. 11–28). New York: OUP.

James, W. (1890). *The Principles of Psychology* (Vol. I and II). New York: Henry Holt.

Jenkins, R. (2008). *Social Identity* (3rd ed.). London: Routledge.

Josselson, R. (1987). *Finding Herself: Pathways to Identity Development in Women.* San Francisco, CA: Jessey-Bass.
Kakar, S. (2007). Family Matters. *India International Centre Quarterly, 33*(3/4), 214–221. Retrieved from http://www.jstor.org/stable/23006083
Kunnen, S. E., & Metz, M. (2015). Commitment and Exploration: The Need for a Developmental Approach. In K. C. McLean & M. U. Syed (Eds.), *The Oxford Handbook of Identity Development* (pp. 115–131). New York: OUP.
Leary, M. R., & Tangney, J. P. (2012). The Self as an Organizing Construct in the Behavioural and Social Sciences. In M. R. Leary & J. P. Tangney (Eds.), *Handbook of Self and Identity* (2nd ed., pp. 1–18). New York: Guilford Press.
Manago, A. M. (2015). Identity Development in the Digital Age: The Case of Social Networking Sites. In K. C. McLean & M. U. Syed (Eds.), *The Oxford Handbook of Identity Development* (pp. 508–525). New York: OUP.
Marcia, J. (1966). Development and Validation of Ego Identity Status. *Journal of Personality and Social Psychology,* 3(5), 551–558.
Markus, H., & Wurf, E. (1987). The dynamic self-concept: A social psychological perspective. Annual Review of Psychology, 38, 299–337. https://doi.org/10.1146/annurev.ps.38.020187.001503
Pasupathi, M., & Hoyt, T. (2009). The Development of Narrative Identity in Late Adolescence and Emergent Adulthood: The Continued Importance of Listeners. *Developmental Psychology,* 45(2), 558–574.
Phinney, J. S., & Rosenthal, D. A. (1992). Ethnic Identity in Adolescence: Process, Context, and Outcome. In G. R. Adams, T. P. Gullotta, & R. Montemayor (Eds.), *Advances in Adolescent Development, Vol. 4. Adolescent Identity Formation* (pp. 145–172). New Delhi: Sage.
Roeser, R. W., Peck, S. C., & Nasir, N. S. (2006). Self and Identity Processes in School Motivation and Achievement In P. A. Alexander & P. H. Winne (Eds.), *Handbook of Educational Psychology* (2nd ed., pp. 391–424). Mahwah, NJ: Lawrence Erlbaum.
Schachter, E. P. (2004). Identity Configurations: A New Perspective on Identity Formation in Contemporary Society. *Journal of Personality,* 72(1), 167–199.
Schwartz, S. J., Klimstra, T. A., Luyckx, K., Hale, W. W., Frijns, T., Oosterwegel, A., Lier, P. A. C. van, Koot, H. M., & Meeus, W. H. J. (2010). Daily Dynamics of Personal Identity and Self-Concept Clarity. *European Journal of Personality,* 25(5), 373–385.
Tajfel, H., & Turner, J. C. (1979). An Integrative Theory of Intergroup Conflict. In W. G. Austin & S. Worchel (Eds.), *The Social Psychology of Intergroup Relations* (pp. 33–47). Monterey, CA: Brooks/Cole.

12

INTERDISCIPLINARY APPROACHES TO UNDERSTANDING CHILDHOOD

Sandeep Kumar

12.1 Introduction

As seen in previous chapters, the nature of the child and childhood have gathered immense importance as areas of study in the last few years. The rapid changes in the social, political and economic arenas and the availability and use of technology have drawn the attention of researchers, practitioners and theorists alike to explore children's worlds and childhood in different ways and from newer perspectives. It is interesting to note that while, on the one hand, these changes have made children's worlds the focus of study from varied lenses, they have equally highlighted the need to study 'disappearing childhood/s' (Postman, 1982) on the other. In such a backdrop, issues, concerns and challenges associated with children, their development and their experiences during childhood become even more significant to know and explore. In earlier chapters of this book, some have already been discussed in the chapters dedicated to childhood.

Let us begin by reflecting on some personal legacies that influence childhood. What is most commonly observed in this regard is the tendency of parents to pre-plan the kind of childhood they would like to give their child/children in relation to their own lived experiences as children. They typically try to nurture and guide their children in terms of what they cherished, valued or were socialised to do, particularly on matters of culture, values and lifestyle, based mostly on their own childhood experience and to some extent on what they perceive as important features and dynamics of a fast-changing society. The dominant tendency to reproduce what one upholds as appropriate, drawn from one's childhood, strongly influences parenting practices. In a sense, what is seen is that parents construct their native theories about

DOI: 10.4324/9781003505501-12

childhood, what may be called 't' theories about childhood and growing up. These are based on intuition and past experience and are informed by everyday knowledge. So, to understand the child and childhood, it is desirable that the little 't' theories be factored in. Apart from this, there is also a fund of academic and research-based discourse available in the public domain in Psychology, Sociology, Anthropology and even Literature, from which different positions and perspectives about the nature of the child and childhood may be drawn.

A dominant strand in understanding children is to perceive them as social beings who develop in social contexts, making the growing process complex and multifaceted. For a long time, and even today to some extent, studies on children and childhood were/are rooted exclusively in the psychological realm. While this provided an important perspective and helped to build a legitimate discourse on understanding children and childhood, it led to the development of understanding, which was somewhat universalistic, not fully factoring in the role of culture and context in children's growth and development. Furthermore, the importance of diversity as a significant factor was also ignored. Over the years, particularly in the last decade, a more interdisciplinary approach began to emerge, as has already been discussed in the earlier chapters on childhood (see Kaur; Gulati in this book). The influence of sociology, the political economy and rights-based discourse became significant forces in shaping the social theory of education. Social theory became a promising lens through which childhood could be understood in a more contextualised and nuanced manner. However, at the same time, it is important to note that there has been somewhat limited exploration of children and childhood from the lens of social theory. Even so, an attempt is made in the following sections to revisit established trends that mark the dominant ways of understanding children and childhood, such as childhood studies from a developmental perspective and those that focus on predominantly psychological aspects. An attempt is also made to go beyond the disciplinary boundaries of psychology and sociology and locate the understanding of children and childhood in a broader framework that considers a more interdisciplinary approach. The idea is to look at children's worlds and childhoods for what they are in terms of how they are lived and experienced.

To substantiate the above, the work by Adler and Adler (1986), in a sociological study of child development, aptly pointed out the danger of failing to conceptualise the child as a social construct. The need to understand childhood as more than a period characterised by 'socialisation' arose. To this was added the dimension of understanding children's socialisation process in terms of 'social criticality'. Almost four decades ago, studies by Wallner and Pohler-Funke (1978) had already highlighted the need to understand the child and childhood from a social point of view. They had emphasised the importance of the 'sociology of childhood', which they explained was not an attempt to undermine the psychological perspective; instead, it was an effort at building a psychosocial perspective informed by both psychology and sociology through their synthesis. While this quest marked the beginnings of what may be designated as the social theory approach, somehow, it did not gain much popularity in studying children and childhood. It did, however, give impetus to the psychosocial perspective. The psychosocial perspective and social theory approach may thus be seen as interrelated. Unfortunately, the interface between psychology and sociology still needs to be adequately represented in the existing body of literature.

Ambert and Anne-Marie (1986) presented an interesting analysis explaining the absence of a psychosocial perspective. In his understanding, women and children were seen at the margins of a larger universal system and given scant attention. To quote,

> Little attention was therefore devoted to children, who were not accepted as significant members although they did occupy their 'proper place' (again like women) in the lives of the more significant ones (men). This insignificance is still granted to children, whereas feminist scholarship has been able to challenge many taken-for-granted assumptions on womanhood of malestream sociology and has contributed to changes within the discipline itself
>
> *(Ambert & Anne-Marie 1986).*

In such a backdrop, the child and childhood failed to become significant foci of study. While the situation has improved steadily over the years, it is only in the last decade that locating childhood in the culture and context in which it unfolds has become important.

12.2 How Do We View Childhood?

The discussion above points towards concerns about research in the area of childhood, wherein children and adults are seen as separate categories. The work of Ennew (1986) drew attention to the problems with this. She pointed out, for instance, that while analysing childhood problems, our conceptualisation of childhood gets marked in two distinct ways. First, we separate and distinguish between child and adult concerning their roles as protected and protecting, respectively; and second, this separation happens with regard to the work that they have to undertake, where a child is denied her/his role/experience as a worker because s/he needs to be protected and be provided education. These two ideas form the base of our understanding of our notions of a child and the life stage of childhood and continue to reinforce adults to prepare children to become adult members of society. Let us look at the implications of this. The emerging ideas suggest that socialisation as the means to steer children towards adulthood is paramount, and family is the appropriate agency to do this and remain the dominant protective context throughout childhood. In effect, the child is separated from his/her society and associates with it only through family. The child thus has what may be termed a 'family life sentence', which means that the child is often shielded and protected by the family at the cost of her/his freedom and autonomy until she/he becomes an adult. The point to be understood here is that such a conceptualisation is not universally relevant in terms of either the cultural or structural development of children and childhood. It considers family and socialisation inseparable and suggests that all children will be socialised by their respective families. It ignores children who live outside the ambit of family life or in varied versions of family life, such as non-intact families, disturbed homes or even not having a home or parents. It does not recognise that the patterns and structures of the institution of family and family life are changing in the contemporary world, and new practices are emerging. Some of these practices are considered deviant from traditional standards of what a family as an institution should stand for. Many moral and legal questions get raised if there are digressions, even though children might be the beneficiaries. The critical point to be raised here pertains to whether the limited framework within which children are studied at present is adequate or whether there is a need to locate one's understanding of children and childhood in a larger spectrum of situations and contexts. In other words, if digression and structural changes in family life are real, is it not important to understand childhood from more varied lenses? The social theory would take into cognisance factors of culture and context and locate the child within them. There is a need to develop a social theory perspective in studying and theorising about children and childhood. The point raised about multiple childhoods in the earlier chapters on childhood also endorses this view.

Further, there are various ways of constructing the idea of childhood, and many frameworks through which this can be done that strengthen our understanding of childhood cannot be denied. That there is often the use of a specific language, pet phrases and terminology to denote children and childhood, which flows from an adult-centric understanding of children, is also true. The problem is that it gives rise to perceptions and understanding about children and childhood based on the notion of 'the other'. The child's own subjective frame of reference and personal sense of agency are entirely ignored. Taking this ahead, if we were to look at meanings, notions and ideas about children from the framework suggested by Foucault, then the point that he made about 'a critical understanding of particular social practices holding intelligibility different from that available to the participants themselves' (1984) becomes extremely valid. It also compels us to ask ourselves whether we can talk about children and childhood in the absence of embedding the understanding in issues like parenthood and domestic ideology, family style and structure such as patriarchy or matriarchy and who holds the reins of power and control. In other words, adults who employ their ideas and perceptions about the growth and development of their children need to reflect seriously on the issues raised so far.

12.3 Sociality of Child and Childhood

The construction of children in social and educational theories has been seen as an oxymoron: we know about children, but they are still unknown; they dwell in our world but appear to be in another world; they are similar to us but exhibit a different sense of being. Jenks (1982) was of the view that

> the difference between the two positions indicates the identity of each: the child cannot be imagined except in relation to a conception of the adult, just as it becomes impossible to produce a sense of the adult and his/her society without first positing the child.

This has also led us to understand the child's conception in the child's absence. We develop our understanding of children concerning their differences from adults and emphasise the process of overcoming these differences in childhood. Thus, adults become the point of reference for understanding children and childhood.

The inherent danger in this is that the child gets defined concerning what she/he will be in the future and not with regard to her/his present position. The child is seen as being in the process of becoming an adult in the future through the process of socialisation. Socialisation has always been seen to be an influential tool for addressing children's concerns through family, school or society, as discussed in the previous chapters. However, the truth is that children actively engage with the social world in which they live, so their experiences become a rich source of understanding of how childhood unfolds. Stretching the same argument to socialisation, it is important to note that socialisation also poses challenges in researching children. It tends to rely on the adults' viewpoint to explain the various dimensions of children's lives. It may thus restrict our understanding of children as veritable social actors.

Another aspect that requires highlighting is that in addition to understanding the social space available to children, the historical trajectory of changes in the conceptualisation of childhood also needs to be understood. There have been many shifts in this. Every shift endorses the view that childhood is never a fixed or inert concept; instead, it has changed and evolved in different social, cultural, economic and political contexts. So, it is imperative to recognise that childhood is socially and historically constructed.

A historical analysis of the available discourse on childhood shows the changing patterns in the ideas of children and childhood. Aries (1962) highlighted through his writings that adults did not construct a separate stage of childhood in the medieval period. Segalen (1986) shared that the child and the young usually shared a common world because no distinctive space existed to demarcate the self during the Renaissance. Augustine spoke about children's innocence stemming from their bodies' helplessness rather than any quality of soul (cited in Herlihy, 1985, p. 228). The previous chapters in this book by Kaur and Gulati carry a more detailed discussion of the historical trajectory of childhood. They may be referred to.

12.4 Objectifying Children and Childhood

In the history of childhood, it can be seen that many raised their voices against children's helpless and vulnerable conditions. Children were the subject of many scientific research studies conducted by adults (Walkerdine, in Henriques et al., 1984). In the nineteenth century, empirical observations of children assumed importance in studying how a child 'develops'. This became the focus point of discussion, initially raised in the late eighteenth century. The study of learning by children also took different forms, such as presuming that children are tabula rasa (Locke), they can be conditioned as was proved by experiments on animals (Thorndike, Watson, Pavlov), they exhibit maturational acculturation (Gesell), they can build schemas and concepts (Piaget) and so on. A critical analysis of all these views indicates that these theorists view the child as an object. Here, it is important to recognise that when we make a child the object of our contemplation, we take a position as the developers of the child. Parents, teachers and all other significant adults may be considered as the developers of the child. This gives rise to a prototype of a child that explains development and growth in various domains, namely psychomotor, affective and cognitive. This prototype is bio-mechanistically driven and governed. The child's social life is ascertained chronologically, based on cause-effect relations and maturational patterns. As developers, we also become supervisors of children's behaviour and start controlling their bodies, thoughts and behaviour. We think what we are doing is in the child's best interest, but the point is whether it is so.

12.5 Childhood in Attachment and Care Perspective

Traditionally, childbearing, child rearing and child care are tasks associated with women. The facilitation of women in performing these roles does not allow them to detach themselves from their children. They are considered responsible for taking care of children at home. This also allows men to escape from the essential task of parenting and fulfil only socially ascribed masculine roles. Such an arrangement does not provide the required parenting to a child; in most cases, the mother takes the primary responsibility for child care. The ethic of care and the development of related emotions and abilities like empathy, nurture, succorance, prosociality, sacrifice and perspective-taking become the pattern for all girls to imbibe. Whereas in the development of a child, the role of the father and all the emotions listed above are crucial for both boys and girls since they are human qualities.

12.6 Educating Children

Education plays a vital role in everyone's life. Educational practices also influence children and their experiences of childhood. The nature of education and the educational opportunities children get in school depend on many factors. One such important factor is the kind of teacher education a child's teacher has received. This is important because every teacher's understanding of children and childhood is shaped at least ideationally by the teacher education programme that he/she attended. What is commonly seen, however, is that teachers, while interacting with children in the classroom, tend to use an adult-centric approach where they are in command. They pre-plan tasks and activities legitimised as fruitful learning experiences for children. So, they provide structured educational opportunities to children with clear-cut goals and learning outcomes in mind. In the process, they often end up restricting the free space available to children to grow and develop naturally, limiting their spontaneity. Let us read a description of a classroom in a play school in Delhi, India, that was observed to understand how this unfolds.

The teacher (Pooja) was enthusiastic about teaching and asked everyone in the class to participate in the activity she had planned for them.

Reena: Samarth, you come in front.

Samarth: Yes, Ma'am.

Pooja: There are three activities available for you. You can choose any one activity for today.

The three activities are painting, reading a storybook in the reading corner, and playing with building blocks. Samarth was excited about the activities but was taking time to decide what he wanted to do. He said building blocks first and then painting.

Reena: No, you can choose only one.

Samarth was still thinking while the rest of the class was getting restless while waiting their turn.

Pooja: Why don't you do building blocks today; they are good.

Samarth nodded. Building blocks were also limited. He could make only two kinds of formations with them.

Take a moment to think about the classroom processes described above. The teacher was prepared with an appropriate activity to help children learn. She also facilitated their learning processes and was deeply interested in what she was doing. At the same time, one can see that the classroom is adult-centric and structured and reproduces conformity.

The class had ample space for children to make choices. However, you can see that the decision-making was in the hands of the teacher. The class was planned based on an 'adult's understanding of the child'. The choices available to Samarth were few and prefixed by teachers. The decision to play building blocks was also not made by Samarth. It was guided by the teacher, which restricted his agency to choose even from within the limited choices.

Further, the possibilities of experimenting with building blocks were also limited. Samarth had little scope to construct or make other than what the curriculum and the teacher had already structured and fixed. Such class activities are organised within a planned framework to fulfil the objectives of the curriculum. The child thus once again gets objectified. Deviating from these norms often creates special labels for children concerning learner readiness, ability, maturity, etc.

With a tight schedule of classes, lunch, playtime, activity time, games, music, art, etc., the school creates a system of regimentation that ends up controlling the lives of children. The adult intention is honourable and ostensibly child-centric, but such tight schedules create an environment where children's demands are eliminated. Foucault (1984) called it an 'institution of confinement', which structures their consciousness and thinking. Children are expected to fall in line.

It is important to note that these micro-practices play a significant role in determining people's lives and reproducing ideas set by adults for children. Schools and teacher education institutions are sites where this reproduction is legitimised, and children get constructed as 'others'.

'Learning is the outcome of the interaction of an individual with the total context and not the single dimension or aspect of a context' (Kumar, 2015, p. 178). However, children's abilities are understood predominantly concerning their school performance, especially academics. There are two crucial concerns here. First, academics are accorded greater value in comparison to other abilities. Second, as Hutchby and Moran-Ellis (1998) argue, the criteria of ability assessment or competency are adult-centric, making a child non-competent compared to an adult. For this reason, educational policies and practices are future-oriented, focusing on what the children will do in the future instead of what they are today. In other words, education is reduced from 'being' to 'becoming'.

12.7 Revisiting Childhood from and for a Child's Perspective

If we wish to change the existing discourse on childhood, we must detach ourselves from prevalent practices. Polakow (1989) held that 'Piaget's notion of egocentrism and the weight of historical individualist constructs bear heavily on the formation of our symbol-systems, they have very little to do with the child's symbol systems, the child's way of making meaning'.

The interpretive perspective argues for the construction of others to be seen from their perspective. In this case, there is a need to understand the reciprocal relationship between education and children and between experiences and children in which children play an active role. We must also develop a balance and permit dialectical perspectives, which incorporate and emphasise individual and socio-cultural forces at play in conceptualising 'children, their experiences and childhood'. This will provide a space to listen to children, understand what they want to tell us in their language and recognise their worldview.

Such a scenario will require a reconceptualisation of childhood and the role of caregivers in it. Parents and caregivers would be required to facilitate autonomy in children in a safe and acceptable environment. At a broader level, the language of the discourse on children and childhood will change as children are brought to the centre of perspective-building.

12.8 Revisiting Socialisation Processes

The concept of socialisation is the outcome of the idea of a society. It gathered attention as the disciplines of Sociology and Psychology emerged as domains of scientific knowledge. The term 'sociological' focuses on a scientific study, contrasting the prevalent subjectivist social theory perspective. We understand socialisation as a process that helps people form a social community and make social life possible. Socialisation is also a social process that significantly impacts the individual's inner or psychological world. The process of socialisation has an inherent sense of morality. It works towards creating a civilised society that adults accept. Thus, inherent in socialisation are ideas of who is considered unsocial, uncivilised, and social and civilised. Along the same line, a new-born child will be categorised as uncivilised and has to go through the process of socialisation to become civilised within the context of prevalent social, political, economic and technological power forces.

Understanding the process of socialisation in the personal realm reduces it to be seen as a process of internalisation of the social environment and cultural practices within which the child is born. This is the narrow psychological lens which focuses on only internalisation and reproduction.

We have already discussed that the ideology of adults plays a significant role in defining children and childhood. This argument can also be extended to explain the dynamics of socialisation. Although adults alone are not responsible for the processes of socialisation, they play an important role as their positions of power allow them to exercise decision-making on behalf of children, who are at the receiving end of socialisation. The socialisation process is primarily based on and emanates from the perspective of social institutions, which facilitate the reproduction of social practices. Those who can reproduce it more appropriately are considered more socialised. From a functional-structuralist point of view, this process in itself is exclusive. This exclusivity, in turn, protects the interests of the elite by maintaining existing positions, hierarchies and practices. This shapes children's lives by directing them towards a prefixed idea. The child is accepted as an object who does not have the agency to resist prevalent socialisation practices. A further consequence of this process is that it focuses more on the product than the process. The socialisation process focuses on strengthening only those outcomes desired by the agent of socialisation. Alanen (1988) points out that this outcome-oriented process imposes two limitations. First, little attention is paid to the process. Second, outcome-based ideas reject other possible outcomes, ignoring children's possible contribution. In other words, adult-centric and output-oriented ideas dismiss the possibilities of generating alternatives.

Various aspects of socialisation and its processes have been critically questioned about its regulating and controlling nature, linearity, being reduced to internalisation, being outcome-oriented, etc. Studies have shown that socialisation includes ideas, practices and notions beyond reproduction. These include aspects that align with the expectations of agents of socialisation.

Another challenge in understanding socialisation relates to the research methods used to conduct studies. First, the nature of the field (human, sentiment, emotions, etc.) and the methods (scientific) used to study it are inadequate to adequately address the issues of development. Identifying a representative sample and conducting research helps only to a certain extent. The idea is not simply to question the existing research. Instead, the focus is on assessing the appropriateness of the method used for exploring the field. Ethnographies, longitudinal case studies, autobiographies, phenomenological studies and cultural analysis are some of the research methods which can contribute to developing an in-depth understanding of children and childhood. This points towards the need to conduct more field-based research to contextualise theorisation through a grounded approach instead of merely reproducing and testing the validity of existing theoretical dispositions. Such research helps us to understand the complexity of socialisation processes, which are generally understood as linear.

Revisiting the ideas of socialisation leads to an acceptance of the child as an actor in their own life and his participation in the entire development process. Burn (1986) indicated that this reconsideration of socialisation provides a different outlook to understanding children and childhood concerning the connection between social practices that a child participates in and social structures. This also provides opportunities to understand and explore children and childhood beyond family and school and, in relation to significant others, to the social, political and economic spheres of life.

12.9 Childhood: An Ever-Evolving Construct

James and James (2008) state, 'a social construction can be defined as a theoretical perspective that explores the ways in which "reality" is negotiated in everyday life through people's interactions and through sets of discourses' (p. 122)' It may also be seen as the negotiation between individuals and social groups in specific contexts in everyday life. This is an ongoing process that takes place daily, along with the negotiations a child undertakes. This engagement of children in everyday social negotiation makes childhood a social construct.

There is a felt need to incorporate the changes in the discourse of childhood studies concerning the freedom of children in order to embrace their active positions as a contribution to their developmental processes. A strong need is to work through an interdisciplinary approach to understand and explore the child's world. For example, we know that the outside exposure of a child with other children has reduced drastically. This is particularly true in metro cities. The geographical spaces available to children are reduced to the home and a small courtyard. Thus, researchers and practitioners in child development and childhood studies need to work with those in the area of geography to develop an understanding of space and its relation to the conceptualisation of childhood and child development. Such collaborations will generate better social and geographical spaces for children and act as a trigger point for public dialogue about childhood.

There is also a need to look at childhood as an evolving process which changes with time, space and context. With such an understanding, we will also be able to disengage with the constructs of universalism and work towards generating a contextual discourse to address the needs of children.

A study undertaken before writing this chapter included children aged 2–14 in a middle-class colony in Delhi, India. The purpose of the study was to know and understand the changes in ideas about games (play) and space from when I was living there as a young child. Informal interactions included questions such as where they spend their time, what games they play, whether their parents supervise them when they are out for play, where they like to spend their time with friends, etc. Approximately fifty children were included in the study. It was found that there is a significant change, like the games they play and the accessible space. Most children reported spending time at home completing their schoolwork, studying, and playing on the phone or watching television if free. None of them mentioned that they went out and sat with their friends in their free time. Most of the games played were on phone or television. The evenings spent in the park were for playing structured games such as badminton. This sharply contrasts the past when children constructed games that were often unstructured and disorganised. The space and freedom to generate their games are not available to children in contemporary times. Children are under the greater supervision of parents. Parents stay with them, even when they play.

Interestingly, children from low-income families continue to create their games since they do not possess games manufactured in the market. They are also under much less supervision of their parents. They responded more confidently to being asked about their favourite place. Some responded that their favourite places were their friend's house or a particular park corner. In contrast, children from middle-income families sought help from parents to respond to this question.

It appears that technology has brought much change in children's lives and has contributed to shaping childhood experiences. Parents also keep details of their children for every minute of their time. This has reduced the free space available to children and left them with little scope to experiment with social spaces.

The above exploratory study corroborates the notion that childhood is an ever-evolving social construct.

12.10 Multiple Childhoods

Moving away from a universalistic notion of childhood, let us explore the idea of diverse contexts and processes of childhood. Time, space, social and geographical context, political and economic context and many more factors contribute to our conceptualisation of childhood and how children live and experience it. Research which explores children's experiences shows a different picture from the ideas of childhood we are generally governed by. For a long time in the history of developmental psychology, research was couched in the quantitative paradigm, which, while being important, presented only one side of the picture, such as how many children live under the poverty line or how many children are in schools or outside school, etc. While these researches served a valuable purpose, they failed to address children's qualitative issues and concerns. The conceptualisation of childhood presented by them was thus incomplete. In this context, the need to undertake qualitative research in the field of childhood has arisen, particularly talking to children and conducting 'research on children – with children'. Wadhwa discussed some ideas in this regard in her chapter.

The vision is to understand and respect the existence of all children with self-respect and dignity without bias, prejudice and discrimination. It also involves knowing about children from their perspective and how they view this world. We must never forget that childhood is different for all children. So, no ideal notion of childhood can be propagated. Such a discourse will be biased and unrealistic. A positive change will lead us to understand the idea of childhoods instead of a singular conceptualisation of childhood. Gulati and Kaur have already discussed this in their respective chapters on childhood. They have already explained how caste, class, gender, religion, cultural background and their intersections provide different kinds of experiences to children. These aspects influence childhood experiences significantly and often act as determining factors in setting limits to possibilities. The kinds of structures, institutions, and social and cultural practices a child lives will silhouette his or her experiences. There are many other aspects which make childhood varied for children, such as being a refugee, belonging to dysfunctional families, single-parent children, war-affected children, children in conflict zones, etc.

Childhood experiences also differ across regional contexts. Children of developing countries are involved in various family responsibilities, such as a girl child still caring for younger siblings at home, cooking food for her family, etc. Boys also go out with their parents to participate in work. So the childhoods of boys and girls are also different in many parts of the world. Children in developing countries also engage in child labour. It also means that in such contexts, education has to fit around work obligations. In contrast, developed countries provide spaces where education becomes a governing factor for doing work, and work should be set around educational obligations.

12.11 Concluding Remarks

Many narratives and stories that exist provide an understanding of children and childhood. The chapter discussed some of the basic ideas emerging from these narratives. Basically, we require to understand children and childhood from a holistic perspective that goes beyond disciplinary boundaries. While studying childhood, we must remember how we can understand children from their perspective and respect their sense of 'being'. This will also influence the way research is undertaken with children and subsequently bring about a change in social practices. A social theory perspective to understanding childhood is also essential to develop policy-based support for children. It is essential to critically assess and evaluate the position of children and adults in a social context. We also have to know the complexities faced by children. This will help us to understand childhood as a social construct (Prout & James, 1990). This requires situating childhood in the framework of social theory.

Children have to be studied beyond the adult conceptualisation of children and childhood. Children are active social entities who construct themselves through negotiations with various practices in society; as Alanen (2001) said, 'studying children in their own right and from their perspectives, ...

taking children as the units of research and focusing the study directly on children and their life conditions, activities, relationships, knowledge and experiences'. (p. 12) This idea will also centre on 'being a child' rather than 'developing a child for the future'.

The notion of an ever-evolving childhood argues that childhood keeps changing over time, context and space. We have to move ahead from the idea of fixedness of childhood. This questions the prevalent ideas of children and childhood and looks at childhood as beyond a 'permanent social category'.

Bibliography

Adler, P. A., & Adler, P. (1986). Introduction. In P. A. Adler & P. Adler (Eds.), *Sociological Studies of Child Development* (Vol. 1, pp. 3–10). Greenwich, CT: JAI Press.

Alanen, L. (1988). Rethinking Childhood. *Acta Sociologica*, 31(1), 53–67. Sage Publications.

Alanen, L. (2001). Explorations in Generational Analysis. In L. Alanen & B. Mayall (Eds.), *Conceptualising Child-Adult Relations* (pp. 11–22). London: Routledge.

Ambert, A.-M. (1986). Sociology of Sociology: The Place of Children in North American Sociology. In P. A. Adler & P. Adler (Eds.), *Sociological Studies of Child Development* (Vol. 1, pp. 11–31). Greenwich, CT: JAI Press.

Aries, P. (1962). *Centuries of Childhood*. New York: Vintage.

Burns, T. R. (1986). Actors, Transactions and Social Structure. In U. Himmelstrand (Ed.), *Sociology: From Crisis to Science? Vol. 2*. London: Sage Publications.

Ennew, J. (1986). *The Sexual Exploitation of Children*. London: Polity Press.

Flandrin, J.-L. (1979). *Families in Former Times*. Cambridge: Cambridge University Press.

Foucault, M. (1984). *The Foucault Reader* (P. Rabinow, Ed.). New York: Pantheon.

Gilligan, C. (1982). *In a Different Voice*. Cambridge: Harvard University.

Henriques, J., Hollway, W., Walkerdine, V., Urwin, C., & Venn, C. (1984). *Changing the Subject*. London: Methuen.

Herlihy, D. (1995). *Women, Family, and Society in Medieval Europe: Historical Essays, 1978-1991*. Berghahn Books.

Hutchby, I., & Moran-Ellis, J. (1998). Situating children's social competence. *Children and social competence: Arenas of action*, 7-26.

James, A., & James, A. (2008). *Key Concepts in Childhood Studies* (p. 122). UK: Sage.

Jenks, C. (1982). *The Sociology of Childhood: Essential Readings*. London: Bats ford Academic and Educational Ltd.

Kumar, S. (2015). *Child Development and Pedagogy*. India: Pearson.

Polakow, V. (1989). Deconstructing Development. *The Journal of Education*, 171(2), 75–87. Sage Publications.

Postman, N. (1982). *The Disappearance of Childhood*. New York: Delacorte Press.

Prout. A., & James, A. (1990). A New Paradigm for the Sociology of Childhood? Provenance, Promise and Problems. In A. James & A. Prout (Eds.), *Constructing and Reconstructing Childhood: Contemporary Issues in the Sociological Study of Childhood* (pp. 7-33). London: Routledge Falmer.

Segalen, M. (1986). *Historical anthropology of the family*. Cambridge University Press.

Wallner, E. M., & Pohler-Funke, M .(1978). *Soziologie der Kindheit*. Heidelberg: Quelle & Meyer.

13

NEW PATHWAYS IN IDEATING CHILDHOOD AND HUMAN DEVELOPMENT

Vikas Baniwal

13.1 Introduction

Any idea of development implies a changed state preferable to the beginning state. This latter state is considered a worthwhile and desirable end to pursue. This logic of development operates deeply in the field of child development, as adulthood is often considered a more desirable and mature state than childhood. The movement towards something "better" is often justified based on criteria that are considered universal. Within human development, theories adhering to such a position "have portrayed humans as perpetually being on their way toward something and as simultaneously lacking in reference to the intended goals" (Lee & Vagle, 2010, p. 1). Thus, when adulthood becomes a goal in developmental theories, childhood becomes a stage of insufficiency.

This view is supported by Neiman (2015), who explains why maturing is the proper course of action – equating childhood with immaturity when things like reason, emotions, viewpoints, knowledge, and intellectual capacity are all seen as being in their infancy. Due to this lack of maturity in reason, children cannot judge the actions and intentions of the adult world, leaving them open to manipulation and control. Neiman contends that the only way to overcome such helplessness is to grow up, which is worthwhile despite its setbacks, annoyances, and frustrations.

Furthermore, the child is seen as a possible site for intervention for various purposes, from developing productive labour to being a good citizen, which is especially true in India, where the child development discourse intersects with notions of nationalism, national development, anti-colonialism, religious beliefs, politics, and the market (See Malik, 2019). In all these

DOI: 10.4324/9781003505501-13

discourses, it is not the present status of a child that matters but the possible status that must be achieved.

At the same time, the notions of healthy adults are not without some qualities of children. For example, it is noteworthy that while arguing for growing up, Neiman (2015) also highlights the importance of being "young at heart" (p. 194), where one is open to learning and experiencing the beauty of life. Such qualities in children are associated mainly with the romanticised ideas of freedom, innocence, and joy. For a child, it is assumed that adult issues are something that one should stay away from, at least temporarily, but one also needs to prepare to handle these issues. So, childhood is seen as something one must overcome to become an adult. This deficit conception of children and childhood (Matthews, 2008) is called developmentalism.

However, while celebrating childhood, the theories akin to Rousseau (1955) and Neill (1995) argue that growing up is a sort of corruption of the inherent goodness of a child. Even if we consider experience an important facet of human life and expect children to learn and understand the ways of the world, both sets of theories question the prevalent ideals of adulthood and critique the rejection of childhood-adolescent ideals as Utopian and impractical. They also question treating a child "as an object and not as a subject of the social process. Viewed as an object to be worked upon, the child becomes a focal point for the imposition of ideals and ideologies" (Spring, 1975, p. 126). Understanding children and childhood as a site for adult intervention is central to developmentalism.

A critique of the normalising force of developmental theories has also been proposed by Walkerdine (1993) and Wong (2007) from a Foucauldian perspective, in which all theories present social relationships, which create and reinforce or question social norms and expectations. Therefore, no process of theorising is bereft of power; instead, it either propagates or challenges the existing structures of power. Theorising is an attempt to justify one conception of social relationships over others. In this stead, developmental theories present particular images of children and childhood, which are normalised to maintain or question the status quo.

From a Foucauldian perspective, it can be argued that developmental theories are used to create a normative ideal of human development based on the beliefs rooted in sources of power (Cohen, 2008) such as industrial, individualistic, liberal, heteronormative, capitalistic, westernised, and religious values. Furthermore, all developmental theories are adult-centric, i.e. rooted in adults' understanding of children instead of children's experiences. They consider children as powerless, weak, dependent, inadequate, immature, and incapacitated, who need to develop into an adult to be otherwise. Adultism, while overestimating adults, "splits off their negative and failing qualities, and projects these onto children while assuming that all virtues such as being wise, kind, and reliable exist only in adults, and therefore adult control must not be questioned" (Alderson, 2020, p.30). Such a position gives immense power to adults over children.

This definition of a child in relation to an adult brings us back to questions such as, "Who is a child?"; "What is childhood?"; "What should it be?" and "What should growing up mean?" While these questions have already been explored and written about through the book chapters, drawing from the discourse in the philosophy and psychology of childhood and education, the following challenges and issues merit discussion.

13.2 The First Challenge

The first challenge within the developmental theories is how they describe child development. The various popular theories that are studied in developmental psychology, such as Piaget's Theory of Cognitive Development, Kohlberg's Theory of Moral Development, and Freud's Theory of Psychosexual Development, "sought to identify orderly sequences of progressive change in the child as he is 'growing up,' aiming at discovering universal, context-independent stages, and phases of development along various dimensions" (Alanen, 2014, p. 122). They gave neat categorisations related to the growing child's age with different stages of development. They spelt out an expected set of characteristics and behaviours for each stage that could be seen in all children. However, the contemporary position that questions universalism and argues for contextualism as a critical factor in every child's development compels us to look at stage theories differently and focus on the role of culture and context.

Taking the debate ahead, interestingly, Jenks (2005) asserts that unlike children themselves, "childhood is a relatively recent phenomenon in the social sciences" (Jenks, 2005, p. 52). Following Ariès (1962), we understand that children were not always visible in society and that their status was always determined compared to adults' intellectual and physical maturity (see Kaur, this volume for a detailed discussion). This perspective focuses on a child's "lack" compared to an adult. These assumptions affect how one structures the various experiences for children, ranging from early childhood care and education, family and parenting, policy planning, pedagogical practices, understanding "popular" developmental milestones, and designing a child's environment. For example, the "discourses of developmental appropriateness and readiness in early childhood education and developmental responsiveness in middle grades education" (Lee & Vagle, 2010, p. 1) reflect the ideology of developmentalism. So much so that "[t]he fear of being childish dogs the steps of every psychologically insecure adult and of every culture which uses the metaphor of childhood to define mental illness, primitivism, abnormality, underdevelopment, lack of creativity, and traditionalism" (Nandy, 1984, p. 365). With this understanding, old age is often understood as a second childhood characterised by dependence, lack of self-control, loss of control over one's bodily functions, and a self-centredness where one cannot consider others' perspectives.

Historically, the assumptions and theories of child development have been important for various reasons: first, they provided a foundational framework to develop expertise in child development. Even though schooling had evolved much earlier, the public education system required developmental theories that could guide practices on a large scale, which has led to the idea of Developmentally Appropriate Practice (Copple & Bredekamp, 2009) worldwide, in which teaching, counselling, and assessments were to adhere to the developmental criteria. Second, they enabled the creation of programmes and courses for colleges and universities so that students can systematically learn about developmental theories and be ready to work in related professions. Third, they promoted these related professions, such as teaching, teacher education, and child and parental counselling. Fourth, they became the basis of policy-programme criteria such as child welfare and planning early childhood care. Furthermore, when childhood was considered a unique stage, separate from other stages, a systematic study of people going through this stage became plausible, which led to the field of childhood studies. Thus, the developmentalist account became the epicentre of justification for power attributed to doctors, intellectuals, and politicians who were largely males to guide parents — largely females (Mattos, 2015).

These assumptions and resulting theories about child development have been important for various reasons: first, they gave a foundational framework to develop expertise concerning child development. Even though schooling had evolved much earlier, the public education system required developmental theories that could guide practices on a large scale. This led to the idea of Developmentally Appropriate Practice (Copple & Bredekamp, 2009) worldwide, in which teaching, counselling, and assessments were to adhere to the developmental criteria. Second, they enabled the creation of programmes and courses for colleges and universities so that students can systematically learn about developmental theories and be ready to work in related professions. Third, they promoted these related professions, such as teaching, teacher education, and child and parental counselling. Fourth, they became the basis of policy-programme criteria such as child welfare and planning early childhood care. Furthermore, when childhood was considered a unique stage, separate from other stages, a systematic study of people going through this stage became plausible, which led to the field of childhood studies. Thus, the developmentalist account became the epicentre of justification for power attributed to doctors, intellectuals, and politicians who were largely males to guide parents – largely females (Mattos, 2015).

Thus, the critique of developmentalism is of "a worldview based on developmental psychology that establishes normative criteria for how a child should develop" (Freedman, 2017, p. 606). These assumptions have changed over time across cultures and social contexts, where it has become more of "a historical and cultural experience and its meaning, its interpretations and its interests reside within such contexts" (Jenks, 2005, p. 53). In the socio-historical approach, instead of limiting the idea of childhood to the adult-child division based on age (the stage concept of childhood) and the developmental concept of childhood, one finds an emergence of the contextualist conceptions of childhood (Alanen, 2014). This conception questions the universal, standard, and milestone-oriented ideas of development – a point already raised in the previous paragraph. This approach can be seen in Vygotsky's conception of dialogue as central to cognitive development as opposed to Piaget's stages of cognitive development; Gilligan's care ethics as opposed to Kohlberg's stages of moral reasoning; and Erikson's psychosocial stages as a move away from Freud's psychosexual stages of development (see Ranganathan, this volume for further elaborations of these theories).

It is essential to highlight that a critique of the universalistic normalising spirit of growing up from childhood to adulthood has not been central only to psychological theories but to philosophical and sociological theories as well. In the philosophical literature, these assumptions have been critiqued significantly by the Philosophy with Children movement. In this movement, philosophers and scholars attempt to show the sophistication of children's thinking by giving evidence to refute the claim that children's thinking is not abstract. The Philosophy for Children movement emerged as a response to the perceived need to enhance critical thinking, communication skills, and ethical reasoning in children. The leading figures of this movement were Matthew Lipman (1976), Ann Margaret Sharp (Lipman & Sharp, 1978), and Gareth Matthews (1980).

Philosophy for Children practitioners argue that the developmental perspective presents children more in light of their inabilities and assigns them an inferior position in society. This guides our various practices and treatment of children so much so that often primary caregivers ignore their own experiences with their children and give importance to the developmental theories while trying to plan the environment and experiences for their children (Matthews, 2009). It presents a deficit conception of childhood where children are seen as incapable of thinking critically and exercising moral reasoning and agency. Burman (2016) also highlights the negligence of cultural and contextual influences on development in the dominant discourse of developmentalism that posits it as universal.

Against the predominant theories of development, Philosophy for Children practitioners argue that developmental psychology is entrenched in physical maturity however, to give a more accurate account of development, "one must first delineate how much maturity is sufficient to develop a particular skill or capacity" (Matthews, 1984, p.117). Secondly, the causality between physical maturity and cognitive abilities must be established to argue for the developmentalist account to be accepted. Furthermore, one would also have to explain how, against the developmentalist account, children can think philosophically. Research is ongoing to answer these questions.

Philosophy for Children recognises the characteristics and attributes of children, such as play, curiosity, wonder, puzzlement, friendship, imagination, and naiveté as potential tools for dialogic inquiry. Children are seen as capable of critical thinking and philosophical inquiry. Children are born curious and ask questions that have philosophical relevance. "Philosophy for Children capitalises on children's natural curiosity to engage them in a philosophical dialogue, i.e. in a deep discussion of questions that have no clear answer and where different points of view can be developed, explained and justified" (Topping, Trickey, & Cleghorn, 2020, p.16). These discussions begin in a very local context but may gradually become universal.

Philosophy for Children looks at the world of children through the eyes of the children and not through an adult lens. These are open discussions in which the facilitator speaks or intervenes only if necessary for the discussion to proceed further while valuing children's voices so that they get to exercise their agency. Hence, Philosophy for Children sessions relieve children of the epistemic injustice they are otherwise subject to. They discuss issues not only directly relevant to their own life but also issues of national and international significance, in which they often display strong moral reasoning and a clear sense of right and wrong with a rational justification. The discussions often build arguments that have been proposed by a seasoned philosopher over ideas such as justice, inclusion, right and wrong, etc., on their own. Matthews believes that instead of comparing children's thinking with pre-defined conceptions of philosophy, it is better "to see whether anything that children say or ask is similar to what some philosopher has once said or asked" (2017, p.55). The basic idea is that one need not necessarily be an adult to think philosophically.

Not only does Philosophy for Children reimagine childhood with better and more respectful treatment for children, but it has also brought about considerable educational achievements. Consequently, the movement is picking pace and is now practised in over 60 countries worldwide. The movement is gaining momentum in schools, colleges, teacher education institutes, and universities (Topping, Trickey, & Cleghorn, 2020, p.16). Considering the specific requirement of the individual context, the movement has taken numerous forms and shapes. The Philosophy for Children (PfC) movement has branched into "Philosophy for Children" or "P4C", "Philosophy with Children" or "PwC", "Philosophical Inquiry with Children", "Philosophical Inquiry", and "Philosophical Enquiry", keeping children and their abilities at the centre.

A critique of the developmentalist assumptions is also visible in questioning the understanding of childhood by the newer sociological approaches (see Kumar, S., this volume for a detailed discussion). In these approaches, children are perceived as individuals with personal experience and agency reflected in their social participation, activities, interactions, experiences, and beliefs articulated in their plays and conversations. This "new" way of doing sociology paved the way for the "everyday-world concept of childhood" (Alanen, 2014, p. 122) that celebrates the lived plural experiences of children or multiple childhoods rather than a singular universal childhood (see Kaur, this volume for a detailed discussion). Thus, instead of understanding childhood as a universal phenomenon, the new approach is to understand it in its plurality as "multiple childhoods" (see Kaur; Gulati; this volume for a detailed discussion). This has significant implications for envisioning children's education and development trajectories.

The concept of multiple childhoods undermines the universality of ideas such as biological age, the distinction between adults and children, understanding of childcare, views about children's employment, and the emotive investments that adults have in children. It also highlights the importance of children's agency and voice. Yet Balagopalan (2014, p. 12) asserts that this position still remains Eurocentric, and experiences of everyday socialisation practices in the "communities in the non-west were to be respected but not desired" (Balagopalan, 2014, p. 13). For example, Carrin (2015) highlights that children in the Santal tribe in India are "expected to control their speech and use metaphors rather than directly express sadness, pain or anger" (Carrin, 2015, cited in Bowen & Hinchy, 2015, p. 321), which indicates that, though young, they are conceived of as persons akin to any adult. The quest to find equal space for expressing non-Western childhood experiences still has a long way to go.

These normative ideals of developmentalism seep into our engagements with children in terms of reliance on developmental goals, developmental milestones, reference to theories proposed in the Euro-American context, conceptualising parenting, defining mental health, disorders, and implicit norms of normality and abnormality. This is more so in the context of education, where the larger attempt is to design a uniform curriculum to cater to the needs of all children. Such attempts overlook the differences mentioned above and lead to mainstreaming at best if not exclusion and marginalisation of alternative voices. By countering developmentalism, it is possible to make space for including diverse perspectives, positions, and experiences. It would entail that the complexity of childhood experiences be acknowledged just as the experiences of adults. Such an approach to child development would help us see children's resistance towards homogenising, totalising, and universalising tendencies of developmental theories.

Another conception of childhood that developed within the "new" sociology of childhood was the structural concept of childhood, which implies

> the existence in a society of a relatively permanent social category "children", and a social and political status that goes with occupancy of the culturally, politically, economically constructed childhood space, in whatever way the category is defined in a particular society
> *(Alanen, 2014, p. 123).*

Understanding the generational concept of childhood, especially in the diversity that characterises Indian society, can lead us to understand the nuances of childhood experiences better.

13.3 The Second Challenge

The second and more specific challenge that these new understandings of child and childhood raise relates to understanding children as moral and epistemic agents. Our understanding of a child ranges from being essentially divine to essentially sinful. However, both these positions take a rather extreme view where, in the former, there will be a fall from the original natural pure state, and in the latter, the child has to submit to be redeemed; both these positions are problematic (Howley et al., 2013, p. 30). As a compromise between these positions, the broader understanding that has emerged is that children have tendencies for both good and bad.

In the domain of morality, many questions about children's construction of morality that recognise their capability and agency have remained relatively unaddressed by developmental theories. For example, Kohlberg's theory of moral development assumes the child to be morally neutral and, following Piaget's stages of cognitive development, learning to be moral through moral reasoning following an age and stage development pattern. On the other hand, Gilligan's "ethic of care" belies a stage theory, recognising important emotions like empathy and prosociality, usually found in girls and women, as the basis of morality. This is a construction of morality based on care, compassion, and concern in which age and context create no bar.

Arguing against the developmentalist theories would imply that we question the oft-accepted theories of cognitive development; for example, adults believe that children have little epistemological grasp, i.e. they cannot tell between truth and false claims. However, Kitchener (1990) highlights evidence to argue that children in Piaget's initial stages can do philosophy as a rational-logical inquiry but not with an awareness of underlying principles or theoretical basis.

> children have a formal logic but not a meta-logic, epistemics but no meta-epistemics, cognition but no meta-cognition, etc. Young children can

> engage in formal deductive inference – they have procedural knowledge – but they do not have an adequate sense of "necessity" and "formal validity" – they lack declarative knowledge and procedural knowledge *about* this procedural knowledge.
>
> *(p.420)*

However, Kitchener proposes a distinction between philosophising about their own experiences and philosophising about ideas they have not experienced. Furthermore, he argues that mere critical thinking is insufficient to call it philosophical thinking; philosophising is a way of life.

Furthermore, highlighting the lack of declarative knowledge, Fedyk, Kushnir, & Xu (2019) argue that intuition is important to children's knowledge. However, it has been marginalised in the epistemological project because verifying, questioning, or tracing the emergence of intuitions is not easy. Further, they argue that "a learner's intuitive epistemology includes a theory of evidence by approximately the age of four" (p.122). This means that children can frequently make accurate judgements about the truth and falsity of epistemic claims. This is akin to the arguments against underestimating feminist epistemology, indigenous, and tribal epistemology (see Pendlebury (2003) for a discussion of feminist epistemology; Carrin (2015) for a discussion of tribal epistemology).

Mascaro and Morin (2015) argue that researchers often confuse children's difficulties in discarding false assertions as a reflection of a conceptual lacuna while ignoring that this could be because of them being trustworthy, attached, or not so bothered about the issue at that moment. Gopnik, Meltzoff, and Kuhl (1999) and Gopnik (2009) provide many examples of children's knowledge. Broadly, the contention is that adult males ignore the knowledge claims of such groups, dismissing them of low or no value. A similar patronising attitude is posed when adult males speak of children's morality. Since children look timid and weak, they are ascribed with highly positive, even God-like attributes.

> [F]irst, the idea of the child as "ritually formed" as he or she goes through the various stages of becoming an adult; and second, the idea of the child as closer to the divine, especially in mythological and iconographic traditions
>
> *(Patton, 2009, p. 218).*

This idea of a child as a divine being leads scholars such as Kakar (1981, p. 27) to note that in India, "thinkers and yogis have not denied the element of nostalgic reverence for childhood in their ideal of the liberated man". This reverence is similar to Neiman's (2015) inclusion of child-like qualities in a grown-up person.

Post-developmental theories see the child as a subject whose articulations may be interpreted but whose unarticulated ideas and lived reality would always be a mystery for the prying eyes of the adults (Kennedy, 1998, p. 31). Such knowledge, being unarticulated by children, is not prone to rationalisation and can be understood as the protest of the Romantics, existentialists, post-modernists, and post-structuralists against the rationalistic enlightenment project. The romantics, such as Rousseau, would highlight the importance of the child's innate ability to grow and respond to the environment, trust the child's impulses, and believe in the child's inherent creativity. Rabindranath Tagore, the Indian poet-philosopher, echoes some of these ideas (see Mukherjee (2020) for a detailed discussion of Tagore's ideas). Existential thinkers will also highlight the importance of a child's subjectivity in order to live authentically. They will question the normalising, standardising, and universal bell-curve approach to development. The ideas of Krishnamurti in the Indian context have many existential themes weaved into his ideas of education and freedom (see Thapan, 2018, for a detailed discussion of some of these themes).

The post-structural and postmodern positions question the possibility of absolute knowledge, reality, and certainty. They question the possibility of universal latent structures waiting to be uncovered. Rather, all understanding is relative to history or society within which attempts at meaning-making are made rather than fact-finding. Here, "singularity is preferred to universality; local knowledge to metanarratives; multiple perspectives and complexity to unity and coherence; diversity to consensus; ambivalence to certainty; meaning making to truth; the possibility of chance in history to natural progress to a preordained end" (Dahlberg, Moss, & Pence, 1999, p. 33). Thus, while appreciating the value of "uncertainty, complexity, diversity, non-linearity, subjectivity, multiple perspectives, and temporal and spatial specificities" (Dahlberg, Moss, & Pence, 1999, p. 33), postmodernism questions any understanding of child or childhood that claims of universality, linearity, homogeneity, and certainty.

In a vein similar to the positions discussed above of the critique of developmentalism by these positions, Murris (2013) argues that not acknowledging children's knowledge and knowing and denying meaningful participation in the processes of knowledge creation, dissemination, and validation is akin to epistemic injustice. Such a position negates the implications of the developmentalist position that "children come to know themselves in relation to the practising of developmentalism's norms and benchmarks" (Taylor, 2018, p. 98) and argues for the consideration of a child as an independent epistemological subject.

This is not to say that the development theories are of no use because they were central to establishing the idea of child-centredness and the importance of considering the child's uniqueness in the developmental project.

Furthermore, "in some contexts, developmentalism is seen as a form of protection against an outcomes-based and standards-driven curriculum, where expectations of preschool children are overly academic" (Kilderry, 2015, p. 119). The attempt, thus, is to revisit these theoretical assumptions to make our practices even more child-centric. The attempt, thus, is to review these theoretical assumptions to make our practices even more child-centric.

In the attempt to give centrality to children's experiences, the idea of Childism is gaining prominence. It "focuses on transforming understandings and practices, not just around children themselves, or even around child–adult inter-generationality, but also around the pervasive normative assumptions that ground scholarship and societies overall" (Wall, 2022, p. 258). This idea has found its place in childhood studies (see Burman, 2016), Philosophy (see Biswas et al., 2023), and literature (see Deszcz-Tryhubczak & García-González, 2023). This is to say that the actual encounters with children must become the basis of theorising rather than the assumptions with which one approaches children and thus understands childhood and literature. The actual encounters with children must become the basis of theorising rather than the assumptions with which one approaches children and thus understands childhood.

Moreover, the modern project of building meta-narratives is not to be dropped because of the failure of the most prominent theories. Instead, this only suggests a need for a robust theory building on firmer grounds. An important aspect to be highlighted here is that in this endeavour, the adults' gaze cannot be the basis for gaining knowledge about children and childhood. Rather, there must be an acknowledgement of children's voices. The negation of developmentalism leads to a reassertion of a child's independence, autonomy, and lived experiential reality.

13.4 The Third Challenge

The third challenge emerges from the omission of understanding children's aesthetic development – developing their sense of beauty. This aspect is absent in almost all theories subscribing to developmentalism. What is seen is that the various theories of development focus on any one aspect of development, such as cognitive, physical, emotional or social, or on some combination of them. Even in the case of the latter, the discussion largely seems to highlight the cognitive aspect of a human being, both individually and socially. Similarly, in the theories of emotional development, the focus is more on emotional intelligence and the management of emotions, which once again supports the view that emotions can be reduced to or are a derivative of reason.

Even if some discussion of aesthetic development is done, it focuses on the performative responses in children – the production of art by children.

However, the criteria that form the basis of evaluating such performances seem to be based on the aesthetic response of adults. It is the adult lens through which we judge children's aesthetics (Lee, 2001, p. 8). Further, it is important to note that some stage theories of aesthetic development have been proposed, akin to Piaget's theory of cognitive development (Wilson & Wilson, 1981). These theories suggest children's aesthetic development depends on their cognitive development; for example, Parsons (1987/1992) argues that children's drawings and their preference for art forms shift from egocentric to other-centric as they grow. Sometimes, their appreciation is also rooted in their moral judgements of the actions depicted in artworks. Parsons (1987/1992) finds a parallel between Kohlberg's stages of moral development and students' responses concerning their judgement of an artwork.

Similar to the critique of Piaget's and Kohlberg's stages of development, the foundational assumptions of these aesthetic theories have been questioned, the argument being that they do not address children's social, cultural, gendered, and emotional contexts. This could be because children cannot express their experiences nuancedly, and their experiences can only be understood by interpreting their responses with a pre-defined framework. This does not let children be seen as independent "human beings" but somewhat limits them to "human becomings" (Lee, 2001, p. 5) who are yet to achieve adulthood. Often, the deficit conception of aesthetics in children "distorts the experience of drawing by disempowering the child, decontextualising their drawing, and re-prioritising white Western and middle-class subjectivities" (Shulte, 2021, p. 63). Thus, there is a need to understand aesthetics within the experiential reality of children, and only after that must one attempt any theorising.

13.5 The Fourth Challenge

This brings us to the last and more fundamental challenge of the possibility of understanding children while not being a child oneself. This challenge arises when we accept that children's experiences and states of mind radically differ from adults, creating a chasm across which the adults try to understand children. To put it in the context of developmentalism, the child's actual position in the social world, succinctly articulated by Kennedy (1998), has been that of a "marginalised subject", "economically disenfranchised", "ontological other", "epistemically incomplete", "cultural outsider", and "marginalised other" (Kennedy, 1998, pp. 30–31). Similar imagination of a child as "incompetent or subordinate", "economic investment", or "means of forming a family and giving status" have been highlighted by Montgomery (2008, pp. 50–77). Thus, the child becomes an "other" to adults, to the knowing gaze of the psychologist, and to the socially shared norms in which the child is being socialised. This viewing of children and their problems from an adult perspective is termed Adultism and Adult-centrism (Goode, 1986).

This marginalisation of children based on developmental theories seems not much different from the marginalisation based on theories highlighting differences among people of gender, class, race, or caste. Their voices have been largely absent; they have been economically dependent and considered akin to property (Kennedy, 1998, p. 30). A parallel can also be drawn between the adult attitude of infantilising children and the colonised one, typified by asserting the superiority of the coloniser's knowledge, power, and discourse (Taylor, 2018, p. 100). Goode (1986, p. 85) finds the position of an adult reforming a child to be parallel to that of a missionary, where adults do not have to justify their actions to children. It is important to draw these parallels because they help us reflect on children's marginalised status.

Nevertheless, even if the otherness of children has been positively construed in the form of an expression of the divine, of the supremely conscious, and of the purest expression of all that is good in humans, the child remains an "other", whose otherness is either below or above the adult, but never an equal. This attitude towards children as the "other", when put into action, constitutes the basis of our social politics of development. They are reflected in our emphasis on one or the other defining aspect of being a child. For example, if we emphasise the physiological differences but the same psychological make-up, then children need to be trained to fully develop or become a source of labour. Neo-Marxists, thus, see "developmentalism as the ideological support for a type of labour discipline that obscures and constrains workers' emancipatory praxis" (Howley et al., 2013, p. 44). But, if cognitive make-up is essential, our education must stimulate them to think. Similarly, if the emotional life of children is kept at the centre, then care, love, warmth, and nurturing become the considerations for development change. A significant assertion here is that aesthetic sensibilities must be developed throughout a human's life if one considers aesthetics an integral part of being human.

While none of these positions is exclusive to parenting or education, the focus keeps shifting. A developmental theory intends to explain development holistically, but a compelling question arises: is such a theory possible? If yes, then would such a theory not make children all the more manipulable? Would it not take the otherness of child and childhood away? One possible response to this way of formulating the question about children and childhood is to think of them as the radical "other" to whom the primary and most essential attitude should be that of responsibility. This idea is reflected in the ideas of Levinas (see Derrida, 1998) for whom there is an irreducible difference between the self and the 'other'. Thus, the self of the adult researcher must accept that the otherness of children is irreducible and unfathomable in its entirety. In this formulation, interestingly, the lack of a complete developmental theory may also seem liberatory because it provides space for divergent voices and children's lived experiences.

13.6 Moving Ahead

As discussed above, in developmentalism, the child is seen as an "other", their experiences ignored, knowledge undermined, capacities undeveloped, aesthetics ignored, and morality invisible. One way in which scholars have attempted to bridge that chiasm of otherness without undermining the differences is through dialogue. Many scholars who argue against developmentalism of different sorts refer to dialogue as a way to question the inherent adultism. Through dialogue, they critique childhood developmentalism by challenging pedagogies rooted in the assumptions and implications of developmentalist theories that have shaped early childhood education. Dialogue questions the notion of universal stages and age norms and recognises the multiple and contextual ways that children learn and grow. Dialogue is a pedagogical approach that values children's diversity, complexity, and agency. By encouraging children to engage in collaborative, Socratic, reflective, dialogical, and inquiry-based conversations with their peers and teachers, an attempt is made to question the power relations and discourses that have constructed children as lacking, deficient, or incomplete and instead affirms their rights, capabilities, and contributions as co-constructors of knowledge and meaning. Dialogue helps transition from the position where children are considered epistemically inferior and passive recipients of knowledge, such that their hierarchically low status is consolidated so that children are empowered and "conscientized" (Freire, 2005). Dialogue, therefore, offers a critical and democratic alternative to developmentalism and invites educators to rethink their practices and policies concerning children. This moves away from the epistemic "incompleteness" or the ontological otherness of children vis-a-vis adults.

Building on these strengths of dialogue, attempts have been made to demonstrate the quality of children's thinking in dialogues. For example, Matthews developed a unique method which consisted of the following steps: "(1) write an original, philosophical story-beginning, (2) share it with the children, (3) write a story-ending based on his dialogue with them, and (4) discuss with them whether the final story did justice to their ideas" (Laverty, & Gregory, 2021, p. 7). Children often vote for the question they wish to explore and develop a community of inquiry to present their ideas open to scrutiny. The community primarily functions on critical, collaborative, caring, and creative thinking ideas. In such attempts, children's philosophical ideas become apparent; for example, Gareth Matthews (1980, 1984, 1994) highlights the following anecdote that suggests the famous dream argument from Descartes: "TIM (about six years), while busily engaged in licking a pot, asked, 'Papa, how can we be sure that everything is not a dream?' " (Matthews, 1980, p. 1).

Similarly, another anecdote raises questions about fairness and justice:

> IAN (six years) found to his chagrin that the three children of his parents' friends monopolised the television; they kept him from watching his favourite program. 'Mother,' he asked in frustration, 'why is it better for three people to be selfish than for one?'
>
> *(Matthews, 1980, p.28).*

Such dialogues show that adults "can profitably reflect on with children questions that should not be considered the exclusive province of professional philosophers" (Matthews, 1984, p. 3). Further, they also demonstrate "the possibility of having a relationship with children that is different" (p. 3) and unique. These dialogues are important not just for pleasure and the excitement of witnessing children engage with such deep questions; rather, "children can help us adults, investigate and reflect on interesting and important questions and that the children's contributions may be quite as valuable as any we adults have to offer" (p.3). Thus, such pedagogical explorations give voice to children and bring their lived reality to the fore in their own words.

As a result of such theoretical perspectives and their relative success in praxis, dialogue has emerged as a prominent method in research with children. Dialogue allows researchers to build new relationships and "facilitate eliciting, hearing, and acting upon children's perspectives, questions, ideas, and experiences" (Siry, 2015, p. 162) and actively involve them in the research process. Dialogue also helps researchers build trust, rapport, and ethical relationships with children and respect their rights, dignity, and agency. Dialogue can also enhance the quality and validity of the research findings, as it enables researchers to co-construct knowledge and meaning with children and to acknowledge the diversity and complexity of their realities. Dialogue facilitates the process of "relational knowing and being known" between children and adults and moves away from the adult-centred perception of childhood and the world of children. Dialogue as a method opens space for seeing together and being with the "other" (Lawrence, 2019). A similar need has been highlighted by Thorne (2007), who argues for the use of dialogue with the more established methods of developmental psychology. Punch (2016) believes that dialogue as a method provides space to the established dichotomies: adult-child, structure-agency, childhood-childhoods, local-global, and universal-contextual to co-exist without one undermining the other.

13.7 Conclusion

The idea behind putting together this chapter as the conclusive one was to reiterate with assertion some of the crucial debates and issues that mark human development, particularly the theories that carry many normative assumptions in their quest to explain the development process. Irrespective of how we understand children's psychosocial development, it is irrefutably true that there are limits to physical growth and development that impact their overall development. The challenge is to conceive of a developmental theory that neither essentialises physical development nor ignores it while conceptualising psychological development.

Further, even if we need to characterise children and their developmental states, we can do so without considering these characteristics necessary because it would give space to acknowledging and addressing diversity. Any essentialising of characteristics of children or childhood has led to a negative estimation of the child as an "inferior version of the adult-as a lovable, spontaneous, delicate being – who *is* also simultaneously dependent, unreliable, wilful and succoured and, therefore, someone who needs to be guided, protected and educated as a ward" (Nandy, 1984, p. 359).

The theory and practice must be congruent with a critical understanding of human development in all these areas because they all are normative, i.e. working with some assumption about "should" and "ought". Hopefully, some of the ideas raised in this concluding note will find expression in envisioning and designing new research on children and childhood. It is also hoped that they will influence policies and practices in schooling, public welfare, children and childhood, and others.

Bibliography

Alanen, L. (2014). Childhood, Concept of. In D. Phillips (Ed.), *Encyclopedia of Educational Theory and Philosophy* (Vol. 1, pp. 121–123). SAGE Publications, Inc.

Alderson, P. (2020). Adultism. In D. T. Cook (Ed.), *The SAGE Encyclopedia of Children and Childhood Studies* (pp. 29–30). Sage.

Ariès, P. (1962). *Centuries of Childhood: A Social History of Family Life.* Vintage Books.

Balagopalan, Sarada. 2014. *Inhabiting 'Childhood': Children, Labour and Schooling in Postcolonial India*. Springer.

Bloom, P. (2014). *Just Babies: The Origins of Good and Evil.* Crown.

Biswas, T., Wall, J., Warming, H., Zehavi, O., Kennedy, D., Murris, K., Kohan, W., Saal, B., & Rollo, T. (2023). Childism and philosophy: A conceptual co-exploration. *Policy Futures in Education*, *0*(0). https://doi.org/10.1177/14782103231185178

Bowen, Z., & Hinchy, J. (2015). Introduction: Children and knowledge in India. *South Asian History and Culture*, *6*(3), 317–329.

Burman, E. (2016). *Deconstructing Developmental Psychology.* Taylor & Francis.

Carrin, M. (2015). Adivasi children and the making of indigeneity in Jharkhand. *South Asian History and Culture*, 6(3), 348–364. https://doi.org/10.1080/19472498.2015.1030872

Cohen, L. E. (2008). Foucault and the early childhood classroom. *Educational Studies*, *44*(1), 7–21.

Copple, C., & Bredekamp, S. (Ed.). (2009). *Developmentally Appropriate Practice in Early Childhood Programs Serving Children from Birth through Age 8* (3rd ed.). National Association for the Education of Young Children.

Dahlberg, G., Moss, P., & Pence, A. (2013). *Beyond quality in early childhood education and care: Languages of evaluation*. Routledge.

Derrida, J. (1998). From Adieu à Emmanuel Levinas. *Research in Phenomenology*, *28*, 20–36. http://www.jstor.org/stable/24659047

Deszcz-Tryhubczak, J., & García-González, M. (2023). Thinking and doing with childism in children's literature studies. *Children & Society*, *37*(4), 1037–1051.

Fedyk, M., Kushnir, T., & Xu, F. (2019). Intuitive epistemology: Children's theory of evidence. In D. Wilkenfeld & R. Samuels (Eds.), *Advances in Experimental Philosophy of Science* (pp. 122–143). New York: Bloomsbury Academic Publishing.

Freedman, J. E. (2017). Disability Studies in Education (DSE) and the Epistemology of Special Education. In M. A. Peters (Ed.). *Encyclopedia of Educational Philosophy and Theory*. Springer.

Freire, P. (2005/1970). *Pedagogy of the Oppressed* (M. B. Ramos, Trans.). New York: Continuum.

Goode, D. (1986). Kids, cultures, and innocents. *Human Studies*, *9*, 85–106.

Gopnik, A., Meltzoff, A. N., & Kuhl, P. K. (1999). *The Scientist in the Crib: Minds, Brains, and How Children Learn*. William Morrow & Co.

Gopnik, A. (2009). *The Philosophical Baby: What Children's Minds Tell Us about Truth, Love & the Meaning of Life*. Random House.

Gunn, A. (2020). Foucauldian Discourse Analysis and Early Childhood Education. In *The Oxford Encyclopedia of Qualitative Research Methods in Education*. Oxford University Press. Retrieved November 28, 2023, from https://www.oxfordreference.com/view/10.1093/acref/9780190643751.001.0001/acref-9780190643751-e-333

Haider, S. (1998). Dialogue as Method and as Text. In M. Thapan (Ed.), *Anthropological Journeys: Reflections on Fieldwork* (pp. 217–267).Orient Longman.

Howley, C., Spatig, L., & Howley, A. (2013). Developmentalism Deconstructed. In J. L. Kincheloe, S. R. Steinberg, & L. Villaverde (Eds.), *Rethinking Intelligence* (pp. 36–58). Routledge.

Jenks, C. (2005). *Childhood* (2nd ed.). New York: Routledge.

Kakar, S. (1981). *The Inner World: A Psychological Study of Childhood and Society in India* (2nd ed.). Oxford University Press.

Kennedy, D. (1998). Reconstructing childhood. *Thinking: The Journal of Philosophy for Children*, *14*(1), 29–37.

Kilderry, A. (2015). Repositioning developmentalism. In M. Reed & R. Walker (ed.). A Critical Companion to Early Childhood (First Edition ed., pp. 116-126). SAGE Publications, Inc., https://doi.org/10.4135/9781473910188

Kitchener, R. F. (1990). Do children think philosophically? *Metaphilosophy*, *21*(4), 416–431.

Laing, R. D. (1978). *Conversations with Children*. Allen Lane.

Lam, C. M. (2009). A Justification for Children's Capacity to Do Philosophy. In E. Marsal, T. Dobashi, & B. Weber (Ed.), *Children Philosophise Worldwide: Theoretical and Practical Concepts*. Peter Lang.

Laverty, M. J., & Gregory, M. R. (2021). Gareth B. Matthews: A Philosopher's Life with Children. In G. B. Matthews (Ed.), *The Child's Philosopher* (pp. 1–28). Routledge.

Lawrence, P. (2019). Dialogical agency: children's interactions with human and more-than-human. *European Early Childhood Education Research Journal*, *27*(3), 318-333.

Lee, N. (2001). *Childhood and Society: Growing up in an Age of Uncertainty*. McGraw-Hill Education.

Lee, K., & Vagle, M. D. (2010). General Introduction: Developmentalism and the Need for Critical Conversations within and across the Fields. In K. Lee & M. D. Vagle (Eds.), *Developmentalism in Early Childhood and Middle Grades Education* (pp. 1–9). Springer.

Lipman, M. (1976). Philosophy for children. *Metaphilosophy*, *7*(1), 17–39.

Lipman, M., & Sharp, A. M. (1978). Some educational presuppositions of philosophy for children. *Oxford Review of Education*, *4*(1), 85–90.

Malik, L. (2019). 'Tayyari Jeet Ki': The Production of Childhood as a Cultural Trope of Developmentalism. In D. Pathak & A. Das (Eds.), *Investigating Developmentalism*. Palgrave Macmillan. https://doi.org/10.1007/978-3-030-17443-9_7

Matthews, G. B. (1980). *Philosophy and the Young Child*. Harvard University Press.

Matthews, G. B. (1984). *Dialogues with Children*. Harvard University Press. https://books.google.co.in/books?id=uNzsER7W_ucC

Matthews, G. B. (1994). *The Philosophy of Childhood*. Harvard University Press.

Matthews, G. B. (2008). Getting beyond the Deficit Conception of Childhood: Thinking Philosophically with Children. In M. Hand & C. Winstanley (Eds.), *Philosophy in Schools* (pp. 27–40). Continuum.

Matthews, G. B. (2009). Philosophy and Developmental Psychology: Outgrowing the Deficit Conception of Childhood. In H. Siegel (Ed.), *The Oxford Handbook of Philosophy of Education*. Oxford University Press.

Matthews, G. B. (2017). Doing Philosophy with Children Rejects Piaget's Assumptions. In S. Naji & R. Hashim (Ed.), *History, Theory and Practice of Philosophy for Children: International Perspectives* (pp. 53–55. Routledge.

Mattos, A. (2015). Feminist Psychology Researches, Interventions, Challenges. In I. Parker (Ed.), *Handbook of Critical Psychology* (pp. 329–338). Routledge.

Mascaro, O., & Morin, O. (2015). Epistemology for beginners: Two-to five-year-old children's representation of falsity. *PLoS One*, *10*(10), e0140658.

Montgomery, H. (2008). *An Introduction to Childhood: Anthropological Perspectives on Children's Lives*. John Wiley & Sons.

Murris, K. (2013). The Epistemic Challenge of Hearing Child's Voice. *Studies in Philosophy and Education*, *32*, 245–259.

Mukherjee, H. B. (2020). *Education for Fullness: A Study of the Educational Thought and Experiment of Rabindranath Tagore*. Taylor & Francis.

Nandy, A. (1984). Reconstructing childhood: A critique of the ideology of adulthood. *Alternatives*, *10*(3), 359–375.

Neill, A. S. (1995). *Summerhill School: A New View of Childhood*. Macmillan.

Neiman, S. (2015). *Why Grow Up?: Subversive Thoughts for an Infantile Age*: Macmillan.

Parsons, M. (1987/1992). *Compreender a arte: Uma abordagem à experiência estética do ponto de vista do desenvolvimento cognitivo* [*How we understand art: A cognitive development account of aesthetic experience*]. Editorial Presença.

Patton, L. L. (2009). Hinduism. In D. S. Browning & M. J. Bunge (Eds.), *Children and Childhood in World Religions: Primary Sources and Texts* (pp. 217–276). Rutgers University Press.

Pendlebury, S. (2003). Feminism, Ēpistemology and Education. In D. Carr (Ed.), *Education, Knowledge and Truth* (pp. 188–202). Routledge.
Punch, S. (2016). Cross-world and cross-disciplinary dialogue: A more integrated, global approach to childhood studies. *Global studies of childhood*, 6(3), 352-364.
Rousseau, J. J., & Foxley, B. (1955). *Émile*. J.M. Dent.
Schulte, C. M. (2021). Childhood drawing: The making of a deficit aesthetic. *Global Studies of Childhood*, *11*(1), 54–68.
Siry, C. (2015). Researching with Children: Dialogic Approaches to Participatory Research. In K. Tobin & J. Kincheloe (ed.). *Doing Educational Research* (pp. 151–165). Brill.
Spring, J. H. (1975). *A Primer of Libertarian Education*. Free Life Editions.
Taylor, A. (2018). Engaging with the Conceptual Tools and Challenges of Poststructural Theories. In M. Fleer & Bert van Oers (Eds.), *International Handbook of Early Childhood Education* (pp. 91–115). Springer.
Thapan, M. (Ed.). (2018). *J. Krishnamurti and Educational Practice: Social and Moral Vision for Inclusive Education*. Oxford University Press.
Thorne, B. (2007). Crafting the interdisciplinary field of childhood studies. *Childhood*, *14*(2), 147-152.
Topping, K. J., Trickey, S., & Cleghorn, P. (2020). *Philosophy for Children*. Educational Practices Series 32. UNESCO International Bureau of Education.
Walkerdine, V. (1993). Beyond Developmentalism? *Theory & Psychology*, *3*(4), 451–469. https://doi.org/10.1177/0959354393034004
Wall, J. (2022). From childhood studies to childism: Reconstructing the scholarly and social imaginations. Children's *Geographies*, *20*(3), 257–270.
Wilson, B., & Wilson, M. (1981). The Use and Uselessness of Developmental Stages. *Art Education*, *34*(5), 4–5.
Wong, J. (2007). Paradox of Capacity and Power: Critical Ontology and the Developmental Model of Childhood. In M. A. Peters & T. A. C. Besley (Eds.), *Why Foucault? New Educational Research* (pp. 71–90). Peter Lang.

INDEX

Note: Pages in *italics* indicates tables

Pages in **bold** indicates figures

Printed in the United States
by Baker & Taylor Publisher Services